BRITAIN AND ISLAM

BY THE SAME AUTHOR

Electoral Reform in War and Peace 1906–1918

The Making of Modern British Politics 1867–1945

The Tories and the People 1880–1935

Lloyd George

Women and the Women's Movement in Britain Since 1914

State and Society: British social and political history since 1870

Storia Della Gran Bretagna 1789–1990 (Britain Since 1789:
A concise history)

The March of the Women: A revisionist analysis of the
campaign for women's suffrage 1866–1914

A Companion to Modern European History, 1871–1945 (editor)

The Pankhursts: The history of one radical family

'Hurrah for the Blackshirts!': Fascists and fascism in Britain
between the wars

'We Danced All Night': A social history of Britain
between the wars

Speak for Britain! A new history of the Labour Party

Britain: Unification and disintegration

MARTIN PUGH

BRITAIN

&

ISLAM

YALE UNIVERSITY PRESS
NEW HAVEN AND LONDON

For information about this and other Yale University Press publications, please contact:
U.S. Office: sales.press@yale.edu   yalebooks.com
Europe Office: sales@yaleup.co.uk   yalebooks.co.uk

Set in Adobe Garamond Pro by IDSUK (DataConnection) Ltd
Printed in Great Britain by TJ International, Padstow, Cornwall

Library of Congress Control Number: 2019941058

ISBN 978-0-300-23494-7

A catalogue record for this book is available from the British Library.

10 9 8 7 6 5 4 3 2 1

MIX
Paper from
responsible sources
FSC® C013056

To Fran, Hannah and Alastair

CONTENTS

ILLUSTRATIONS

1. The Mezquita, Cordoba, Spain, where both Christians and Muslims worshipped. Jim Gordon / CC-BY-2.0.
2. The 'Rainbow Portrait' of Queen Elizabeth I, *c.* 1600, incorporating Islamic fabrics and jewels worn at the Tudor court.
3. General William Palmer, British Resident at Lucknow, with his Muslim wife Fyze (seated), their children and several of Fyze's relations, painted in 1785.
4. A typical Victorian dismissal of Turkey's capacity for reform, *Punch*, 1877.
5. The Shah Jahan Mosque, Woking, Surrey, the first purpose-built mosque in Britain, 1889. RHaworth / CC-BY-SA-3.0.
6. British anger at Turkey's alliance with Germany in the First World War, *Punch*, 1910, republished 1914.
7. Norman Hassan, an Arab merchant seaman who lived at South Shields, with his English wife, pre-1914.
8. Winston Churchill, Gertrude Bell and T.E. Lawrence at the Cairo Conference, 1921. University of Newcastle Department of Archaeology.
9. General Allenby, high commissioner in Egypt, and King Faisal, Britain's choice as King of Iraq, 1921. Hulton Archive / Getty Images.

PREFACE

'Apparently England is ever forgetting that she is at present the greatest Mohammedan empire in the world.'

The words of the Victorian traveller-explorer, Sir Richard Burton, in the introduction to his translation of *The Arabian Nights* (1886) echo uncomfortably down the decades. Between 1947 and the 1970s, the British abandoned their empire in a remarkably short space of time and, on the surface, with surprisingly little trauma or controversy among the general public at least. But there was a downside: they never mourned its passing, forgot all about it during the 1950s, and later found it hard to come to terms when the empire came home to them. Loss of empire is only one of the many respects in which British national identity has unravelled during the last 40 or 50 years. The British relationship with Muslims has been one of the casualties. In 2017, many British mosques found it expedient to declare an 'open day', designed to encourage the public to come in and learn a little about Islam. But this is a sad reflection of the fact that today the whole subject is clouded by an immense amount of ignorance, misconception and prejudice. The worst symptoms of this are the regular misrepresentations of Muslims in the popular press, the tendency to blame all Muslims for the faults of a few, the publication of Islamophobic books about the supposed subversion of Europe, and the survival of UKIP as an anti-Muslim party.

Against this background this book is unashamedly educational, intended as a corrective to prejudice; it is aimed at a general audience, and especially a non-Muslim audience, in the hope of getting things into perspective. It is often argued that history does not repeat itself; but it would be more accurate to say that it does not repeat itself *exactly*. No one, looking at successive invasions of Afghanistan by the British twice in the nineteenth century and by the Russians and Americans in the twentieth and twenty-first, can fail to see the same cycle being repeated by politicians ignorant of history. In Britain, the anti-Muslim propaganda of the medieval Crusades was resurrected in Victorian times under the influence of the Evangelical revival and the needs of politicians like W.E. Gladstone, who painted shocking caricatures of Muslims and especially Turks. More recently, the Victorian concerns about Islam as an obstacle to progress have been revived as the conflict-of-civilisations thesis by foolish American presidents and academics and repeated by several ignorant British prime ministers. We were even entertained to a faint echo of the Victorian propaganda during the EU referendum campaign, when Boris Johnson tried to scare voters with the claim that some 70 million Turks were about to obtain membership of the community!

The troubled relations between Islam and the West have inspired others to delve into the subject – for example, in the American context with *What's Right with Islam?* (2004) by Imam Feisal Abdul Rauf. I have found this approach stimulating, because from a British perspective it does not seem particularly plausible. It is a very American book, which starts from the assumption that America's gift to the world is liberal capitalism, and consequently gives no thought to the idea that Islam is arguably closer to socialism than to capitalism! The author even characterises American society as a modern manifestation of the Abrahamic ethic, which seems to stretch things rather far. His claim that US society is Islamic does remind one of its religiosity, which is so unusual for an advanced Western country. By contrast, Europe has largely emancipated itself from religion and Britain has become an especially secular society. This may be helpful, in the sense that it is comparatively easy for Muslims to retain their own values, while also adapting to British habits and traditions; but it is also a complication, in that it gives grounds for those who purport to defend Britishness by championing Britain as a Christian country under threat from a resurgent Islam.

In the first instance, this book is a modest attempt to explain how radically British relations with Muslims have fluctuated over the 1,400 years since the foundation of Islam: from the fanatical propaganda associated with the Crusades, to the pragmatic collaboration with Muslim states inspired by the Protestant Reformation, the appreciation of the extensive common ground between Islam and Christianity in the eighteenth century, and Britain's pose as a defender of Islam (in the shape of the Ottoman Empire) by the early nineteenth century.

In particular, we need to recognise what an extremely long record Britain has of interference in the Islamic world, in terms of rearranging its boundaries in India, Pakistan, Bangladesh, Iraq, the Ottoman Empire, Jordan, Palestine, Lebanon, Egypt and Sudan, as well as attempting to control its policies and change its rulers. As a result, we have acquired over two centuries a dangerous addiction for meddling in Muslim countries which has almost always proved to be counter-productive. The habit is very much alive today among politicians, diplomats and experts, and is responsible, at least in part, for modern domestic terrorism.

Historical perspectives also help to correct the obvious misperceptions about Islam. Today we are understandably obsessed with what is a very limited part of Islam in several countries of the Middle East and North Africa. Yet the biggest Muslim country in the world is Indonesia, notable for its relaxed approach to religion and its democratic practice. The book also gives much attention to India. We should remember that when Richard Burton referred to Britain as a great Muslim power, he was thinking of India, where, in the eighteenth century at least, the British fell in love with Muslims. Even today, independent India – with approximately 200 million Muslims – is one of the world's largest Muslim societies, yet it does not figure as prominently in discussions about Islam as it should. As a result, Islamophobes tend to overlook the fact that so far from Islam being incompatible with democracy, for over 60 years Indian Muslims have been practising liberal democracy.

As a historian, I have tried to put Muslim experience into a truer perspective by showing, for example, how far Muslim societies in the past have engaged with Westernisation and modernisation and adopted liberal democracy, often obstructed, rather than aided, by Britain. I emphasise the importance of the First World War in leading Britain into her modern role in perpetually intervening in the affairs of the Muslim world and in rearranging the boundaries of Muslim states, a habit that has become completely counter-productive.

I have explained that the Muslim experience in Britain since the 1950s has been very similar to that of earlier immigrants, like the Jews from the 1890s onwards, but also more complicated because Britain suffers from the almost complete collapse of her sense of national identity, which was at its peak between the late-Victorian and inter-war eras.

The book places the Islamophobic scaremongering in historical context by showing how similar it is to the anti-Semitic propaganda of the inter-war period, reflecting the same need to identify external enemies. I have also exposed the exaggerations and errors of the Islamophobic literature of the last 30 years, including some of the absurdities it has generated, such as scares about *Winterval*.

Finally, the book offers a corrective to the remorselessly negative tone that fills the speeches of politicians and the pages of newspapers (with the honourable exceptions of the *Guardian* and the *Observer*). To this end, it examines the ways in which Muslims have already succeeded in becoming part of the British mainstream, especially through participation in the economy, in sport, in politics and in the celebrity culture which is so characteristic of our society today. We are seeing – though not in the newspapers – a process of quiet social *convergence* between the Muslim and non-Muslim communities in Britain which makes the controversies over multiculturalism seem almost irrelevant.

Martin Pugh
Slaley, Hexham, Northumberland

ACKNOWLEDGEMENTS

I would like to record my thanks to various people who have helped with the writing of this book, including Professor Eugenio Biagini, Dr Lewis Mates, Dr Maurice Milne, Dr Nisar Mir and Camille, Sadat Yildiz my Turkish barber, Noor Ali of Morrisons, and Beacon Confectionery of Nuneaton. As always, I am grateful to the staff at the library of the Newcastle-upon-Tyne Literary and Philosophical Society, who were consistently helpful and efficient over my efforts to locate sources. My thanks also to the publisher's anonymous reviewers for their comments and corrections.

Indirectly, but fundamentally, I gained the original inspiration to write the book long ago, from my experience as a lecturer during 1969–71 at the Aligarh Muslim University in India. I am grateful to my students there, including P.S. Mohd Moideen, A. Jamaluddin, K. Abdul Rasheed, Seyed Mahmud, Mohd Ali and the late Mohd Basheer, as well as members of staff including Professor Nurul Hasan, Professor A.K. Nizami, Professor Irfan Habib, Dr Arshad Ali Azmi, Dr. N.A.Siddiqi, Dr Athar Ali, Dr Safi Ahmad, Dr Z.U. Malik and Dr Z.U. Siddiqi.

I am obviously indebted to the authors of many books dealing with aspects of the subject, but especially to Jerry Brotton, *This Orient Isle: Elizabethan England and the Islamic world* (2016); Christopher de Bellaigue, *The Islamic Enlightenment* (2017); Peter Frankopan, *The Silk*

Roads: A new history of the world (2015); James Fergusson, *Al-Britannia, My Country* (2017); Nader Hashemi, *Islam, Secularism and Liberal Democracy* (2009); Kenan Malik, *From Fatwa to Jihad* (2009); Pankaj Mishra, *From the Ruins of Empire: The revolt against the west and the remaking of Asia* (2012); Ziauddin Sardar, *Balti Britain* (2008); Sayeeda Warsi, *The Enemy Within* (2017); and Philip Lewis and Sadek Hamid, *British Muslims: New directions in Islamic thought, creativity and activism* (2018).

I am grateful to the following for permission to include the illustrations in this book: the marquis of Salisbury, the British Library, *Punch*, the Shah Jahan Mosque, Richard I. Lawless and Exeter University Press, the Department of Archaeology (Bell Archive) Newcastle University, Popperfoto/Getty Images, the Hulton Archive, the Aziziye Mosque, Beacon Confectionery, and Lewis Pies.

CHAPTER ONE

ISLAM

'A KIND OF CHRISTIANITY'?[1]

The Prophet Mohammed was born at Mecca, in the Arabian Peninsula, around AD 570. Following the early death of both parents, he was brought up first by his grandfather, and then by his uncle. Mecca stood on a major trade route in the Hejaz, which ran from the Yemen northwards towards Syria. He became experienced in the trade of the Arabian Peninsula and was employed by a widow, Khadija, to look after her goods; later she married him and had seven children by him. Accounts that have come down to us suggest that this was a marriage of equals. Mohammed depended on her emotionally and never took another wife during her lifetime; she, for her part, was the first to recognise his genius.[2] Although known as a reflective youth, Mohammed showed no indications of any desire to found a new religion – until the year 610, when, at about the age of 40, he received his first revelation, in which the Angel Gabriel declared him to be a messenger of God. The revelations continued until his death in 632, but it was not until 613 that he began to preach publicly.

At this stage, he emphasised the oneness of God, the exercise of goodwill towards all people, the care of the poor and the terrors that lie in wait on the Day of Judgment. The local Arabs, who were mostly polytheists, were familiar with the ideas of the Jews and Christians, whom they called *ahl al-kitab* or the 'People of the Book'. They did not regard

1

Christianity and Judaism as entirely separate or distinct from their own thinking and values, but more as indicative of tribal variations. Arabs appreciated some of these traditions as being compatible with their own ideas, and consequently they felt under no particular pressure to convert, as all were members of the Abrahamic family. But the Arabs did admire the idea of a revealed text, and some felt the need for an Arab monotheism in a society dominated by polytheism.[3] Following disputes with the local community in Mecca, Mohammed's clan withdrew its protection from him, and in 622 he and his followers fled to Medina – an event celebrated as the *Hijrah*. Consequently, 622 marks the first year in the Islamic calendar. From his base at Medina, Mohammed extended his control over Mecca and the entire peninsula.

Today it is not generally appreciated that when Christians first heard of this new prophet they often assumed that his teaching amounted to a variation – or perhaps a heresy – within Christianity, rather than an entirely new religion. There was ample corroboration for this view. Initially Mohammed himself had not claimed to be founding a new religion, but rather to be redirecting his followers to the study of the gospels. As Mohammed grew up among Jews and Christians, he was inevitably influenced by them, especially as his main spiritual teacher was a Nestorian Christian. In a society marked by the pagan worship of many gods, Judaism, Christianity and Islam distinguished themselves by their common belief in monotheism. Believing in one all-powerful God, they disparaged the myths, demons and sprites favoured at that time by much of society in Arabia-Syria. All three communities were 'People of the Book', who drew on the Abrahamic tradition and the Old Testament; Abraham was the patriarch, or founding father, of Judaism, Christianity and Islam alike. Muslims thus embraced his belief in one God and venerated the succession of prophets through Isaac, Jacob and Moses, up to and including Jesus. For them, Mohammad came as the last in the line of these prophets, and his task was to bring a final clarification for the 'People of the Book': 'Today I have perfected your religion for you and I have completed my blessing upon you.'[4] As a result of this clarification, everyone would be able to abandon arguments about doctrine and concentrate on good works.

Consequently, the adherents to the three religions had much in common, in terms of both their religious ideas and the cultural attitudes and social habits that characterised the region and the era in which they lived. As a result, today their cultural practices are often assumed (incorrectly) to enjoy some specific religious sanction. One example of the common culture involves the similar approach of Jews, Christians and Muslims to hair, which had been a symbol of authority in the Middle East well before Islamic times. For male Muslims, the practice was to retain the beard as a sign of authority and to distinguish them from women and non-believers. In Judaism and early Christianity, women concealed their hair from all men, apart from their husbands. Another example is the harem, which existed in Middle Eastern countries long before the advent of Islam. As Islam extended its control over existing societies, it usually adopted the harem. This was justified in the Qur'an to the extent that modesty for women was commended, but the harem was essentially a sign of social status and wealth, indicating that a family's women did not need to work.

Since their emergence towards the end of the second millennium BC, Jews had been noted for their rejection of idol worship, their belief in one God and their focus on the Hebrew Bible and the Torah, which had been revealed by God to Moses on Mount Sinai. Jews and Muslims shared a belief in revelation, prophecy and Satan. The two communities ate kosher food, avoided pork and shellfish, practised baptism, circumcision, fasting and arranged marriages, dressed modestly to avoid revealing the contours of the body, and disapproved of usury.[5] From this brief sketch, it is clear that a good deal of Judaism and Jewish culture reappeared under Islamic society. When establishing himself at Medina, Mohammed expected to be favourably received by Jews, and he adopted several Jewish practices, including the direction of prayer towards Jerusalem. However, as they rejected his claims, he modified these practices and introduced Mecca, in place of Jerusalem, as the direction of prayer. Over many centuries, Jews were to enjoy fair treatment under

Islamic rule, and they flourished by comparison with their treatment in the Christian West.

For their part, the early Muslims frankly recognised that they stood within the Judaeo-Christian tradition. The Qur'an incorporated many of the biblical stories familiar to Christians about the creation of the world, Adam and Eve, Noah's flood and the exodus from Egypt. Muslims saw themselves in a three-part tradition, whose first stage began three thousand years earlier with the Jews. Subsequently, Christianity had emerged as an improved version, originally seen as a sect within Judaism; and the early Christians had defined themselves with respect to Judaism. In the third and final stage, Islam appeared as a purified and simplified form that superseded Christianity. This was felt to be necessary, because Muslims believed that Christians had introduced into the practice of the religion all kinds of dubious notions, elaborations and misunderstandings that had not been part of the original. Islam provided a *clarification* and a return to a truer, simpler, stricter form. This was a view that many Christians themselves were to welcome, especially during the Protestant Reformation in the sixteenth and seventeenth centuries (although it was to overlook the central disagreement about the divinity of Christ).

Consequently, early Islam was not a missionary movement. It perceived no permanent hostility between Muslims and Christians; it accepted that Muslims could marry Jews and Christians; and Mohammed himself allowed Christians to worship in his mosque.[6] Under Muslim rule, Jews and Christians enjoyed freedom to worship; and although a tax was levied on them, it was lighter than taxation under the Byzantine Empire that Islam replaced. Christians could make pilgrimages to the Holy Land, they went to study at Cairo and Cordoba, and they commonly rose to major government positions in the Muslim states. As a result, despite some Christian martyrs under early Islam, Muslim–Christian relations were generally good before the advent of the Crusades towards the end of the eleventh century.

Moreover, conversion from Christianity to Islam was comparatively simple, in that Islam never developed the extensive theology characteristic of Christianity. Islam maintained that God remained almost an abstract idea and unintelligible, except through faith, devotional practice and the intellect. For a convert, the first step was to show submission to God's will by reciting the Profession of Faith before witnesses. This was the first of the five basic rules, or 'pillars', of Islam: 'There is no God but Allah, and Mohammed is the messenger of Allah.' The second pillar was an act of submission, involving prayers five times a day – at dawn, midday, mid-afternoon, sunset and after nightfall. Devotees washed their hands, feet and face before praying, and used a prayer mat which usually had a defect, designed as a reminder that only God is perfect. Usually the prayers took place communally, including at noon on Fridays in mosques; but they could be undertaken in private and public places individually. In a mosque, the proper direction of prayer towards Mecca was indicated by a niche in the wall. The third requirement was that the believer should contribute a sum, usually 2.5 per cent of income or property, to be spent on charitable purposes. The fourth involved fasting during the month of Ramadan, the ninth month in the Islamic calendar, between dawn and sunset (the date being set through astronomical observations). This was an opportunity for reflection and prayer, and especially a time to be generous to the poor. At dusk, Muslims broke their fast with a light meal, followed by a family gathering later for a larger meal. Ramadan ended with a feast (Eid al-Fitr) that might last for several days. However, Ramadan was more flexible in practice than it appears, as many exemptions from fasting were accepted for the sick, the elderly, pregnant women, those who had recently given birth, young children, students taking examinations and travellers.[7] Finally, the believer who was able-bodied and who could afford it had an obligation to make a pilgrimage (known as *Hajj*) to Mecca at least once in his life-time. Historically, the numbers who did so were actually quite small, though the figures vary a lot: as late as 1880, estimates range from 25,000 to 200,000; numbers rose significantly in the 1960s, 1970s and 1980s, reaching 1.3 million by 2000.[8] The *Haji* celebrates the reunion of the Muslim community and the idea of human equality.

In common with Christians, Muslims believe in a Day of Judgment, preceded by a series of cataclysmic events, when all human beings will appear before God to have their sins and virtues weighed. Some Muslim scholars today regard the moral degradation of modern society as an indication that the Day of Judgment is near (as do many Christians, especially in the United States). The Qur'an contains many descriptions of the next stage, when believers go to Paradise, where they enjoy sensual and spiritual pleasures, luxuries, comfort and gratification, including the attentions of divine maidens known as *houris*. Infidels go to Hell for eternity, though disobedient believers go only for a period, the length to be determined by their sins. These convictions set Islam and Christianity apart from most other religions. Hindus, for example, regard the idea of Hell as wholly appalling. Similarly, Muslims share with Christians an expectation of the Resurrection, heralded by various manifestations. For Muslims, this includes the appearance of a *Mahdi* – a leader who will restore the purity of the faith and free Muslims from injustice. Mankind will then assemble for Judgment; God will appear; and all the prophets, including Jesus and Mohammed, will take their rightful place alongside him.

Muslims believe that God communicated his will to man through various prophets, or messengers, and that his will now exists in the form of the Qur'an, or 'recitation'; this is regarded as the eternal, complete and infallible word of God. Approximately the length of the New Testament, the Qur'an comprises 114 chapters, varying in length from 3 to 286 verses. It represents the revelations made to Mohammed, memorised by his followers, collected after his death and written down, in Arabic, under the direction of the third caliph, Uthman, around 650. As Mohammed is widely believed to have been illiterate, the Qur'an is regarded as his (only) miracle. Some scholars argue that he wrote it himself, suggesting that his work as a merchant would have required an ability to read and write. Many Muslims consider that it cannot be translated into other languages – though in the 1000s a Persian version did appear, and then in the 1100s a Latin translation; but only the Arabic version is the Qur'an. The additional sources for Muslim belief are found in the *Sunna*, which record the sayings, actions and behaviour of the Prophet and represent a supplement, giving guidance on issues not resolved in the Qur'an. The *Sunna* is found in a large collection (known as the *hadith*), which comprises oral reports that go all the way back to Mohammed. Much controversy has been generated as to the *hadith*'s reliability, because its accounts originate with a number of witnesses; indeed, some Muslims reject the *hadith* and prefer to find guidance only in the Qur'an.

However, although the Qur'an is authoritative, it is also susceptible to different interpretations. In any case, it is inconsistent on certain topics. For example, the prohibition on alcohol is generally taken as absolute, but was not part of Mohammed's original message. Somewhat ambiguously, the Qur'an urges: 'O believers, do not approach prayer while you are drunk, until you know what you say.' And one *hadith* reminds unrepentant Muslims that they will be denied the reward of drinking wine in the afterlife.[9] Inevitably, situations and problems arose to which it was difficult to find guidance in the Qur'an, and some later Muslims, such as the Pakistani philosopher Fazlur Rahman (1919–88), rejected literal interpretations on the grounds that they were valid only for the time and place in which the original revelations occurred.[10] Rahman contended that Muslims should study the historical context of the revelations, in order to understand the spirit of Islam and then apply it to modern conditions. This approach, he felt, would enable Muslims to handle better the problems presented by the modern world.

Despite the extensive common ground in the beginning between Muslims and Christians, there were naturally some differences (though arguably no greater than the differences among Christians themselves). While Muslims honoured Jesus as one of the great prophets, they did not regard him as the Son of God. Even the Prophet himself was not seen as a divine figure, but as another 'messiah', or messenger, to whom God had revealed himself: 'Mohammed is merely an apostle before whom many apostles have come and gone.'[11] Muslims also looked askance at the Christian idea of the Holy Trinity, because it suggested a deviation from the key principle of monotheism. This, too, was a criticism accepted by many Christians. Similarly, the majority of Muslims rejected the idea of saints as being inconsistent with monotheism, and saw the worship of saints as superstition. Although Muslims, like Christians and Jews, recognised Adam as the first human being, they rejected the claim that he passed on his original sin to the rest of humanity: their view was that Adam and Eve repented and God forgave them.[12] For Muslims, the notion of original sin was a 'doctrine of despair', as an individual could achieve salvation through genuine repentance, without any need for confession to a religious intermediary.

Nor did Islam develop the elaborate hierarchy or the priesthood that became characteristic of the Church: no priest intervened between the believer and God. Prayers were led by an *imam*, but he could simply be any good, knowledgeable Muslim, and not necessarily a priest. In addition, there were the 'men of knowledge', known collectively as *ulema* (or *ulama*) – a term that covered *imam, ayatollah, mullah* and *mufti*. These titles, however, were honorific and did not represent any formal rank or office. The *ulema* interpreted religious law, issued opinions (called *fatwas*), or taught in schools. From the eighth to the thirteenth century, the *ulema* became an influential educated elite and played an important role in educational, political and legal affairs; in later centuries, they sometimes formed the opposition to change in Muslim societies, especially when they were undermined by Western innovations; in consequence, they led the resistance to Western rule. The *fatwa* was a legal opinion issued by a *mufti*; it carried authority, but was not legally binding. Its origins lay in the early period, when there were few schools and little literacy, and when consequently only a few people enjoyed sufficient knowledge of the Qur'an to be able to pronounce on Islamic principles. A *fatwa* was often a personal ruling, and, in case of disputes, the various parties might appoint their own *muftis* and receive differing *fatwas*. But sometimes they dealt with major issues, such as war and domestic policies – as in 1876, when an Ottoman sultan was deposed by *fatwa*. Under European rule, the *fatwa* was used to mobilise the population against the unbelievers.

However, although Islam was relatively simple and straightforward, it did develop a number of different sects and beliefs – even though Mohammed had warned that Muslims should not allow themselves to be divided into factions. Before he died in 632, Mohammed nominated his successor, Abu Bakr. Abu Bakr stipulated that, according to Arab tradition, a new leader must emerge from a consensus in the community. He was succeeded by the second caliph, Umar, who extended Muslim control into Syria and Palestine. However, after his death in 644, the role was given to Uthman – a controversial decision that meant passing over one of the Prophet's sons-in-law, Ali, whose supporters felt that he was the nearest in blood to Mohammed. Ali was chosen in 656, on the death of Uthman, but his murder in 661 left a permanent schism in Islam. Those Muslims known today as Sunnis constitute 80 per cent of Muslims; meanwhile, the Shias – who support Ali and regard his successors as usurpers – form a majority only in modern Iran, Yemen and Azerbaijan, though they are numerous in Iraq, southern Arabia and on the Indian sub-continent. Traditionally, Sunnis have been regarded as the more conservative branch of Islam and Shias as the more revolutionary. Shias expected the emergence of a *Mahdi*, or 'chosen one' (a divinely guided leader sent to earth to unite Muslims prior to the end of the world), and they were widely seen by the imperial powers as a threat to the status quo.[13] Another splinter group are the *Alawites*, or 'upholders of Ali'; founded in 1021, they are concentrated in modern Syria, Lebanon and Turkey. Seen as extremists within Islam, they have much in common with Christianity, including the idea of the Resurrection and the Second Coming; they also celebrate Christian festivals, including Epiphany, Pentecost and Easter.

Sufism, an important school within Islam, developed from the eighth century onwards among Muslims who wanted to focus more on their inner spiritual life, rather than on the external manifestations. It arose partly as a reaction to the austere, authoritarian character of orthodox Sunni Islam; it had a great emotional appeal, especially to rural Muslims. Sufis believed in attaining a spiritual detachment from the pleasures of the mortal life, and they sought to follow a moral and saintly path. They promoted the idea of union with God through overwhelming love for him and through mystical experiences, which resulted in a kind of holy intoxication. Some achieved this through ritual trance dancing (hence the 'whirling dervishes'), walking on hot coals or lying on a bed of nails. Organised into monastic orders, the Sufis became key promoters of learning and culture by founding universities or *madrasas*. Sufis designated many saints and organised pilgrimages to their tombs, which became very popular among rank-and-file Muslims.[14] However, to orthodox Muslims,

the Sufis' extreme veneration for Mohammed seemed to verge on conferring supernatural qualities on him; as a result, efforts were later made to
purge Islam of what many considered to be superstition.

⬡ ❖ ⬡

Despite the common origins of Islam and Christianity, Islam has long
been misunderstood and misrepresented in Western societies, particularly over such matters as women, polygamy, sex, sexuality, slavery and
jihad. Westerners today are largely unaware that Islam is a relatively
egalitarian religion which does not endorse differences of birth, caste,
wealth or race. In fact, it denounces privilege as un-Islamic, though this
has not prevented the emergence of elites and aristocracies over time.
Converts often find the egalitarianism a refreshing change. In this spirit,
a number of Muslim states have, in modern times, adopted policies of
socialist Islamism. And while Islam has always recognised differences
between men and women, believers and unbelievers, and slaves and
freeborn, historically the differences were significantly less under Islam
than in other societies, especially as regards women and slaves.

For the British, it has always proved difficult to get the institution of
slavery into its true perspective. They have tended to close their minds to
the fact that for a long time the British profited enormously from the slave
trade, preferring to emphasise the later campaigns against the trade and
the efforts made to eradicate it in the Muslim parts of Africa during the
Victorian period. In fact, although Islamic law sanctioned slavery (and it
could not easily be abolished, because it was acknowledged in the Qur'an),
it was not the same institution as in the West. The position of slaves was
notably better than in classical times or in nineteenth-century America, in
the sense that under Muslim rule they enjoyed certain rights, and slave
owners were under certain obligations. As the manumission of slaves was
recognised in the Qur'an as a meritorious act, they were commonly freed
after seven years. Also, the children of slaves were born free.[15] There was
little stigma attached to being an ex-slave, and some prominent slaves rose
to high positions in Muslim societies. These included the janissaries, who
became the sultan's soldiers in the Ottoman Empire, and the Mamluks,

10

who became rulers in Egypt. Over time, the institution was steadily whittled away. In 1830, the Ottomans emancipated Christian slaves, and they prohibited the slave trade in 1857. In 1846, the governor-general of Tunis freed the (largely black) slaves using Islamic justifications: the cruel treatment of slaves was inherently un-Islamic, and the enslavement of Muslims by Muslims was illegal under Islamic law. This action set a precedent for others to follow. Saudi Arabia and Yemen held out longest, only abolishing slavery as late as 1962.

From the start, Islam recognised two essential communities: the overall brotherhood of Muslims and the family. The centrality of family life made Islam an essentially conventional and conservative society, broadly in line with Western social practice. The family was the key institution, standing half-way between the traditional tribal communities of the Arabs and the individualistic families that later became characteristic of Western society. In this context, the status of women was really an extension of the existing culture of Arabia-Syria in a patriarchal society – that is, women were largely subordinate to their male relatives, had to obey their husbands and could be disciplined by them.

On the other hand, there was nothing in Islamic doctrine to prevent the education of women, and any opposition to female education was a reflection of prevailing social attitudes, rather than ideology. Indeed, in the context of traditional Arab society, Islam represented a progressive, reformist movement that condemned misogyny, forbade female infanticide, insisted that if any money changed hands on marriage it should be given to the wife as payment for her household labour, and guaranteed women property rights that they did not enjoy in the West until the nineteenth century. Under the patriarchal Arab society, a deceased man's property passed to his nearest male relative on the father's side. However, the Qur'an changed this by making strict provision for wives, daughters, sisters and grandmothers, who all received a fixed share of the inheritance, with the remainder going to the senior male.[16] This fell short of equality, as a woman's share was only half that of a man (and not all women were aware of their rights); but the result was that wealth was more equally distributed than in Christian societies. After a divorce, a wife was permitted to obtain a financial settlement from her ex-husband. The Qur'an forbade any coercion of women as far as property was concerned: women retained control of their marriage dowry and enjoyed freedom of dealing.[17] They were thus free to operate in business if they so wished (and as Mohammed's wife, Khadija, did).

On the other hand, the behaviour expected of women in public is unclear, and it remains uncertain whether they were obliged to remain in seclusion and to wear the veil, for the evidence is inconsistent and ambiguous. The early Muslim community did inherit certain social customs, including veiling and seclusion from the surrounding society. And the Qur'an refers to the veiling of Mohammed's own wives; but it is not clear whether that was a special provision to give them some privacy in a crowded household full of visitors, rather than a general prescription. In Arabia, the practice varied greatly and, while women were advised to dress modestly and chastely, there was no unequivocal rule that Muslim women must wear the veil. In effect, the practice spread later, during the Middle Ages, and especially among wealthier, urban families; it was far less common in rural areas and in the desert. Although it is difficult to generalise, the conclusion must be that female dress was primarily a matter of custom and culture, rather than a strictly religious phenomenon. It varied from one society to another and changed considerably over time. Change could be accomplished by gradual shifts, designed to meet different situations over a long period of time. For example, in modern Istanbul women may be seen in a full range of dress, from Western fashions to the *burqa*. As late as the 1970s, some female students at the Aligarh Muslim University in northern India would leave their homes each morning wearing a veil, to travel by cycle rickshaw; half-way to the university they would discard the veil and spend the day unveiled. They would then repeat the process in reverse on their way home.[18] In modern Saudi Arabia, the most conservative of Muslim countries, some women wear the veil when in the country, but abandon it when abroad. And while older women wear thick veils, younger ones use such thin material that their faces are fully visible.

Women were given a lower status in the Qur'an:

Men are in charge of women, because Allah has made some of them excel the others, and because they spend some of their wealth. Hence righteous women are obedient, guarding the unseen which Allah has guarded. And those of them that you fear might rebel, admonish them and abandon them in their beds and beat them.[19]

As in Christianity, early Islam saw women as a source of support and comfort: 'He created for you mates from among yourselves that ye may dwell in tranquillity with them.' The Qur'an also permitted a man to have up to four wives, provided he could support them. But this represented a *limitation* on previous practice. Moreover, the taking of several wives came about after a battle which left large numbers of war widows and thus an unbalanced population.[20] In these circumstances, polygamy seemed desirable, if the ideal of marriage and family was to be generally attained. However, it was an expedient and a cultural phenomenon, appropriate in special circumstances: most marriages were to be monogamous. Over time, practice changed, so that in the modern era it became rare for Muslim men to have more than one wife. Turkey abolished polygamy altogether in 1926.

For Muslims, marriage itself was a contract, rather than a religious ceremony. The *hadith* also insisted that a woman could never be married without her consent. While marriages might be arranged between families as a means of uniting them, this was not the same as a forced marriage, which Islam does not sanction. Although Islam permitted the betrothal of girls at a young age, it was forbidden to hand a bride over to her husband before she was ready for marital congress. A couple could divorce by mutual agreement, and a woman could obtain a divorce in the courts by proving a matrimonial offence, such as cruelty, desertion or failure to maintain her. The husband also had responsibilities towards his ex-wife: 'Divorced women should be provided with an affordable provision. This is incumbent on the righteous.'[21]

Attitudes towards sex have also been the cause of some misunderstanding between Muslims and Christians. From the outset, Muslims felt that Christianity had a problem with sex, amounting almost to an anti-sexual bias; meanwhile Islam adopted a more honest and straightforward approach. Contrary to Western assumptions about its puritanism, the Qur'an fully accepted the human need for sex and did not blame Eve for the fall from grace, as the Bible does. Islam taught that the gratification of sexual desire was a positive good and to be enjoyed – within marriage; it was public sexual display that was an evil and that undermined marriage. Hence the Muslim idea of Paradise included a sensuous and sexual life. Sex even became an element in the humour and poetry of Islamic society, which invented humorous names for the penis and the vagina.[22] Conversely, the idea of celibacy was seen as unnatural and was discouraged in the *Sunna*. The introduction of celibacy into Christianity by the Catholics was always regarded as perverse and inexplicable, not least because it represented an attempt to undo the work of God, who had made man a sensual being.

In modern times, the increasing liberalism of the West has given Islam a reputation for being homophobic. In so far as it is true, this feature underlines the religion's Judaeo-Christian roots, for Christianity was also homophobic for most of its history – and continues to be so in parts of the world, notably Africa. However, there is a good deal of uncertainty and disagreement about the authority for homophobia. Like the Bible, the Qur'an frequently refers to the story of Lot, his wife and the men of Sodom; but some interpreters argue that it is not clear what this means. Passages in the Qur'an can be cited as condemnation of homosexuality. And in parts of the *hadith* the Prophet reportedly said that it was unnatural and a crime, like adultery: 'What, do you come to male beings, leaving your wives that your Lord created for you? No, but you are a people of transgressors.'[23]

On the other hand, however, some Muslims argue that the references to homosexuality are oblique, not direct, and that same-sex sexuality is mentioned without condemnation; also much of what is reported in the *hadith* is of dubious authenticity and is, in any case, inspired by culture, not ideology.[24] Modern interpretations of the Qur'an suggest that it disapproves of lust and coercion in *all* circumstances, regardless of sexual orientation: 'You approach men instead of women lustfully; you are rather a people given to excess.' Thus the story about Lot is not about homosexuality, but is a critique of male sexuality in the form of rape and aggression; similarly the condemnation of Lot's wife was for her infidelity.[25]

Whatever conclusions are reached about the Islamic view of homo-sexuality, the practice in Muslim societies is another matter altogether. In homoerotic Arabic, Persian and Turkish poetry, it was entirely acceptable for men to praise and court boys, express their love for them, admire their beauty and develop relationships; although there was apparently no word for homosexuality, the idea was expressed as 'sensibility to beauty'.[26] It was commonly believed that sex with women was chiefly for purposes of reproduction (which was also the view taken by the Christian Church), while sex with boys was for pleasure. Yet this, too, is contested on the basis that Islamic tradition did not see the main justification for sex as procreation; the Prophet himself taught that sex was a pleasure.[27] In the early modern period, when trade and piracy brought Europeans and Muslims into frequent contact, Western observers often claimed that sex between men was common, especially in North Africa. It ought to be said that the reports were strongly associated with the enslavement of captives. It was reportedly common for young men who had been captured by the Barbary pirates to be bought by wealthy Moors; they acted as valets and cooks for their masters, but also shared their beds.[28] Petitions for ransoming slaves claimed that the Moors 'do frequently bugger the said captives', and in 1677 Thomas Baker, the English consul at Tripoli, wrote that homosexuality was quite acceptable there.[29] Although it is clearly difficult to generalise, on balance it does appear that Muslim society was more tolerant of same-sex relationships than European society, which became increasingly homophobic during the nineteenth century.

Today, Western observers show as much concern about the more political features of Islam – including the state, the law and terrorism – as about its customs and social practices. *Jihad* is casually, but erroneously, linked with the Christian idea of 'holy war' or crusade. In fact, it simply implies 'struggle' or taking pains to achieve something; thus, in the seventh and eighth centuries the greater *jihad* was an internal struggle to achieve personal purity.[30] In the Qur'an, the three words employed for war are *harb, qitar* and *jihad*. But *jihad* is rarely used, and none is used for aggression against enemies or unbelievers. As the early Muslims were surrounded by tribes who regularly engaged in war, they were obliged to defend themselves; but any requirement to fight occurred in a specific context.[31] *Jihad* was consequently practised along the frontiers with Byzantium and Spain. In the Muslim lands – known as *Dar al-Islam* – there was tolerance of unbelievers; but in territory beyond Muslim rule – *Dar al-Harb* – there was a collective and divinely sanctioned duty to expand, so that the whole world would eventually embrace Islam. This, however, could be attained by teaching and good example, and not necessarily by war.

In time, as it became obvious that Muslims could not convert the entire world, the leaders began to reconsider how to deal with non-Muslim populations. The presence of Muslims as a minority in South Asia (which was not *Dar al-Islam*) complicated traditional thinking about Islamic rule and undermined assumptions about a perpetual state of conflict between Muslims and non-believers. A distinction was drawn between aggressive non-believers (who were to be invited to convert to Islam) and the 'People of the Book', who were not to be fought unless they attacked first and who could, on agreeing to pay a tax, remain free to practise their religions.

Later complications arose where Islam was actually in retreat, such as in British India after the Mughals had been supplanted. Muslims in such areas usually accepted non-Muslim authority, rather than engage in warfare. For pragmatic Muslim rulers who wanted to make alliances with one enemy to help them deal with another, it was possible to draw on supporting evidence in the Qur'an about making a truce with non-believers and on the practice of the Prophet himself, who had settled with the Meccan armies.

A further problem was that despite injunctions to unite, the Muslim world insisted on dividing itself up into nations: the first Arab Empire began to break up as early as in the 700s. The process accelerated under European colonial rule and encouraged attempts to rethink Islamic ideas about international law. Responding to the pressure of colonialism, some Muslims developed what is known as the 'apologetic interpretation of *jihad*', first advocated by the Indian, Sayyid Ahmad Khan. This holds that fighting is justified only to resist persecution or aggression. Against the background of the 1857 Indian Rebellion, in which some Muslims had participated, he contended that since the British permitted Muslims to practise their religion freely, there was no case for waging *jihad* against them. Going even further, most modern Muslim countries have rejected the traditional view that the Qur'an divides the world into *Dar al-Islam* and *Dar al-Harb*, and have abandoned any idea of using *jihad* to justify a state of war. They recognise the sovereignty of other states, while retaining the idea of Islamic unity as a symbolic objective. Although Islam acknowledges the importance of martyrdom in a moral or spiritual cause, it condemns the martyr who seeks glory and prestige. Sunni Muslims consider the deliberate pursuit of martyrdom to be tantamount to suicide, which is specifically condemned. However, Shia Muslims take a different view, honouring a long list of early martyrs and making pilgrimages to their shrines.

Among the most distinctive features of Islam, by comparison with Christian society, was the role of the state. The persecution suffered by the early Christian communities implanted in them a strong tradition of the separation of religion and the secular authority. Admittedly, some rulers attempted to qualify this – notably kings who claimed to rule by divine right; but this notion was robustly challenged and dismissed. Christian communities largely followed the biblical injunction to 'Render therefore unto Caesar the things that are Caesar's; and unto God the things that are God's.' As a result, for Christians the Church came to assume a large institutional role: it was much more than just a building. For Jews and Muslims, on the other hand, the synagogue or mosque was essentially a building for worship. The upshot was that Muslims did not develop the idea of secularism, as in the West, and in Islam there was no separation of the religious and the secular authority. During the Middle Ages leading Muslims were known to look down on the state, even to the point of declining posts from the emperor.

This tradition had important consequences for the identity of Muslims. Whereas Christians usually developed a political focus, Muslims relied more on their religion as the basis for their identity: their religion transcended all other loyalties.[32] It was only later that they began to define themselves more as Turks or Persians or Egyptians and to espouse nationalist and patriotic loyalties. As a result, most Muslim states lacked a stable state at the centre and never evolved an acceptable means of changing government. The ruling institution of the Islamic state was known as the *Caliphate*. It was presided over by a caliph, who was chosen for (and who claimed authority from) his connection with Mohammed; but he had no spiritual powers himself – merely the duty of maintaining the legacy of the Prophet. Each of the first four caliphs – known as the 'rightly guided' caliphs, because they closely followed Mohammed's ideals – was a personal relation of the Prophet. However, disputes about the succession arose from the start. With the expansion of Islam, the Caliphate had lost its centrality by the ninth century. In the eleventh century, the Seljuk Turks marginalised the caliph, and the sultan emerged as the chief secular authority. Under the Ottomans after 1290, he effectively became caliph; Ataturk finally abolished the Caliphate altogether in 1924.

Complementary to this neglect of secularism is Muslim law or *Sharia*, meaning 'the path which God wishes men to walk'. Whereas in Western Christian countries the law is determined by and enforced by the state, and regulates a man's relations with the state and his neighbours, in Islam the *Sharia* incorporates his relationship with God and his conscience. The law is binding upon individuals, but is not enforced by the state. Its provisions apply to Muslims who live within Islamic territories, but does not apply in non-Muslim countries. The *Sharia* reflects the view that men are unable to discern right from wrong and consequently need guidance. The law is thus divine and eternal.[33] Thus, whereas secular Western law tends to change and reflect shifts in society, by medieval times Islamic law had become rigid, incorporating crimes against religion, including unlawful intercourse, false accusation, drinking alcohol, theft and robbery. However, from 1917 onwards, the Muslims of the Ottoman Empire began to reform Islamic law, and – except for on the Arabian Peninsula – the *Sharia* was limited to family law, inheritance and endowments. During the twentieth century most Muslim countries came to base their civil and criminal law on European models and secular courts. Countries like Tunisia and Egypt have largely abolished *Sharia*, and India and Pakistan tend to absorb it into a system of national, secular courts.[34]

This survey of some of the key ideas associated with Islam serves to underline one important point: though commonly seen as rigid and eternal, in many ways the religion clearly has changed and adapted. Slavery, for example, is no longer taken for granted, and women are not everywhere treated as inferior to men. While for centuries it was assumed that Muslim states were properly ruled by sultans or kings, this notion was never explicitly sanctioned, and most Muslim states have abandoned monarchy. Emerging from a common cultural background, Jews, Christians and Muslims have all moved away from their origins, albeit in different ways. But Muslims have not always and in every respect been the slowest to change: up to 2017, for example, Orthodox Jews would refuse to sit next to a woman in an aeroplane (for this reason, the Israeli national carrier, El Al, frequently moves female passengers).

The idea that Islam and Christianity were great religious enemies from the start is one of the great fallacies generated by the Crusades. The origins of the myth are best viewed in the geographical-cum-political context of early Islam, when, aside from the Persian Empire, its expansion was constrained by the various Christian powers, including Byzantium, the Frankish Kingdom, Poland and Hungary. But this did not reflect significant religious differences. At the death of Mohammed in 632, Islam was arguably the most dynamic civilisation in the world. Its remarkable expansion in the next century was helped by the general exhaustion of the Byzantine and Persian Empires, both divided by religious and social discontent. Many people had become so oppressed by Byzantine rule that they welcomed the Arab invasion: Christians, Jews and Samaritans all gave them assistance and found the Muslim regime less onerous, especially in terms of taxation.

Yet the main explanation for the rapid spread of Islam lay with the tribes of the Arabian Peninsula, who had traditionally expended much of their energy in attacking one another. Islam introduced them to the concept of Muslim brotherhood. After winning over Medina and Mecca, the Prophet then extended his alliances to the other tribes. Once they had become believers, they turned their aggression outwards, enabling Islam to extend its range dramatically. This was achieved without a professional army: the Arab warriors believed that their success was proof of divine inspiration. The emergence of this force proved timely, in that it energised trends already apparent in Arabia. Arabs felt the need for unity, and their desire for a higher form of religion was already indicated by Judaism, Christianity and the appearance of other prophets from the local tribes.[35] In effect, Mohammed gave a focus to the existing forces, making for a national revival among the Arabs.

Mohammed's two immediate successors advanced Islamic power across Arabia, Palestine, Syria, Mesopotamia, Asia Minor and Persia. The Battle of Yarmuk in Jordan in 636 – which saw 30,000 Muslims defeat 100,000 Byzantines – was a turning point. The Muslims had captured Jerusalem by 638 and Syria by 640; from 642 they advanced into Egypt, and then spread more slowly along the North African coast, through modern Libya, Tunisia, Algeria and Morocco, until in 709 their forces crossed the Straits of Gibraltar and occupied Spain. Eventually, the Arab armies were checked in France at the battle of Poitiers in 732, and by 759 they had withdrawn to south of the Pyrenees. Meanwhile, attacks on the Roman Empire's capital Constantinople were also repulsed, at least until 1453; but Islamic forces advanced eastwards into the whole of Afghanistan by 664 and Sind by 712. Any further advance into India was held up until the annexation of the Punjab in 986, but a combination of armed forces, traders and missionaries then extended Islam's influence from the Indus valley, along the plain of the Ganges to Bihar and Bengal by 1290.

The Qur'an's message of compassion and mercy was widely embraced in Africa, where it reached as far south as Mali and Nigeria during the ninth century thanks to commercial contacts. Muslim traders from Gujarat in India also helped to extend Islam further east to Sumatra and the Malay Peninsula by 1290, and subsequently to Java, the Moluccas, Borneo and the Philippines. In Indonesia, Islam interacted with Hinduism, Buddhism and other local religions to produce a hybrid version. Indonesians also found Sufism very appealing. Whereas Hindu society divided people by caste, Islam placed all believers on an equal footing and was thus very appealing to those at the bottom of the scale. As Indonesia was so far from the centre of the Muslim world – before the twentieth century, few made the pilgrimage to Mecca – its version of Islam developed independently, acquiring the tolerant, easy-going character of the local society.

Initially, this Islamic expansion was primarily an Arab achievement, directed from the capital in Damascus by the leadership of the Umayyad dynasty. However, its character changed under the Abbasid dynasty (750 to 936). This period saw a growing emphasis on conversion, which depended not so much on coercion as on the compelling appeal of the new religion. In Europe, conversion was a particular feature of Islamic rule in Spain. Meanwhile, the centre of Islam was transferred from Syria to a new capital, Baghdad, founded in 762, where the Abbasids developed a prosperous and sophisticated empire presided over by an autocratic caliph and a non-Arab ruling elite comprising the commercial, administrative and land-owning classes. Closer to Persian influence, Baghdad stood in the agriculturally rich valley of Mesopotamia and at the intersection of several trade routes. Under the Abbasids, Islamic civilisation flourished in the spheres of agriculture, industry, commerce and culture. With up to a million people, Baghdad itself became one of the world's greatest cities. Innovations included crop rotation (which enabled several harvests to be produced each year), novel irrigation techniques and the development of new fruits and sugar cane. The non-Muslim people, known as *dhimmis*, benefited under this system, for – though second-class citizens – they could freely practise their religions, enjoy property rights and be employed by the state. As yet, Western Europe was not prepared to be so tolerant towards those outside the Church.

During the eleventh and twelfth centuries, the Islamic world was subject to new invasions from the Seljuks, a Turkish people from Central Asia. The Seljuks captured Baghdad in 1055, but became converts to Islam. Then, from 1300 onwards, a new Turkish power arose in the shape of the Ottomans. They initially attacked Byzantine territory in the west, but in the later 1300s occupied Muslim lands and absorbed the Seljuks into the Ottoman Empire, which continued to expand until 1600.

The chief cultural centre of the original Arab empire had been in Damascus, but over time greater centres evolved – not only in Baghdad, but also in Cairo, Constantinople and Cordoba. The foundation of Baghdad coincided with the introduction of paper-making, leading to the growth of public libraries and programmes of translation from classical works into Arabic. This process lasted for 200 years and, in this multicultural empire, was carried out by Greeks and Christians, as well as Muslims.

During the ninth and tenth centuries, the Muslim rulers became dependent on slave-soldiers, known as Mamluks, who converted to Islam. After 1250, the Mamluks ruled Egypt and the adjacent regions. However, weakened by famine and the Black Death, they were supplanted by the Ottomans in 1517. Cairo became famous for al-Azhar, built in 970 originally as a mosque, but which developed into a university and a pre-eminent centre of Arabic-Islamic learning. Al-Azhar had no formal admissions, courses, departments or examinations. The students, who came from all over the Middle East, Afghanistan, India and parts of Africa, were often financed by religious endowments.

The success of Islamic-Christian civilisation was epitomised by Cordoba, known as 'the ornament of the world', where Christians and Muslims could worship at the same mosque-church. Many people there converted to Islam because they found it attractive, not because of coercion. At its height, the city of Cordoba had half a million inhabitants, a famous university, 1,600 mosques, 900 public baths, street lighting and many libraries: the library of the caliph, Abd al-Rahman, reportedly contained 400,000 volumes.[36] Beyond the cities, the population of Spain benefited from the tolerance and egalitarianism of the Muslim rulers, manifested in a fairer distribution of land. In addition to such crops as rice, citrus fruits, sugar and cotton, the Arabs developed pottery, textiles, paper, silk and mining. Many of the troops who arrived with the invasion stayed on and intermarried with the local people, as did new waves of Berber and Arab immigrants during the eighth century. A similar cultural cross-fertilisation occurred in Sicily, where the Arabs bequeathed many words to the local dialect, as well as such tangible things as cotton, oranges, sugar-cane, dates and mulberries, and the irrigation they required. When the Normans conquered the island, rather than suppress the Arab influence, they adapted to it, making use of Arab architecture, poetry, soldiers and administrators; they even minted coins with Arabic inscriptions. Travellers commented that in Palermo local Christians spoke Arabic and dressed like Muslims. As a result, Sicily became another route for the transfer of Islamic knowledge to Western Europe.

Scholars who fled from Athens and Byzantium found the atmosphere of these Islamic centres relaxed and welcoming, free from anti-intellectualism and the fear of heresy. One caliph, al-Ma'mun (813–33), faced with a group of Muslims who felt it was unnecessary to look beyond their own religious writings, ordered the provincial governors to summon all the local scholars and force them to accept that the Qur'an had been created, not spoken by God. Severe punishment was meted out to anyone who resisted. From the eighth century onwards, and right through the medieval era, these Islamic centres preserved the knowledge inherited from the Greeks and extended it in many areas, including astronomy, chemistry, medicine, mathematics, philosophy, optics, anatomy, engineering and geography. Advances in particular fields included the discovery of the circulation of the blood through the heart; the calculation of the earth's circumference (at 22,400 miles, it was only 22 miles out); the identification of the symptoms of smallpox and measles; the recognition that light travelled from the object to the eye and not the other way round; the development of modern hospitals handling surgery, contagious diseases and mental illness; and theories of flight, algebra and quadratic equations.[37] During the ninth and tenth centuries, Muslim mathematicians adapted the concepts of Indian mathematics to create the numerical system used today, based on Arabic numerals (rather than the unwieldy Roman ones) and units of ten, as well as a decimal system, fractions, algorithms, algebra and geometry. Alchemy also reached a peak in Muslim society in the Middle Ages. Though often seen as magic, it laid the foundations for modern chemistry. Muslim alchemists pioneered scientific methods by keeping precise records of their experiments – a practice that later became standard procedure. For Muslims, cosmology (or the study of the universe) embraced both the physical and the spiritual world and was thus, in effect, a means of trying to understand God's purpose in creating and ordering the world. Muslim scientists also practised the most advanced astronomy of the Middle Ages, building the first observatories and using trigonometry to measure the angle between the sun and the horizon. Astronomy was favoured by Muslims because it helped with Islamic worship, notably ascertaining the times of daily prayers, and determining the times of sunrise and sunset (which dictated the duration of fasting).

The Arabs also enjoyed commercial links, especially with Spain, Sicily, southern France and Byzantium. As a result of this, Europe gained a wide range of products and institutions, ranging from coffee, chess and toothpaste to botanical gardens (including plants such as roses and tulips), public libraries, universities and hospitals. Knowledge of the distillation of alcohol was a further benefit: for example, a clear spirit flavoured with juniper berries (a proto-gin) – initially regarded as a tonic or medicine – appeared around 1055 on its way from the universities of Baghdad to the monasteries of Western Europe. Such familiar English words as alcohol, algebra, alchemy, jar, arsenal, cotton and coffee were derived from Arabic roots. These extensive intellectual and economic contacts between Islam and the West were later to be heavily downplayed in the wake of the Crusades; but they clearly had a profound cultural impact on Christian Europe.

CHAPTER TWO

THE MYTHS OF THE CRUSADES

During the centuries of Islamic expansion, England lay in comparative obscurity on the north-west margins of Europe. Until the fourth century, Christianity was not widespread, though bishoprics had been established at London, York and Colchester. After the withdrawal of the Roman legions in 401–02, the country was divided among several Anglo-Saxon kingdoms, and for a time Christianity was largely extinguished except in Wales, Ireland and parts of Scotland. The period of invasions left church life a modest affair, with few bishops, great buildings, religious houses or educational institutions. However, a turning point came in 597, when Pope Gregory sent Augustine on an evangelistic mission to the Anglo-Saxons, extending the influence of Rome and an organised ecclesiastical system to England. Conversion to Christianity was still going on in England in the sixth century, only a few years before Mohammed founded Islam. By the seventh century, England had become dominated by the Christian kingdoms, Mercia, Northumbria and Wessex, and by the tenth century it was largely united under Wessex. Even in this early period, the Saxon rulers seem to have been aware of the rise of Islam. Offa, who became king of Mercia in 757, asserted his control over English trade and used reform of the currency to bring it into line with that of Charlemagne; Offa even issued gold coins bearing the words 'There is no God but Allah alone.' As he was on bad terms with the archbishop of Canterbury (following his attempt to create a new archbishopric), it may be that his motive was to assert his own authority in religious matters.

From his base as the first archbishop of Canterbury, Augustine began to introduce the influence of Mediterranean learning to England. The bishops accepted received doctrine from Augustine, St Wilfred and the Venerable Bede, and reverenced the authority of Rome. In particular, Augustine made the biblical account of Adam and Eve and the devastating loss of Eden the central issue for the early Church. Christians focused on Adam's sinfulness and his attraction into evil by Satan, but they placed the blame primarily on Eve, thereby initiating centuries of misogyny in the Church.[1] This emphasis marked an early contrast with Islam, which identified Adam's role as the original Prophet of God, rather than emphasising his sinfulness. For Muslims, any error by him was not a crime for which mankind should suffer; and if there was any blame attached, it was shared equally by Adam *and* Eve. On the other hand, while the influence of Rome distanced English Christians from Muslims, some of the monastic orders were much closer to the spirit of Islam. The early Cistercians, for example, adopted a simple and austere approach, shunning idols, paintings and coloured glass.

The Norman Conquest in 1066 gave England closer links with the Continent – both because her kings ruled large parts of France and because of the domination of Catholicism over her intellectual life. Despite this, England remained geographically remote from the world of Islam. Beyond enjoying an awareness of Islam as a heretical movement, there was little direct knowledge about it, and the Arabian Peninsula remained almost completely unknown to Europeans; hardly anyone visited Mecca or Medina, although several propagandists claimed to have been there and to have witnessed the *Hajj*. It is thought that the first to have attended was an Italian, Ludovico di Varthema, in 1503. But up to the sixteenth century, most accounts were second-hand, based on hearsay. English scholars such as the Venerable Bede derived a little knowledge about the 'Saracens', as they were known, from the Bible. Bede related that the Saracens were the descendants of Ishmael, the son of Abraham's second wife, Hagar; but as she was a 'bondswoman', it followed that all Saracens were of low origins – including the Prophet. Along with other eighth-century Christians, Bede hoped for the conversion of Muslims; but there was almost no missionary activity, and contemporaries agreed that Christians were too sinful to attract recruits.[2]

The most immediate source of understanding about Islam came from Spain and Sicily, both centres of Islamic-Christian culture. There, Islam was cast in a largely positive light, thanks to the experience of visiting Christians, who commonly embraced the language, ideas and culture of the Arabs and flourished under Muslim rule. English scholars travelled to Cordoba and Toledo, and in time even as far as Baghdad, while Christian pilgrims enjoyed access to Jerusalem. They benefited from the work of Islamic scholars, who translated Greek texts that were transferred to other parts of Europe. Among the Englishmen who undertook these visits in the twelfth century were Adelard of Bath, Michael Scott, Daniel of Morley and Thomas Brown, who even adopted an Islamic identity as Kaid Brun.[3] Around 1143, the first translation of the Qur'an was undertaken by Robert of Ketton at the instigation of Peter the Venerable, the abbot of Cluny. It was entitled *The Religion of Muhammad the Pseudo-prophet*. Worried about the growing influence of Islam, Peter wanted anti-Islamic propaganda to be better informed. The translation was full of errors, but even so it remained the standard version until 1649, when a good English translation appeared; this was itself superseded by George Sale's translation in 1734.

However, at least a few Christians enjoyed enough knowledge about Islam to be able to correct some of the misapprehensions. In the 1140s, Otto of Freising commented that reports about 'Muslim idols' were highly improbable, because:

> It is known that the whole body of Saracens worship one God and receive the Old Testament law and the rite of circumcision. Nor do they attack Christ or the Apostles. In this one thing alone they are far from salvation – in denying that Jesus Christ is God or the Son of God, and in venerating the seducer Mahomet as a great prophet of the supreme God.[4]

In 1460, Pope Pius II conceded:

> There are many points of agreement between Christians and Muslims: one God, the creator of the world; a belief in the necessity for faith; a future life of rewards and punishments; the immortality of the soul; the common use of the Old and New Testaments; all this is common ground. We only differ about the nature of God.[5]

Medieval England also shared other ideas with Muslims – for example, the ban on usury, which was condemned in the Qur'an and in the Christian scriptures. For centuries, usury was regarded as immoral. The English circumvented this by relying on Jews, who settled in England after the Norman Conquest, as moneylenders. They were exploited by kings in need of ready cash and blamed by the public when the economy declined. On the other hand, as usury underpinned the foreign trade on which English prosperity depended, it came to be seen as a necessary evil, especially in the sixteenth century. Thus, the Act against Usury of 1571 did not ban it, but set a limit of 10 per cent interest on loans. But as the expansion of trade tempted moneylenders to raise the level, a further regulatory proclamation was announced in 1581.[6] As so often, Christians and Muslims started from the same position and professed similar beliefs, but found ways of compromising their principles.

Christians found it increasingly difficult to adopt an objective and rational view of Islam, despite the availability of translations of the Qur'an. The explanation for this lay in the growing concern in the medieval Church about Christian heresies. In this context, it was inevitable that Islam should be regarded as the worst of the heresies. As England remained essentially a Continental power, and intellectually Catholic, she was almost inevitably influenced by the concerns of the Catholic Church in Europe and its obsession with the world of Islam. Consequently, in the Middle Ages Muslims were commonly – if absurdly – characterised as pagans and the Prophet either as a heretic/dangerous schismatic, or as an impostor/idol/false god. He was portrayed as an instrument of heresy, driven by some diabolical inspiration to divide Christendom. In 'The Man of Law's Tale', Chaucer reflected the hostile view, referring to Mohammed as 'Mahoun our prophete', which was doubtless typical of the period. Medieval romances about the wars fought by the Emperor Charlemagne against the Saracens routinely depicted golden images of Mohammed, and the popular imagination had him as a fiend or devil who lured his followers to destruction by false promises.

The standard account of his early life revolved around a number of fictitious episodes. As evidence of his capacity for deception, he was said to have tricked a wealthy widow into marrying him. He was supposed to suffer from falling sickness, the result of being dazzled when the Angel Gabriel came to him. He was said to have taught milk-white doves to rest on his shoulders and pick grain out of his ears. It was claimed that he hung pots of milk and honey from the horns of a bull to symbolise the prosperity and abundance that would accrue from following him. One of the more elaborately absurd stories in circulation had Mohammed as a cardinal living in Rome and aspiring to become pope; on being frustrated, he took revenge by quitting the Church in order to found a rival religion.[7] Among the travesties, the most lurid purported to describe his death. It was claimed that he died from an epileptic fit, or by poisoning, and that his body was eaten by pigs. Another story had it that his body was left on a dunghill and was kept for 30 days before being placed in an iron coffin and carried to the roof of the temple at Mecca, where it hung in the air between four magnetic lodestones.

These lurid accounts epitomised the conundrum that Islam posed for medieval Europe. The extensive common ground between the two religions raised major questions about whether Islam in fact represented a stage in Christian evolution or even heralded the final days of the world. Its sheer success in spreading across the world underlined the uncomfortable fact that Christianity's claim to be the superior world civilisation now looked rather dubious. The flourishing world of Islam posed a real challenge to the complacency of medieval Europe: that largely agrarian, feudal, monastic society was now faced with a dynamic, intellectually vital religion. How best to deal with it? The readiness of Islam to accommodate Christians by allowing them to practise their religion and make pilgrimages to the Holy Land betrayed a disturbing confidence in the ultimate triumph of Islam. It was thus only too tempting to damn the Prophet as a charlatan and Islam as the work of the Devil, and to mobilise the Christian states against its political-military might.

⬭ ✤ ⬭

Although England was territorially too remote to be directly affected by the expansion of Islam, her rulers were inevitably influenced by Continental concerns. As early as 759, Christian Europe had begun to push back against the apparently inexorable expansion of Islam, notably in Spain. In that year Arab forces withdrew beyond the Pyrenees following their defeat at Poitiers. By 950, Aragon, Navarre and Castile had been restored to Christian control. However, the re-conquest of Spain against the Caliphate of Cordoba was a protracted affair that did not accelerate until after the Arab defeat at Tolosa in 1212 and that eventually culminated in the fall of Granada to the Christian forces in 1492. Thus began the eclipse of the remarkable Arab-Spanish civilisation that had flourished there. A tolerant Islamic society was replaced with a narrow, bigoted brand of Christianity. After 1492, Muslims were given the option of converting to Christianity or being expelled. Some 3 million eventually left Andalusia, but in the process they helped to spread its culture and learning around the Mediterranean, North Africa and the Middle East.

Meanwhile, in the east, Islam continued to expand. The empire of the Seljuk Turks challenged the Byzantine Empire, which in 1025 extended from the Balkans and Greece, across the whole of Anatolia, to the western regions of Persia. When the two forces met at Manzikert in 1071, the Seljuks destroyed the Byzantine army and began to move across Anatolia towards Constantinople. Eventually, in 1095, Alexius I, the Byzantine emperor, keen to restore control over Asia Minor and northern Syria and to shore up his domestic position, asked the Western European powers

30

for help against the Seljuk Turks, thereby triggering the start of the Crusades. However, the incoherence of this great enterprise was evident from the outset, for Alexius had no interest in recapturing Jerusalem from the Muslims – even though this was ostensibly the aim of the First Crusade. For their part, the Western Crusaders, especially the Normans, felt disinclined to help Byzantium, which they despised and resented. Nonetheless, in November 1095, Pope Urban II used the meeting of the Council of the Church at Clermont to support Alexius, by issuing a rousing appeal to launch a Holy War for the recovery of Jerusalem. It was to be regarded as a kind of penance for its participants. This resulted in the First Crusade in 1096, which led to the re-conquest of Jerusalem, the massacre of its Muslim population in 1099, and the formation of several Crusader states in Tripoli, Antioch and Edessa along the Levantine coast.

Driven by self-interest and opportunism as much as by religious fervour, crusading soon became a habit. A Second Crusade took place in 1145–49. However, by 1186 the Muslim armies under Saladdin had surrounded the Crusader territory. In 1187, they annihilated the Crusader army and recaptured Jerusalem, a setback from which crusading never fully recovered. This prompted the Third Crusade in 1188–92, the episode that saw the most notable English involvement. The death of King Henry II in July 1189 brought Richard I ('The Lionheart') to the throne for the next ten years, during which time he rapidly emerged as the movement's most effective leader, if a rather barbaric one: in 1191, within weeks of making a truce with his opponents, he broke the agreement and executed 2,700 Muslim prisoners.

Crusading was an expensive business. Richard declared that he would sell London to finance his crusade, which in the first year cost him 70 per cent of his entire annual revenue. He spent £14,000 (21,000 marks) simply on preparing the fleet for the Third Crusade. The money for crusading was generally raised by imposing taxes on revenues, property and profits. In his day, Henry II had introduced a profits tax known as the Saladdin Tithe. This involved reaching agreement between the royal government and parliament and thereby created a useful precedent for future wars.

Despite Richard's efforts, the Third Crusade ended in stalemate, leading Pope Innocent III to call for a Fourth Crusade in 1201–04.

A Fifth Crusade was launched in 1217–29. But although Christian rule over Jerusalem was briefly restored between 1229 and 1244, Crusader control remained precarious and limited to the coastal strip of Palestine. At this point, historians begin to lose count – partly because so many very minor crusades were sent to Palestine, but mainly because they were increasingly launched from other parts of the world, including the south of France, Spain, the Baltic and Egypt.

The Crusades stamped their indelible mark on English identity. They formed a heroic episode, generated some of the iconic English figures, resulted in the adoption of the red cross as a symbol of England and created a narrative that was to be resurrected later in the Victorian period. Yet the fact remains that they loom much larger in European history than in the history of the Muslim world; and even in Europe, their impact was largely erased during the period from the Reformation to the eighteenth century. Moreover, as one leading historian of the subject has put it: 'Most of what passes in public as knowledge of the Crusades is either misleading or false.'[8] Consequently, their significance must be heavily qualified in a number of ways.

The most obvious is that they proved to be a failure. Up to the Eighth Crusade, in 1291, the crusading movement only temporarily recovered control of Jerusalem and failed to reverse the advance of Islam, except in Syria, or even to establish a permanent presence in the Holy Land. As the Turks spread across Anatolia, their aim was to extend Islamic power, rather than to make converts. They followed the Islamic thinking that Christians and Jews should be allowed to practise their religions, so long as they accepted Islamic rule. This tradition meant accepting anyone who wished to convert, and Islam was a comparatively easy religion to adopt. Many of the Anatolian Muslims were themselves descended from nomadic converts, who embraced religious practice more easily than Muslims in Arabia. Consequently, the Turks readily adopted local Christian saints and local Christian customs. In addition, conversion to Islam brought the advantage of lower taxes and greater influence.

It is also arguable that not only did crusading fail, but it even undermined Christendom, in that it eventually weakened the Byzantine Empire, which lost its ability to protect Christians against the expansion of Turkish power in south-east Europe. This was partly because the invaders never formed a united front against the Muslim world. In 1204, the Crusaders turned on Byzantium, captured Constantinople and installed a Latin Empire until 1261. Even among the English kings, the response to papal appeals varied a good deal. We are familiar with the crusading zeal of Richard I, but he was far from typical. The English contribution to the First and Second Crusades was slight. For example, King William II, known as 'Rufus' (1087–1100), entirely lacked religious piety and took a highly sceptical view: in conjunction with Anselm, the archbishop of Canterbury, he actually forbade the people – and even the clergy – to participate in the First Crusade.

King John (1199–1216), who is nowadays regarded as a capable and intelligent ruler, also showed much less enthusiasm for crusading than did his brother, Richard. This reflected his disputes with Pope Innocent III over appointments and revenues; in theory, England was subject to Rome, but in practice the king and the royal courts controlled these matters. Innocent disputed his choice for archbishop of Canterbury, took the side of the English clergy and the religious houses from which John was trying to extract extra taxes, and eventually excommunicated the king in 1209.[9] Fearful of internal revolt and invasion from Europe, in 1213 John dispatched a mission to the sultan of Morocco, seeking military support and reportedly offering to convert to Islam. Although this initiative failed, it is interesting, since it prefigured the sixteenth-century Tudor policy of trying to engage the Muslim powers against Continental opponents: Henry VIII consciously adopted the cause of King John. In this context, it is not surprising that John – unpopular on account of high taxation and dependent on paid mercenaries for support – tried to steer clear of the Crusades. He only symbolically took the Cross in 1215, shortly before being obliged to accept Magna Carta; but this was seen as a cynical manoeuvre, intended simply to strengthen his domestic position.

More generally, the motivation for participating in the Crusades was, at best, a mixture of the secular and the religious. The clergy were not free agents, and by the thirteenth century their role was modest. Some took their vows, but never actually set out to the Holy Land; others went, but only under instruction from their superiors.[10] Other Crusaders were sent as a punishment or a penance, or went as refugees to avoid retribution at home (some of them having been banished by the king for several years). There were also material considerations: some went because they had been dispossessed. However, the idea that younger sons (who enjoyed limited opportunities at home) were tempted by the prospect of making their fortunes in the Holy Land is now considered less significant than previously.[11]

On the whole, the Crusaders were not very interested in the culture of Islam, and while it clearly represented a more civilised, sophisticated and urbanised society, they remained largely on its margins. In the Holy Land itself, the impact of the Crusaders was mitigated, because those who lived in the Crusader territory along the coast of Palestine cooperated with the local people, on whom they relied for supplies of food. Also, from the eleventh century onwards, Christian merchants, especially the Venetians, supplied the Muslims, despite repeated threats of excommunication against 'all those faithless and impious Christians who . . . provide the Saracens with weapons, iron and wood'.[12] The French also early on developed commercial relations with the enemy, a prelude to their formal military cooperation with the Ottomans in the sixteenth century. As a result of social and commercial contact, some Christians became assimilated with the Arab population via marriage, and adopted their tastes and habits. The wars, after all, were short, seasonal affairs, leaving the invaders to enjoy long periods of peace, when they developed the habit of compromising with local society. The Europeans took to wearing long, flowing robes, enjoying oriental houses with courtyards, fountains and gardens, and even taking regular baths – all of which were condemned by the Christian fanatics as consorting with Satan.

Above all, crusading rapidly lost whatever original purpose and coherence it had enjoyed. It was easily abused by popes, who used the newly raised armies to target their own enemies. In addition, by the time of the Fourth Crusade in 1202–04, the movement had turned inward against Christian heretics and dissidents of all kinds. The most notorious example was the 'Albigensian Crusade' waged against the Cathars in the Languedoc area of France during 1209–29, which degenerated into a crude seizure of land. In effect this crusade amounted to a war of conquest by the king of France, involving the massacre of thousands of Christians and heretics.

Although no crusades were launched specifically against the Jews, they rapidly became indirect victims, being condemned as opponents of the Cross and seen as a challenge to Christianity. In 1096, the first Crusaders initiated the massacre of Jews as they passed through the Rhine valley, reportedly leaving every Jew dead in towns such as Cologne and Mainz. This soon became a habit in the lands through which the Crusaders passed. In Jerusalem, they slaughtered Jews (who were regarded as deserving of protection by Islam), along with the Muslims. During 1189–90, anti-Jewish riots and massacres also occurred in several English towns. Of course, anti-Semitism pre-dated the Crusades by many years, but the crusading movement legitimised violent attacks on Jews everywhere: as Jews had killed Christ, so it was claimed, all Jews could be held responsible. William Rufus, who sympathised with the Jews and disliked religious extremism generally, had foreseen that the fanaticism and ill-discipline of the Crusaders would have unhappy consequences. In 1290, the Jews were exiled from England by Edward I.

Eventually, under the influence of royal leadership, crusading deteriorated into a series of imperialistic territorial seizures: the Crusaders grabbed Lisbon (not especially close to the Holy Land); and in 1191, when King Richard's ships were blown off course and ended up in Cyprus, he decided to take that island, which remained in Christian hands until 1571. In 1202, during the Fourth Crusade, the European forces found themselves unable to raise enough funds to pay the Venetians for their ships and supplies. They therefore accepted the Venetians' offer of a moratorium on their debts, in return for helping the Venetians to capture the Dalmatian port of Zara (modern-day Zadar) – despite the fact that it was a Christian city under the rule of a Crusader, the king of Hungary.

Such actions reduced crusading to an increasingly incoherent and opportunistic movement. The very idea of the Crusades as a great ideological conflict between Islam and Christianity, or as a war between two civilisations, was shown to be highly exaggerated – if not totally implausible. In any case, by the late fourteenth or early fifteenth century, the European powers had become too divided and distracted. England and France, for example, were engaged in their Hundred Years' War. Only Hungary and Poland were ready to lead new crusades against the Ottomans. But three crusades – in 1396, 1444 and 1448 – all proved disastrous, and effectively marked the end of serious crusading. Europe abandoned the Balkans, along with the remainder of Byzantium, taking a stand in Hungary, Croatia and Poland.

What was the impact of the Crusades in the Muslim world? There was much uncertainty about the motives behind the attacks. The Crusades were not generally seen as religious in character, or as 'official' holy war. At best, they were assumed to be part of the general Christian advance into Spain and Sicily. Some Muslims, arguing along the same lines as Christians, suggested that they were a punishment from God or a divine test of their faith, intended to draw them into advancing against Constantinople or Rome.[13] The early Crusades enjoyed an advantage, in that there was little enthusiasm for a *jihad* among the population of Syria, and a complete lack of unity among Muslims, especially in the areas targeted by the invaders. Although leadership and coordination improved later, the Crusades never engaged the Muslim world as a whole.[14] Saladdin spent more time and effort on the internal consolidation of his territory and on fighting other Muslims. In any case, Islam was far more concerned about the advances of the Mongols under Chingis Khan from 1220 onwards, followed by attacks led by Tamerlane during the later fourteenth century and culminating in the defeat of the Ottoman Sultan Bayazid in 1402. However, the Mongols' conversion to Islam mitigated the threat and promoted their assimilation into Muslim society. Within half a century, Mongol rule had collapsed and the Ottomans had rallied.

Subsequently, the expansion of Islam continued apace through modern Algeria and Morocco, the Yemen and Iraq, and through sub-Saharan Africa as far as Ghana. In 1453, Constantinople fell to the

Ottoman Sultan Mehmet II, who thus brought an end to Byzantium and extended Turkish territory through Anatolia, Greece and the Balkans. Expansion continued in the early sixteenth century: Sultan Selim I took Aleppo and Damascus in 1516 and occupied Egypt in 1517. Subsequently, the Ottomans defeated Hungary in 1526 at the Battle of Mohacs and laid siege to Vienna in 1529. In 1542 the Turks overran Hungary, an alarming reversal of the expansion of the Christian kingdoms across eastern Europe.

But Ottoman power suffered from two weaknesses: there was a tendency to get diverted by conflicts with the Safavid Empire in Persia; and the empire enjoyed less command of the sea. Defeat at the naval battle of Lepanto by a coalition of Christian forces in 1571 restricted the Turks' control to the Eastern Mediterranean; but even this represented only a temporary setback lasting two years. For most of the next 500 years, Islam remained as great a threat to Western Christendom as it had been at the start of the Crusades. Not until the major setbacks between 1683 and 1699 in its wars with Austria and Poland was the Ottoman Empire finally put onto the defensive.

At an ideological level, Muslims believed that the Crusaders contaminated their lands both physically and spiritually. They regarded worship of the Cross as idolatrous and deviant. The Crusades provoked extreme criticisms of the Christian belief in Jesus as God incarnate, and condemnation of the account of his birth: 'They believe . . . that their God came forth from the privates of a woman, and that a woman was made pregnant by their God . . . anyone who believes [this] is quite mad.'[15] More generally, the Crusaders were seen as boorish, dirty and uncivilised people, deficient in sexual morality and lacking concern for the virtue of women. Muslims visited bath-houses daily, and in time some Christians began to copy them; but Muslims were shocked to find that they retained their pubic hair.[16] On the other hand, the Christians seemed capable of improvement; and in any case, it was necessary to deal with them during the lengthy periods of peace that followed the various treaties between them. The major long-term effect was to promote trade between Europe and the Levant, especially via Alexandria and Acre. This was acceptable under Islamic law, though the popes tried to ban Europeans from trading with Muslims under threat of excommunication. They failed, because the profits were too attractive.[17] Europe wanted spices and alum, and the Muslims sought timber and iron in return.

Despite its failures, crusading continued sporadically through the fourteenth, fifteenth and even sixteenth centuries. It was, however, largely a nominal strategy adopted when it suited rulers to gain respectability, arouse enthusiasm or divert attention from internal problems. As late as 1511, for example, King Henry VIII dispatched support to King Ferdinand of Spain against the sultan of Morocco. Henry dignified this assistance with the title of 'crusade'; however, he had no belief whatever that crusading served a sacred purpose – the expedition was merely a pragmatic act of policy. The English duly arrived at Cadiz, drank too much local wine and vandalised the town. Ferdinand sent them home and concluded a treaty with the Moroccan sultan instead. The expedition was more of an end than a beginning.

Meanwhile the development of heresies within Christendom served only to exacerbate the late-medieval disparagement of Islam. Martin Luther was one of many who interpreted the advances of the Turks as a scourge inflicted by God in order to punish Christians for their failings. As a result, he condemned attempts to organise new crusades, on the grounds that 'to make war on the Turks is to rebel against God, who punishes our sins through them'.[18] Christians, he thought, should tackle their own divisions before attacking the Ottomans. But Luther also wanted information about Islam to be spread, so as to promote the refutation of its errors: 'once the book of Muhammad has been made public and thoroughly examined in all its parts all pious persons will more easily comprehend the insanity and wiles of the devil'.

It was during the sixteenth century that humanist scholarship promoted a more detached view of the Crusades, although continuing fear of the Ottomans and admiration for the heroism of the medieval knights sustained the traditional attitudes. The significance of the crusading era was also undermined by the long-term commercial and social contact with the Eastern Mediterranean, especially during the reign of Elizabeth, and above all by the impact of the Protestant Reformation. Not surprisingly, later historians have been severe in their assessments of the Crusades. As early as the seventeenth century, this view was heralded by Francis Bacon, who disparaged them as 'the rendezvous of cracked brains that wore their feather in their head instead of their hat'.[19] By the eighteenth century, the retreat of the Ottoman Empire encouraged a more relaxed approach, and anti-clericalism led to denunciations of medieval Christian fanaticism. David Hume condemned the Crusades as 'the most signal monument of human folly that has yet appeared in any age'. And Edward Gibbon dismissed them as episodes of 'holy madness', whose proponents were 'destitute of humanity and reason'.[20] Not until the early nineteenth century did the renewed fascination with medievalism, Romanticism and Evangelicalism see a revival of the traditional view of crusading as a noble enterprise. However, one of the most eminent modern historians of the Crusades, Sir Steven Runciman, condemned the entire movement as 'one long act of intolerance in the name of God which is the sin against the Holy Ghost'.[21] In reality, there was no 'clash of civilisations', as some twentieth-century commentators and politicians have claimed, but rather a series of sordid power struggles and a waste of resources for no measurable gain.

CHAPTER THREE

THE IMPACT OF THE REFORMATION

As early as the reign of Henry VIII (1509–47), the hostile view of Muslim societies associated with the Crusades had been undermined. Although the merchants of the Tudor period struggled to compete with superior forces in the shape of Venice, Istanbul and the North African pirates, they managed to import luxury goods from the Ottoman Empire and Persia, including 'Turkey carpets', wall coverings with Islamic designs, silks, sugar, cotton, wine and such novelties as rhubarb. By the 1560s, 250 tons of sugar arrived each year from Morocco alone. At court it became fashionable for men, including the king, to adopt Turkish silk and velvet clothing, as well as turbans and scimitars. Much of what we see as the Tudor style was actually inspired by the Ottomans. Not that the Tudors were especially tolerant of Islam, but they dealt pragmatically with the people whom they variously called Turks, Moors, Saracens, Ottomans, Persians and Mahometans.[1] Many European traders recognised the common ground with Islam and appreciated the sobriety, discipline and toleration characteristic of Muslim societies. They also felt obliged to show respect for a superior civilisation: there was no question of carving colonies or spheres of influence out of Islamic territory. Europeans could not but be aware that the North African Muslims with whom they traded looked down on them, refusing, for example, to drink from the same cups. They commented unfavourably on their skin, bleached white by extreme cold, and on the tight-fitting clothes that seemed immoral.[2]

Just as important as commerce in discrediting the idea of a clash of civilisations between Islam and Christianity was the Protestant Reformation of the sixteenth century. Following Henry VIII's break with Rome in 1531, the English Reformation led Britain into a protracted struggle with the two great Catholic powers, Spain and France, for the next 300 years. The long-term effect was to define Britain as the leading Protestant power; but more immediately, it posed a far greater threat to England than Islam, and effectively destroyed the rationale for crusading activities. In this situation, the Islamic empires actually became a valuable balancing factor in European diplomacy. Henry's readiness to deal with the Muslim powers was far from eccentric during the sixteenth century. Both King Francis I of France and Queen Elizabeth I of England (who was excommunicated by Pope Pius V in 1570) took the policy of collaboration much further. Francis shared common enemies with the Ottoman sultan in the shape of the Holy Roman emperor, Charles V, and King Lewis of Hungary. 'I cannot deny that I wish to see the Turks all-powerful and ready for war,' he admitted, 'to weaken the power of the emperor.'[3]

For the Ottomans, it was highly advantageous that sixteenth-century Christendom should seem incapable of uniting against them; indeed, the sultan, Suleiman the Magnificent (1520–66), reportedly encouraged the imams of Constantinople to pray for the success of Luther. For the Turks, a major ally in the west of Europe offered a valuable counterweight to the Holy Roman Empire. The two powers engaged in diplomatic talks and French ambassadors were received in style by Suleiman, who planned to advance from the Balkans towards Hungary and Vienna. Suleiman also put the Turkish fleet at the disposal of the French, to help tip the strategic balance in their favour, and in 1541 Francis invited it to use Toulon as its base.

The military collaboration involved Francis frankly asking Suleiman to advance against the king of Hungary while he attacked Charles V. The result was a disastrous defeat for the Christian forces at the Battle of Mohacs in 1526, followed by the siege of Vienna in 1529. This Franco-Turkish collaboration lasted for several decades. Although Francis was condemned as a traitor to Christianity, he was not deterred. If there was any element of ideology or religion in the relationship between the French and the Turks, it was clearly superseded by the exigencies of great-power rivalry and by the wider conflict between Catholics and Protestants. Assumptions about an inherent or permanent hostility between Islam and Christianity were further discredited by a prolonged period of Muslim–Christian cooperation in terms of commerce, pilgrimage, diplomacy and strategy that lasted all through the sixteenth and seventeenth centuries.

If Queen Elizabeth (1558–1603) avoided going as far as Francis into an Islamic alliance she devoted much time to cultivating the Muslim powers. After coming to the throne, she spent ten years dodging a marriage with her dead sister's husband, the Catholic Philip II of Spain, and she was denounced as 'the pretended Queen of England' by Pope Pius V. Her reign was consequently dominated by frustrating the schemes hatched by Philip and the pope to 'subdue the English Turks' and expunge the Protestant heresy from Europe. But Elizabeth's policy was driven by another concern. Always short of funds, she saw the lucrative trade of the Eastern Mediterranean as a valuable prize, and her pragmatic approach to religion left her uninhibited in pursuing it. To this end, Elizabeth used freelance diplomats, such as Anthony Jenkinson, who in 1553–54 reached Aleppo, where he negotiated with the Ottoman sultan, though he could not speak Turkish, and secured a trading agreement for England. Thereafter Jenkinson found the going harder. Dispatched to Persia via Central Asia, he learned that there was no market for English woollen cloth. On a second visit to Persia in 1562, he found the Shias less relaxed than the Sunni Ottomans: suspect as a pagan and an infidel, he was followed by a servant who was equipped with a bucket of sand to cover the steps that polluted the shah's palace.[4] In rejecting Jenkinson's overtures, the shah was influenced by the Ottomans, with whom his relations had improved, who thought the English were trying to profit from divisions between the two Muslim powers. In general, both rulers remained sceptical and somewhat indifferent to the English; after all, Jenkinson represented an obscure and peripheral island, whose very whereabouts were uncertain. This attitude places Elizabethan England – today a major focus of British pride – in a more modest light.

By contrast, the English found it easier to engage with Morocco in a trade that clearly indicated a mutual interest in war with the Christian powers: the English valued Moroccan supplies of saltpetre, and in return exported armaments. After the defeat of the Spanish Armada in 1588, the danger of a Spanish invasion diminished; but Elizabeth's success tempted her to adopt a forward policy. In 1600, she received with great ceremony Muhammad al-Annuri, an envoy from the sultan of Morocco. Ostensibly the delegation was to further Morocco's exports of sugar, which was much in demand among the Tudors. But al-Annuri was under instructions to agree a Protestant–Muslim military alliance against Spain. The intention was to promote an invasion, leading to the recovery of al-Andalusia, the southern part of Spain that had sustained a sophisticated Islamic-Christian civilisation, and a joint campaign to seize Spanish colonies in the Americas and the Far East. However, this ambitious scheme came to nothing and was abandoned when James I succeeded to the throne in 1603.

In the context of a Christendom now divided between Reformation and Counter-Reformation, Catholics blamed Satan for using the Turks to stir up the heretics against the true Church. For their part, the English Protestants commonly regarded the crusading era in a distinctly hostile light, as a time when England had been led astray by the machinations of papal politics and the vaunting ambition of Catholic princes. The Protestant critics were right in thinking that, among other things, the Crusades had been used as a means of extending papal authority and imposing uniformity on Christendom; they saw this as a waste of resources and a distraction from true religious purpose. Luther argued that God himself had sent the Turks as a visitation for the sins of the Christians, and Protestants convinced themselves that the Turkish army was an instrument of God. In effect, the expansion of the Ottoman Empire was now interpreted as a standard by which to measure Christianity, for it offered a reflection of God's judgment on the secularism and corruption of the Church and its leaders.

During the sixteenth century, both sides were at pains to emphasise their common ground, now that it suited the interests of state. Edmund Hogan, a merchant used by Elizabeth in talks with Abd al-Malik, the sultan of Morocco, reported him as being hostile to Spain on account of the pope and the Inquisition. Going further, Hogan had found him to be 'a very earnest Protestant of good religion and living, and . . . bearing great affection to God's true religion used in your Highness's realm'.[5] To paint the sultan as being virtually a Protestant was highly optimistic, but it suited Elizabeth, who wanted her sales of arms to a Muslim to enjoy some respectability. This frame of mind was complemented by the Ottomans. In 1574, their government told the Lutherans:

> You for your part do not worship idols, you have banished the idols and portraits and bells from churches, and declared your faith by stating that God almighty is One and Holy Jesus is his Prophet . . . but the faithless one they call [the pope] does not recognise his Creator as One, ascribing Divinity to Holy Jesus, and worshipping idols and pictures which he has made with his own hands.[6]

The Turks were interpreting Lutherans as virtually Muslims, partly on account of appreciation of the common ground, but also because it suited them to accentuate divisions within Christendom.

There were other considerations that promoted a more sober perspective on Islam. However unpopular with some Christians, a Muslim alliance would give England the backing of some of the world's most powerful empires. The Tudors could hardly ignore the fact that their century was dominated by the rise of no fewer than three great Muslim civilisations: the Safavids in Persia, the Ottomans based in Anatolia and the Mughals in northern India. These empires enjoyed superiority in the early modern world not only in a military and territorial sense, but also because of their impressive cultural achievements in art, architecture, science and literature – achievements that placed them far above the Europeans in the early modern era. In the West, there has been a revival of the traditional assumption that these empires were somehow always in decline and bound to give way to rising European power; but in fact they proved to be much more enduring than the later empires of Britain, France and the United States.

Seventeenth-century England was well informed about the Ottomans through *The Generall Historie of the Turkes* (1603) by Richard Knolles, who wrote of 'the glorious empire of the Turks, the present terror of the world'. Another measured discussion appeared in 1704, in the shape of Joseph Pitts' *A True and Faithful Account of the Religion and Manners of the Mohammetans.* Conversely, even at this stage English observers disparaged the effete and decadent character of the Ottoman Empire and regularly predicted its imminent demise. 'This mighty empire hath passed the noon and is declining apace,' claimed Sir Thomas Roe, who was England's ambassador at Istanbul, in 1621.[7] Yet the Ottoman Empire, already over 300 years old, survived for another 300. Even on the eve of its disappearance from history in the First World War, the empire was a formidable force. And its demise was almost accidental – as Turkey only narrowly opted to join what was to prove the losing side in the war. It finally ended in 1924, by decision of Kemal Ataturk.

Under the Safavid dynasty, Persia attained its political and cultural peak, especially during the reign of Shah Abbas I, who ruled from 1588 to 1629. Its main achievements included miniature painting, calligraphy, building mosques, garden design, improved water supplies and the wholesale reconstruction of cities such as Isfahan. Persia's prosperity at this time was enhanced by the duties paid on large quantities of goods arriving via the Silk Road from Central Asia and greatly in demand among Western Europeans. As a Shia Muslim state, Persia took up arms against the Ottoman Turks (who were Sunni Muslims) throughout the sixteenth century, an antagonism that was readily appreciated in the West, as it helped to relieve Europe of the pressure of the Ottomans.

The Mughal Empire was founded in 1526 by Babur, one of a succession of Muslim invaders who crossed the north-west frontier to conquer the plains of the Punjab and Ganges valley, making their capital at or near Delhi. Under Babur's successors, Humayun, Akbar, Jahangir and Shah Jahan in the later sixteenth and seventeenth centuries, the Mughals extended their control through the entire sub-continent from Kashmir in the north to Bengal in the east and almost to the far south. The economy of Mughal India flourished partly because of the influx of gold and silver into Western Europe, much of which then found its way to India in pursuit of the luxury goods manufactured there.[8] Mughal rule also engendered an artistic school based on miniature portraiture, an acclaimed style of landscape gardening and an architectural tradition that culminated in the building of Akbar's vast new capital, Fatehpur Sikri, near Agra, Humayun's Tomb in Delhi, and Shah Jahan's memorial to his wife, the Taj Mahal at Agra. This empire declined under the concentration of French and British forces during the seventeenth century, but did not come to an end until 1858.

Above all, it was through the Ottoman Empire that the English became deeply involved with the Muslim world. The empire had been founded by Osman Gazi in 1299, but attained its peak after the capture of Constantinople in 1453; from the reign of Mehmet II to that of Suleiman the Magnificent – from 1446 to 1566 – the empire became the most powerful state in the world. Under Suleiman, it comprised over 30 million people on three continents, at a time when England's population stood at 4.5 million. Constantinople, with a population of 700,000 by 1600, was the largest city in the world, attracting craftsmen and artists from many other countries. They helped to make it a centre for ceramics, mosques, palaces, *hamams* (Turkish baths) and markets. The regular influx ensured that Constantinople was a thriving commercial centre and also a sophisticated, cosmopolitan metropolis. Remarkably, 40 per cent of its population was non-Muslim; these were mostly Christian, but included 10 per cent who were Jews. The latter played a valuable role in developing the economy through the supply of finance and investments for its enterprises, and they enjoyed a more comfortable life than was generally possible in the Christian West. In fact, under the sultans, the empire was notable as a model of tolerance towards people of diverse races and religions. Mehmet II adhered strictly to Islamic rules by allowing freedom of worship; he exempted the Greek clergy from taxes and left them to administer the Orthodox Church; he permitted the Church to fund schools and welfare by levying its own taxes; he granted the Greek courts power over marriage and inheritance; and he named the patriarch, who became an official of the Ottoman state.

Most English people at this time gained their familiarity with the Muslim world at second hand, notably through the work of the Elizabethan and Jacobean dramatists, including Christopher Marlowe, Philip Henslowe and William Shakespeare. In scores of plays they featured Muslims, including the Prophet himself. This had the advantage of requiring a good deal of colourful and dramatic costume and props.[9] It also lent itself to some of the traditional stereotypes about Turks. In Shakespeare's plays they tend to be associated with sensuousness, lasciviousness and deception. In Elizabethan England, the phrase 'to turn Turk' meant to adopt Islam or to be treacherous. The phrase was also employed in *Much Ado About Nothing*, where it implied becoming a prostitute.[10] However, Shakespeare also painted a sympathetic view of Muslims. In *Othello* he told his audience: 'The Moor is of a constant, loving, noble nature' – code for the view that Muslims made reliable allies, in contrast to the many deceitful and hypocritical Christians. In 1596, when the English attacked Cadiz, they enjoyed the support of North African Muslims. The event was referred to by Shakespeare in the *Merchant of Venice*, where the prince of Morocco is, in effect, recommended as a worthy match for Portia (for whom read Elizabeth herself).

Despite the reaction triggered by the Reformation, sixteenth-century England inherited the medieval era's prejudices and grotesque stories about Islam and the Prophet. Critics liked to dismiss Islam as 'a hodge-podge of sundry religions'; and some visitors continued to feed the pope with optimistic assurances to the effect that the Ottoman sultan or the shah of Persia was about to be converted to Christianity. However, disparagement of Islam was increasingly blunted by the Reformation, in that Protestants drew analogies between Islam and Catholicism as a way of attacking Rome. Moreover, the more absurd claims about Muslim society were increasingly discredited by improved sources of information. John Seldon, one of the best-informed Arabists, corrected the common fallacy about Muslims as pagan idol-worshippers: 'all the world knows that the Turkes are forbidden images by their Religion'.[11] In 1597, an anonymous book entitled *The Policy of the Turkish Empire* offered readers a reasonably accurate picture, enumerating the key features of Islam in terms of the belief in one God, regular prayers, the one-month fast and almsgiving.[12] In 1649, a translation of the Qur'an from the French – but 'newly Englished' – appeared, though without either the publisher's or the translator's name, which suggests it was still seen as subversive.

The English enjoyed contact with the eastern empires largely through Mediterranean commerce. But pilgrimages also continued, usually taking in the Church of the Holy Sepulchre, the Garden of Agony, the Mount of Olives, Bethlehem, Jericho, the Jordan Valley, the Dead Sea, Syria and Egypt. Typically, visitors would travel by sea to Venice and thence to the Holy Land or to Constantinople. Some of the European visitors corroborated traditional stereotypical notions of the Turks as barbaric and treacherous, and throughout Anatolia and Palestine they had to endure poor roads, dirty lodgings and bad food (though this was no worse than travellers experienced in England at the time).

Despite these derogatory views, however, wider contact with Muslims gradually introduced a more balanced – even sympathetic – view. Many Europeans commented on the hospitality, civility, neatness and cleanliness of the Turks, who were 'much addicted to baths'.[13] Some drew a distinction between Islam, which they saw as suffering from false prophets, and Muslims themselves, who often compared favourably with European Christians on account of their simplicity, sobriety and reverence; Turkish society had fewer idlers, scholars and lawyers, but also wasted less time on horse-racing, hunting, hawking and amorous entertainments.[14] It is obvious that these characteristics appealed to the more Puritanical mentality of the seventeenth century. They are also sentiments that have been echoed more recently by Europeans who see Muslim society as commendably modest and sober by comparison with the indulgence and ill-discipline of Western countries.

At a social level, English travellers noted that Muslims enjoyed sitting around drinking coffee. The visitors initially thought it tasted like soot, but accepted that it was good for the digestion. Not until the second half of the sixteenth century was there enough demand for coffee in the West to make regular imports worthwhile. Muslims also found a niche in English society via public houses, which were sometimes named 'Saracen's Head', 'Turk's Head' or the 'Trip to Jerusalem'. In 1393, when Richard II required publicans to hang up a sign indicating their trade, some proprietors cast around for something novel or eye-catching. The adoption of these names had followed the return of knights from the Holy Land, some of whom incorporated a Turk's head in their armorial bearings. Almost certainly, the publicans hoped to use the connection to boost their standing.

From the sixteenth century onwards, another form of contact with Muslim countries involved gardening and the import of plants from Anatolia and the Eastern Mediterranean. In this way the English acquired some of their characteristic garden plants, including shrubs such as Philadelphus (mock orange) and Syringa (lilac), herbaceous plants such as alchemilla, gypsophila and helleborus (lenten rose), and many bulbs such as alliums, anemones, chionodoxa, colchicums, autumn crocus, cyclamen, fritillaries and, above all, tulips. Of the 14 tulip species growing in Turkey at this time, only four were indigenous, the rest having arrived from Central Asia via the Silk Road. Their cultivation became an obsession, especially in the reign of Sultan Ahmed III (1703–30) which was known as the 'Tulip Era'. By the middle of the sixteenth century, tulips had reached Germany and Flanders and were imported into England in the reign of Elizabeth. Their spread was accelerated by the religious controversies of the day, as Protestant refugees from Holland found them a convenient and valuable item to carry with them as they fled from Catholic persecution.[15] During the Civil War and the Restoration – from the 1640s to the 1660s – English enthusiasts exchanged and sold prized tulip bulbs at high prices. Whereas the Turks appreciated narrow-waisted, high-pointed flowers, more like today's lily-flowered tulips, the English preferred rounded, cup-shaped blooms. An easily managed plant, tulips fitted well into the formal squares and parterres typical of English gardens of this era. But the tulip was not a natural in England's wet, cool climate, and by the eighteenth century it had moved indoors via a multitude of tulip societies and shows.

❀ ❄ ❀

By far the most important opportunity for contact with the Muslim world lay in attempts to muscle in on the lucrative trade through the Mediterranean to Asia Minor and Persia. During the first half of the sixteenth century England played little part in this, partly because of the hostility of Venice and Genoa, but also because of the frequent attacks on shipping by pirates from North Africa and Turkey. One expedient for the English lay in using Venetian ships for their trade.

But Anthony Jenkinson, who was employed by the Russian tsar after 1559 as his representative in Bokhara, found a way around the problem. In 1561, he led a mission to Persia on behalf of both Russia and England in the name of the English Muscovy Company, with a view to opening up the trade in precious stones, silks, tapestries and carpets. The Persian trade proved to be so profitable that it effectively delayed the development of trade between English ports and Turkey. However, it involved a dangerous route through Central Asia and dealings with an uncertain power. The English had hoped that they could develop friendly relations with the Persian merchants on the basis that Protestant Christians had a good deal in common with Shia Islam, which was the dominant religion and which set the Persians at odds with the Sunni Muslims of the Ottoman Empire. However, despite the religious similarities, there proved little mileage in this tactic.

All these expedients were rendered irrelevant from the early 1580s, when Queen Elizabeth's government recognised that the cultivation of the Ottomans was too important to admit of further delay: they offered England a potential ally against Spain and, because they controlled half of the Mediterranean, access to a profitable trade. It proved advantageous that England had not participated in the Ottoman defeat at the Battle of Lepanto. Elizabeth, who had no time for popular prejudices against the Turks, sent the sultan gifts and letters of friendship. She went out of her way as a Protestant to impress on him that she hated idol-worship (code for Catholics) as much as Muslims did. And she released Muslims serving as galley slaves on captured Spanish ships and sent them home.[16]

At an official level, Elizabeth followed up her friendly advances in 1582 by sending William Harborne to Constantinople. Her external policy was a partly privatised affair, as Harborne acted as the queen's representative, but was also an employee of the Levant Company, which actually paid his salary. On arrival, Harborne was shocked at being asked to remove his shoes on entering a mosque, but he soon settled in. He sufficiently impressed the sultan, Murad III, that he gained a guarantee of the safety of English ships and the right to trade and establish consulates. He also managed to secure a reduction in the customs duties paid by English merchants. In 1581, the queen had issued letters patent to 'The Company of Merchants of the Levant', and had granted them a 12-year charter, with monopoly trading rights. It was subsequently renewed in 1592, when some 53 merchants were trading under its aegis. James I, who was more sceptical of the Ottomans than Elizabeth had been, nonetheless renewed the charter in 1605. By the 1620s, English merchants were sending goods worth £250,000 a year to Turkey, and by the end of the century a quarter of all English trade was with the Ottomans. In this way began a formal relationship between the English and the Ottoman Empire that was to endure, despite complications, for 400 years.

In his capacity as the first accredited ambassador at Constantinople, Harborne did his best to persuade Turkey and Persia to make peace. He also sought to tempt the sultan into a pact against Spain:

> In my small judgement I think it nothing offensive to God to set one of his enemies against the other, the Infidel against the Idolaters, to the end that whilst they were by the ears, God's people [the Protestants] might respite and take strength.[17]

He used his influence to secure the release of Christian slaves in Constantinople and on the Barbary coast. Visitors also toured the slave markets, where they bought Christian slaves (at exorbitant prices) in order to free them. However, slavery in the Middle East should not be confused with slavery in the New World. Although Islamic law denied basic rights to slaves, it was far less harsh, allowing them both wealth and power. Both the Seljuks and the Ottomans often took booty in the form of slaves, who were incorporated into the army, where they were among the most loyal elements. The most able of these slave-soldiers were trained up as commanders, and some were appointed as regional governors. Under Mehmet II (1444–46 and 1451–81), they also occupied key positions in the central administration of the empire. In thirteenth-century Egypt the slaves, known as Mamluks, had taken control of the country while retaining their status as slaves.

English ambassadors at Constantinople were obliged to offer lavish and novel gifts to the sultan (who considered them 'tributes' from an inferior power) and to government officials (which were effectively bribes). In 1605, James I granted the Levant Company the large sum of £5,322 as a present to the sultan. In 1599, the requirement for novelty was met by the dispatch of an elaborate organ, along with its builder, one Thomas Dallam.[18] On arrival, the organ was installed in the seraglio of the sultan, Mehmet III, who had had 19 of his brothers killed there. The sultan demanded an immediate performance. This was tricky, as to play it Dallam had to turn his back on the sultan – an offence punishable by death. Fortunately, the sultan was gracious; he enjoyed the performance and Dallam managed to retire backwards from his presence, escaping with his life. Politely declining Mehmet's invitation to remain as court organist and enjoy the services of two wives, he returned to England.

It is an indication of the relative status of the two countries that the Turks were slow to follow the English example in establishing formal diplomatic relations. Not until July 1607 did one Mustapha arrive in London, claiming to be an emissary or agent of the sultan. The English representatives in Constantinople reported that Mustapha was actually an impostor; but, as he seemed an affable fellow and adopted the local customs, it was deemed prudent to provide him with board and lodging, especially as no one wished to offend the sultan. However, King James did not even give him an audience until September, as he thought it demeaning for a Christian monarch to receive a Muslim, and suspected that his goal was actually to exacerbate the dissension among Christians. Fortunately, when Mustapha returned to Constantinople in 1608, he gave a favourable report of his reception, which pleased the sultan.

The major complication in Elizabeth's policy, as Harborne realised, was the conflict between the Ottomans and Persia, which had reached a pinnacle of wealth and power under Shah Abbas I (1587–1629). For some time, English policy was largely taken out of Elizabeth's hands by the freelance activities of Sir Thomas Sherley, his brother Anthony and son Robert who enjoyed the patronage of the earl of Essex. The Sherleys were opportunists and buccaneers, and in 1598 Thomas cheerfully accepted a commission from Essex to travel to Persia with a view to promoting trade and engineering an alliance between Shah Abbas and the European powers against Turkey. On arrival, they passed the gruesome spectacle of 20,000 decapitated heads of Uzbeks, recently defeated by Shah Abbas; but after kissing his feet, they were lavishly entertained and taken to see the new capital at Isfahan. The Sherleys helped him to train an infantry, and gave him tips on fortifications and the use of muskets and artillery. Anthony Sherley claimed, falsely, to be Elizabeth's envoy and returned to Europe carrying letters for the pope, the Habsburg emperor and other rulers; but his son, Robert, was left behind as a hostage. Elizabeth's government had no time for the Sherleys, who were monitored by the agents of both England and Turkey. However, the accession in 1603 of the more anti-Turk James I raised their status, and Anthony was granted a licence 'to remain beyond the seas'. In 1608, Robert Sherley was appointed the shah's ambassador to the European powers and made his escape, though he was shadowed by the English ambassador in Constantinople on behalf of the Levant Company. When Robert reached London, decked out in his robes and turban, no one took his ideas for a Persian alliance seriously, and his position was subsequently undermined when a second Persian ambassador arrived. Both were sent back to determine who was the fraud. Despite their ceaseless travelling, the Sherleys never made Persia more than marginal in English calculations (unlike the Ottoman Empire). But as freelance diplomats, they did at least demonstrate that Englishmen could function comfortably in a Muslim society in the seventeenth century.

For her part, Elizabeth naturally came under attack from the Jesuits for her pro-Turkish policy, but she denied any disloyalty to Christianity, justifying it as an English national interest. However, her stance reflected more than simply hard-headed pragmatism. At a time when the English were struggling to contain the controversies unleashed by the Reformation, the example of the Ottoman Empire gave pause for thought. It did not go unnoticed that at Constantinople the communities of Muslims, Jews and Christians managed to co-exist beneath the overall umbrella of Islam, a reflection of the instruction in the Qur'an: 'Let there be no compulsion in religion.' As yet religious toleration was very far from being acceptable in the Christian countries, and among the dissenting sects Islam was increasingly held up as a model. As a result, seventeenth-century Protestants often expressed themselves 'desirous that Turkey should overrun Christendom to gain their liberty from Catholic rule' or ready 'to live under ye Turk because of liberty of conscience'.[19]

Those Protestants who wanted to interpret the scriptures in a rationalist manner focused especially on the idea of the Trinity as an inexplicable mystery, arguing that there was no reference to it in the Bible. In this they found themselves at one with Muslims, who had always seen the Trinity as a deviation, providing grounds for the suspicion that Christians believed in three gods. In 1694, Archbishop Tillotson, commenting on the Trinity, admitted: 'I do wish we did not have it' – a frank recognition that it represented the weakest part of Christianity. Some Anti-Trinitarians – or Unitarians, as they later came to be known – decamped to more tolerant places, including Basel, Poland, Transylvania and even Damascus, where they appreciated the more relaxed view taken by the Ottomans. By contrast, the Habsburg emperor aspired to impose an orthodox Catholicism on Transylvania, but was deterred by the proximity of the Ottoman army. It is striking that during this period, European visitors passed on messages to the shah of Persia and the Ottoman sultan, inviting them to convert to Christianity, while on the other hand influential Muslims in Constantinople suggested that the English had adopted a position so close to that of Islam that a simple confession of faith would bring them into the community. While such rumours doubtless reflected the role of romantics and opportunists in the diplomatic exchanges between East and West, they were not without some significance. In effect, Unitarianism had begun to act as a bridge between Christianity and Islam. This interaction underlines the extent to which the Reformation had effectively sidelined the crusading era as a discredited cult, a leftover from a more superstitious age.

During the seventeenth century, the discussion about Islam and Christianity moved a little away from the propagandists into the hands of scholars and academics. This trend was symptomatic of the desire to escape the censorious tone of medievalism for something more empirical, notably a new emphasis on the rational study of Oriental history, religion and languages. One reason for this lay in the need felt by many Christians to improve the accuracy of the biblical texts. Some parts of the Old Testament were written in Hebrew and Aramaic, and the study of those languages required a knowledge of Arabic. In addition, Arabic was the language of astronomy, mathematics and science. Of course, this objective was not without controversy, as the Puritans believed that too much knowledge simply undermined one's faith; consequently, the practitioners of Oriental languages had a hard time during the mid-seventeenth century.

An Arabic dictionary had been produced back in the 1590s; and in 1632 a chair in Arabic studies was established at Cambridge. Improved understanding would, it was hoped, help to demonstrate the roots and traditions of the moderate English Church at a time when the rival extremists of Calvinism and Catholicism were tearing Christianity apart. To this end, scholars explored the links with the Eastern Orthodox Church and with Arab and Aramaic Christianity. The most significant promoter of these aims was William Laud, an influential figure under King Charles I, who became bishop of London (1628–33) and archbishop of Canterbury (1633–45). Once regarded as a secret papist, Laud actually wanted the Anglican Church to adopt a moderate theology. He was tolerant in matters of doctrine and is now regarded as having sought to promote compromise and conciliation in the Church. He donated 1,300 manuscripts to the Bodleian Library, a quarter of which were Oriental, and established chairs in Hebrew and Arabic at Oxford. In 1636, Laud made the crucial appointment of Edward Pococke, who had spent four years in Aleppo learning Arabic, to the chair of Arabic. Pococke shared the fashionable desire to study religion in a rational and informed manner and was sceptical about Christian mysteries, such as the Trinity. In 1650, he published the *Specimen Historiae Arabum*, which discussed the culture, literature and history of Islam in a sober, scholarly way for the first time.[20] Taken with the 1649 English translation of the Qur'an, the book enabled people in England to study an objective account of Islamic thought and civilisation, a huge advance over the absurdities of the medieval era.

On the other hand, the positive relationship between Muslims and the English in the Elizabethan period was severely handicapped by the fact that throughout the sixteenth and seventeenth centuries the English were continually antagonised by the activities of Moorish pirates in the Mediterranean and the Atlantic. The immediate stimulus for this arose from the success of Ferdinand and Isabella in finally expelling Islam from Spain in 1492. Seeking compensation for their losses in Andalusia and thirsting for revenge, many of the exiles took up piracy from bases at Tangiers, Algiers, Tunis and Tripoli. These 'corsairs' or 'Moors', as they were known, soon dominated several thousand square miles of sea – from Morocco to the Straits of Gibraltar and along the North African or Barbary coast, even up to Palestine. During the seventeenth and eighteenth centuries an estimated 20,000 Englishmen were captured by the corsairs, most of them ending up as slaves.[21] Although this generated much propaganda about the North African states as barbarous and tyrannical, Mediterranean slavery was not comparable to that practised in the Americas. European slaves often felt they were well treated and better off than they had been at home, and in time saw their captivity as an opportunity to start afresh in life.[22]

Dealing with the threat proved complicated, as the Ottoman sultans had a habit of outsourcing their commercial policy in the Mediterranean. The most notorious pirates in the early seventeenth century, Oruc and Hizir, were based at Tunis and then at Algiers from 1516. In 1518, Hizir asked for Ottoman support against the Spanish, offered his services to the sultan and was even appointed governor of Algiers. Subsequently, Suleiman appointed him admiral of the Ottoman fleet and awarded him the honorary title of Khair-ud-din. In this capacity he built up the Ottoman fleet, raided the coast of Spain and fought along with the

French to capture Nice. In 1551, the sultan used Khair-ud-din's successor to take Tunis from the Knights of St John (the pirates had built up Tunis as a naval base and capital of an Ottoman province). In effect, the Barbary states of Tripoli, Tunis and Algiers were autonomous, but were governed by appointees of the sultan, on whose behalf they collected taxes. It suited Istanbul to turn a blind eye to piracy as a way of undermining the European states by disrupting their trade and intimidating their coasts, although, when under pressure to suppress it, the Turks would pretend to take appropriate action. Even after the Turkish defeat at Lepanto in 1571, which deprived the corsairs of Turkish protection, they simply took to smaller-scale raiding. All this proved frustrating for the European powers, but they were slow to devote enough naval force to the Mediterranean. In 1583, the sultan signed a treaty with England guaranteeing the rights and liberties of English nationals living under Islamic rule, allowing freedom of religion, free passage by land and sea, and providing protection from pirates, though this was largely nominal.

Yet while the friction over pirates inhibited regular English trade, it hardly impacted on the English tradition of unofficial piracy against Spain, which was enthusiastically supported by the Protestants. During the 1580s and 1590s, the privateers who regularly left Bristol and Plymouth benefited from a mutual understanding with the Moors of North Africa on account of their common enemy. The Muslim rulers allowed them to organise celebratory bonfires following news of the defeat of the Spanish Armada. Admittedly, when James I succeeded Elizabeth in 1603, he renounced her relaxed view of the corsairs and pursued a policy of peace with Spain; in particular, he announced that all prizes seized from Spanish ships were to be returned. By 1604, the war with Spain had ended. However, the king's measures proved largely counter-productive and prompted the English pirates to rely even more on the Moorish ports for sanctuary. Popular sympathy for the men who plundered Spanish ships only impeded the king's attempts to suppress piracy. Even members of James's government, including his lord high admiral, acquiesced in the buccaneers' escapades by accepting a share of their booty. Moreover, as James ran down the navy, which numbered only 37 ships by 1607, many Englishmen who had served in it subsequently turned to piracy as a means of support. In this situation, attempts to eliminate piracy were simply unrealistic. James eventually issued a pardon to the 3,000 or so English pirates.

In fact, from 1608 onwards English piracy reached its zenith under the informal leadership of the notorious John Ward, who lived a life of prosperity among the Moors. Ward had served in the Royal Navy, but he resented the official restrictions on the tradition that allowed English ships freedom to plunder their national enemies, and he recruited ex-servicemen and deserters for his escapades. After seizing a French ship, he sailed to Tunis, where he made a pact with the local Turkish pirate, Kara Osman, who granted him use of the base in return for a share of Ward's booty. King James proclaimed Ward and others outlaws in 1609 and closed all English ports to them. As they had taken to attacking English ships, they were now accused of having 'turned Turk'. They had even begun to share with the Turks their knowledge of navigation, how to employ artillery on board a ship and how to use fast sailing vessels in place of the galleys rowed by slaves.[23] This sympathetic relationship between the buccaneers of the two nations stood in contrast to official criticism of Moorish corsairs and efforts to promote regular trade, and demonstrates how ambivalent relations between the English and Muslims could be in the seventeenth century.

However, English attitudes hardened especially after 1617, when a Moorish pirate vessel managed to enter the Thames estuary. Around this time, the aggrieved relatives of people who had been seized in the coastal villages of Cornwall and Devon also started to petition parliament to take action to suppress piracy, and in 1620 and 1621 expeditions of Royal Navy ships were dispatched to the Mediterranean. However, they enjoyed little success, although they did free some Christian captives at Algiers. Sir Thomas Roe, the ambassador at Constantinople, attempted to persuade the sultan to suppress piracy altogether, but without success, though he, too, managed to liberate some slaves in Turkey and more at Algiers in 1624. However, as Algiers and Tunis renounced their allegiance to the Ottomans at that point, things deteriorated even further. In 1634 it was estimated that there were 32,000 captive English slaves in Tunis and Algiers alone.[24] The English were reduced to raising a collection to pay for their release. As late as 1645, a raiding party landed on the Cornish coast and kidnapped 234 men, women and children. It was not until after the restoration of Charles II in 1660 that piracy was finally brought under control. This was more easily accomplished when the English acquired Tangiers as part of Charles's dowry from the Portuguese princess, Catherine of Braganza. Tangiers was perfectly placed, using only four men-of-war, to intercept any ships that tried to pass through the straits. Although Britain failed to maintain Tangiers, she did extend her presence in the Mediterranean during the eighteenth century at Gibraltar and Minorca. Significantly, she relied on the Muslim Barbary states to supply these imperial outposts against the challenge of the Catholic powers, a consideration that somewhat mitigated British irritation over piracy.

There was, however, a further complication. During the reign of Charles I, the English felt humiliated by reports that a large proportion of English slaves and captured soldiers had 'turned Turk' – in this case, converted to Islam. While the late Bernard Lewis claimed (without evidence) that conversions to Islam were minimal, it is now clear that in 1619, in Algeria alone, there were 200,000 Christian converts – 'Renegados' or 'Levantines' as they were known, with a further 500 joining them each year. Christians who did not believe in the Trinity were often called 'Mahometans', which created the impression of even more Muslims. All this was embarrassing. Contemporaries asked whether it meant that Islam was the superior religion. Was it the true revelation of God? Would it eventually replace Christianity?[25]

Why were there so many converts from Christianity to Islam and so few from Islam to Christianity? Despite a widespread belief in England that the Turks practised forcible conversion, in fact generally they did not seek converts from vanquished opponents, preferring simply to collect taxes, fines or services from them. The idea was spread by slaves who had been ransomed or escaped, and then claimed to have been the victims of compulsory conversion.[26] In fact, converts were usually willing, especially if they had experienced religious persecution in Europe. Protestants were especially appreciative of Muslim society; it was relatively tolerant, had no idols or monastic orders, and was based on individual study of the religion instead of passive acceptance of it from priests.[27] But the main advantage lay in linking oneself to a more powerful empire and a superior civilisation. Converts found that the relatively egalitarian spirit of Islam allowed employment and advancement for those from modest backgrounds. In Morocco, the royal executioner was one 'Absalom'; as a former butcher from Exeter, he evidently had the right skills![28] Samson Rowlie, a merchant from Great Yarmouth, was captured in 1577, castrated and converted to Islam as Hassan Aga; he rose to become chief eunuch and treasurer of Algiers and adviser to the Ottoman governor.[29] Although the English chose to regard Rowlie's conversion as nominal and temporary, he became too wealthy and powerful to want to return. Other prominent converts included John Ward, the pirate, who became 'Yusuf' and lived out his days at Tunis.[30] Even more shocking was the case of Sir Francis Verney, a member of a respectable Buckinghamshire gentry family. Following a family dispute and the sale of his estates, Verney left for Morocco in 1608, joined the mercenaries and became a pirate.[31]

Although the Wards and Verneys were denounced for treachery in poems and plays, the religious significance of their conversion is unclear. The Tudors did not use the word 'Muslim', referring rather to Turks. Conversion was easy, as it involved little challenge to one's beliefs. Englishmen who lived for some years in Muslim states usually adopted the local lifestyle, which naturally included the religion. The experience of conversion varied considerably. Muslims were not especially charitable towards slaves, who could not expect to be freed simply by converting to Islam, although many owners did free them on conversion. At its best, conversion took place in Istanbul before the sultan and the imperial scribe, who sprinkled gold dust over his record of the event. The convert recited: 'There is no other God than God, and Mohammed is his messenger.' He was presented with a purse, some white muslin for a turban and a cloak, before being taken to the imperial surgeon for circumcision. Converts often celebrated the event by adopting a new Islamic name.

The reign of Elizabeth marked a period of unusually close involvement between the English and the Muslim world, founded on a combination

of religious tolerance, commercial gain and military necessity. By cultivating alliances with Muslim powers at both ends of the Mediterranean
her governments went some way to safeguarding a beleaguered England
against the challenge of Catholic Spain. Their commercial contacts
enabled the English to maintain a network of envoys, who were in effect
spies, with a view to keeping them well informed about any emerging
threats. However, all this changed quite abruptly under James I after
1603. The new king, who had spent years at loggerheads with the
Presbyterians in Scotland, adopted a narrower and more ideological view
of religion. After *Othello*, playwrights quickly abandoned their practice of
including Moors and Turks in their writings. Although a sound Protestant,
James had no desire to inveigle the Ottomans or the Moroccans into war
with Spain. Indeed, he antagonised many people by proposing to marry
his son to the king of Spain's daughter. He showed more interest in developing English opportunities in the New World and less in the conflicts
taking place in Europe.

CHAPTER FOUR

INDIA AND THE ANGLO-MUSLIM LOVE AFFAIR

'Apparently England is ever forgetting that she is at present the greatest Mohammedan empire in the world.'[1] The words of the great Victorian traveller-explorer, Sir Richard Burton, in the introduction to his translation of *The Arabian Nights* (1886) serve as a powerful reminder of how extensive was Britain's relationship with Muslim communities – above all in India, home to around 30 million Muslims in the seventeenth century. Mid-Victorian and twentieth-century British views of Muslims as fanatical and iconoclastic have obscured earlier attitudes, which were much more sympathetic. It was in India that the British became most fond of Muslims, and there that the relationship acquired an element of romance.

For all the Victorians' self-confidence in the superiority of their civilisation, when the relationship with India began in the seventeenth century the British played a distinctly subordinate role. The early modern world was dominated by three great empires: the Ottomans, based in modern Turkey but stretching far beyond it; the Safavids in Persia; and the Mughals in India. Apart from their military might, all three boasted impressive cultural achievements in terms of art, architecture, science and literature that made them superior to the Europeans of the time.

When the British sought to trade with India at the start of the seventeenth century, they found the country under arguably the greatest of the

Estimate of Muslim populations *c.* 1880 (in millions)

British India	40
Indonesia/Malaysia	30
Ottoman Empire	22
North Africa	18
Arabia/Syria	11.5
Persia (Iran)	8
Central Asian Khanates	6
Egypt	5
Afghanistan	3

Source: Wilfred S. Blunt, *The Future of Islam* (1882, 2007 edn), pp. 28–9.

Mughal emperors, Akbar, who ruled from 1556 to 1605. It cannot be overemphasised that the original British envoys were obliged to come to his court as supplicants for his favours. Current British obsessions with the glories of the Tudor period build on inflated patriotic traditions about the heroism of that era. In popular history, the reign of Elizabeth I has inspired a cult of the invincible *Gloriana* and her unauthorised pirates, Drake and Hawkins. Yet by comparison with the opulent and grandiose Mughal state, the Tudor court was a shabby little affair on the margins of Europe. In the East Indies, the British as yet lacked the military muscle to compete with the Netherlands, Portugal and Spain, which were already established there, and any idea of forcing the Mughals to trade with them would have been unrealistic. Consequently, when the queen granted a monopoly of British trade in the East to 'The Company of Merchants of London Trading into the East Indies' by royal charter in December 1600, this was an expression of hope, and the gains were to be attained by careful diplomacy rather than by force.[2]

However, with the permission of the Mughal court, trade developed after 1623. Not surprisingly, the seventeenth century saw some fluctuations in the commercial fortunes of the new company, before it began to become a really profitable venture. Although the early British visitors dealt with an empire ruled by a Muslim elite, only about a fifth to a quarter of its population was Muslim. Akbar set a model for tolerance in religious affairs by appointing non-Muslims as provincial governors and revenue officials, and by encouraging a remarkable intellectual cross-fertilisation between the ideas of Islam, Hinduism and other religions. Moreover, among the wider Muslim population, religious practice was less than orthodox, as many were actually converts from Hinduism; they remained ignorant of the strict requirements of Islam and were open to the retention or infiltration of Hindu practices into their daily lives. Muslims also varied widely in both numbers and character across the sub-continent. As Arab traders, they had been present on the western coasts for hundreds of years, constituting a fifth of the population in Malabar (modern Kerala). They enjoyed a big majority in Sind and the other provinces of modern Pakistan; they made up around half of the population in Bengal, and just under half in the Punjab; but they accounted for as little as 5 per cent in Madras and Tamil Nadu. Many Bengali Muslims (whose descendants nowadays live in Bangladesh) were low-caste Hindus who had converted to Islam as a means of raising themselves in the social scale. Meanwhile, those in the North-Western Provinces and in the Ganges valley were the descendants of Muslim invaders. They had established themselves as landowners, soldiers, scholars and civil servants, and now constituted a ruling class.[3] It is tempting to assume that this status was in itself a factor in promoting Anglo-Muslim relations, for in many of their colonies the British developed the habit of associating with the current or former rulers as a useful prop to their control. However, in India this was as yet a marginal consideration, especially as Muslim power went into a steady decline. There were more significant factors that promoted Anglo-Muslim relationships in the seventeenth and eighteenth centuries.

Although the British eventually came to regard their position in India as conditional on a separation of races and an assumption of European superiority, in the early period this was far from being the case. In fact, in many ways they enjoyed remarkably close and relaxed relations, especially with Indian Muslims. Why was this so? The first element in the explanation is that the British approach to religion had undergone some changes over time. After the puritanical zeal over religious ideas and observance that was typical of the sixteenth and seventeenth centuries, attitudes calmed down considerably; it was as though a great ideological storm had eventually blown itself out. Indeed, the eighteenth century was marked by the gradual development of toleration towards the various dissenting sects and churches, and even to a rather relaxed view of religion among many Anglicans. Aristocrats were commonly agnostics by this time, even though they respected the outward forms of Anglicanism. This, of course, paved the way for a significant loss of influence by the Church of England as the population expanded and people moved into urban areas during the Industrial Revolution in the later eighteenth century.

Against this background, it is understandable that some British visitors to India felt able to come to terms with non-European and non-Christian peoples, while a few even recognised the sophistication of Indian civilisation and took a scholarly interest in its culture. One notable and influential example was Sir William Jones (1746–94), a distinguished Orientalist who mastered Arabic and Persian as a young man, became a student of Indian history and a Bengal judge in 1778, and founded the Asiatic Society of Bengal, the first learned society devoted to Indian studies. Jones loved the free and simple life of such regions as Arabia and Kashmir, and was keen to make Asia more accessible to Europeans; he felt little sympathy for the East India Company, which appeared to introduce an unwelcome element of avarice and corruption into a cultured society. Noting the contribution of Indians to arithmetic, geometry and logic, he hailed their discoveries of the game of chess, the decimal scale and the science of grammar as proof of 'yet higher pretensions to praise of a fertile and inventive genius'.[4]

In any case, British attitudes towards religion in India were, in the early years at least, heavily moderated by the East India Company itself. Admittedly, both Christianity and Islam had developed a powerful missionary impulse, in complete contrast to Hinduism, whose adherents generally showed no desire to save souls from eternal damnation, arguing instead that men should do their best to live a morally decent life according to the rules of the society into which they had been born. However, the company had no interest in saving souls; its philosophy was 'Orientalist', in that it believed that Indian culture and institutions should be left alone as far as possible. Consequently, it had no desire to admit Christian missionaries, who were, at best, a complication in its commercial activities and, at worst, a cause of antagonism among the local people. In addition, some of its employees quickly succumbed to the charms of Asiatic society – foreshadowing what was later called the Romantic Movement, they admired what they saw as its simplicity and moral superiority by comparison with Western Europe.

Another major explanation for Anglo-Indian relationships is that the early British visitors to India found themselves largely isolated in very small European communities. Consequently, they soon sought company among the local population, especially those who lived outside the main British centres of Calcutta, Bombay and Madras. As a result, many Englishmen, following the earlier example of the Portuguese, not only adopted an Indian lifestyle, but also developed a remarkably extensive Anglo-Indian social life involving relationships with Indian men and women. 'Here in the heart of the city,' wrote one Englishman in Agra, 'we live after this country in the manner of meat, drink and apparel . . . after the custom of this place sitting on the ground at our meat or discourse. The rooms are in general covered in carpets and with great high round cushions to lean on.'[5] The company's employees commonly consumed Indian food, ate rice with the right hand (because the left was used for ablutions), wore loose-fitting Indian clothes which were suited to the climate, smoked hookah pipes, chewed betel nut for improved digestion, learned the local languages and enjoyed the pleasures of the *hamam*. William Fraser, who was assistant to Sir David Ochterlony, the British Resident at Delhi, learned Persian and Arabic, kept a harem of seven Indian wives, gave up beef and pork for the benefit of his Hindu and Muslim guests, wore Mughal clothes and was 'half asiatic in his habits . . . has a real and profound understanding of [Indian] inner life . . . Hindi and Persian are like his two own mother tongues.' Fraser enjoyed what William Dalrymple has called 'a hybrid lifestyle so forming a sort of Anglo-Mughal Islamo-Christian buffer zone between the Mughal world and the world of the Company's Residency'.[6]

It is worth noting that although this social life involved Hindus, the British generally found social relations easier among Muslims. The explanation is probably that although Muslims were numerous in India, they represented a minority, along with the British. For the Europeans, it was usually the practices and customs of the Hindu majority that surprised and shocked them most, and the contrast starkly underlined how much Christians and Muslims had in common in both religious and social terms. The British were more likely to socialise with Muslims because many Hindus regarded them as untouchable and refused to eat with them. Britons were known to have themselves circumcised with a view to enjoying better relationships with Muslim women.[7] As a religion, too, Hinduism was certainly more alien. For example, its adherents were genuinely appalled by Christian ideas such as Hell and damnation. Even Lord Cromer, who was invariably critical of Muslims in Egypt and India, commented that 'the religious fabric of Islamism is much more readily comprehensible to the European mind than the comparatively subtle and mystical bases of Hinduism'. In any case, at the higher social levels, Indian Muslims were often flexible in their social behaviour and happily engaged with English habits. For example, alcoholic drink was freely available in the form of arrack, a spirit similar to brandy and produced from coconuts, which the English took to very readily. Arrack was reportedly 'good for the gripes . . . in the morning a laxative and in the evening an astringent'. When Muslims dined with English people, they commonly consumed alcohol and reputedly held their drink well. They were also intrigued by British bottled beer on account of the bubbles that burst forth when it was opened.

Perhaps the most notorious Anglo-Indian of the eighteenth century was Major James Achilles Kirkpatrick (1764–1805), the British Resident at the court of the nizam of Hyderabad, the most distinguished of the princes who ruled the largest Indian state. There, in the midst of one of the greatest centres of Islamic culture, it was tempting for him to adopt the local style; and since his employment required him to be on close and friendly terms with the local ruler, it was sound tactics, at least up to a point. Kirkpatrick adopted Muslim dress, wore Indian 'mustachios', used henna on his hands like a Muslim nobleman, and even kept a harem at the back of his house.

However, Kirkpatrick went considerably further. He fell in love with a 14-year-old girl, Khair-un-Nissa, who was the daughter of a nobleman and was a *Sayeeda* – that is, a direct descendant of the Prophet. He married her, fathered two children by her, and converted to Islam. Although the girl's family pressed for an abortion, her mother felt that if it were not for the sectarian religious divisions he could easily have married Khair 'in the same manner that he might have had her before the distinctions introduced by Moses, Jesus and Mohamed were known to the world'.[8] When Khair became pregnant in 1801, the British authorities, concerned about local reactions, instituted an inquiry into the relationship and considered whether Kirkpatrick could now be relied upon from a political point of view. However, Kirkpatrick was a brilliant soldier and diplomat, who had managed by diplomatic means to secure the withdrawal of the French and had persuaded the nizam to sign a treaty with the British, bringing his huge state into alliance. He had been a decisive force in consolidating British power in the sub-continent. Apart from shortening his time as Resident, there was not much to be done – especially as Kirkpatrick was determined to remain loyal to his wife and their children. Like so many British servants in India in this period, he annoyed his superiors but got away with it.

The relatively fluid approach that characterised attitudes towards race and religion before the nineteenth century has never received due attention either in orthodox Indian nationalist writing or in the conventional British historiography. The explanation consists in the racist propaganda subsequently developed by the Victorians, who condemned those who 'went native' and fervently believed that British rule could be maintained only through a strict separation of the races and by promoting the idea of the British as a super-race. By contrast, the more relaxed attitudes of the early Anglo-Indian relationship involved a personal-political rationale. During the seventeenth and eighteenth centuries, some employees clearly lost faith in the East India Company and developed sympathies towards the native princes. Their conversion to Islam and their readiness to undergo circumcision were seen as indicative of a fundamental shift in loyalties. As early as 1616, the British ambassador in Delhi, Sir Thomas Roe, had drawn up an agreement with the Mughal emperor that reflected his fear of British defections to Islam. He wanted all British converts to be delivered into the hands of the company. After initially refusing, Shah Jahan eventually agreed to Roe's request. However, the British had little way of controlling the behaviour of fellow countrymen who were widely scattered across the sub-continent and chose to change religious affiliation once they had left the company's employment. Sometimes – among men keen to enrich themselves quickly – the motive for conversion lay in opportunism, rather than in the appeal of the religion itself. In one case at Surat in 1652, for example, some 23 men abandoned their employment with the company to serve under the local princes. Apparently, the Mughal government found it worthwhile to place its agents in the British community to seek such recruits.[9] However, this practice gradually declined as the Mughal government lost effectiveness during the eighteenth century. On the other hand, if the British were to pursue an effective diplomacy at the courts of the Indian princes, it was desirable for their representatives to, at the very least, learn the local languages and develop some familiarity with the local culture. Indeed, official British policy recognised this need by negotiating a multitude of treaties with Hindu, Muslim and Sikh princes with a view to mitigating the alien quality of their rule. In time, the princes even came to be regarded as a bulwark against the rise of nationalism; though this proved rather over-optimistic, many did become genuinely pro-British.

(((())) ✤ (((())))

From the British perspective, the real problem with relationships such as Kirkpatrick's lay not in sexual relations, but in his insistence on *marriage* to an Indian. Sex itself was less of a problem and one that could be managed. It was inevitable that young British men, cast adrift in exotic parts of the world, would discover that varied sexual activity was one of the advantages of having an empire. For a time, the East India Company tried importing English women, giving them board and lodging on the understanding that they were to get married after a year; but this caused so much scandal that the scheme was abandoned.[10] It proved simpler to allow the men to make their own arrangements with Indian mistresses, who were known as *bibis*.

However, this caused major complications in the army. In India, only 12 per cent of soldiers were permitted to marry, and in practice only 5 per cent did so. As the authorities never for a moment imagined that English soldiers would remain chaste – even if they were married – a free market in sex inevitably developed. But this had the effect of spreading venereal disease very widely among the troops, so much so that during the nineteenth century around a third of British soldiers were unfit for active service at any one time. For this reason, each regiment maintained a number of women for the use of their men in lock hospitals and had them regularly inspected for signs of disease. During the nineteenth century, campaigns to suppress vice sometimes led the authorities to close down these lock hospitals, but as 'the boys went back to syphilis' this did not last long.[11] Underlying these arrangements, but largely unspoken, was the fear that if denied access to heterosexual relations, the men would develop feelings for each other, which would undermine discipline and fighting spirit. The lock hospitals helped the troops to remain manly. In the long run, British soldiers who had completed their term often opted to stay in India, where they might gain employment on the railways and marry local women. As a result, by 1901 the mixed-race or 'Eurasian' population had reached 89,000.

The dilemma faced by the military authorities underlined the undoubted fact that empire offered extensive opportunities for irregular forms of sex that would have been far more risky, or embarrassing, if indulged in at home. As John Masters, who served as a Gurkha officer on the north-west frontier between the wars, put it:

70

Ours was a one-sexed society . . . there was always an unnatural tension . . . some tried sublimation, some chased polo balls and some chased partridges, some buried themselves in their work, some went to diseased harlots and some married in haste . . . and a few homosexuals followed their secret star with comparative comfort in that large and easy-going country where there are so many sins that there is no sin except inhospitality.[12]

It is estimated that around a quarter of upper-class men did not marry in the eighteenth century; in time, as attitudes hardened and the law on same-sex sex became more severe, they found domestic society uncomfortable. As a result, same-sex sex became increasingly associated with joining the army and with leaving for the empire; both Africa and Australia offered plentiful opportunities. Some of the great heroes of British imperial expansion, including General Charles Gordon, Lord Kitchener and Cecil Rhodes, had no interest in women; they made a practice of employing young, unmarried men, and are usually regarded as passive homosexuals.

In India, the British discovered much earlier that, as in most countries outside the Judaeo-Christian societies of Europe and the Middle East, attitudes towards same-sex relationships were relatively relaxed. Indian men routinely touched each other in conversation, or held hands briefly when negotiating crowded bazaars, without implying anything beyond mild friendship. But some went further and engaged in what the British delicately referred to as 'the special Oriental vice'. As viceroy, Lord Curzon attempted to regulate the sexual behaviour of the princes – initially because he thought they cultivated affairs with English women, but also because some engaged in same-sex relationships. Perhaps sensitive because he had himself had relations with men earlier in life, Curzon even drew up a list of princes with homosexual tendencies. 'I attribute it to early marriage,' he commented. 'A boy gets tired of his wife, or of women, at an early age, and wants the stimulus of some more novel or exciting sensation.'[13] When he discovered a homosexual young prince, he sent him to the Imperial Cadet Corps, which he had founded, to learn some self-discipline. But as his advisers pointed out, this was no solution, as the prince was certain to meet other young men from England who had already had such experience. At this level of society, it was impossible for officialdom to eliminate homosexuality. The Punjab was the centre of a notorious homoerotic establishment in the form of the triangular friendship of Henry Lawrence, Herbert Edwardes and John Nicholson. They were in love with one another and with the young male protégés – both Christian and Pathan – that they collected around them.[14]

From a military point of view, the British – influenced by martial-race theory – felt convinced that they could categorise Indians into the effeminate races, such as Bengalis, and the martial races from the Punjab and the north-west of the country. The Muslims of the latter region fitted neatly into British theories about martial-races, and not surprisingly they became strongly represented in the British army, along with Sikhs. Many of the Muslim soldiers came from districts where the land was poor and families appreciated the additional income and prestige that came with the army connection. Money was sent home to help build mosques and pay for schools and pilgrimages to Mecca. For their part, the British took care to conciliate the Muslim troops by holding separate assemblies for prayers and sports; they also arranged for their meat to be slaughtered by a Muslim in the approved manner. 'Colonel sahib has made excellent arrangements and takes great trouble for us Musalmans,' wrote one soldier in the First World War. 'His arrangements for our food during the fast were very good.'[15] The flaw in this relationship arose when Muslims were required to fight outside Hindustan or north-west India, and against fellow Muslims – as in the Afghan War of 1878–80, when the Pathans often deserted. As a result, by the 1890s the British had stopped employing Muslims in frontier wars.[16]

Moreover, the British tendency to equate fighting qualities with conventional masculinity turned out to be rather naïve. In fact, manliness and homosexuality coexisted notably among the Pathans of the North-Western Provinces, who were much admired by the British for their fighting qualities. John Masters observed that Pathans were unlike effeminate Western homosexuals: 'They often wear roses in their long hair, and I frequently wish I could see a Pathan entering a gay cocktail party given by Manhattan fairies.'[17] He recalled one famous Pathan song, entitled 'Wounded Heart', which reportedly began with the words: 'There's a boy across the river with a bottom like a peach; but alas I cannot swim.' Despite changing attitudes towards homosexuality, Pathans continued to find a role in the British forces. As late as 1915, one wrote from England to his lover, complaining at his transfer: 'But now I have a beautiful white boy. He is my mess mate and I am very happy.'[18] Captain Kenneth Searight, who was stationed in Darjeeling, Peshawar, the Punjab and Rajasthan from 1909 onwards, left a manuscript account of his sexual relations with Pathan teenagers.[19] These relations worked, because Pathans could be frankly and assertively homosexual without detracting from their manliness, and this appealed greatly to some British soldiers and officials. Their feelings could be contained without much difficulty in a world where it was normal for higher-class men to have servants and juniors who ministered closely to their needs without arousing suspicion. The official world recognised the martial qualities and largely turned a blind eye to the private behaviour.

However, this positive relationship between Englishmen and Indian Muslims became complicated over time. Even before the growing disapproval in the Victorian period, there was a case for saying that some British men were fraternising with the enemy. As the Mughal Empire dwindled during the eighteenth century, nothing could wholly obscure the fact that the British had effectively usurped its power. No doubt the British tried to mitigate the alien quality of their rule by leaving the Mughal emperor in place in Delhi as a symbol of Muslim greatness and by making treaties with Muslim nawabs, who enjoyed effective internal control in their states, subject to advice and pressure from their British Residents. Beyond that, the British supported and cultivated Islamic culture in those cities where it flourished, including Lucknow, Delhi and Hyderabad. In Delhi, the last of the Mughal emperors, Bahadur

Shah Zafar II, presided over a brilliant court; he himself patronised art and literature, wrote Urdu and Persian poetry, as well as works on Sufism, created gardens and designed buildings. To some extent, this was undermined by the British, who humiliated him by taking over the administration of Delhi and removing his name from the coinage; more and more he came to be confined to the Red Fort and was simply paid a pension. But although many officials increasingly regarded Delhi and the other Islamic capitals as centres of corruption and decadence, their survival went some way to maintaining the notion of Muslim prestige and achievement.

More importantly, British disparagement of Indian Islam reflected the decline of political power among Muslim rulers, though it over-looked the fact that Islam itself was not in decline. On the contrary, during the eighteenth century learned Muslims were energetically devel-oping their religious traditions. This took the form of the building of Islamic libraries, the growth of shrines (for example, in the Punjab, where the Chishti Sufi order produced many new teachers), the gath-ering of learned Muslims at the Firangi Mahal seminary at Lucknow, the writing of tracts by famous teachers such as Shah Waliullah and Shah Abdul Aziz in Delhi, and the maintenance offered to learned Muslims by princes, including the nawab of Arcot. The British themselves contributed to the development of Islamic studies by founding the Calcutta Madrasa, the Delhi College and the Mohammedan Literary Association of Madras. However, they were slow to appreciate that beyond the higher levels of Muslim society religious revivalism reflected a reaction to alien rule. Repelled by the social behaviour of the British, their eating, drinking and sexuality, many Muslims aspired to purify and revive their own religion, rather than become more closely involved with the culture and habits of the Europeans. By 1800, some Muslims had begun to demand an end to the relaxed accommodation with other religions typical of the Mughal era, and sought to assert a stricter Arabic form of Islam.[20]

British thinking was also complicated by widespread assumptions that Muslims were under an obligation to wage holy war or *jihad* against non-Muslim rulers, though in practice this was far from being the case.[21]

The misapprehension arose largely from the context in which the Qur'an was originally written. Amid the warring tribes in seventh-century Arabia, Muslims felt vulnerable, and so divinely instituted war was simply inevitable if they were to be defended. But this was always qualified, as God was forgiving, and those who paid taxes and gave alms were to be left in peace. In later times, the question as to whether Muslims were required to take up arms largely depended on context and circumstance, especially on relations with local communities of unbelievers. When Islamic powers were engaged with major imperial armies, they found it desirable to enjoy divine authority for their campaigns. But in the case of British India during the eighteenth and nineteenth centuries, this was hardly the case. As Muslim power had not merely stopped expanding, but had actually started to dwindle, the case for holy war was far less obvious. Although some Indian Muslims argued that the British role in Hindustan had made the region *Dar al-Harb*, or 'Abode of War', and thus a military target, others countered that the British represented an improvement on the Hindu Maratha princes who were otherwise dominant; and neutral opinion simply advised Muslims to accept that as India was a country in which Islam could be freely practised, they could thus live at peace.

As the British went some way to maintaining an illusion of Mughal power, even when the reality had gone, it was possible to argue that their rule maintained or even protected Islam, though some felt sceptical about this. Bishop Heber observed that 'If a fair opportunity offered, the Musulmans would gladly avail themselves of it to rise against us. But this is from a political or a religious feeling.'[22] But Heber recognised that many Muslims chose to believe that the East India Company ruled in the name of the Mughal emperor. Consequently, there was no clear obligation to resist them, and in practice most Indian Muslims settled down to make the best of their situation by pursuing their occupations and paying their taxes. There were occasional revolts, including millenarian movements among Muslims in Bengal and the Moplah (Mappila) Rebellion on the Malabar coast, but these were very localised and were as much social in character as religious. The key to stability lay in having the Muslims of Punjab and the Ganges valley continue to see the British army as *their* army, in that it offered defence against the invasions that traditionally came from across the north-west frontier; this notion retained its credibility so long as the army did not venture further afield. Only the British interventions in Afghanistan in 1839 and 1878 undermined the illusion.

Towards the end of the eighteenth century, however, changing ideas at home began to undermine the comfortable relations prevailing in the East India Company's early life. In particular, those who had been influenced by the ideas of the Evangelicals, the Utilitarians and the liberal free traders took an increasingly dim view of its privileged position. From the point of view of free traders, for example, the company's habit of withholding supplies of tea from sale in order to boost the price was a practice blatantly against the public interest; consequently, the removal of its trading monopoly became an important objective. Also, young men who went out to India between the 1780s and 1820s increasingly looked down on the easy-going attitudes of the older men and believed that they had adopted the lax standards of the natives. As for the Utilitarians, they were almost as critical of society at home as in India, but in the empire they faced fewer obstacles to implementing their innovations. Once appointed to administer an Indian district, they imposed reforms without consulting local opinion; for them, India was, in effect, a huge laboratory in which to try out new ideas for land taxation, for example. Above all, the company was undermined by a revival of religious fervour, promoted partly by concerns about industrialisation and partly by a reaction against the worldliness and complacency of the contemporary Church. This manifested itself in the Evangelical movement within Anglicanism and in the rapid growth of Methodism. Moved by a fundamental belief in human depravity and in the need for Christians to be active in their faith, Evangelicals were critical of what they saw as the backwardness and decadence of Indian society, and were consequently keen to promote missionary work to save the heathen; for them, the English purpose must be to improve India, not simply to make money there. But in this enterprise, the men of the East India Company represented a huge obstacle, for they had largely accepted Indian society as they found it and refused the admission of missionaries to the country.

Over time, however, the Evangelicals gained influence, especially in parliament, as the abolition of the slave trade demonstrated. After 1800, keen Evangelicals deliberately infiltrated the East India Company, getting their supporters onto the board of directors – men such as Charles Grant, who became chairman. Increasingly, the company dispatched young men who held similar views: the Punjab, in particular, was noted for the collection of Evangelicals, including Henry and John Lawrence, Henry Havelock, John Nicholson and Sir Herbert Edwardes who served there. As a result of their influence both in parliament and within the company, policy inevitably changed.

For the company, the problem lay in the fact that parliament needed to renew its charter every 20 years. The new drafts of 1813 and 1833 disrupted matters by abolishing the company's original monopoly on trade and by forcing it to admit missionaries to India. Not that their impact should be exaggerated: by 1851, there were only 339 ordained missionaries in India for a population estimated at 151 million and their efforts were largely focused on the south. On the other hand, although the missionaries never made many converts, they were terribly conde-scending towards Indians and their presence proved disruptive, espe-cially in the army, where some officers attempted to encourage the men to convert. The appointment of Reginald Heber as the first bishop of Calcutta in 1814 represented a major complication, as he took a very dim view of Indians generally. Through his hymns, Heber propagated the idea of a holy war waged by Christianity against the vile heathens of the sub-continent. He was shocked at meeting the elderly British Resident in Delhi, Sir David Ochterlony, who usually dressed in pyjamas and turban, who maintained 13 Indian wives (including a young Brahmin dancing girl who had converted to Islam) and who proposed to bring up his children as Muslims. For the new recruits to India, the kind of cosmopolitan English–Hindu–Muslim regimes run by Ochterlony were absolute anathema.

The role of the reformers was accentuated by the shift in official policy associated with Lord William Bentinck, governor-general from 1827 to 1835. Bentinck was typical of the young men who had been influenced by Evangelicalism and was the first governor-general to arrive in India as an out-and-out reformer, rather than as someone who focused on the commercial success of the company. The result was a collection of humanitarian reforms, including an end to flogging in the army, the abolition of the slave trade between districts, the adoption of English as the official language, and the abolition of thuggee (a form of banditry with religious sanction) and suttee (the burning of widows on their husbands' funeral pyres). In the process, the whole character of the company changed. Whereas originally it had enjoyed a buccaneering approach, seeking trade for its employees and profits to keep its shareholders happy, during the 1800s it focused more on the mundane work of collecting the land revenues, becoming in the process more of a bureaucracy than a commercial organisation.

It is tempting to place the blame for the 1857 revolt, traditionally known as the Indian Mutiny, on this shift from commerce and conservatism to Westernising improvement and reform. However, it is worth noting that the British innovations largely affected the practices of the Hindus, such as thuggee and suttee (or sati). Indeed, the Mughals themselves had unsuccessfully attempted to abolish suttee. By contrast, Muslims were little affected by the reforms, the obvious exception being the adoption of English, which threatened the role of Persian among the educated Muslim class in Hindustan. Nonetheless, the reforms were indicative of a general view of Indian society, and increasingly the British characterised Muslim communities as decadent, especially those at famous Islamic centres such as Lucknow, which were still ruled by Muslim princes.

After Bentinck's departure in 1835, India enjoyed a quieter phase until 1848, when a new, young and dynamic reformer, Lord Dalhousie, arrived as governor-general. Less cautious than his predecessors, Dalhousie set about a series of measures designed to stimulate the economy, including canal building, railways, telegraphs and cheap postage. His reputation as the man who did most to bring about the mutiny of 1857 lay largely in his high-handed treatment of the Indian princes, who numbered around 600 and still ruled over half the sub-continent. By a variety of means, and using a mixture of excuses, Dalhousie annexed many Indian states, including Mysore, Sind, Punjab and Nagpur, as well as several smaller ones. But his greatest miscalculation came in 1856, when he took over the Kingdom of Oudh (Avadh), based on Lucknow. This state had 10 million people and 24,000 square miles of territory, and was a major focus of Muslim culture and prestige. Although the British had granted the nawab a 21-gun salute and had given him the title of 'king' in 1819, they had treated him disrespectfully over the years, grabbing bits of his territory from time to time and securing loans from him. The annexation shocked Indian opinion, because the nawab had been completely loyal and there was no real justification; it was an imperial land-grab, which Dalhousie claimed would bring in substantial extra land revenues. As the British had deliberately elevated Oudh as a rival to the declining Mughals in Delhi, this action was almost calculated to be counter-productive for the overall British strategy.

The high-handed treatment of Oudh was symptomatic of a wider arrogance affecting the British by the 1850s. Britain's own development in terms of manufacturing industry and her admired system of government had generated a confidence in the inevitability of progress, provided the obstacles were cleared from the path. Consequently, they did not stop to consider the effects of annexations or the danger of distancing themselves from native traditions. It was, for example, normal for Indian rulers to associate themselves with local religious practice as a means of consolidating their position; and for many years the British had followed their example. They routinely supported the maintenance of temples, mosques, the water tanks in front of mosques and shrines by overseeing the collection of taxes paid by pilgrims. In Mysore, following the defeat of Tipu Sultan, one of the greatest Muslim leaders, the British built new mosques and offered employment to some of Tipu's officers. Moreover, if learned Muslims or Hindus disliked the prospect of working under the British system, they could usually move to take employment with one of the many remaining princely states; this acted as a useful safety valve for an alien regime.

However, during the 30 years before 1857, the authorities withdrew much of their previous participation. In 1833, the government abolished the pilgrim taxes and ended all official association with religious ceremonies. In Oudh, some 50,000 royal troops suddenly lost their employment, and only 15,000 were taken on by the Bengal Army. Previously the nawab had paid somewhere in the region of a million rupees to pensioners around the court, but his functions were absorbed by a new Resident who had little sympathy with these arrangements. Many Hindus, Muslims and Eurasians who had enjoyed high-level employment under the nawab found themselves unemployed. Also, the lax collection of land revenues from the farmers was replaced by a stricter and more unpopular British administration. Muslim *zamindars* (land-owners) who had previously acted as intermediaries and had bargained with the local princes now found themselves lacking access to the more formal British administration.[23] Consequently, disaffection with the British was not just a matter of princely resentment among those who were displaced: almost all levels of society, urban and rural, were united against the British – at least in Hindustan, the area stretching from Bengal north-west through Bihar and Oudh to Agra and Delhi.

Despite this, the rebellion that broke out in 1857 was not a national revolt, but a regional one, largely confined to Hindustan. Nor was it primarily a religious uprising, although contemporary British opinion saw it largely in this light. Though triggered by a military mutiny among both Hindu and Muslim troops, the soldiers' actions reflected the growing dissatisfaction among the civilian populations from which they were drawn. By contrast, the armies of Bombay, Madras and the Punjab remained largely calm in 1857–58. Also, the revolt lacked any real leadership or coordination, its pattern being more a reflection of local factors and the antagonism of certain nawabs, rajahs, landowners and farmers who felt displaced or threatened by the shifts in British policies.

Nonetheless, contemporary British opinion in the aftermath of the revolt commonly held that Muslims had been the key element, giving leadership and motivation and mobilising the Hindu sepoys. This, however, was scarcely consistent with the evidence that the British had put far more pressure on Hinduism than on Islam. Many Brahmins had become afraid that the British were attempting to undermine their caste through the introduction of railways, by allowing widows to remarry, by allowing those who changed religion to inherit property and by depriving convicts in jail of the right to enjoy separately prepared food. This accounts for a certain religious fervour among Hindus that was largely lacking among Muslims.

Despite the evidence, contemporary commentators were initially misled into seeing the revolt as Muslim inspired, because in Delhi the rebels dragged the reluctant, elderly Bahadur Shah out of his seclusion with a view to using him as leader of the ramshackle movement; subsequently the authorities tried him and exiled him to Rangoon. But he was no more than a figurehead and had no aspirations to restore the Mughal Empire. More relevant was the effect of British rule in gradually restricting the activities of freelance Muslim military adventurers in the north. Also, Muslim employment in the legal and revenue departments in Bengal and the North-Western Provinces was curtailed, as posts as magistrates and collectors were taken over by British men. Bentinck's decision in 1829 to abandon Persian as the official language in favour of English finally heralded the eclipse of Muslims in the bureaucracy. As a result, by 1856 only 54 of the 366 men who held judicial and revenue posts that paid over 50 rupees were Muslims.[24] Some were replaced by Bengali Hindus, who adapted to the English language more readily. This helps to explain why Muslims joined the revolt in the towns around Delhi, where they felt displaced as a ruling class by the British; there was nothing to be lost by a change in the system.

Yet even in the North-Western Provinces, Muslims were no more prominent in the rebellion than Hindus. In Bengal and the Punjab, where Muslims were in a majority, they remained largely uninvolved, even the princes refusing to throw in their lot with the rebels. Where Muslims were affected, it was chiefly as small landowners, farmers and taxpayers, rather than as Muslims per se. Prior to 1857, British officials had overthrown titles to land in the case of those who could not produce sufficient legal documentation and had imposed a stricter system when reassessing the land revenues. In Oudh, they also pushed aside many of the local *taluqdars*, who acted as intermediaries between the farmers and the government over the collection of land revenue; the British refused to tolerate delays in payment and were much more systematic in collecting the revenues. As the *taluqdars* had around 600 small forts, they acted as rallying points for anyone who wanted to defy the authorities. The widespread desire to reject revenue demands and reclaim rights to the land accounts for the swift collapse of British authority in much of the countryside in 1857. Here the rebellion was a genuine social revolt, but participation involved a large element of opportunism on the part of both Hindus and Muslims, rather than any ideological or religious inspiration.

Whatever the cause, the impact of the 1857 rebellion on the British was profound. The massacres of British people – and especially of women and children – permanently warped British attitudes towards Indians, and the realisation that they had nearly been forced out of the country altogether made them much more cautious. Most of the blame was pinned on the company, whose role was terminated in favour of crown rule. The army, in many ways more culpable, was simply reorganised so as to disband the sepoy regiments from Oudh and reduce the number of Indian troops from 240,000 to 140,000, in the process limiting the role of Muslims in favour of Sikhs and Gurkhas. The Evangelicals' claim that the revolt was God's way of punishing the British for not doing more to convert the natives was widely rejected, and there was a general retreat from ideas about improving and Westernising Indians during the next half century. A royal proclamation expressly denied that there was any intention of changing Indians' religious allegiances. Missionaries were still allowed to operate, but without government encouragement; there were, in any case, fewer missionaries, as some of the societies had diverted their resources to Africa. The British recognised that most princes had kept clear of the revolt, including Muslim ones with large armies, like the nizam of Hyderabad. For the future, the wisest strategy seemed to be to consolidate British relations with the princes by avoiding threats to their position, granting them gun salutes, awarding them honours like the new Star of India, engaging them in sports such as cricket, polo and pig-sticking, inviting them to durbars, and encouraging them to see Queen Victoria, who became empress of India in 1876, as filling the place of the Mughal emperor.

After their initial shock, the British moderated their suspicion of Muslims as the inspiration behind the revolt, taking the view that a Muslim was a dangerous opponent, but a good friend. Several revolts by the Wahabis, designed to restore Mohammedan rule, were serious enough to provoke British military expeditions in 1858 and 1863. The involvement of Muslims in the assassination of a chief justice in 1871 and of the viceroy, Lord Mayo, in 1872, also appeared to confirm the pessimists' view. However, British policy remained largely unaffected by such events. In 1871, as a means of discrediting the whole idea, the viceroy deliberately invited a Bengal official to write a book entitled, *The Indian Mussulmans: Are They Bound in Conscience to Rebel Against the Queen?* Lord Canning, the governor-general after 1857, simply declined to follow suggestions from London to wreak special revenge on Muslims. He told the prime minister: 'I beg you not to ask for anything to be done against the religion of either race . . . I do wish to leave both religions alone, and to treat them with indifference in the real sense of the term.'[25] In future, British policy was to be based on abstaining from interference in Muslim religion and on avoiding any expropriation of their position as property owners. Judicious concessions would be employed to help segregate 'the party of sedition' from the majority of peaceful Muslims.

However, despite Canning's even-handedness, Muslims were inevitably affected by the growing distance between the races in India. This trend was not wholly attributable to 1857, but rather to long-term developments in the British community. By the nineteenth century, it had increased greatly in size as a result of improvements in communications. Originally the journey to India by sea around the Cape of Good Hope had taken six months, but by the 1860s, with the coming of steamships, it was down to three months. A faster route lay through the Mediterranean, overland through Egypt to the Red Sea, thence to the Indian Ocean and

Bombay. By the 1830s, this journey could be accomplished in only two months, and in 1843 the Peninsular and Oriental Steam Navigation Company began regular voyages for mail and passengers. The opening of the Suez Canal in 1869 enabled P&O to reduce the journey to one month. As a result, the English community increased in size and changed in composition, as more women made the journey. Not only did wives accompany their husbands, but young, unmarried women – known as the 'Fishing Fleet' – arrived. Victorian society was obsessive about the necessity for marriage; but as women outnumbered men in the population (partly because so many young men in their twenties and thirties departed to work in the empire), many women remained unmarried. By the 1860s, of the 10 million women in the population of the British Isles, nearly a quarter lacked a husband; a third of those were widows and the remaining two-thirds were spinsters. Consequently, expeditions of middle- and upper-class girls travelled to India during the colder months from November to February with instructions to find a husband. In order to assist, and to give themselves something to do, the ladies at each British station organised a full social programme based at the club, where they did their best to bring the sexes together. Here there were no Indians (apart from servants) and the opportunities for friendship between British men and Indian women diminished; indeed, anyone who avoided the all-English social life was seen as eccentric and even as a threat to the Raj.

Consequently, the old practice of establishing families with Muslim women largely disappeared, and even the taking of mistresses dwindled. Those British officers who persisted in taking wives or mistresses from the native community found themselves transferred to remote and unhealthy parts of the Raj – a situation depicted by George Orwell in his novel, *Burmese Days* (1934). The government never banned mistresses for fear that the men might be provoked into marrying them: a wife was worse, because she would enjoy the same status as her husband, whereas one could at least pretend that a mistress did not exist. The continued provision of women for the troops by the army caused endless controversy and embarrassment, but it was justified as a necessary exception to the general rule. By the late nineteenth century, Indian princes would often travel to England, where they met English women. Short of actually preventing the princes from leaving India, there was not much the authorities could do. But as far as possible, the British followed the principle of keeping the races separate outside their official and working relations. They were ready to placate respectable Muslims by offering concessions to those who had something to lose by opposing the Raj; but this was as far as the relationship was to go.

CHAPTER FIVE

BRITAIN AND THE MANAGEMENT OF ISLAMIC DECLINE

During the eighteenth century, the relationship between Islam and the British entered a remarkably benign phase – and not just in India. The British began to take a more relaxed, even subdued, attitude towards religion generally, partly as a reaction against the fanaticism of the previous two centuries, the civil wars in England and the religious wars in Europe. In 1689, Britain even passed the Toleration Act, which admittedly excluded the Catholics and Unitarians, but did allow Dissenters freedom of worship under licence from a bishop. If Britain lagged behind Muslim practice, the act was at least symbolic of the gradual progress towards religious and civil freedom over the next century. We have an indication of a pragmatic attitude that emerged especially among the upper classes from the experiences of Lady Mary Wortley Montagu, whose husband became ambassador at Constantinople in 1716. Not only did she appreciate the more rational approach of Muslims, but she noted approvingly the response of people such as the Albanians, caught between Christianity and Islam. Not especially sophisticated, the Albanians were known to attend the mosque on Fridays and church on Saturdays; they reasoned that when the Day of Judgment came, they would enjoy the protection of the true prophet – even though they felt at present unable to decide who that was! Lady Mary, who disliked the tendency among Christians to develop sects, mysteries, novelties and controversies, thought it merely sensible to recognise the similarities between the two religions.

Even more significant was the fact that, as Islam itself had entered a phase of contraction after centuries of expansion, it could not be represented as the threat it had once been. The Mughal Empire in India entered a period of decline in the face of British expansionism from 1707, culminating in its eclipse in 1858. In the 1680s, the Austrians checked the protracted Ottoman offensive, and their success at Kahlenberg, outside Vienna, in 1683 proved decisive in lifting the siege of their capital. After this point the Ottomans were effectively on the defensive on several fronts. The Austrian Habsburgs recovered Hungary in 1699 and went on to take parts of Serbia, including Belgrade, and Transylvania in 1718. Meanwhile the Russians seized the Crimea, the north coast of the Black Sea and the area around Azov, to the north-east of the Black Sea, between 1768 and 1792. The Ottomans were also obliged to grant Russia and Austria the right to intervene on behalf of the Christian subjects living in their empire.

However, to describe this as a spectacular decline for the Turks would be an exaggeration; the shrinkage of the empire was in fact a very protracted affair, and included many to-ings and fro-ings. The Ottomans reversed the Russian capture of Azov in 1711; they lost Greek territory to the Venetians, but recovered it in 1715; they pushed the Austrians out of Belgrade, Serbia and Bosnia in 1737–39, leaving them again in control of almost all of the Balkans. By 1739 they had largely recovered the lost territory. Yet despite these rear-guard actions, Islam had clearly passed its early dynamic phase, leaving Muslims to consider how to handle an era increasingly marked by European expansionism. The explanation for the long survival of the Ottomans lay less in their own strength than in the anxiety of the European powers about preventing Ottoman territory falling into the hands of their rivals. They simply found it useful to maintain it in decline.

The two changes – territorial and ideological – were complementary, in that it became easier for the British to be objective (or at least pragmatic)

about Islam, now that it had ceased to be such a threat, and thus to appreciate the common ground. Eighteenth-century critics recognised that Christianity had come about to refine the pagan religions but had got itself lost in a maze of mysteries and imported rites that had been avoided by Islam; to some extent, they accepted the claim that Islam offered a means of purging Christianity of its corruptions.

The publication in 1739 of what was seen as a good translation of the Qur'an by George Sale helped to clarify the elements in Islam that were appreciated in the eighteenth century. It had kept to its original simplicity, resisting temptations to elaborate the religion. It lacked a priesthood. It did not involve miracles. And it took a rational anti-Trinitarian view: 'Do ye believe that God hath a Son? Praised be God, he is most rich, and hath no need of any person.'[1] Anti-Trinitarianism, known later as Unitarianism, enjoyed support in high places. Henry St John, Viscount Bolingbroke, a secretary of state in 1709–14, argued that the doctrine of the Holy Trinity enabled Muslims to say that Mohammed had rightly established the unity of the supreme being, as opposed to the polytheism introduced by Christians. Of course, there was a vigorous counter-attack against this view, manifested in the foundation of Trinity Colleges at Dublin, Cambridge and Oxford. Critics claimed that the Unitarians were actually closer to Islam than to Christianity: they were even suspected of being Muslims in disguise, whose real aim was to prepare for a further advance of Islam across Europe. Up to a point, the Unitarians endorsed these claims both by itemising the common ground and by suggesting that the Prophet had never intended to create a new religion, but rather to re-establish the true, original Christianity.

Another aspect of the debate lay in the attitude towards Heaven or Paradise in the two religions. Critics of Islam had often focused on its alleged sensuousness, as evidenced by the claim that Paradise was populated by *houris* – women with whom the saved would be able to enjoy relationships. Such views had always been ridiculed by Christian theologians. But Muslims countered this with the argument that Christianity suffered from inhibitions about human sexuality which it sometimes tried to deny. When the body was resurrected, so ran the argument, this would involve both the body and the bodily functions, including eating, drinking and sex; all this was to be seen as healthy and as a correction against undue prudishness.

Among the most eminent of the participants in discussions about Islam was the historian Edward Gibbon (1737–94), who adopted a characteristically eighteenth-century view. Gibbon famously observed that but for Charles Martel's victory over the Moors in 732, Islam would have continued to spread into northern Europe, and thus 'the interpretation of the Koran would now be taught in the schools of Oxford'.[2] Cynical towards Christianity, Gibbon condemned all manner of Christian practices: its claims to miraculous powers as proof of validity, the worship of relics, the use of images, the invocation of saints, the use of the Cross as a symbol, the mystery of the sacrifice of the body and blood of Christ, monastic life, celibacy and the growth of a priesthood.[3] He felt that monotheism had liberated men from pagan superstition, but it had been corrupted by the superstition that led to the religious fanaticism that was alive in his own times, as the anti-Catholic Gordon Riots of 1780 demonstrated. Conversely, Gibbon was among those eighteenth-century men who saw Islam as preferable, in that it was un-mystical, undogmatic, tolerant and simple; Muslims, he thought, believed there was one God and one Prophet (which was not correct).[4] Gibbon also appreciated the way Islam promoted civic qualities and duties, including honour, charity, hospitality and justice; in this way it had a bonding effect on society.

Perhaps surprisingly, this sympathetic view survived the spread of evangelical Christianity in the late eighteenth and early nineteenth centuries, as is evident from the comments of the great historian and political commentator, Thomas Carlyle (1795–1881). Fascinated by the role of great men in history, Carlyle inevitably homed in on Mohammed. Rejecting medieval accusations of him as a scheming imposter, Carlyle commended him as 'a true prophet', noting that he was not a God, but a God-inspired man.[5] Not that Carlyle was uncritical. Of the Qur'an he wrote:

I must say, it is as toilsome reading as I ever undertook. A wearisome, confused jumble, crude, incondite, endless iterations, long-windedness, entanglement.[6]

But he praised Mohammed for his 'total freedom from cant', his sincerity and his emphasis on the giving of alms. Noting that after a quiet, unexceptional life, he did not experience revelations until he was over 50, Carlyle described him as: 'A silent great soul; he was one of those who cannot but be in earnest; whom Nature herself has appointed to be sincere.'[7] And he advised fellow Christians to recognise that as Islam had stood for 12 centuries and had 180 million adherents, or about a fifth of mankind, it was unlikely to be a falsehood. Like Christianity, it believed in one God and commanded men to 'be resigned to God'; as such, it was surely 'a kind of Christianity'.[8]

Against this background of softening British attitudes, by the late eighteenth century the strategic policy of governments had become increasingly dominated by the triangular relationship between Britain, Turkey and Russia. Although her role in defeating the French revolutionary and Napoleonic forces made Russia appear a potential ally, this was complicated by her long-term support for the Orthodox Christians in Greece, Serbia, Bosnia, Bulgaria and Romania, which provided a convenient cover for intervention at the expense of the Ottoman Empire. Since 1774, Russia had enjoyed a formal right to intervene on behalf of the Orthodox Christians and for Russian pilgrims to access the Holy Land. Her annexation of the Crimea in 1783 proved especially offensive, as it was populated by Muslims, and during the 1790s she kept chipping away at Turkish territory.

Eventually, Russian aggression so worried William Pitt, the British prime minister, who took office at the end of 1783, that he concluded it was politic to revert to the earlier tradition of allying with Turkey to check the southward advance of the Russians. He felt that religious considerations should simply be ignored. Interestingly, Pitt also considered that the Ottoman Empire was going to last a long time, despite the challenges it faced, and it was therefore worth the trouble of cooperating with it. At the time, however, Pitt's thinking was not popular. In any case, he suspended his policy because, in 1792, the Turks and Russians reached a peace treaty at Jassy in Romania that settled the border between them.

On the other hand, Pitt had clearly mapped out the future, in which Britain played a key role in managing the decline of the Ottomans. Strategic calculations were to be radically changed following the outbreak of the French Revolution in 1789. This resulted in Napoleon's invasion of Egypt in 1798, which was intended as a means of attacking Britain in India, but which also dramatically underlined Turkish weakness. Although Britain managed to defeat the French fleet at Abouqir Bay, to evict French forces and restore Ottoman rule, Napoleon's initiative proved to have a stimulating effect on nationalist sentiment and was thus disruptive for Ottoman control in the Balkans. As yet, however, Britain was a long way from seeking a permanent occupation of Egypt, and she evacuated her troops in 1802 and restored Turkish sovereignty. For the time being, she remained content with naval mastery of the Mediterranean.

However, the conclusion of the Napoleonic Wars in 1815 left Russia as the strongest power in Europe, thereby reviving British concerns about the southern Slav expansion. Trapped by ice-bound seas in the Baltic and in the Far East, the Russians inevitably regarded the warm waters of the Black Sea as conferring a major strategic advantage, provided she could maintain a sufficient naval force there. This, however, would enable her to threaten Britain's increasingly important trade routes through the Eastern Mediterranean and across Egypt to India. Consequently, in British eyes, the maintenance of Ottoman control across the narrow waters of the Bosphorus and the Dardanelles began to loom as a major national interest.

From the British perspective, it was Ottoman rule over Greece that dragged to the fore the question of how to manage Turkish decline. After 1815, Europeans had revived the practice of the Grand Tour, though this at first involved travelling in France and Italy (Greece being regarded as a sad relic of its former days and the Greeks themselves as rather degenerate). However, appreciation of Greek culture began to increase. When Lord Byron made his first visit in 1810, he felt antagonised by the tyrannous rule of the Turks and was also dismayed at the British themselves, who were busily loading crates of what were to become known as 'the Elgin marbles' onto ships at Piraeus. By 1821, when the Greeks rose in revolt against the Turks, British liberal opinion had become very sympathetic towards struggles for national independence. Some 30,000 Turkish troops rapidly subdued the revolt, while others were suppressing uprisings among the Christians in Moldavia and Wallachia, looting churches and mutilating bodies in the process.

However, not everyone was persuaded by these events. The reactionary duke of Wellington, for example, frankly opposed Greek independence, arguing that they were better ruled by Turkey, 'our ancient ally'. From his perspective, nationalism was contagious – and especially dangerous in Ireland. In the event, the British government contented itself with urging the Turks to introduce some reforms, leaving it to volunteers to go to fight for the Greek cause in the war from 1822 to 1824. Byron returned to join the fight in 1824, but died from either tick fever or malaria, exacerbated by excessive bleeding by his doctors. His personal sacrifice saw him acclaimed as a hero, more in France than in Britain, and provided a major moral stimulus to the Greek cause.[9]

Meanwhile the Russians issued an ultimatum to the Turks, who responded by seizing Russian ships at Constantinople and imprisoning their sailors. Marked by appalling atrocities, the rebellion spread to central Greece, the Peloponnese and Macedonia, dragging on until Russia, France and Britain eventually offered mediation in 1827. The Russians really wanted the creation of a large Greek state under their protection, but to Britain it looked like another attempt to extend the tsar's control. In any case, mediation was rejected by the Turks. The three powers gathered a fleet, which was intended to separate the rival forces but became unintentionally involved in the destruction of the Turkish-Egyptian fleet at the battle of Navarino. The equivocal stance of the British government was reflected in the fact that it apologised to Turkey for this action, as it continued to regard the Ottoman Empire as a useful element, rather than as something to be swept aside.

For the Turks, Greek independence threw into sharp relief the need to avert the collapse of their European territories under the combined threat from Russian imperialism and Balkan nationalism. For a time, the danger seemed acute. In 1828, 65,000 Russian troops crossed the

River Danube heading south towards Constantinople. Although half of them died from disease, the Russians renewed their offensive in 1829, reaching Adrianople (Edirne), only a short march from Constantinople. With Turkish forces in disarray and the Russian fleet dominating the Black Sea, it appeared for a time as though the Ottomans were about to collapse and that their territory would be partitioned by the European powers. However, lack of support from Austria and the other Western powers restrained Tsar Nicholas, who contented himself with making the Romanian provinces of Moldavia and Wallachia autonomous, but under Russian protection. The by-product of these Turkish defeats was the formation of a small Greek state comprising Athens and the Peloponnese, which was guaranteed by Britain, France and Russia in 1830. While Britain had not played a major role in Greek independence, its intervention demonstrated the potential of her strategy of managing the Ottoman decline through a combination of judiciously curtailing the empire, while largely preserving it as a buffer against the Russians. Nonetheless nothing had really been resolved. The existence of an independent Greece gave inspiration to the other Christian nationalities in the Balkans and complicated British policy in the long term by ceding the moral high ground to the anti-Turkish view.

Britain had got off lightly over Greek independence, enjoying some credit for the outcome without actually doing much. But during the 1850s, the management of Ottoman decline rapidly became more complicated and costly. Greek independence highlighted the danger of further Russian advances, especially in the Crimea, which the Turks expected to be used as a military base to challenge their rule in the Balkans and Constantinople. This was the fear that eventually led to the Crimean War of 1853–56. Tension had increased in 1833, when it emerged that the Russians had made a secret agreement to extend military protection to Turkey, in exchange for a promise to close the straits at Constantinople when requested by Russia. This appeared to be a means of giving Russia control of the Black Sea and landing an army at

Constantinople before Britain had time to resist it. 'It becomes an object of great importance for the interests of Great Britain to consider how Russia can be prevented from pushing her advantage further,' wrote Lord Palmerston in 1833, 'and to see whether it is possible to deprive her of the advantage she has already gained.'[10] He empowered the ambassador at Constantinople to summon the British fleet from the Mediterranean if ever the city was threatened by Russia.

Despite these underlying concerns, however, the Crimean War was an unnecessary and ill-conceived one, sparked by conflicts over access to religious sites by Orthodox Christians, Armenians and Catholics that were exploited by the Great Powers. The Ottomans, as the authority in Palestine-Syria, found themselves caught up in these disputes among the Christians; but when subjected to pressure from the Russians, they felt able to resist on the basis that they enjoyed support from France and Britain. At the time, the British and French claimed that they were defending the Ottomans against a barbarous Russian bully. The French Emperor Napoleon III hoped to restore the status his country had enjoyed under Napoleon I, while some (though not all) British politicians were keen to check Russian expansionism in the Mediterranean.

Despite the obvious political-strategic motivations, the war also involved a significant religious element – at least on the part of Tsar Nicholas I, who believed that he was engaged in a religious struggle, almost a crusade, on behalf of Orthodox Christianity. Many Russians regarded it as their divine mission to liberate Orthodoxy from the domination of the Ottoman Empire and to restore Constantinople as the centre of Christianity in the East, as it had been under the Byzantines. During the 1840s, various Christian groups had been active in the Holy Land, investing in churches, schools, hospitals and bishoprics. Every Easter, 15,000 Russian pilgrims (for whom the shrines of Palestine were an object of passionate devotion) would arrive in Jerusalem, travelling through the Caucasus, Anatolia and Syria. Catholics and Protestants from Western Europe, whose fervour had long since moderated, were shocked and repelled at the intense emotion shown by these Orthodox pilgrims. By contrast, the Muslims appeared to them to be restrained, dignified and almost secular in their attitude.[11] Some observers feared that the Russians were sponsoring pilgrims and missions as a means of preparing the way for a physical takeover of Palestine. Conflicts, including fights between Orthodox and Latin Christians over access to churches and shrines, compounded this impression.

The Ottomans, caught between the rival Christians and their governments, seemed inclined to give way to Russian pressure. In 1851, the situation reached crisis point when the French, who had established a commission with the Turks designed to resolve the question of religious rights, began to threaten extreme measures and to warn of the superior French naval strength in the Mediterranean. At this point, Britain did, in fact, have an alternative to maintaining the Ottoman Empire by risking war with Russia. In the long run, Turkey could be partitioned: the only immediate complication was that Austria, Russia and Britain were unable to agree how to do this. Yet since 1844, Britain and Russia had had an agreement on what to do if Turkey collapsed, and for this reason the two powers expected to be able to cooperate on a solution during the crisis of the 1850s. However, the British ministers in Lord Aberdeen's fragile coalition government (1852–55) were divided. Palmerston, the influential ex-foreign secretary, resisted any attempt to partition Turkey, arguing with good reason: 'Turkey is not a dead or dying body, but on the contrary it possesses powers of life and national resources which render it worth maintaining as a useful element in the European balance.'[12]

For their part, the Ottomans had formally recognised the Russian annexation of the Crimea in 1792, but they had never really accepted the loss of the territory. They were also antagonised by the brutal treatment of the Muslim people in Russia's southern borderlands. Starting in the early decades of the nineteenth century, Russia had evicted thousands of Muslims and had brought in Christian settlers in their place. They had also destroyed mosques and prevented Muslims from travelling to Mecca. However, as the Turks had come off worst in the wars of 1806–12 and 1828–29, they no longer felt strong enough to stop the Russians by themselves. Consequently, they looked for an alliance with the Western powers, who shared their fears of Russian aggression.

That alliance rapidly materialised in 1853, when the Russians issued an ultimatum to Turkey, invaded the Danubian provinces and sank the

Turkish fleet at the battle of Sinope. This provoked a coalition of French, British, Austrian, Sardinian and Turkish troops, who initially landed at Varna on the Romanian coast of the Black Sea to check the advances across the Danube. When the attack failed to materialise, these troops were transferred to the Crimean Peninsula, where the main conflict was taking place. In the Crimea, the allies won a victory at the battle of Alma and laid siege to the Russians' naval base at Sebastopol. Despite a series of costly battles at Balaclava and Inkerman, the Russians failed to lift the siege and they abandoned the city in October 1855, bringing the war to an end.

However, the significance of the Crimean War was rather mixed. From a domestic perspective, the war became famous for the exploits of Florence Nightingale; it was sanctified by the Charge of the Light Brigade; and it resulted in Alma, Balaclava, Inkerman and Sebastopol appearing as street names all over the country. But it also exposed the incompetence of Lord Aberdeen's coalition government, and generated much criticism of the amateurishness of the army and of the political system, especially among assertive middle-class Radicals. Eventually, a number of reforms – including the abolition of the practice of buying officers' commissions and peacetime flogging in the army – would be enacted under W.E. Gladstone's post-1868 government. Despite its incompetence, the army's heroics led to the creation of a new honour, the Victoria Cross (1857), and to the growth of the cult of 'muscular Christianity' – that is, the idea of British imperial expansion as the occasion for Christian soldiers to wage righteous wars. In churches it became increasingly common to sing the hymn:

Onward Christian soldiers, marching as to war,
With the cross of Jesus going on before.

This notion was reinforced by the Indian Mutiny of 1857, which also conferred prestige on an incompetent army in the context of what was represented as a struggle for civilisation.

On the other hand, it is far from clear that the war resolved the issues that had led to it in the first place. The Turks, usually neglected in British accounts, suffered 120,000 casualties, nearly half of their troops.

Although they enjoyed a victory, retained their territory and in effect stopped Russia from trying to turn their empire into a client state, they regarded the war as more of a humiliation, as it seemed to make them dependent on the Western powers and forced the Ottoman state into serious indebtedness.

For the allies, the war kept the Russians in check – but for only a short period. In any case, the Crimea was of little strategic significance. Indeed, it is arguable that for Britain the chief importance of the war lay in giving her the opportunity to destroy Russian ships and naval installations in the Baltic. In 1856, the Treaty of Paris imposed a ban on Russian warships in the Black Sea, which served British purposes admirably. But the Crimean War did not change the fundamentals at all, as the allies lacked the military strength to inflict a serious defeat on Russia. While the British remained dominant at sea, the Russians were left as the major land power. Not only that, but they were extremely difficult to get at, given their huge continental land mass. They could afford to wait a little. Above all, it was questionable whether Britain could afford to repeat the mistake she had made in order to prop up the Ottoman Empire in another war.

It was not long before the Crimean settlement was dramatically undermined by the Franco-Prussian War of 1870–71, which enabled the Russians to take the opportunity to renounce the 'Black Sea' clauses in the Peace of Paris. In this situation, Britain had too small an army to tackle the Russians alone. But with France defeated by the Prussians, and the Austrians also defeated by them in 1866, any idea of reviving the alliance of 1853 was wholly implausible. Consequently, the 1871 London Convention actually sanctioned the Russians' action, giving them the right to maintain warships in the Black Sea, though Turkey had the right to open the Dardanelles to foreign warships even in peacetime.

Even this proved to be temporary, as the question of Ottoman decline re-erupted spectacularly in 1875–76 because of a revolt among the Slav population of Bosnia and Herzegovina against Turkish rule that was suppressed with some brutality. By 1877, the Russians had grasped the opportunity to intervene against the Turks on behalf of the Christian population, and by the end of the year they had largely overrun the

Balkans, reaching San Stefano (only a few miles from Constantinople). At this point, they imposed the Treaty of San Stefano on the Turks, creating a large Bulgarian state which most observers saw as merely a Russian puppet. But in so doing they had overplayed their hand. This time the powers intervened via the Congress of Berlin with a view to curtailing Russian gains. In effect, they were now adopting the policy long anticipated – agreeing between themselves how to partition the Ottoman Empire. Prime Minister Benjamin Disraeli claimed that he had secured British interests by gaining the island of Cyprus, the so-called 'key to the Mediterranean'. Sadly, Disraeli had a weak grasp of geography and strategy, and his ignorance of French meant that he had little understanding of what the Congress was deciding! With no suitable harbour for the navy, Cyprus was useless as a base from which to defend Egypt and Britain's route to India, and it subsequently became irrelevant when Britain occupied Egypt. Cyprus also proved to be a source of trouble for Britain for many years to come – a classic example of a counter-productive intervention in Muslim affairs.

With the Eastern Question, Disraeli was really indulging in politics, and for a time he succeeded in playing the patriotic card. As with the Crimean War, public opinion was easily aroused, and music-hall audiences happily chanted: 'We've fought the Bear before and while we're Britons true, the Russians shall not have Constantinople.' By calling the fleet up to the Dardanelles and mobilising Indian troops Disraeli came perilously close to another war with Russia. Fortunately, his cabinet refused to take any further risks. Meanwhile, at Berlin, the powers split Bulgaria, creating a new state of 'Eastern Rumelia' along the line of the Balkan mountains as a buffer against Turkey. Sounding like something out of a Gilbert and Sullivan operetta, Eastern Rumelia disappeared from history in 1885, when it amalgamated with the rest of Bulgaria. Austria was to occupy and administer Bosnia and Herzegovina, though the provinces remained nominally under Turkish suzerainty; and Serbia, Montenegro and Romania were recognised as independent.

These events effectively undermined the basis of British policy towards the Ottoman Empire. In mid-century, Palmerston had insisted on the necessity of maintaining it against Russian pressure. But by the

1870s, Gladstone, his successor as Liberal leader, had adopted the opposite stance, ostensibly on moral grounds, though his view was really the more realistic one. Disraeli had meanwhile seized the patriotic, Palmerstonian cry and polarised politics over external policy. However, in the long run Disraeli's fellow Conservatives, notably Lord Salisbury (who was prime minister for most of the 1885–1902 period), concluded that Disraeli had backed the wrong horse: they recognised that Gladstone had been right about Turkey and that the pro-Turkish policy was futile. Britain no longer had the capacity to manage Ottoman decline effectively by propping her up whenever threats arose. The Turks' vulnerability both to Balkan nationalism and to Russian aggression even called into question the feasibility of doing so. In the long run, the creation of national states in the Balkans – though admittedly the cause of a series of regional wars – represented a more effective barrier to Russian expansionism than a declining Turkey.

In other parts of the Ottoman Empire, British policy showed more continuity, especially in Egypt and Sudan. But this line proved equally complicated, partly because it required indirect management involving London, Cairo and Constantinople, but also because of the emergence of nationalism within the Islamic world. In the process, Britain was led into the first of what turned into a whole catalogue of mistakes in Egypt and Sudan; these interventions, though largely counter-productive, foreshadowed what in the twenty-first century has become almost a habit of interference in the affairs of the Muslim world.

Egypt's strategic position at the eastern end of the Mediterranean, on the route to India, raised the question of how far Britain could manage the territorial decline of the Ottomans. More fundamentally, it posed a dilemma for the British about whether Islam was capable of modernisation and reform, or was irredeemably backward and obscurantist. These issues divided British opinion through both the nineteenth and the twentieth centuries. As long ago as 642, Muslim forces had occupied Egypt, displacing the rule of the Byzantines. However, the Jews and

Christians who comprised most of the population had been left in place; they served in government and enjoyed protection for their churches. After a series of Muslim rulers, Egypt fell under the control of the Mamluks, a slave dynasty whose members rose to high places in government. After 300 years, they were superseded by the Ottomans, who seized the opportunity to gain not only the economic riches of Egypt, but a new status as protectors of Islam's holy places at Medina and Mecca. As a result, Cairo prospered as a centre for Islamic learning, especially at al-Azhar, the famous mosque-university. During this period, a majority of Egyptians were converted from Christianity to Islam.

However, in time Egypt became somewhat peripheral to Ottoman interests, as did other Arab centres. The economy declined and the country fell into disarray, exposing it to foreign intervention. This arrived dramatically in 1798, when Napoleon Bonaparte led his armies into the region. Although counter-attacks at sea and on land by the British had expelled the French by 1803, this episode had important consequences. It made Egyptians realise that they could no longer count on the Ottomans for protection, and it opened the country to European influences. From the chaotic conditions following the departure of the French emerged a new leader, Mohammed Ali Pasha. Nominally administering Egypt on behalf of the Ottoman sultan as viceroy (or khedive from 1867 onwards), he was the effective ruler from 1805 to 1849. A ruthless but effective leader, determined to modernise his country, Mohammed Ali created a centralised administration and a powerful army, extended his empire across Syria and Arabia, and in 1831 even invaded Anatolia. With Constantinople itself under threat, the sultan appealed to Russia for help, raising the prospect of a partition of Ottoman territory by Russia and Egypt. France and Britain then intervened to force the Russians to back off, and the Egyptians withdrew from Anatolia. However, in 1839 the Turks were again defeated by the Egyptians and the Turkish navy defected to Mohammed Ali, making the dissolution of the Ottoman Empire seem possible. Again, this was averted by the intervention of Lord Palmerston, who was keen to maintain the Ottomans; he did not want to occupy Egypt – simply to prevent the intervention of the French, who had been training the Egyptian army. Beyond the strategic aim of safeguarding communications with India, the only British interest lay in using Egypt as a source of supplies of cotton. Palmerston managed to impose the Treaty of London in 1841, which forced Mohammed Ali to reduce his army from 90,000 to 18,000 men, disband his war industries and return Syria to Turkey. Britain and France cooperated to check Russia, but were divided over the French desire to allow Egypt to become independent of Turkey – a move that seemed likely to lead to a French protectorate.

Keeping Egypt at arm's length was a sound objective for Britain, but it proved elusive in practice. The French had unleashed the idea of modernisation and development, which materialised in a scheme to construct the Suez Canal. The idea had originated with the 1798 expedition and was favoured by Ferdinand de Lesseps, the French vice-consul in the 1830s. The death of Mohammed Ali in 1849 set back the plan, but it was adopted in 1854 by another viceroy, Said Pasha, who signed an agreement allowing de Lesseps' Canal Company to build and operate the canal. The idea had been resolutely opposed by Palmerston, who tried to persuade the Turks to frustrate it; but the Egyptians went ahead regardless. In 1863, a new khedive, Ismael, took over and pushed the canal to completion in 1869. Ismael had great ambitions: he hoped to extend Egyptian control over the Sudan, to become fully independent of the Ottomans and to use the wealth generated by the boom in Egyptian cotton (a by-product of the American Civil War, which interrupted supplies) to obtain foreign loans to promote the development of the country.

However, although the canal was a great asset, it inevitably involved Egypt in prolonged intervention by foreign powers, as Palmerston had foreseen. In 1863, Britain pressured Turkey into issuing an ultimatum to the Suez Canal Company on the grounds that its act of concession had never been ratified by the Ottoman government. This led to some bargaining between Turkey, France and Britain which forced the company to relinquish many of its rights and powers, in return for a payment by the government of 130 million francs in compensation for the labour and land involved. As Ismael was already in serious debt, this settlement proved disastrous for Egypt: he had little understanding of finance and was soon paying interest on the debt at between 12 and 26 per cent.[13]

Egypt's public debt increased from £3.3 million in 1863 to £68 million by 1876. In 1875, Ismael decided to sell 176,000 of the company's 400,000 shares. The British prime minister, Benjamin Disraeli, hastily raised £4 million with a loan from Ferdinand de Rothschild, giving Britain a 44 per cent holding in the canal. British shareholders in the canal received a return of 8–9 per cent.

W.E. Gladstone condemned the purchase as 'an act of folly fraught with personal danger', realising that it would entangle Britain in the domestic affairs of Egypt. The shares, he said, would be 'the almost certain egg of a great African Empire that will grow and grow'. As Egypt's public finances deteriorated, Britain and France sent their representatives to devise fresh arrangements, so that by 1876 Egypt's debt charges had reached £16.5 million each year, or two-thirds of the revenue from the canal. The debt was managed by a dual Anglo-French board, on which Sir Evelyn Baring (later Lord Cromer) was Britain's representative. Egyptian cultivators were henceforth taxed heavily in order to pay the British and other bond-holders who had bought into the country's debt. 'My country is no longer in Africa,' protested Ismael, 'we are now part of Europe.' Although Britain and France were not technically ruling Egypt, they pulled the strings. They forced Ismael to accept English officials and pressurised the Ottomans into ordering him to abdicate. In 1877, Baring was appointed 'commissioner for debt' and thereafter he remained the key figure in the government of Egypt until 1908.

By this time, a nationalist movement had developed in Egypt comprising several elements: Muslims who were keen to unite against foreigners; a body of middle-class, liberal constitutional reformers, and the army, which was the most significant. 'The army is the only native institution which Egypt now owns,' observed *The Times*, 'all else has been invaded and controlled and transformed by the accredited representatives of France and England.'[14] The army demanded a written constitution for Egypt, but the leading British officials – Sir Auckland Colvin, Sir Edward Malet and Baring – found it hard to take the nationalist demands seriously, and they dismissed the leading figure, Colonel Ahmed Arabi, as 'an illiterate fanatic' – a gross caricature of a courageous leader who enjoyed the confidence of both the army and the people.

Meanwhile in Britain, Disraeli's imperialist policy had been rejected by voters. The post-1880 British government under Gladstone wanted to avoid direct military intervention in Egypt and maintain cooperation with the French, and felt that if any intervention to check the disorder became necessary, it would come better from Constantinople. However, in 1881 the French began to urge direct action in order to stem what was described, without any evidence, as an anarchic situation in Egypt. Gladstone took a realistic view of Arabi and the movement for reform: 'I am not by any means pained at the rapid development of a national sentiment and party in Egypt.' He endorsed Arabi's 'Egypt for the Egyptians' cry as the only realistic solution to the problem.[15] However, Gladstone was undermined by the British representatives on the spot, who simply could not believe that an Oriental people was capable of governing itself.

In 1882, a proposal by Malet to send Arabi and several other officers into exile provoked a popular uprising and rioting in Alexandria, in which several hundred people were killed. As a result, Arabi and the army effectively took over responsibility for keeping order. Abandoning everything he had previously said, Gladstone now dispatched 20,000 troops under Sir Garnet Wolseley, who defeated Arabi at the battle of Tel-el-Kebir and sent him into exile, thereby making it virtually impossible for the Egyptians to govern themselves. His action also put an end to the dual control with France, leaving the British completely responsible for Egypt. However, the British pretended that their control was purely temporary, and to this end Egypt never became a British colony, but was known as a 'condominium'. A legislative council and general assembly were created, but as they enjoyed no powers they were a mere sham. In effect, the country was ruled by Lord Cromer from 1883 to 1908. An experienced imperial administrator, Cromer was not known as 'over-Baring' for nothing. Patronising, arrogant and conventionally racist in attitude, Cromer largely lacked sympathy for Muslim society, which he regarded as backward, intolerant and incapable of change. Any evidence of improvement he attributed entirely to British influence.[16]

❀ ✿ ❀

Yet having seized control of Egyptian affairs, the British were uncertain how far they had to go to secure existing imperial interests. In India, the local representatives had usually argued that in order to maintain one territory it was necessary to control the areas adjacent to it: Burma, for example, was to be annexed, as it lay to the east of British Bengal. This line of argument was capable of almost indefinite extension, however implausible it became. In the case of Egypt, British eyes were fatally drawn south to the vast land of Sudan, which had been annexed by Mohammed Ali in 1831 and was thus in a sense Egyptian territory. And because Egypt was indirectly Ottoman, it was also a Turkish responsibility. The underlying case for trying to control Sudan was that the River Nile passed through it, making it crucial to the stability and prosperity of Egypt itself. However, the validity of this claim remained dubious: Cromer argued that even if Muslim rebels held the Upper Nile valley, they would not actually threaten Egypt. Another popular domestic argument for British control lay in suppressing the slave trade, which constituted the chief economic activity in Sudan, though this objective was largely beyond any imperial power: Major General Charles Gordon had already spent some years trying to stop the trade and had failed.

The immediate pressure for British intervention arose in 1880–81 on the appearance of one Mohammed Ahmad, who proclaimed himself the 'Mahdi' at Kordofan, some 125 miles south-west of Khartoum. The oppressiveness and unpopularity of Egyptian rule generated thousands of willing followers for him. After winning over the Sudan, the Mahdi proposed to march on Egypt and eject the Turks. His movement carried a powerful message in the Muslim world, because of the tradition that at some time a Mahdi would emerge to complete the work of converting the world to Islam. His coming would coincide with that of the Anti-Christ. Then Jesus would descend to earth and join the Mahdi. Although he was branded a false Mahdi by orthodox Muslims, many people flocked to him, largely in reaction to the unpopularity of the government. As the British had disbanded much of the Egyptian army, the Mahdi had little difficulty in defeating the forces sent against him. The revolt rapidly spread to the Red Sea and throughout the country south of Khartoum; it started to pose some danger of spilling over into Egypt itself. Soon the Egyptian garrisons were besieged and Khartoum was threatened.

In this situation, Cromer thought the sensible thing was to evacuate all forces and simply abandon the Sudan; but the Egyptian government continued to insist that possession of the Sudan was essential to the stability of Egypt.[17] With virtually no roads or railways, a single telegraph line and only partial river communications down the Nile, the country looked inaccessible and chaotic. But, as many previous British governments had found, in an imperial crisis it was difficult to resist the popular pressure to stand firm. The press demanded an expeditionary force, and Queen Victoria, who was partisan and excitable, believed that General Gordon would be able to settle matters in a couple of months.

The cabinet, more realistic than the queen, decided it would be best to evacuate the British forces from the country and concentrate on Egypt. Unfortunately, to this end they decided in January 1884 to dispatch a force under Gordon, who had served as governor-general of Equatoria, the area south of Sudan, in 1874–76. Ominously, the foreign secretary had three times suggested Gordon's appointment to Cromer, who had consistently declared that it would be a mistake![18] Gordon's reputation as a militant evangelical Christian made him a provocative choice for a country experiencing a wave of Islamic revivalism. On the other hand, Gordon stood high in popular esteem at home as a classic example of 'muscular Christianity' who had fought in the Crimea. He was also considered to be good at handling wild and uncivilised peoples. Conversely, he was regarded by those who knew him as eccentric, even slightly mad, and throughout his career he had shown a rather relaxed attitude towards the orders issued by his superiors.

Despite these reservations, Gordon departed for the Sudan in January 1884. On arrival in Khartoum, he immediately flouted British policy by suspending the abolition of slavery and actually contemplated handing government over to a prominent slave trader. This was a situation that had often occurred in imperial history; in India, local governors had frequently seized new territory in contravention of their orders from a distant government in London which feared the costs of reckless expansionism. Free of immediate control from London and Egypt, Gordon then decided not to evacuate, but to postpone his departure from Khartoum, arguing that there was no one to rule the country. In adopting this reckless position, he completely underestimated the extent of the rebellion and his own vulnerability until it was too late.

Once it became known in London that he had become besieged in Khartoum, pressure built up to send a relief force to rescue him. But Gladstone and his cabinet concluded that Gordon had never intended to evacuate the country and that he was conning them into sending more troops. 'I called him at the outset inspired and mad,' complained Gladstone, referring to the messages he sent to Baring and the khedive, 'but the madness is now uppermost.'[19] Eventually, the much delayed relief expedition arrived just too late, finding that Gordon had been killed in his palace at Khartoum. A few months later, the Mahdi also died and he, too, became a national hero – as the leader who had liberated Sudan from Egypt, defeated the British and restored his people to the true expression of Islam.

Gladstone briefly attracted a great deal of criticism as the 'Murderer of Gordon'. However, it is an indication of how superficial British attitudes towards imperial expansion were that within a short time the controversy had blown over and the country had lost interest in the Sudan. With Gordon dead, the drama had gone. There was little interest in occupying the territory, and fears that an Islamic rising in Sudan would threaten Egypt were discounted as unrealistic. For some years, the British kept away from the country, but by the mid-1890s the old idea of the Nile Valley as a unity was revived and affected both cabinet ministers and Lord Cromer. They were also influenced by the activities of the Italians in the Horn of Africa and by a French expedition to Fashoda, near the headwaters of the Nile. The result was a new expedition in 1896, when Lord Salisbury's government dispatched a force under Sir Herbert Kitchener, who won the battle of Omdurman in 1898 and reoccupied the country. Yet despite all this effort, the British never turned the Sudan into a formal British colony, preferring to rule it under a condominium until the 1920s.

❁❁❁

Britain's experience in Egypt and Sudan demonstrated the limitations of her strategy for safeguarding her imperial and commercial interests. The Napoleonic invasion of Egypt, the Greek war for independence, the Crimean War and the Russo-Turkish war of 1877–78 underlined how much British external policy in the nineteenth century was bound up with attempts to manage the territorial decline of the Ottoman Empire. However, that empire remained so extensive and attracted so much interest from France, Russia, Italy and the Balkan nationalities that it was increasingly beyond British power to control the situation or to check the erosion of Ottoman territory. Consequently, its dismemberment continued to gather pace up to 1914. Yet the efforts to retain some control had implanted a habit of intervention in the British official mind that was to influence British policy throughout the twentieth century and beyond.

CHAPTER SIX

THE VICTORIANS, ISLAM AND THE IDEA OF PROGRESS

'Let the great world spin for ever down the ringing grooves of change.' The confident tones of Alfred, Lord Tennyson in celebration of railways in particular, and Victorian progress in general, underline a marked shift in British thinking during the nineteenth century. After the comparative tolerance of the eighteenth century, the Victorian era saw a distinct deterioration in British attitudes towards Islam, culminating in an almost fanatical view of Muslims by the later nineteenth century. While there is a variety of explanations for the long-term trend, the fundamental one lay in the impact of the process of industrialisation that had set in during the late eighteenth century and that had left Britain apparently the world's leading power by the 1850s. For the 6 million visitors to the Great Exhibition at the Crystal Palace in 1851, the triumphs of industrialisation were too obvious to require debate. National income increased from £523 million in 1851 to £916 million by 1871; and annual per capita income in 1860 stood at £32 in Britain, compared to £21 in France and £13 in Germany, for example. Railways represented the most dramatic symbol of British economic success, with a 6,000-mile network in 1850 rising to 13,000 miles by 1871.

Yet railways were only the visible expression of a pervasive belief in progress in this period. The Whig view, articulated by historians such as T.B. Macaulay, held that Britain had undergone her revolution successfully in the seventeenth century and had emerged with a balanced and stable form of government, backed by judicious representation and an open, liberal society, in contrast to the autocratic regimes of continental Europe that were subject to regular political upheavals and instability. Many Victorians convinced themselves that their success was underpinned by something distinctive in the English national character or experience – perhaps influenced by the cool, misty climate, which fostered a practical, non-ideological temperament that made for self-help, industriousness and political stability. Even when confronted with the evidence produced by mid-century investigations into widespread poverty, many Victorians retained their self-confidence, arguing that if industrial development continued for another generation it would inevitably generate employment and spread prosperity for all who were able and willing to work.

This confidence in progress was certainly distinctive of the era; during the twentieth century, it was largely destroyed by evidence of economic decline, loss of empire, two world wars and the threat of nuclear war, to take only the obvious factors. At the time, this mentality inevitably influenced the way in which Victorians regarded other societies, including European ones that were actually very similar. Easy generalisations about French or Italian people that now seem preposterous were quite routine even among progressives and reformers. For example, some of the advocates of women's suffrage felt unconvinced that the right of women to vote was appropriate for the emotional women of the Mediterranean countries, who lacked the sober qualities of the Anglo-Saxons and Scandinavians. How much more sceptical were they about societies elsewhere in the world? Fortified by what appeared to be British superiority, many Victorians took for granted the backwardness of Muslims, doomed as they were to obscurantism by their religion and trapped by beliefs that rendered them incapable of reform. The obvious way out lay in the missionary route, designed to raise them to British levels, though many felt that Muslims were usually resistant to such pressure.

On the other hand, Victorian confidence in social progress failed to satisfy national needs entirely. Indeed, among some contemporaries it generated a critical reaction against the modern world, a nostalgic hankering for the supposed stability, harmony and hierarchy of the lost medieval world, and a need to re-create the national past in Romantic form. Industrialisation and urbanisation were creating a booming but rather vulgar society that was in some ways out of control, posing a threat to deference and stability, and that was losing touch with British traditions. Consequently, while boldly celebrating the glories of industrial society, Victorians also cherished the – often imaginary – attractions of medieval life. Victorian Romanticism left its mark on art and architecture, literature and even politics. Successful industrialists built grand houses and Manchester warehouses that resembled Italianate palaces, and newly minted suburbs such as at Saltaire in Yorkshire were endowed with tall, slender towers suggestive of the urban landscape of Renaissance Italy. Victorians restored dilapidated houses with the crenellations and towers of medieval castles, and constructed country homes in the Gothic style associated with medieval Christianity.

While Romanticism had earlier been fashionable among intellectuals, for some it enjoyed a major boost in the 1830s and 1840s in the shape of the Gothic architecture of Augustus Pugin and the popular writing of Sir Walter Scott. To some extent, Victorian medievalism was also complemented by religion, in that some enthusiasts (including Pugin) became converts to Catholicism, another route back into an earlier era. Pugin advocated the revival of 'Christian' architecture as a stage towards the creation of a more Christian society and a restoration of the spiritual integrity of the Church.[1] Along with Queen Victoria, Scott did much to familiarise the English with an appealing, if imaginary, picture of Scotland in the medieval age, replete with tartan, kilts and clans, while novels such as *Ivanhoe* (1819) and *The Talisman* (1825), which was set during the Third Crusade, conjured up an exciting and romantic picture of feudal England.

To be fair, Scott was writing, often at speed, about a period of which he knew relatively little. He did not offer merely a rose-tinted view; on the contrary, he depicted the irrational side of the Crusades, the fanaticism of the Christians, and the humanity of Saladin. However, he wrote for a public already enchanted by an imaginary notion of the Middle Ages; *Ivanhoe* sold 10,000 copies in its first two weeks alone.

Scott's readers happily used his books to suit their own predilections: they took Ivanhoe as a champion of medieval chivalry, treated Richard I as a national hero fighting for the Cross, and effectively reinvented the whole idea of the Crusades, largely obliterating the barbaric record of the Christian invaders in favour of a sanctified and romantic version of knighthood and chivalry.[2] Victorian medievalism also involved such colourful manifestations as the revival of medieval jousting tournaments at Eglinton (Ayrshire) in 1837, which was attended by Queen Victoria and Prince Albert; Parham in 1875; and Earl's Court as late as 1912. Even that staid bourgeois, Prince Albert, sat for his portrait incongruously bedecked in knightly armour.

It suited English medievalists to fit Victorian India into their feudal perspective, by seeing it as a society based on hierarchy and deference that would appreciate a benevolent paternalistic policy. Thus, India played its part in the medieval fantasy. This reached a climax in 1877, when – inspired by Disraeli – the viceroy, Lord Lytton, presided over an imperial durbar in Delhi. There the queen was proclaimed as empress before a huge assembly of princes, Muslim and Hindu. Lytton (himself a romantic medievalist) believed he was giving the Indian nobility a 'fountain of honour' and 'its feudal head'. Along with a College of Arms to order the Indian peerage, the leading princes were given banners emblazoned with coats of arms and, in 1878, a new order – the Order of the Indian Empire – to complement the Star of India (1861). India's present was being re-created from its feudal, Mughal past.[3]

Towards the end of her life, Queen Victoria succumbed to this aspect of medievalism through her fascination with her Indian Empire, its culture and traditions. After 1887, she employed a Muslim, Abdul Karim, known as the 'Munshi', as her 'Personal Indian Clerk' and then as her 'Indian Secretary'. She acquired this interest through the enjoyment she derived from her new and antiquated title as 'Empress of India'. Yet the queen never visited India and her understanding remained fairly limited. Karim and his family occupied an isolated position in England, and many people assumed that he was a Hindu, not a Muslim. Within the government and the royal household, he was strongly resented, partly because he represented another 'John Brown' figure enjoying the queen's affections, but also because officials feared that she allowed him to see state papers (something the queen flatly denied) and was influenced in a pro-Muslim direction. She took up the case of a friend of the Munshi, Rafiuddin Ahmad, suggesting to Lord Salisbury that he should be appointed as a Muslim attached to the British embassy in Constantinople; he would, she suggested, be helpful in restraining the Turks and in placating Muslim opinion on India. The queen was correct in thinking that in India the potential significance of Abdul Karim was never really appreciated. For Indians, it would have been immensely flattering to know that a fellow Indian enjoyed the trust and affection of the queen-empress. However, the advisers and politicians, especially those in India itself, were generally too unimaginative and conservative to see the relationship as an asset, calculated to help consolidate the British position in the post-Mutiny era.

As the role of Disraeli and Lytton suggests, the fascination with past traditions extended into politics via the reaction against industrial society and urbanisation. It took institutional form in the shape of the Primrose League, a Conservative organisation founded in 1883. Its founders claimed that it intended to honour 'the genuine English volunteer type known to our forefathers as chivalry . . . on the basis of the old orders of knighthood'.[4] To this end, the league called its male members 'Knight Companion' and 'Knight Harbinger', its leader the 'Grand Master', and its local branches adopted the Middle English title 'Habitation'. This was a modern party-political organisation cast in the form of a lost medieval world that offered reassurance in a period of rapid social change; but its success indicated the attractions of an erroneous conception of the chivalry and heroism of the Crusades that proved enduring.

The Catholic converts of the Victorian era are a reminder that a revival of religious fervour after what many Christians saw as the worldliness and complacency of the eighteenth century represented another complication in Victorian attitudes towards the Muslim world. For Muslims, Catholicism had departed a long way from the original faith. But by the early nineteenth century, Christian attitudes increasingly reflected the spread of Evangelicalism, which was now influencing British policy at home and abroad. Taking a more emotional and zealous approach to their religion, the Evangelicals emphasised the authority of biblical scriptures, personal conversion and the doctrine of salvation through faith. They adopted a highly critical view of Catholicism, which they saw as the stronghold of superstition and obscurantism, and they pointed to the economic backwardness of many Catholic countries, by contrast with the progressivism of most Protestant states – a view that was routinely extended to Muslim societies, too. Convinced that man was basically depraved, the Evangelicals were energetic in trying to save souls. Their belief in the scope for improvement inevitably made them highly critical of lax standards and moral failings among Asian and African societies, and thus active in missionary work and in efforts to eliminate the slave trade, which they associated with Muslim societies in Africa. Later in the century, evangelical Christians often embraced a militant imperialism, reflecting their belief that the British had a missionary duty to extend the benefits of good government to Indians and Africans.

They were even more concerned about developments at home, as a hugely swollen population was increasingly concentrated in sprawling towns, where many became effectively lost to Christianity. According to the religious census of 1851, only two out of five people now attended a place of Christian worship on Sundays, dipping to only one in four in London and the major cities. In effect, the Anglican Church had failed to follow the population and it felt obliged to spend large sums of money building 1,750 new churches between 1840 and 1876, as well as creating elementary schools, Sunday schools, emigration societies and missionary organisations.

Moreover, religion became politically controversial once again. In 1844, nonconformists founded the Church Liberation Society, whose objective it was to disestablish the Anglican Church. By working through the Liberal Party, it eventually achieved its aim in Wales. In 1859, Charles Darwin's book, *The Origin of Species*, offered a new challenge by arguing that evolution had occurred through natural selection, rather than divine intervention. Meanwhile, Irish immigration boosted the Catholic population, which, taken along with the conversion of some prominent Anglicans to Catholicism and the creation of 13 new Catholic bishops in 1850, suggested to some that a Catholic offensive was under way.

Christianity also became entangled with several political controversies. When, for example, politicians considered divorce reform in 1857 (which removed the church courts from the process) or debated votes for women after 1866, many of them immediately sought biblical authority in the shape of St Paul's Gospel for guidance. This was especially characteristic of the rising generation of politicians, such as W.E. Gladstone, a High Anglican who became Liberal leader after 1868 and brought an emotive religious appeal into both domestic and foreign politics as the outstanding spokesman of the 'nonconformist conscience'. In effect, the various challenges posed to Christianity in general, and to the Church of England in particular, inhibited the balanced approach towards Muslims that had characterised the previous century. This was especially so when moral-ideological feelings became entangled with imperial-strategic considerations.

The cumulative effect of the belief in progress, the return to popularity of the crusading idea, and the emergence of Evangelicalism in public life was to invigorate the high-handed British attitude towards Islam and the country's policies towards the Muslim world. Pragmatic politicians of the older school, such as Palmerston, had been inclined to overlook the ideological considerations that inhibited others from collaborating with the Ottoman Empire. But increasingly, moral factors became mixed up with imperial concerns, effectively undermining the more relaxed approach towards Muslim societies. In particular, the Victorians became especially concerned about the extensive collection of Muslim territories that stretched from Egypt, through the Ottoman Empire and Persia to the Central Asian territories in the area between the Caspian Sea, Russia and China (including Khiva, Bokhara, Kokand and Turkmenistan), and on finally to Afghanistan in the south-east. Seen from the Victorian perspective, the Central Asian countries represented a standing rebuke to the very idea of progress: they were essentially survivals from an earlier and more barbarous era. Fortified by their determinist outlook, many Victorians felt certain that Afghanistan and the Central Asian khanates simply could not survive in the modern world, and nor should they. Either they would modernise, which seemed unlikely, or they would be superseded by superior civilisations capable of dragging them into the nineteenth century.

Inconveniently, these societies lay in an extensive and remote belt of territory between two superior states: tsarist Russia to the north-west and imperial Britain to the south-east, in the shape of the Raj. It seemed inevitable that they would absorb the decaying societies of Central Asia. But while such developments were all in the name of progress, the opportunity offered for Russia to advance posed a threat to British control in the Indian sub-continent – in the form of the unstable state of Afghanistan. This prospect was made all the more alarming by the 'Indian Mutiny' of 1857.

British policy was greatly complicated by the geography of Central Asia, which was so remote as to be immune to the naval power that she usually brought to bear on recalcitrant Oriental territories. In this situation, the simplest expedient was to employ young army officers and medical men, whose talents were appreciated in the courts of the khans, as agents and spies who could travel through Central Asia and then report back on communications, political conditions and especially on any forward movements by the Russians. However, as Britain's eyes and ears in the 'Great Game', they had (as spies invariably do) a tendency to try to enhance their own employment prospects by exaggeration and alarmism. In 1832, one Captain Alexander Burnes reached Bokhara and reported that it would be possible for British exporters to drive Russian commerce out of Central Asia and effectively make the region a buffer for British India – a distinctly over-optimistic assessment.[5]

For the British, by far the most acute and intransigent element of this problem was Afghanistan. Between the seventh and tenth centuries its population had steadily been converted to Islam, leaving only small numbers of Buddhists, Animists and Jews. But beyond Islam, Afghanistan enjoyed no unifying features; it came together as a country only in the eighteenth century, and it remained a ramshackle collection of tribes and territories that were not easily governed from Kabul. Afghanistan's geographical position at the crossroads between the Middle East and

Asia had always left it vulnerable to invading forces, though its rulers had occasionally launched their own invasions into northern India. By 1826, the country had been more or less united by its amir, Dost Mohammed, though he faced threats from an exiled former amir, Shah Shuja. Keen to keep on good terms with Dost Mohammed, the British sent Captain Burnes to his court at Kabul. Burnes, who got on well with the amir, suggested that Britain should make an alliance with him. However, this proved complicated, as Dost Mohammed wanted British help in recovering Peshawar from the Sikh ruler, Ranjit Singh. The British, however, declined to assist, as the latter seemed a stronger and more reliable ally. From the British perspective, the problem consisted partly in trying to define the north-west frontier between the Raj and Afghanistan, and partly in deciding what sort of frontier the empire should have. The combination of poor communications and the unstable tribes in both British territory and Afghanistan made it unrealistic to impose the kind of stable administration that the British applied to most of the Raj; but it was otherwise difficult to decide exactly how and where to defend their territory from any future Russian advance.

The British obsession with Russia during the nineteenth century was justified to the extent that she was steadily expanding in three directions: the Baltic, Siberia and Central Asia. Russia's aggrandisement towards Persia and the Ottoman Empire left British governments increasingly alarmed about her intentions. The publication in 1829 of *On the Practicability of an Invasion of British India*, by Colonel George de Lacy Evans, fuelled their fears. In 1830, two key politicians, Lord Palmerston, as foreign secretary, and Lord Ellenborough, as president of the Board of Control for India, chose to interpret any move by Russia, however small, as part of a systematic process of expansion designed ultimately to destroy British strategic and economic interests in Asia.

On the other hand, most informed British representatives considered their fears alarmist, because a Russian challenge was simply not feasible. In the mid-1820s, Russian control extended roughly from Georgia to the

Caspian Sea and the Aral Sea, about 1,500 miles from Afghanistan and the borders of the Raj. The country between the two powers was rather empty, lacked resources and boasted few roads and no railways. All that made it very difficult to arrange for a modern European army to cross it in good order, particularly since the army was dependent on sufficient fodder being available for the baggage animals carrying its supplies. This became abundantly clear in 1839, when a Russian army actually did attempt to march south from Orenburg towards Khiva; however, it rapidly succumbed to disease, cold and hunger, and eventually had to turn back. Ignorance about Russian intentions obviously made things seem worse than they were, and to remedy this the Bombay government developed a rudimentary intelligence service designed to generate a supply of information about Russian commercial activity in Central Asia – the assumption being that trade would indicate the likeliest route for an approaching Russian army. British agents also surveyed the land, and particularly the passes through the mountains where an enemy force might best be checked. To this end, they travelled through Sind, Baluchistan and Afghanistan to Persia and Turkestan, gaining access to the courts of the local khans.

Ultimately, those who felt that British interests could best be safeguarded by what later became known as 'masterly inactivity' argued that if any hostile force ever did cross Central Asia, it would be resisted by the Afghans. Despite the influence of Palmerston, policy was largely determined by Sir Charles Metcalfe, India's governor-general, and by the Whig-Liberal politicians at home who saw the Russian threat as a rather distant prospect. They argued that Britain's best policy was to identify the likely geographical advance of a hostile army, either via Bokhara, Kabul and the Khyber Pass to Peshawar, or via the southerly route from Persia, Herat, Kandahar and the Bolan Pass into Baluchistan. Meanwhile, Britain should concentrate her strength along the line of the Sutlej River, where she enjoyed the support of the Sikh ruler, Ranjit Singh. Beyond that, Britain should cultivate the amir of Afghanistan, preferably installing a pliable figure who would allow the British access to counter a Russian threat.

However, the advocates of a forward policy pointed to the flaws in this. No amir could be relied upon to cooperate, and the Afghans themselves were reluctant to accept the sort of amir deemed desirable by the British. Moreover, although the policy of masterly inactivity usually prevailed, during the 1830s events somewhat undermined this approach. By 1836, the British were afraid that the Russians were encouraging the shah of Persia to take Herat (which he was certainly keen to regain from Afghanistan). Herat was an ideal base for an invasion advancing to Kandahar and the River Indus, thereby avoiding the mountainous route in the north.[6] In 1837, the shah laid siege to Herat. In this undertaking, he was (according to the British ambassador at Teheran) encouraged by Russia, which supposedly saw the move as a way to bolster its influence in Persia. If this was indeed the case, the opportunity was not seized by the Russians.

Nonetheless it greatly alarmed some on the British side. Amir Dost Mohammed offered cooperation with Britain, in return for support in controlling Herat and in recovering Peshawar; the British declined his proposal. In 1837, the amir accepted a Russian agent at Kabul, whereupon Captain Burnes withdrew and the British decided to abandon Dost Mohammed, preferring to support the rival claims to the throne of Shah Shuja, the former amir. At this point, the Persians withdrew from Herat and the crisis quickly subsided. But instead of recognising this, the new Indian governor-general, Lord Auckland, supported by Palmerston, continued to pursue the aim of removing Dost Mohammed and replacing him with a more pro-British ruler.[7] Auckland's misjudgement resulted in Britain's first invasion of Afghanistan – the model for a succession of similarly ill-conceived ventures over succeeding centuries.

During 1839, the so-called 'Army of the Indus' approached via Sind and Kandahar, reaching Kabul in August. Thereupon it installed Shah Shuja as amir and left a British Resident, William Macnaghten, with him in Kabul. By November 1839, less than a year after they had set out, most of the troops had marched back to India. However, the military success rapidly collapsed: the new amir had little control over the country; he was unacceptable to most Afghans; and he maintained himself only by means of British force, at a cost of a million pounds a year. Subsequently, the British cut their subsidies to the Pushtun tribes, which responded by blocking British communications between Kabul, the Khyber Pass and Kandahar. In 1841, a major rebellion broke out, led by Dost Mohammed's son; and by January 1842, the British had decided to evacuate the Kabul garrison. In the protracted retreat to Peshawar, all the British troops but one were killed, and by 1843 Dost Mohammed had returned as amir.

Apologists for the First Afghan War claimed that the amir would be reluctant to antagonise Britain again, as she had demonstrated her capacity to mount an invasion. But it seemed even more true that Britain would avoid further interference as being costly and ineffective. In reality, the First Afghan War was a complete humiliation for the British. Moreover, like so many interventions by Britain in the Muslim world over the centuries, the war proved to be counter-productive. It did nothing to deter the Russians, who, while having no plans to threaten India, could see how easy it was to frighten Britain by putting pressure on her in Asia. Tsar Nicholas made the point in 1839 by sending an army south, towards Khiva (see above), suggesting that if anything the Afghan War had stimulated Russia, rather than deterring her. The war also demonstrated the limitations of British power. Like the Crimean War – also technically a victory – Britain had not been able to weaken Russia either militarily or strategically, and had not been able to deter her from forwards movements in Central Asia.

⊗ ❀ ⊗

At the time, the 1839 invasion of Afghanistan appeared to be a mistake that would not be repeated. It undermined British efforts to present themselves as the defenders of Islamic states, and was followed by a return to a more conciliatory policy involving the granting of subsidies to the amir. Dost Mohammed remained on the throne until his death in 1863 and managed to restore a degree of stability to the country. In 1857, he even signed a treaty of mutual respect and friendship with Britain – a reflection of the concern felt about Russia by both sides. For the British, the wisdom of this was proved during the 'Indian Mutiny' in 1857, when, despite pressure from his people, Dost Mohammed stayed neutral. And for Dost Mohammed, the value of the alliance was demonstrated in 1863, when the British intervened on his behalf to push the Persians out of Herat, allowing him to annex the city.

However, policy towards the Muslim world had now become increasingly controversial at home, in a trend exacerbated by the Crimean War. That conflict had set the two leading Liberals, Gladstone and Palmerston, on a collision course in foreign policy. After the latter's death in 1865, the antagonism was continued by the Conservative leader, Benjamin Disraeli. Keen to seize the patriotic mantle of Palmerston for his party, Disraeli did his best to portray Gladstone as unwilling to stand up for British imperial interests, especially when challenged by the Russians. This polarisation in politics reached a dramatic peak following a revolt by the Christians in Bosnia and Herzegovina against Turkish rule that broke out in 1875 and led to war between Turkey and Russia in 1877. In this situation, the Disraeli government – less because it was pro-Turkish than because it was anti-Russian – determined to back the Turks, on the grounds that Britain's imperial interests dictated that she maintain the Ottoman Empire as a barrier to Russian expansionism through the Black Sea and into the Eastern Mediterranean. The opposing view was twofold. First, for those who saw the Ottoman Empire as a corrupt and failing regime, it seemed increasingly futile to try to prop it up against the rising tide of national self-determination in the Balkans. Second, there was now a compelling moral consideration: reports in the *Daily News* and *The Times* claimed that some 12,000 Bulgarians had been killed by the Turkish forces suppressing the revolt. This transformed an issue of foreign policy into a question of 'Christian civilisation' against 'barbarism'.

Even so, the conflict would not have grown into a major political issue but for two contingencies. During 1873–75, the famous American preachers D.L. Moody and I. Sankey had toured Britain, sparking off a new Evangelical revival. When the Bulgarian atrocities issue was taken up by Gladstone, his meetings seemed to his audiences to be something of an extension of the Moody-and-Sankey campaign. Gladstone certainly possessed the evangelical style and fervour in full measure, and as a High Anglican he was a devout Christian, always apt to see politics through a moral perspective.[8] The second contingency was Gladstone's sudden return to politics after his retirement following his electoral defeat in

1874, which was bound to impart unusual interest to the issue he chose to adopt. This involved a personal-religious element. Gladstone detested Disraeli and apparently believed that the latter's policy was influenced by his Judaic sympathy for the Turks and his hatred for Christians (though there is no evidence for this). In addition, as many High Churchmen had become antagonised by the Public Worship Regulation Act 1874, introduced by Disraeli's government, they found it easy to join with the nonconformists, who were already attracted by Gladstone's moral fervour.

The agitation began in August 1876, and Gladstone inaugurated his campaign by writing a pamphlet – 'The Bulgarian Horrors and the Question of the East' – in early September. According to his daughter, 'Papa rushed off to London . . . pamphlet in hand, beyond anything agog over the Bulgarian horrors, which pass description.' Within a matter of days, it had sold 40,000 copies. In one famous sentence Gladstone wrote:

> Their Zaptiehs and their Mudirs, their Bimbashis and their Yubashis, their Kaimakams and their Pashas, one and all, bag and baggage shall, I hope, clear out from the province they have desolated and profaned.

But he went further:

> There is not a cannibal in the South Seas whose indignation would not arise and overbook at the recital of that which has been done . . . which has left behind all the foul and all the fierce passions that produced it, and which may again spring up in another murderous harvest from the soil soaked and reeking with blood.

Referring to the Qur'an as 'that accursed book', Gladstone claimed the Turks had indulged in 'abominable and bestial lusts' and had committed actions 'at which Hell itself might almost blush'. His language was, at best, emotional and over-the-top; at worst, it was bordering on racist: 'The Turks are, upon the whole, the one great anti-human species of humanity.' Having offended against humanity, he argued, the Turks had lost all claim to moral and material support from the other powers.

Several qualifications may be made about his extreme language. A typical Victorian, Gladstone allocated his Muslims to categories, so that Indian Mohammedans were 'mild', the Spanish Moors 'cultured' and the Syrian Arabs 'chivalrous'. His condemnation was largely reserved for the Turks, on the grounds that they upheld the idea of empire, which violated the principle of self-determination and was based on state violence rather than government by law and popular consent.[9] When he appeared at Blackheath in London, where 12,000 people heard him in the pouring rain, he was more restrained, perhaps in deference to his Liberal colleagues who were moved less by the plight of the Balkan nationalities and more by fear of Russia. His provincial tours proved a triumph: at Birmingham, for example, some 30,000 people turned up to cheer him for a speech at the Bingley Hall.

Despite these qualifications, however, there is no evidence that Gladstone, though very well read and informed about religion, really knew much about Islam. He viewed it as a political problem in the shape of Turkey, and his emotive language lent respectability to extreme pre-existing prejudices about the Turks which became a permanent element in public debate. Many Victorians convinced themselves that the Turks lacked self-control and had inflammable minds, so that English women were always at risk from them. Obsessed with the harems known to exist in Oriental countries as hotbeds of vice, they accused the Turks of sexual depravity, religious fanaticism and political corruption. Such prejudice persisted into the First World War, when thousands of Muslims fought on Britain's side and convalesced in English hospitals. In 1915, the *Daily Mail* caused a scandal by publicising the awarding of the Victoria Cross to Khudadad Khan. The authorities then made efforts to prevent Muslims from mixing with English nurses, as it was feared they would be subject to temptation. Embarrassingly, it emerged that English nurses liked to fuss over their Muslim patients; but officialdom considered that this behaviour posed a serious threat to the principle of maintaining a racial distance from colonial people.

However, while the prejudice shown by Gladstone against Turkish Muslims may have been widespread in the late-Victorian period, it is qualified by evidence of a more sympathetic view of Islam, especially among middle-class nonconformists. During the late-Victorian and Edwardian era, Islam gained some respectability thanks to a number of well-connected converts. There were an estimated 5,000 British Muslims at this time, and 10,000 by 1924, of whom 1,000 were thought to be converts. The converts sometimes compromised by retaining their English names and dress, but adapted to Islam by avoiding the consumption of pork and alcohol. Conversion was comparatively easy, especially for Unitarians, who were intellectually well disposed to Islam because they shared its view of the Trinity. Many nonconformists and middle-class teetotallers found the Prophet's reputation for living an austere life very appealing. The first purpose-built mosque was the Shah Jahan at Woking in 1889. As Woking had no Muslims, this seems odd; but the moving spirit, one Dr Gottlieb Leitner, was chiefly moved by the need for an educational institution to study Islam and provide for students coming from India. London was the obvious choice, but high property prices forced him to look at Woking instead. The mosque fell into disuse after 1900, but it was revived by Khwaja-ud-Din, a visiting Indian lawyer who devoted himself to the Woking Muslim Mission thereafter.

Among the converts was William 'Abdullah' Quilliam (1856–1932), a wealthy Liverpool lawyer, who had been brought up as a Wesleyan Methodist and was influenced by Unitarian thinking. On a visit to Morocco in 1882, he developed an interest in Islam and converted in 1887. His book, *Faith of Islam*, was read by Queen Victoria. Quilliam was unofficially recognised as the leader of British Muslims by the Ottoman sultan, the shah of Persia and the amir of Afghanistan. He made many converts in Liverpool, where he established a mosque in a terraced house in 1891, as well as the Muslim Institute; however, foreign critics claimed that he diluted the faith in order to attract converts. A more eminent convert was Henry Edward John Stanley, the third Baron Alderley (1827–1903), a leading Liberal, diplomat, Orientalist and linguist. He visited Mecca in 1860, where he reportedly converted to Islam. As a Muslim, Stanley closed the public houses on his Cheshire estates. He was buried according to Muslim rites by the imam from the Turkish embassy. Marmaduke 'Muhammad' Pickthall (1875–1936) was an Anglican clergyman's son who travelled in Palestine and Syria in the 1890s and learned Arabic. His sympathy for Turkey in the Great War led him to convert in 1917. Pickthall became noted for tackling conventional prejudices head-on in lectures on 'Islam and Progress'; he edited the *Islamic Review* and *Islamic Culture*, and his much-praised translation, *The Meaning of the Glorious* Qur'an, was authorised by al-Azhar University. For Pickthall and others, the attraction of Islam consisted partly in an appreciation of its egalitarianism and in a reaction against the conservatism and privilege of the Anglican Establishment.

Among those who empathised with Muslims in this period, the most famous was the Victorian traveller Sir Richard Burton (1821–90), who, in his introduction to his 1882 translation of *The Arabian Nights*, reminded readers of England's responsibilities as the greatest Muslim power.[10] There were more Muslims than Christians in the British Empire at this time. Experience in the Indian army in the 1840s made Burton realise his gift for languages and for disguise, which led to a role in the intelligence service and to travel in many Asian and African territories. In 1853, he managed to visit Mecca (forbidden to non-Muslims) disguised as a Pathan, and later Egypt as a Sufi dervish. Burton was a classic example of the British pro-Arabist tradition. He complained that in the examinations for the Indian Civil Service, Britain was neglecting Arabic, hence her failure to manage Afghanistan, Egypt and Sudan: 'Now Muslims are to be ruled by raw youths who should be at school and college instead of holding positions of trust and emolument.'[11] Yet even Burton's influence was mixed. His published translation of the *Arabian Nights* gained him £10,000 and celebrity status, but it also made him notorious because it retained the sexual fantasies of the original tales. The eroticism shocked many contemporaries, including his wife, Isabel, who destroyed his papers and published an emasculated version in 1886; she cut 215 pages of the 3,115 in the original, because 'I want to give to the English public for family reading the real thing' and enable the student 'to realize what the Arab really is'.[12] To this extent, for all his Arab sympathies, Burton effectively complemented, even corroborated, the hostile late-Victorian view of Muslims as sensuous and decadent.

Indeed, it was easier for late-Victorian champions of the Muslim and Arab world to influence the intellectual and political elite, rather than the general public. Like Burton, Wilfrid Blunt (1840–1922), diplomat, poet and hedonist, travelled extensively in the Middle East and Egypt. He abandoned his original Catholic faith and became sympathetic towards Islam at a time when it was generally equated with fanaticism. Blunt believed not in the clash of civilisations, but in the common humanity of East and West; he argued that, as Christians and Muslims had virtually abandoned any hopes of converting one another, they could now live in harmony.[13] A forerunner of T.E. Lawrence, Blunt loved the Islam of the Bedouin, which he saw as a purer version of the religion than that of the Ottomans.[14] As he also supported Irish nationalism, he became a critic of imperialism generally, which he regarded as driven simply by a desire to exploit colonial people. He even tried to convince Gladstone of the merits of Arabi, but was ignored. Influenced by the Persian thinker al-Afghani, whom he met in Egypt, Blunt sympathised with pan-Islamism, which he regarded as a bulwark against European subjugation and as a means of responding to the challenge of the West. He even saw himself as a prophet for the revival of Islam, which he thought would come via the overthrow of Turkish rule.

Yet, again like Burton, Blunt complemented the conventional Gladstonian view through his attitude towards the Turks; indeed, despite his eccentricity, Blunt took a realistic view of the Islamic world and the role Britain might play in it. He started from the view that the Turks had corrupted Islam and that their claims to the Caliphate were always dubious. He anticipated, as was common at the time, the collapse of the Ottoman Empire, and the move of the Caliphate to Mecca and of its capital to Damascus or Baghdad. This, he thought, would allow Islam both to reform and to recover its spiritual character: 'It is to Arabia that Mussulmans must look for a centre for their religion'; in this way they would 'escape the mundane glory of vast palaces', political intrigue and despotic government.[15]

Britain, according to Blunt, had a role in all this. Because of their separation from the European Catholic tradition and the crusading states, the British could approach Islam in a liberal way; indeed, Muslims saw the British as Unitarians and thus as part of Islam. '[Britain] cannot destroy Islam, nor dissolve her own connection with her. Therefore, in God's name let her take Islam by the hand and encourage her boldly in the path of virtue.'[16] As Mecca would in effect be under Britain's protection, this would strengthen her position in India, and allow Queen Victoria to preside over the Arab world. The Foreign Office remained unconvinced by all this – not because it doubted the inevitability of Ottoman collapse, but because it felt unable to control the process of dismembering the empire. Despite this, Blunt's vision proved influential in forming the pro-Arabism of Lawrence's generation.

What Blunt and Burton overlooked was that Gladstone's extreme portrayal of the Turks was wildly at odds with their record during the nineteenth century. They were on the whole less rigid and racist than the British in their empire. Contrary to Western propaganda, the Ottoman Empire was quite tolerant of diversity: it sustained a flourishing multicultural society, in which a majority of people spoke their own languages – Serbian, Greek, Bulgarian, Arabic – rather than Turkish. Although Ottoman rule was based on Islamic law, within this framework the Christian and Jewish communities enjoyed partial autonomy in such matters as charities, marriage, divorce, inheritance and even taxation. For four centuries, this relaxed approach served the empire well. While Muslims were dominant, there was no systematic repression of Christians. Admittedly, Christians were subject to certain restrictions. If they wore a fez, they were required to sew a strip of black cloth on it; they were not eligible for the higher government posts; they were excluded from the army, and paid an exemption tax instead.[17] And while Western critics might criticise the inefficiency of Ottoman government, this was actually to the advantage of the Christians and other non-Muslim groups.

Faced with discontent from nationalists in the Balkans and complaints from Christians about unequal treatment, the Turks undertook constructive steps to make their empire more viable. Under Sultan Mahmud II, an imperial edict of 1839 introduced the general principle of equality for all subjects, regardless of religion, including guarantees of life, property and honour. This principle was reaffirmed in 1856. Some Christians were then appointed to provincial councils and to the Grand Council of State. At this point, the Ottomans also abolished the two traditional forms of discrimination – the poll-tax or *jizya*, and the ban on non-Muslims bearing arms. This was part of the move towards a common citizenship for all Ottoman subjects. That year, 1856, also saw a ban on the trafficking of black slaves, a regular source of concern among Western governments. Conservative Muslims complained that this offended Islamic law, but the Ottomans backed down only to the extent of allowing the slave trade to continue in the Hejaz.

However, European critics were inclined to dismiss the reforms as a failure that did nothing to reverse Ottoman decline and was undertaken simply to appease Western governments. This was scarcely true, for the reforms were implemented by Turks who appreciated Western ideas and culture and accepted that innovations were necessary in order to strengthen the empire. A crisis such as that of 1876 may have influenced the timing of reforms, but no more than that.[18] The Turks calculated that reform would help to reconcile the non-Turkish population to the status quo and inhibit any tendency to rebel; they expressed this aim as the fusion or brotherhood of all subjects. Admittedly, the weakness of the policy lay in the reluctance of the Christians themselves, who, in Crete, Serbia and Bosnia, increasingly preferred to organise rebellions. Consequently, Christians made a great deal of internal trouble for the Ottomans. This was not just targeted against the empire, but also involved disputes among themselves – so much so that they were regarded as incorrigible rebels against all forms of authority. The greater willingness of Muslims to accept authority was seen as a major difference between them and the Christians. As a result, the Turks became increasingly resentful of interference by Western governments on behalf of Christian communities in the Balkans and Greece, and especially aggrieved about the activity of missionaries, many of them Americans, who provided education for the Christians and revived the traditional denunciation of the Prophet as an imposter. Christian missionaries caused a good deal of trouble by promoting a sense of Christian superiority and by encouraging revolutionary nationalism. As a result, in 1875–76 the Turks felt that Western interference on behalf of the Bosnian Christians gave them a privileged position which was unjust to the Muslims.[19]

Yet although the British were generally unwilling to recognise the redeeming features of Muslim states, they appear to have been sobered by the invasion of Afghanistan. For a time, that restored a degree of consensus about the folly of precipitate interventions in that country. In any case, the strategic position of the Raj was strengthened by the seizure of Sind in 1843 and the occupation of the Punjab in 1849, which made India contiguous with Afghan territory. Britain decided to create a separate North-West Frontier Province between Afghanistan and the Punjab in the north. To the south, Sind was ruled arbitrarily by British commissioners, who simply used irregular troops to chase troublesome tribesmen across the border. The only further possible improvement in Britain's strategic position required placing troops at the Bolan Pass to check a southern invasion and at Peshawar to stop a northern attack. To go any further forward, so the argument ran, would only help the Russians by provoking the Afghans. This frontier was about as secure as it was possible for Britain to achieve. Beyond this, Lord Mayo, the Indian viceroy (1869–72), maintained a shrewd policy of cultivating the amirs by offering them subsidies, but not arms; giving them territorial backing if required, but otherwise abstaining from interference in their territory.

Unhappily, the policy of benevolent neglect was undermined by developments in Afghanistan and Russia. After the death of Dost Mohammed, the country suffered a period of civil war among his 12 sons (a common phenomenon in Muslim societies). Between 1869 and 1879, several innovations in government and education were implemented by Amir Sher Ali, including the introduction of a postal system, as well as military reforms that resulted in an army of 37,000. Yet his innovations failed to impress the new viceroy, Lord Lytton (1876–80), who persisted in regarding Afghanistan as 'far too weak and barbarous' to be capable of resisting Russia. Such fears were exacerbated by the determination of a new tsar, Alexander II, to resume expansion in Central Asia. To this end, the Russians occupied Tashkent in 1865 and Kokand in 1866; they created a new province of Turkestan and turned Bokhara into a protectorate in 1868, followed by Khiva in 1873 and Kokand in 1876. In effect, the Russians had created what they saw as a protective barrier between themselves and the British; they were doing no more than the British had done by taking over Sind and the Punjab.

As there was little Britain could do about this expansionism, the Russians refused to talk to her about their objectives or their border. They grew more confident, not because they planned to invade the Raj, but because they appreciated that any forward moves by them could stir discontent in India, and were thus a good means of putting pressure on the British. For their part, Indian officials now began to argue that Britain's strategic position had deteriorated, as she could not impose control on Afghanistan in the way the Russians could on the Central Asian khanates. As a result, the post-1874 government under Disraeli and Lord Salisbury (the foreign secretary) decided that a return to a more forward policy was required. In 1876, they occupied Quetta, the key to the Bolan Pass in the south. They also appointed a singular new viceroy, Lord Lytton, a feudal-minded peer who lived in a Victorian Gothic mansion in Hertfordshire; Lytton confessed himself ignorant of India, and disliked sitting on the viceregal throne because it aggravated his piles. However, the romantic novelist in him proved unable to resist Disraeli's scheme for plunging back into medievalism by proclaiming Queen Victoria 'Empress of India' and treating the princes to a lavish spectacle.[20]

Meanwhile in India, pressure for a forward strategy mounted through Sir Bartle Frere, a former Bombay governor, who criticised British policy as too defensive. 'Orientals generally misunderstand our present inaction,' pronounced Frere. 'If it is once understood that nothing will move us until the Russians appear on our frontier we shall certainly hasten that event by a great many years.'[21] This appealed to the new viceroy, though the foreign secretary, who felt alarmed by Lytton's imagination, cautioned him: 'I think you listen too much to the soldiers . . . you should never trust experts.' But to no effect. Although the viceroy journeyed to India with instructions to try to extend British influence in Afghanistan by persuading the amir to accept a British mission in Kabul (which would, in effect, control his external relations), Disraeli did not give him a mandate to invade Afghanistan. However, Lytton, ignorant of diplomacy and Indian affairs, committed an error familiar in imperial history by misinterpreting his instructions. Consequently, in July 1878, when a Russian mission was received by the amir at Kabul, he responded by sending a British mission, which was turned back at the Khyber Pass in September. The idea had been foolish, since Sher Ali had already indicated that he would not receive the mission. Thus, instead of placating the amir, Lytton had over-reacted and tried to force the pace.

British troops advanced to Kandahar and Jalalabad, while Sher Ali escaped into Russia. In 1879, the British imposed a new treaty that gave them control of the Khyber Pass and Afghan foreign policy, and a permanent representative in Kabul. Briefly it appeared that Britain had successfully reduced Afghanistan to the status enjoyed by Bokhara under the Russians. In fact, the Second Afghan War followed the same dismal cycle as the first and foreshadowed the (considerably) later invasions by Russia (in the shape of the Soviet Union) and the United States. It was not difficult to send a Western army across the border, to seize Kabul, to displace the amir and to find a more pliable alternative. But thereafter the question of managing the country remained as elusive as ever.

Later in 1879, the British mission in Kabul under Sir Louis Cavagnari was massacred, and the following year Gladstone returned to power, committed to reversing Disraeli's policy. Lytton thereupon resigned. Although an army under Sir Frederick Roberts defeated the Afghans at Kandahar, this did nothing to alter the futility of the invasion. The British invited a nephew of Sher Ali, Abdul Rahman Khan, to become amir and withdrew their forces from Kabul. In effect, Britain now accepted that although she had the capacity to invade, she lacked the ability to control the country. The best to be hoped for was that Abdul

Rahman Khan would be able to form a government stable enough to create a barrier to the Russians. Over the next 20 years the 'Iron Amir', as he became known, was largely left alone to reconstruct the country and create a centralised and autocratic state backed by generous British subsidies. His approach was in a sense modernising, but not progressive: he simply wanted to isolate his country. He used his resources to suppress all opponents and operated a system of informers and secret police. In effect, his regime was a model for British policy in the Muslim world in the twentieth century. Appreciating that Britain's concern was basically defensive, Khan remained on friendly terms, maintaining Afghanistan as a buffer state and treating all contacts with foreigners as un-Afghan and un-Islamic. He claimed to rule on the basis of the *Dar al-Islam* – that is, the defence of the land of Islam.

In the aftermath of the Second Afghan War it became clear that Britain had effectively lost the Great Game, for she was no longer prepared to risk going to war in Central Asia. In 1884, the Russians extended their control from Khiva to Merv, and in 1885 they routed an Afghan army at Panjdeh, between Merv and Herat in the west of Afghanistan. British instincts made them mobilise 25,000 troops at Quetta; but it was 500 miles to Herat, and the British were keen to avoid another war, as indeed were the Russians. The Gladstone government sensibly recognised that to send troops further would only force the Russians to advance; it was not worthwhile for either side to undertake another conflict in such a remote area. A compromise was reached, allowing the Russians to remain in Merv. If they had wanted to invade India, they now had several possible routes.

Another such incident occurred in the early 1890s, when the Russians explored the Pamir mountains, an area between Afghanistan and China. Britain despatched an expedition under Colonel Francis Younghusband to challenge them. But eventually the two powers agreed to define a narrow corridor of territory from Afghanistan to China that separated Russia from British India. This, of course, was no real defence for the

Raj, but it was reassuring as an indication that the Russians were willing to accept that the two powers did not need to fight each other.

In effect, Britain had downgraded the importance of Afghanistan in the belief (justified, as things turned out) that India was not now under threat – a judgement that was corroborated during the First World War. But she did concede ground in Asia generally. In 1895, the naval authorities advised that they could not get British ships to Constantinople before the Russians, and the following year, when Tsar Nicholas II visited London, Salisbury gave him to understand that if the Ottoman Empire collapsed, Britain might accept a Russian occupation of the straits.[22] Russia was also tightening her influence in Persia, despite the appointment in 1888 of Sir Henry Drummond Wolff to Teheran with a mandate to extend British commercial and political domination. Again, geography was the problem, for Teheran was beyond British naval power in the Persian Gulf, but was dangerously close to the Russian border. As a result, the Russians felt confident that they could extend their commercial role at British expense.

The wisdom of non-interference in Afghanistan became obvious after Abdul Rahman's death in 1901, when the throne passed to his son, Habibullah. It was he who set the country on the road to modernisation, especially through educational reform (employing Muslims from British India) and military reform (using Turkish instructors). Habibullah also liberalised the political system, by allowing the return of exiles, and initiated the building of hospitals, hydro-electric plants, factories and roads, all of which undermined British assumptions that Islamic states were incapable of improvement, unless led by Western powers.

The climax of Britain's failure in Central Asia came in 1904, when the Russian railway system finally reached Tashkent, thereby making it feasible to transport a large army up to the Indian border and keep it supplied. This development prompted the commander-in-chief in India, Lord Kitchener, to demand huge troop reinforcements. Yet there was no question of finding the men he required, because by this time the government at home was far more concerned about redirecting its forces to cope with the greater threat now posed by Germany. Fortunately for the British, the Russians felt exactly the same way. The result was the

Anglo-Russian Entente of 1907. In view of the weakness of Britain's position in Central Asia, this settlement was extremely favourable for her, and was an indication of how worried the Russians were about Germany: they agreed to keep their agents out of Kabul and to communicate with the amir through the British.

However, if Afghanistan was becoming more marginal for Britain, other Islamic countries, notably Persia and Turkey, occupied an increasingly important position. This shift of priorities did little to modify the unsympathetic attitudes that had resurfaced during the Victorian era. Even Gladstone unexpectedly resumed his atrocities campaign in 1895–96. This followed a revolt in a remote region between the Caspian Sea and the Black Sea of the Christian Armenian population, which was still under Ottoman control. In fact, the cause of the trouble lay with the Armenian revolutionaries, who had killed thousands of Turks at the start of the rebellion. In putting down the revolt, the Turks in turn massacred Armenians. This led Gladstone to resume his denunciation of Constantinople as a cruel and lustful Oriental despotism. If the controversy aroused by events in such a remote region was largely ignored by the European powers and passed fairly quickly, the Armenian massacres kept alive hostile perceptions of Islam.

Thus, the end of the century saw British attitudes towards Muslims apparently set in concrete. In Egypt, Lord Cromer had recently retired, still convinced that Islam was basically incapable of change. In India, a much younger imperialist, Lord Curzon, was fortified by his belief that Orientals were invariably deceitful, treacherous and corrupt. Though, to be fair, Curzon took a dismal view of most people: the Greeks he considered unfit for democracy, because they were 'just awakening from the night of four hundred years of Turkish oppression'. That said, his arrogant view of non-British people was tempered to some extent by his readiness to recognise that certain civilisations had achieved great things in the distant past, including Muslim ones. On his travels around India, he was impressed by the evidence of the art and architecture of the Mughal era, of which the Taj Mahal was only one outstanding example. He created a Department of Archaeology, with a view to preserving and restoring India's treasures and to encouraging Indians to be more appreciative of them.

By the turn of the century, Curzon's prejudices were no more than routine. We find them echoed in the views of younger British imperialists, such as Winston Churchill. As a young correspondent, Churchill had gained some experience of Muslim societies on the north-west frontier of India and in the Sudan in the late 1890s. In 1897, attacks on the British forts at Malakand and Chakdara on the north-west frontier of India triggered a punitive expedition led by General Bindon Blood in which Churchill participated as a war correspondent. And in 1898, he managed to join General Kitchener's force, as it advanced down the Nile to reclaim Khartoum from Muslim control. In the wake of these expeditions, he penned *The River War* (1898) and *The Malakand Field Force* (1899). In *The River War* he famously wrote:

> How dreadful are the curses which Mohammedanism lays on its votaries. Besides the fanatical frenzy, which is as dangerous in a man as hydrophobia in a dog, there is this fearful, fatalistic apathy ... Improvident habits, slovenly systems of agriculture, sluggish methods of commerce, and insecurity of property exist wherever the followers of the Prophet rule or live. A degraded sensualism deprives this life of its grace and refinement; the next of its dignity and sanctity.[23]

Churchill's observations at this time were positively Gladstonian – a concoction of Victorian assumptions about progress, Romanticism, Social Darwinism and British racial superiority. Even in later life, he still referred to the Sudanese rebels as fanatics. Of the Afghan tribes, he claimed 'their religion is miserable fanaticism, in which cruelty, credulity and immorality are all equally represented'. Under the influence of Islam 'all rational considerations are forgotten ... they become ... as dangerous and as sensible as mad dogs: fit only to be treated as such'.[24]

Confronted with these effusions, it is worth remembering that Churchill was 23 years old, with a young man's superficial knowledge and an urgent desire to make a name for himself. He has been described as heavily influenced by monotheistic Judaeo-Christian traditions, but if so he would surely have shown more understanding towards Islam. He was also distinctly impressionable, attracted by novelties and inclined to change his mind fairly easily. Above all, Churchill was in love with words, which helps to explain why so much that he wrote and said seems exaggerated and done for effect. He picked up conventional ideas and discarded them just as easily. For most of his generation, the racial superiority of the British seemed nothing less than obvious and the British Empire a force for good. For him, empire arose when 'civilised men rule over the uncivilised, without their consent for the sake of the mutual improvement of the rulers and ruled'.[25] Consequently, frontier wars against militant Muslims were episodes when 'the forces of progress clash with those of reaction'. Churchill was reaching adulthood just in the period when mid-Victorian confidence in British industrial society as the epitome of progress was being badly dented, but its impact on him was not very evident until around 1906–08, when he first entered office as a Liberal.

However, some qualifications may fairly be made about the young Churchill's views. Like many British people with extensive experience in India, he readily acknowledged that Muslims made brave fighters and thus, potentially, good allies if properly managed. More importantly, Churchill recognised that in Egypt and Sudan, rebellions by Muslims – however fanatical they appeared – could be inspired by proto-nationalistic sentiment, rather than by religious fervour. As in the Indian rebellion of 1857, a rebel movement often took on symbols, language and leadership from Islam largely because that was immediately available. In his maturity, Churchill recognised the Mahdi as 'foremost among the heroes of his race', saying he did not know 'how a genuine may be distinguished from a spurious Prophet, except by the measure of success'.

In time, Churchill acquired a more sophisticated view of British policy in the Muslim world. In particular, he recognised the futility of the forward policy, especially on the north-west frontier, where the tribes could be temporarily subdued but nothing really changed. As a junior minister in the Edwardian Liberal government he encountered another Islamic revolt in Somalia, which, according to the British authorities, was inspired by yet another 'mad mullah'. Churchill pointed out that any attempt to control the interior of Somalia would not be worth the cost and would only be temporary anyway. He also learned to make distinctions between the different Muslim societies. He found it hard to see his opponents in Sudan and on the north-west frontier as anything but fanatics, but he became attracted by the desert Arabs, their culture and their sense of honour. In 1897, during the Greek–Turkish war over Crete, which resulted in thousands of Cretans being killed, he was again in full Gladstonian mode, denouncing Lord Salisbury's readiness to back 'the cause of Moslem barbarism'. Churchill condemned the policy for prolonging 'the servitude under the Turks of the Christian races'. But he was also looking ahead:

> It is foolish because as surely as night follows day – the Russians are bound to get to Constantinople. We could never stop them even if we wished. Nor ought we to wish for anything that could impede the expulsion from Europe of the filthy Oriental.[26]

Churchill did not realise how close he was to the complete dismemberment of the Ottoman Empire. In the years leading up to 1914, Britain, despite her treaty commitments and her pro-Turkish tradition, was finally to abandon her long-standing relationship with the Ottomans.

CHAPTER SEVEN

ISLAM – WESTERNISING OR ORIENTALIST?

After the repulse of the Ottoman forces besieging Vienna in the late seventeenth century, Islam went onto the defensive for two centuries, not simply territorially and militarily, but in a more profound sense. As Europe began to transform the world during the eighteenth and nineteenth centuries, with a series of scientific, industrial and technological innovations, Muslims felt obliged to take stock. Traditionally, Muslims had regarded Islam as the final revelation after Judaism and Christianity, and had consequently not shown much interest in learning Western languages or in travelling to Christian Europe, which was in any case prohibited by Islamic law, unless for a specific purpose, such as ransoming captives. For many centuries during the medieval and early modern era, Islam had influenced the West with its intellectual and scientific insights; but now it appeared to have lost its lead. The imposition of European colonial rule on Islamic countries in the nineteenth century provoked some Muslims into a complete rejection of Western culture and values and the adoption of *jihad*; but others argued for a revival and renewal within Islam to make it fitter for the modern world. The question inevitably arose how far Islam should now be prepared to take on board Western ideas and practices. There was no simple or final answer. Even in the twenty-first century, some Muslims condemn ostensibly Islamic countries for taking a wrong turn, abrogating the Holy Law and adopting alien ideas, laws and customs.

During the nineteenth century, the British often assumed that modernisation was improbable because Islam was too obscurantist, backward and dogmatic; hence it would prove unable to adapt to the modern world and inevitably be overtaken by the West. Ernest Renan, the French intellectual, pronounced: 'Islam is the reign of dogma, it constitutes the heaviest chains which have ever shackled humanity.'[1] In particular, Renan considered Islam and modern science to be incompatible. Faced with the impressive record of Arab and Persian scholars in science and philosophy, he simply dismissed them as apostates who had rejected their religion. In fact, earlier Islam had satisfactorily combined science with ethics; the Reformation had undermined this achievement in so far as it challenged religious authority in general.

The British, confident in their political and economic achievements, usually regarded Islam as a hindrance. As for Egypt, Lord Curzon loftily explained, 'civilisation is foiled by a country which refuses to be civilised, which will remain uncivilised to the end'.[2] Admittedly, the imperial administrators believed they could improve the economies of such countries; but in the political sphere, Westernisation was considered to be largely unrealistic. 'Free institutions,' wrote Lord Cromer, 'must, for generations to come, be wholly unsuitable to countries such as India and Egypt.' The transfer to liberty would be the work of centuries, and parliamentary institutions were 'thoroughly uncongenial to Oriental habits of thought'.[3] It would, however, be mistaken to attribute these views simply to late-Victorian racist ideas, for Curzon and Cromer took almost as dismal a view of the British people's capacity to participate in a free political system, which is why they opposed votes for women. In effect, late-Victorian disparagement of the intellect and capacities of Asian and African people reflected the fear among conservatives that they and their ideas were on the retreat in Britain in an era of parliamentary reform, expanding trade unions and an emerging socialist movement. In this context, empire often appeared a desirable refuge – a place where one could hold out against democratic change under the protective umbrella of patriotism.

Moreover, what really alarmed some imperialists was not so much that Muslims were completely resistant to modernisation and

Westernisation, but that some at least embraced the prospect too enthusiastically. While reform was often imposed from the top, it is easy to overlook the extent to which the initiative for it came from Muslims themselves in the societies of Asia and Africa. During the nineteenth century, Muslims in India, Egypt and the Ottoman Empire embarked upon radical Westernising strategies, as did those in Afghanistan, Persia and Turkey during the 1920s, to take some of the most notable examples. For the imperialists, this process was dangerous because it was frequently linked with an emerging sense of nationalism.

The case of India is particularly interesting as a corrective to the usual assumptions about Muslim resistance to reform. It is also significant, simply because there were no fewer than 62 million Muslims in British India by 1900. Moreover, the role played by the British was largely indirect, as Westernisation occurred partly through Muslim initiative, rather than simply as a top-down policy of the sort that provoked controversy elsewhere in Muslim societies. Although the British displaced many Indians from respectable occupations during the nineteenth century, they also created opportunities. Even before British rule, the state administration and the legal system had been major employers. By the 1850s, Muslims held 72 per cent of the judicial posts open to Indians in the North-Western Provinces, a reflection of their traditional influence in the region, though by the 1860s their share was declining, a trend that strengthened efforts to promote English education among Muslims.[4] Of these, the most prestigious were the thousand or so covenanted posts in the Indian Civil Service, a career for which many English public schools prepared their boys. Entry to the ICS was open to all via an examination system, though by 1887 only a dozen Indians had succeeded. Lord Lytton complemented this in 1879 with a statutory service, to which men of some social standing could be recruited via nomination: by 1886, 27 Hindus, 15 Muslims, two Parsis and two Sikhs had been appointed. From 1879 onwards, the British were gradually forced out of the uncovenanted posts, leaving opportunities for

Indians. Professional opportunities also expanded through the formation of colleges for law, medicine and engineering and the three universities at Calcutta, Bombay and Madras. As a result, by the late-1880s
most of the subordinate judges and magistrates were Indians.

In effect, the British had created a ladder of advance for Indians.
However, many contemporaries believed that certain Indians, notably the
literate classes of Bengali Hindus, were especially suited to climbing up
through the system. The assumption was increasingly made that Muslims,
by contrast, failed to compete effectively and represented a backward
class. Admittedly, in regions such as Bengal, the Muslims were largely
poor, landless labourers who had little education and few aspirations.
Conversely, many of the Muslims who lived in 'Upper India' – that is, the
cities of the Gangetic Plain, the north-west and the Punjab – were the
descendants of an invading class comprising wealthy and educated men,
who became lawyers, administrators, *literati*, landowners and warriors.
They were by no means backward. In the North-Western Provinces and
Oudh they held 45 per cent of the uncovenanted posts in 1886–87, for
example, though only 19 per cent in the country as a whole.[5]

Yet although these Muslims were not obviously backward, it was they
who felt most acutely that the impact of British rule had been to disadvantage them, and that they were losing out in the competition with
other Indian communities. In the aftermath of 1857, some also argued
that Muslims must overcome the suspicion that they had been responsible for the rebellion by showing their readiness to come to terms with
British rule. The leading exponent of this view was Sir Syed Ahmed
Khan (1817–98). A reforming Muslim, Sir Syed discouraged his fellow
Muslims from a literal reading of the religious texts, urging them to
reinterpret miracles as metaphors. Sir Syed's chief strategy for Muslim
advance lay in expanding education. In an 1872 report he disparaged
the existing Muslim schools, books and syllabus in the most emphatic
terms:

> [They] deceive and teach men to veil their meaning, to embellish
> their speech with fine words to describe things wrongly and in irrel-
> evant terms . . . to puff themselves up . . . with pride, vanity and

self-conceit, . . . to speak with exaggeration, to leave the history of the past uncertain, and to relate facts like tales and stories. All these things are quite unsuited to the present age and to the spirit of the time, and thus instead of doing good they do much harm to the Muhammadans.[6]

Sir Syed's diagnosis was stark: 'If the Muslims do not take to the system of education introduced by the British,' he argued, 'they will not only remain a backward community but will sink lower and lower.'[7] He wanted much more than a reconciliation between the British and Muslims. In effect, he aspired to convince fellow Muslims that it was possible to study Western literature, political ideas, medicine and science while remaining a good Muslim: 'If you wish to attain honour, prosperity and high position, strive to acquire a high English education which is the only means for your real improvement,' he advised the students.[8] One who did just that, Mohammed Iqbal (1877–1938), was educated at the universities of Cambridge and Munich. He went further by denouncing Indian Muslim society as backward and corrupt and the *ulema* as reactionary. Iqbal argued that there would never be a material improvement in the condition of Indian Muslims unless they reinterpreted the Qur'an and took up the science and technology of the West.

Yet these aims represented a formidable challenge for orthodox Muslims, who believed that knowledge was entirely contained within the Qur'an and suspected that anything not found in the Qur'an was probably anti-Islamic. This led to prolonged disputes among Muslims, especially about the compatibility of scientific advances with their religion. However, interpretation was hindered by the brief and opaque references to scientific matters scattered through the Qur'an:

Allah causes the night to pass into the day and the day to pass into the night . . . Do you not know that Allah knows what is in the heavens and on Earth. All that is in a Book, and that is an easy matter for Allah . . . He who has created seven stratified heavens. You do not see any discrepancy in the creation of the compassionate. So fix your gaze, do you see any cracks? . . . We have adorned the lower heavens with lamps, and We turned them into missiles launched against the devils; and We have prepared for them the punishment of the Fire . . . Do you not see how He created for you seven heavens superimposed on one another? And placed the moon therein as a light and made the sun a lamp?[9]

Those who felt like Sir Syed argued that to study the laws of science was in effect to understand all the better the laws created by God for the universe and could not therefore be seen as un-Islamic. However, this argument was never really resolved. For example, some believed that the dissection of bodies and organ transplants was incompatible with Islam, while others argued that the needs of the living came before those of the dead, or that permission from the next-of-kin was acceptable. Well into the twentieth century, Muslims continued to debate the propriety of coming to terms with scientific advances. Even meteorological predictions were seen as suspect by some, on the basis that only God can know the weather. Genetic engineering and cosmetic surgery were thought to tamper with the will of God. Others debated whether man's ability to travel to the moon had been anticipated in the Qur'an.

During the late-Victorian period, Sir Syed's approach was rejected even by modernisers such as Jamal al-Din al-Afghani, a Persian thinker and activist who visited many Muslim countries, but was strongly swayed by his anti-imperialism. Dismissing the English as 'thieves of unknown extraction', al-Afghani disparaged Sir Syed as a deluded Westerner who aimed 'to weaken the faith of the Muslims, to serve the ends of the aliens, and to mould the Muslims in their ways and beliefs'.[10] It hardly helped his standing with Muslims that he had been knighted by Queen Victoria.

In the face of this scepticism, an obvious means of accommodating Indian Muslims to the British system was to send young men to study in London. By the 1890s, they comprised around a quarter of Indian students in Britain. Largely drawn from wealthy families from the north-west, they typically studied law or medicine and prepared for the Indian Civil Service examinations. However, their experience proved mixed. They usually appreciated the political freedom and the absence of social inhibitions they found in England. They saw little in Christianity to challenge their faith and were not susceptible to missionary pressure. However, the students were shocked by the poverty, drunkenness, materialism and class inequality, and realised that England was less democratic than it appeared on the surface. Concluding that Christianity had made little impact, they contrasted it with the greater charitable sense found in India, especially among Muslims, for whom alms-giving was a requirement.[11] The students also reacted against the inconsistency in the English approach: they were expected to absorb Western values, but not to become fully Westernised. Discrimination, which by the end of the century included surveillance of Indian students, also heightened their sense of nationalism. As a result, the English experience sometimes backfired. Sheikh Abdul Kadir was one of those who rejected parental aims by deciding not to enter the ICS examinations, out of hostility to the British. Faiz-i-Hussein, who studied law at Cambridge, went home to found the Lahore branch of the Muslim League.[12]

An alternative strategy lay in India itself. Sir Syed founded a Translation Society (later the Scientific Society of Aligarh) in 1864, followed in 1875 by the Mohammedan Anglo-Oriental College at Aligarh, which had 300 students and gave degree classes from 1881 onwards. Lord Lytton laid the foundation stone in 1877 and the first headmaster was an Englishman, H.G.I. Siddon. In 1920, the institution gained its charter as the Aligarh Muslim University. Although Sir Syed aimed to promote the advance of Muslims, he believed strongly in the unity of Hindus and Muslims as part of a single Indian nation, and the first students to matriculate comprised three Muslims, one Hindu and one Sikh. Yet orthodox Muslims remained wary of Western education and sometimes condemned Sir Syed as a *kafir* (unbeliever) and even an atheist.[13] However, much was done to reassure the doubters. The schools initially established at Aligarh taught Urdu, Persian and English, though English was the medium of instruction. Students were also required to say prayers five times daily. Ramadan was strictly enforced, with meals, music and singing banned for Muslims. The approved uniform for students comprised a black Turkish coat, white pyjamas, fez, shoes and socks, with exemptions during the hot weather. In time, the university established additional departments in Oriental and Islamic Studies, English, History, Political

Science, Chemistry, Mathematics, Astronomy, Geography, Sunni Theology, Shia Theology, Arabic Language and Literature, Persian, Urdu, Law, Botany, Zoology, Sanskrit, Education and Engineering.

During 1902–04 a struggle ensued over the establishment of a women's college. At length, a school for girls was set up in 1907, some 50 students being conveyed, veiled, by sedan from nearby districts. But this was opposed by several leading figures within the college, who claimed that to place the women's school and the college close together would lead to lax moral standards.[14] As a result, a women's college was not formed until 1929, and it affiliated to the university in 1930. The female students continued to be educated separately.

Despite the criticisms from orthodox Muslims, the problems encountered by the initiative at Aligarh were less to do with religion and more with the political complications. Originally, Sir Syed had believed that Muslims should work with the British system and keep out of politics as the best way of helping their community. However, his aims were greatly complicated by the foundation of the Indian National Congress in 1885 and further upset by the creation of the All-India Muslim League in 1906. In 1886, Sir Syed pronounced that India was not ready for representative or popular government, and even damned Congress as subversive. Conversely, Jawaharlal Nehru argued that it was right to encourage Muslims to acquire a Western education, because this would enable them to participate in the national movement. For its part, the Muslim League proposed to work for the interests of all Muslims, rather than to appease the British (which is how they saw Sir Syed's conciliatory tactics). In 1920, when Mohandas Karamchand Gandhi and his main Muslim collaborators, Mohammad Ali and Shaukat Ali, visited Aligarh, they sought to persuade the authorities to join the Non-Cooperation and *Khilafat* campaigns against the government. Mohammad Ali not only denounced the government and those who cooperated with it as Satanic, but he also disapproved of the teaching of science at the university.[15] When rebuffed by the loyalists at Aligarh, the Muslim nationalists formed a new Muslim institution, the Jamia Millia Islamia, which subsequently moved to Delhi and became the Jamia Millia University. Muslims were now effectively split by the appeal of nationalism.

Yet even apart from the emergence of nationalism, the idea of Muslims abstaining from politics was more complicated than it appeared. Although the British Raj was an imperial autocracy, it was far from being an *unqualified* autocracy. As the historian T.B. Macaulay had observed back in 1835, 'India is perhaps the only country in the world where the press is free while the government is despotic.' During the 1870s and 1880s, Indians received some interesting lessons in the operation of the liberal British system of government, partly because Indian affairs became the subject of party political controversy at home. Lord Northbrook, viceroy from 1872 to 1876, was a Whig who clashed with Lord Salisbury, the Conservative secretary for state for India, and resigned; Lord Lytton, his Conservative successor, quit when the Liberals won the 1880 election; and the new appointee, Lord Ripon, was a reforming Liberal who reversed Tory policies. Gladstonian Liberals sympathised with Indian aspirations to self-government, just as they supported those of the Greeks, Italians and Irish. By contrast, leading Conservatives like Salisbury especially disliked the 'educated natives' and praised autocratic government in India as preferable to popular institutions. For Indians, these disagreements suggested that it was now worth taking an interest in the outcome of British elections, cooperating with supportive MPs at Westminster, and studying the tactics of the Irish nationalist movement.

They also noted that in 1874 a British government pressurised Northbrook to remove the already low tariffs on British exports to India; and they could hardly miss the controversy in Britain over the creation of the 'Empress of India' title for Queen Victoria. In 1878, Salisbury attacked the press, which was an obvious focus for educated Indians and for criticism of the British: Bengal alone had 39 newspapers at this stage. Although India had enjoyed freedom of the press since 1835, the new Vernacular Press Act undermined this by giving district officers the power to see proofs, to confiscate objectionable material and printing machinery, and to allow magistrates to demand written pledges from publishers and printers not to publish anything likely to cause disaffection. This was especially offensive because it did not apply to English-owned or English-language newspapers. However, Lord Ripon, who believed that Britain must either cooperate with educated, middle-class

Indians or repress them, repealed Lytton's Vernacular Press Act in 1882, despite the opposition of his legislative council and most British officials. Ripon also attempted reforms designed to widen Indians' participation in government by allowing them to be elected to the provincial councils and to the viceroy's legislative council, thereby fostering the development of a 'loyal opposition'. However, this was vetoed by the Council of India in London, and so Ripon introduced an elected majority into the local municipal and local boards, which he said was 'chiefly desirable as an instrument of political and popular education'. Above all, Ripon's attempt to extend the powers of Indian judges in cases involving Europeans (the Ilbert Bill) caused an outcry among the British residents.

These events proved to be of great significance for Muslims and Hindus, in that they offered a model for organising peaceful campaigns, agitations and petitions against government policies. Moreover, they demonstrated that British power was not monolithic: it existed at several levels – from the local level in India to the provinces, the viceregal administration in Calcutta and the parliament and ministries at Westminster. It was thus possible to play off one level against another, as Gandhi was to demonstrate during the First World War; Indians could even campaign in Britain, as well as in India.

Muslims, however loyal, were not slow to participate in the politics of British India. They were especially provoked in 1904 by the decision of Lord Curzon to partition Bengal into an eastern and a western province. Although Curzon claimed that this would be more efficient and would offer more employment for Muslims, it was very controversial because it split the 41 million Bengalis into a Muslim-majority province and a Hindu-majority province. While some Muslims, led by the nawab of Dacca, supported partition, others joined the Congress-led agitation against it. The British extended their divide-and-rule tactics through the Morley–Minto reforms of 1909, which greatly extended Indian representation through elections that offered Muslims separate electorates. For example, they had six of the 27 seats in the Imperial Legislative Council. This reflected the viceroy's response to a demand by a Muslim delegation in 1906.

However, the underlying significance of the controversies in India from the 1870s to 1914 lay in involving Muslims in public affairs, thereby undermining claims that circulated widely in the twentieth century about the incompatibility of Islam and democratic politics. In effect, Indian Muslims enjoyed a period of over three-quarters of a century of political participation, both formally and informally, up to independence in 1947. It is easily forgotten that reform in India proceeded much as it had in Britain between the 1830s and the 1920s: formal voting rights were extended in stages and non-voters (such as the Chartists, the Irish and the feminists) took an active part in public campaigns, even though they remained formally excluded from the system. In the process of participation in a liberal-but-autocratic system, Indian Muslims developed a culture of political democracy that was to be carried over into independence. This process is never achieved quickly, whether in Europe or in Asia. In twentieth-century Russia, for example, the country moved from tsarism to Bolshevism, and then to a nominal democracy after the fall of communism, but leaving the appetite for autocratic leadership largely undiminished, because the culture of political democracy had never had an opportunity to develop as it did in India.

The experience of Westernisation among the Muslims of Egypt proved different from the story in India – partly because it involved a radical policy imposed from the top, but also because the stimulus was *French* rather than British. Yet it was seen by Egyptians as a transforming experience. 'My country is no longer in Africa,' claimed the khedive, Ismael, in 1878. 'We are now part of Europe.' Certainly, the process began dramatically in 1798, when Napoleon invaded Egypt as a step towards his plan for threatening British India. Three hundred years of Mamluk-Ottoman neglect had produced a dwindling economy, a population down to only 4 million and the decline of educational institutions such as al-Azhar. Suddenly Egyptians confronted Europe's most dynamic civilisation, intellectually invigorated by the ideas of the Enlightenment. Although the military presence of the French lasted only three years before they were ejected by the British, they brought with their troops an array of scholars, such as Nicolas-Jacques Conte, who invented the graphite pencil and devised a scheme to invade Britain by balloon. The experts included botanists, astronomers, chemists, artists, cartographers and archaeologists, who often displayed a genuine interest in the culture and history of Egypt which few of the British showed.

Although shocked, the Egyptian elite reacted positively to the French. It may have helped that, as the French were regarded as the most secular society in Europe, they were seen as posing less of a challenge to Islam. According to one of the country's leading religious intellectuals, Abdulrahman al-Jabarti, Muslims could not accept the French Enlightenment notion that all men were equal before God or that worldly matters were separated from divine; but they did recognise that Napoleon's invasion must be the will of God.[16] Thoughtful Egyptians like al-Jabarti were genuinely impressed by the French enthusiasm for knowledge and literature and by the interest they showed in Egypt's own culture. They enjoyed demonstrations by the French chemists, saw the benefits of their approach to public health, and appreciated their application of the idea of equality before the law. As a result, al-Jabartis's student, Hassan al-Attar, took up the task of reconciling Islam with the secular knowledge of Western society. In the space of nine years, no fewer than 2,000 European and Turkish books had been translated into Arabic.

In many ways, the key figure in Egyptian Westernisation was Mohammed Ali, who defeated the British forces in 1801 and ruled on behalf of the Ottomans from 1805 to 1849. Frankly recognising Egypt's backwardness, he gave the necessary support to the intellectuals and educators, and determined to employ the country's resources to finance Western technology. A million acres of additional land were brought under cultivation, resulting in a huge increase in cotton production in the Nile Delta; and cooperation with the French was maintained by employing their engineers to construct dams across the Nile. Western technology was imported to develop Egyptian industries. Mohammed Ali also appointed Hassan al-Attar as rector of al-Azhar University to extend the syllabus, and from 1825 students were sent to France to study, with a view to creating a new generation of Egyptian modernisers.

On the other hand, there were limitations to the extent of Egypt's Westernisation. Mohammed Ali's project was strictly a top-down strategy, widely resented beyond the enlightened elite. Smallpox vaccinations, for example, provoked popular unrest which had to be forcibly suppressed. Ali's rule was strictly autocratic, leaving no room for the evolution of a democratic culture, as in India. This involved the expropriation of the Mamluks' farms and an attack on the land held in the form of endowments by the *ulema*, which was their power base.[17] He also had the Qur'an printed for the first time, another means of strengthening the government in relation to Islam. The state appropriated the entire grain crop and enjoyed a monopoly of foreign trade. Public works schemes were implemented by gang labour, in which thousands died. Using French advisers, Mohammed Ali drastically reformed the armed forces, keeping families at home (rather than following the troops), training officers at military colleges, copying European weapons and ships, and adopting European tactics, including the infantry square, the bayonet charge and flanking attacks by the cavalry. This resulted in an efficient army of 150,000 men.

However, the ideological foundations of these innovations were far from secure. Egyptian intellectuals showed themselves reluctant to come to terms with European thinking. They commonly rejected the idea of political and social freedom. They were puzzled by the European desire to keep searching for new species in the animal world. They also noticed that the result of French political ideas was a rather anarchic society, as indicated by the revolutions of 1830 and 1848. By contrast, Muslims were seen as having a greater respect for authority. They did, however, attempt more subtle ways of reconciling French thinking with their own traditions. They argued that the idea of liberty had actually been anticipated in Islam by 'justice', equality by 'charity' and patriotism by religious zeal, none of which was very plausible.[18] Those who wanted to reform Islamic education also encountered opposition. Despite his anti-Westernism, al-Afghani criticised Muslim education and believed Egyptians had to catch up with the West. When he taught mathematics, philosophy and theology at al-Azhar, he offended the conservatives, who considered him an atheist.[19]

Nor were orthodox Muslims impressed by French religion; indeed, they regarded France as Catholic only in name. In effect, the French were so sophisticated that they no longer seemed to need religion. Their Christianity was so full of irrational notions – including sainthood, celibacy and the eucharist – that it could not defend itself against modern knowledge.[20] Western medicine in the shape of anatomy also posed a problem for a time, because Islamic law banned the dissection of bodies. However, Mohammed Ali established a medical college under a French surgeon, who proceeded by degrees to overcome the prohibition. One might begin with the dissection of a dog (especially if it was not a Muslim-owned dog); skeletons could be obtained from the cemetery; human dissection might be practised on the bodies of black slaves. In 1827, the first official dissection finally took place.

Nor was there much progress over women's education. Reformers argued that equal educational provision for the sexes was acceptable by pointing to the Prophet's wives, who had been literate, according to the *hadith*. But women's education remained unpopular. Later in the century, Lord Cromer claimed that 'the position of women in Egypt, and in Mohammedan countries generally, is a fatal obstacle to the attainment of that elevation which should accompany the introduction of European civilisation'.[21] Educating women was an obvious remedy, but he alleged that this would mean attacking one of the pillars of Islam, as the Prophet had relegated them to an inferior position. As Cromer devoted himself to resisting the improved status of women in Britain (especially the right to vote), this looks like another convenient argument to justify the treatment of Muslim women under British rule. Western governments generally interested themselves in the condition of slaves and Christians under Muslim rule, but ignored the status of women. However, the case for female emancipation was eventually made, notably by Qasim Amin, a lawyer who had worked in Paris, in *The Liberation of Women* (1899). Amin argued for women's education, the abolition of the veil and a reinterpretation of the Qur'an with a view to eliminating polygamy. By stages, polygamy was banned in Turkey, Iran and Tunisia. There was also an increase in the economic role of women. They had always been part of the agricultural labour force in Egypt and Turkey, but modernisation increased the demand for female workers. As the wars in the Balkans drew men into the Ottoman army, so women increasingly worked in industry and the professions, in effect laying the ground for the later policies of Kemal Ataturk, who insisted that Turkey would never catch up with the West unless women were emancipated.

Yet despite the qualifications, Egypt under Mohammed Ali had undergone a major transformation. In barely 50 years he had dragged the country from medievalism to the edge of modernity and had created a centralised government that was the basis for an Egyptian nation state. The pace of change was maintained under the next two khedives, but then accelerated when Ismael Pasha succeeded in 1863. He instigated 8,400 miles of irrigation canals; increased the railway track from 275 miles to 1,185 miles; built 430 bridges and 500 miles of telegraphs; reclaimed 1.5 million acres from the desert; trebled Egypt's exports; and expanded the number of the country's schools from 185 to 4,685 by 1875. As *The Times* commented in 1876, Egypt had 'advanced as much in seventy years as many other countries have done in five hundred'.[22]

The flaw in the modernisation strategy lay in Ismael's financial mismanagement, and in particular in the building of the Suez Canal. Its opening symbolised the modernisation of Egypt and was celebrated by having Verdi write the opera *Aida*. But the government's indebtedness led to intervention by British bondholders and the UK government's purchase of 44 per cent of shares in the canal for a mere £4 million. By 1876, Ismael had suspended payment on treasury bills, and in 1879 he was deposed as khedive by the Ottomans, in favour of a new regime backed by Britain and France. The intervention culminated in 1882, when the British invaded and placed Egypt effectively in the hands of Lord Cromer until 1908.

Cromer's account of his administration is patronising and compla-cent. He took the country's debts in hand and implemented some improvements, including the abolition of forced labour, the building of the Aswan Dam and the Delta Barrage, and the creation of an Agricultural Bank. However, Cromer exaggerated the benefits of British rule and ignored what had been achieved previously. In some ways, Egypt went backwards in this period. Preferring to confine Egypt to the production of raw materials to supply British manufacturers, Cromer damaged Egyptian industries by imposing duties on local manufacturing. Above all, he was hostile to popular government and quite unable to come to terms with the political evolution that had occurred by the 1880s. He doggedly insisted that any move towards self-determination was inhibited by Islam.

However, this was manifestly untrue. One of the country's leading Muslim scholars, Jamal al-Din al-Afghani, advocated modernisation on the basis that science, reason and liberal government were quite compatible with Islamic teaching. The British sent him into exile on account of his support for popular uprisings. They found it difficult to come to terms with the emergence of an Egyptian nationalist movement sustained by three main elements: the army officers, Muslims who resented Western interference in their country and constitutionalists protesting about despotic rule. Inevitably, the pressure of the constitutionalists for parliamentary representation attracted the opposition of the British, the khedive and the sultan in Constantinople alike. Many of the journalists and lawyers who sustained this movement enjoyed a French education and regarded the removal of British influence as a central objective – a sentiment that was hardly flattering to the British view of themselves as the champions of parliamentarianism.[23]

After 1900, the nationalist movement became more focused. In 1904, the Anglo-French Entente meant that the nationalists lost the support of the Paris government. In 1906, a dispute with Turkey over Egypt's frontier in Sinai shocked the British, because Egyptians largely supported the sultan, who was evidently seen as a lesser evil than Cromer and even appeared as a symbolic leader for pan-Islamic sentiment. In the same year, clashes between British troops and villagers at Denshawi exacerbated anti-British feelings and led Mustafa Kamil, the new nationalist leader, to undermine Cromer by visiting London, where he won the sympathy of the new Liberal prime minister, Henry Campbell-Bannerman, and the foreign secretary, Sir Edward Grey. Cromer resigned, complaining that he was not getting enough support. He refused to take Egyptian nationalism seriously and protested, with some reason, that it was 'deeply tinged with Pan-Islamism'. In effect, Cromer represented the dead-end of British imperialism in Egypt, frustrated by an Egyptian demand for modernisation and Westernisation that he was not prepared to accept.

As in Egypt, the immediate stimulus to Westernisation in the Ottoman Empire was the shock posed by European military aggression, especially from Russia. For the Turks, the only balancing factors were the British, who resisted Russian advances, and the Austrians, who feared Russian control over the Slavs of the Balkans. But even they grabbed Ottoman territory – the Austrians in Bosnia and Herzegovina in 1878 and 1908, and the British in Cyprus in 1878 and Egypt in 1882. The French took Tunisia in 1881 and the Italians Tripoli in 1911. As a result of these and other depredations, Ottoman territory shrank from 1.34 million square miles in 1750 to 1.14 million in 1850 and 910,000 in 1900.

However, Westernisation in Turkey proved to be a very protracted process, partly because of the difficulties in controlling such a sprawling Empire and partly because, in contrast to Egypt, the opposition to change was well entrenched, especially in the army. The Ottomans' difficulties were also compounded by economic exploitation. From 1854 onwards, they took out loans with the European powers, but the extra production this financed was not enough to pay off their debts. Consequently, a loan of £36 million taken in 1865 actually produced only half that amount, once the earlier debts had been deducted.[24] Unfortunately, much of the territory lost to foreign powers, such as northern Bulgaria, was the most productive and had been developed by state revenues. Moreover, the war of 1877–78 cost the Ottomans 800 million French francs paid in indemnities to Russia. They were also handicapped by *capitulations* which had existed for several hundred years: Europeans paid very low customs duties and taxes on goods entering Turkey, but the practice was not reciprocal. Capitulations made it almost impossible for the Turks to protect their own industries as other countries did. As a result, by 1914 Turkey had only a very small manufacturing base.

On the positive side, by the nineteenth century Turkish intellectuals had become familiar with European political ideas, including nationalism, which, like the Egyptians, they took from France. Once again, Britain was a negative influence, especially in the shape of her notorious ambassador, Sir Stratford Canning, an arrogant bully who treated the sultans with disrespect in the belief that he would always be supported from London. Although the intellectuals aspired to strengthen Turkish nationalism, this was not easily reconciled with the multinational character of the empire; as a result, national identification remained fairly weak. At this stage, Turkish nationalism was largely secular in character, in effect reliant on diminishing the role of religion, and was thus regarded as alien by the Muslim majority. Those who displayed too much sympathy for European ideas attracted severe unpopularity. One eighteenth-century sultan, Ahmad III, for example, actually lost his throne for this reason, while grand viziers were sometimes executed for being pro-European.

As a result, the promotion of Westernisation proved to be a complicated and dangerous project, even when backed by the sultans. Faced with the military and economic power of Europe, Turks wanted to modernise – but not at the cost of losing their soul. Westernisation took many acceptable forms, including the adoption of military reform, educational innovation and industrial and technological techniques, but Turks feared the corrosive culture and destructive politics of European societies.

The limitations of Ottoman modernisation are obvious from the experience of the first modern reformer, Sultan Selim III (1789–1807). He and his advisers focused on military reform, in the belief that that would be enough and everything else could be left intact. Cautiously, Selim imported European weapons and instructors to train the troops, introduced drill, a command structure and European uniforms. The new army proved to be a success, even when tested against the French. However, Selim lacked confidence and determination in the face of domestic opposition. The traditional heart of the Turkish army was made up of the janissaries or 'slaves of the sultan' – men who were recruited through a child-levy, never married and lived entirely in barracks. They formed a standing army of around 30,000, but over the decades had become over-privileged and corrupt. Opponents of reform claimed that Selim's new force was designed to replace the janissaries, leaving the conservatives with no means of defending their traditions. As a result, in 1807 the janissaries rebelled after hearing that some troops had been told to wear European uniforms; they demanded the disband-ment of the new army and the removal of reformers from the govern-ment. The sultan was attacked while saying prayers, deposed and hanged.

The obvious lesson from this experiment was that a reforming sultan was unlikely to make progress unless he enjoyed the backing of the mili-tary. This was taken on board by Mahmud II (1808–39) who spent years reassuring the opponents of reform before making his moves. He was generous to the religious leaders and filled government posts with men who were personally loyal to him. But Mahmud also symbolised Westernisation by adopting European coats and trousers in public, mixing freely with non-Muslims, and employing a German, Helmuth von Moltke, to reorganise the army. Meanwhile the janissaries discred-ited themselves by their failure against the Greeks and Russians, and by attempts to extort money from the population. Thus, in 1826, when Mahmud adopted reform, he was in a stronger position. Although the janissaries rebelled, 6,000 of them were killed, overcome by a combina-tion of a reliable military corps and the civilian population. From this point on, the army became a tool for reforming sultans and viziers, and thus a major Westernising element in Turkey.

Even so, Mahmud II moved cautiously, concentrating on reforms to the administration and army. He reorganised Ottoman government along European lines, with ministers and ministries with specific, defined responsibilities. He paid civil servants regular salaries, as a means of curtailing corruption. He created a cabinet and a legislative body to enact new laws. He also initiated a postal system, a register of popula-tion and the empire's first newspaper. But implementing reforms proved difficult, simply because, at the lower levels, the administrators had little notion of European systems, having grown up with Ottoman traditions. Mahmud concluded that improved knowledge of European languages was a vital means for widening their understanding. In the past they had learned Arabic and Persian, but now training schools and a Translation Office were opened to teach French. In this way, a new generation of Turkish civil servants gained an understanding of European ideas and practices, which eventually they carried forward into the highest offices of the empire.

Yet all Westernising innovations were subject to the objection that to imitate the foreigners was ultimately to become one of them. The Ottoman reformers adopted two main expedients for getting over this argument. One (though it could not often be employed) lay in demonstrating the immediate effectiveness of change. For example, in both Istanbul and Egypt the adoption of European methods for dealing with the plague hugely curtailed the number of deaths; between 1836 and 1850 it was eradicated from the Ottoman Empire. The other way was to exploit the authority of the Prophet himself. The reformers pointed out that Mohammed had used the military tactics of his enemies, which made it a legitimate ploy for contemporaries.[25] Beyond that, reformers had to rely on the authority of the sultan. In 1838, for example, Mahmud issued a decree that human dissection was now permissible. As a result, visitors to the medical school in Istanbul found the students happily dissecting the bodies of Africans.[26]

The next sultan, Abdulmecid I (1839–61), relied heavily on the younger generation, in the shape of Mustafa Resit Pasha. He was a prototype for the reformers: despite his origins in the traditional system, he had travelled in Europe, observed Mohammed Ali's reforms in Egypt and acted as Ottoman ambassador in London and Paris. Mustafa Resit and his supporters became known as the 'men of Tanzimat' – 'those who put things in order'. Although they appreciated European achievements, they did not aspire to turn Turkey into a mere echo of Europe, but somehow to combine Ottoman customs and religion with new ideas.[27]

The Tanzimat reforms involved restructuring the tax system by abolishing tax farming and making taxation fair and regular. A new penal code guaranteed citizens security for their property and lives. There was a regular system of military conscription applicable to all Muslims. These measures were shrewd, in that they did not pose a challenge to Islamic traditions or to Turkish customs. But they involved a radical shift in the idea of the state, whose responsibilities now extended across a whole range of social and economic matters previously left to individuals or private organisations, including schools, welfare, communications and services, such as the supply of water. This represented a major step towards a European notion of the state and the idea of individual rights for the people.

Tanzimat was complemented by the spread of newspapers, which had previously been run by non-Muslims. The year 1860 saw the publication of *Tercuman-I Ahval* ('Interpreter of Conditions'), the first independent Muslim-owned newspaper. It was edited by Ibrahim Sinasi, who had spent five years in Paris and who spoke French, Arabic and Persian. Sinasi returned to Istanbul in 1854, keen to promote parliamentary democracy and Turkish nationalism, as well as to reform the Turkish language to make it less flowery and more effective in expressing both technical terms and modern political ideas. As a clean-shaven Turk, he appeared to personify pro-European attitudes. A republican, he wrote much about justice and rights, but little about religion. However, his work was forced to stop in 1865 when a nervous government introduced censorship, leading Sinasi to flee to Paris until 1869; but in the long term among ordinary Turks he helped to popularise European ideas – including natural rights and freedom of expression – by using a simpler, less elaborate language. By 1871, 25 Turkish newspapers were being published, and by 1876 the number had risen to 130. By pioneering an independent press critical of the government, Sinasi shocked his contemporaries, but in the process he helped to build a culture of democracy in Turkey.

Central government saw less change, in that the Council of Ministers advised the sultan without being subject to any wider control. Moreover, the implementation of reform proved to be slow at the local level. For example, the introduction of technical and scientific subjects and new languages involved building new schools, but by 1867 barely 3 per cent of pupils attended them. The biggest weakness of the Tanzimat reforms lay in economics, where major increases in state revenues proved elusive. Here was a cultural problem, in that the officials, who had little knowledge of economics, simply left trade to the non-Muslims. Financial handicaps grew worse under Sultan Abdulaziz (1861–76), largely because Turkey's wars increased the national indebtedness.

As a result, many Ottoman bureaucrats became convinced that reform would have to go further, to include not just the technology of the West but also its democratic political institutions. To this end, some reformers gathered to form the Young Ottoman Society in 1865 to propagate their ideas through newspapers and pamphlets. Optimistically, some Young Ottomans believed that Islam was fundamentally democratic and capable of adapting to a constitutional system. But they represented an educated elite, whose democratic ideals enjoyed little purchase among the mass of the people; indeed, in a society where only 15 per cent of people were literate, the very idea of democracy remained largely unknown. They hoped that if all the communities were allowed to vote, in time they would develop a new nationality for the empire. This was utopian, since most Turks felt loyalty primarily to the regime and to their religion.

Nonetheless, in 1876, under the new Sultan Abdulhamit II, the Young Ottomans managed to introduce the first Ottoman constitution. Conservative Muslims argued that anything like a parliament was an innovation alien to the ideas of the Prophet. However, the Qur'an had nothing to say about constitutions, and the reformers pointed to verses in which Mohammed was urged by God to take counsel with his followers, as evidence that the idea of representation was compatible with Islam. In practice, the main object was to prevent any impression that a new constitution had been forced on the country by foreigners. In the event, the 1876 constitution provided for a two-chamber parliament, a system of cabinet ministers, an independent judiciary, freedom of religion and graduated taxation. However, this was limited by the extensive powers retained by the sultan to make laws without parliamentary approval, to veto parliament's legislation, to dissolve parliament, to make war and to declare a state of emergency. Unfortunately, Abdulhamit proved to be intolerant of the criticism caused by Ottoman failure in the war of 1877–78 – so much so that he dissolved parliament in 1878 and proceeded to rule autocratically, like a traditional sultan, until his overthrow in 1909. Admittedly, he continued the Tanzimat reforms in the economic sphere, especially by building new roads and railways, and managed to reschedule the Ottoman debt. Meanwhile, the European powers contented themselves with their control over the Public Debt Administration, which allowed them to collect Turkish revenues for their own benefit. But none of them, including Britain, attempted to use their influence to encourage the sultan to accept the democratic constitution. Britain preferred the empire to remain like Egypt, in hock to her investors under a traditional government.

Yet although Abdulhamit kept the lid on Turkish constitutionalism for many years, he could not destroy it. His autocracy simply stoked the resentment of a new generation of reformers, known as the Young Turks, who believed the empire would not survive unless it adopted democracy. However, they lacked the power to overthrow autocracy by themselves. It was the Turkish military, and its extensive involvement in political organisation, that was basically responsible for the next stage in the empire's evolution.[28] Students in the army's medical school set up revolutionary cells and formed the Committee of Union and Progress (CUP), which was a prototype for a political party. By 1907, the troops had become restive because they had not been regularly paid; and they felt that the sultan's government was failing to allow them the supplies necessary to contain revolts among Macedonians, Bulgarians and Greeks. As a result, in 1908 the troops in Macedonia rebelled, killing the senior officers sent to subdue them. Thereupon Abdulhamit agreed to restore the constitution and hold elections in November and December of that year. The resulting parliament reflected the multicultural society of the Ottoman Empire, comprising 140 Turks, 60 Arabs, 25 Albanians, 23 Greeks, 12 Armenians, 5 Jews, 4 Bulgarians and 3 Serbs. The CUP won a narrow majority and proceeded to replace the sultan's vizier with their own man.

However, they took office at a precarious moment, as Bulgaria declared itself independent and the Austrians annexed Bosnia. The new government was blamed for this by opponents of Westernisation. Reactionary Muslims, backed by some troops, staged a counter-revolution in Istanbul in 1909, marched on parliament and dispersed the CUP. However, Abdulhamit, welcoming their intervention, mistakenly sided with the conservative elements. Thereupon the army in Macedonia immediately converged on Istanbul, combined with the CUP and deposed the sultan in favour of his brother, Mehmet V; in effect the army and the CUP now held power.

Thus, 1909 marked the culmination of a long period in which the army had become the focus for Turkish nationalism, following its adoption of the political ideas, the educational systems and the languages of Western Europe. It was from this milieu that Mustafa Kemal, later famous as Ataturk, emerged from his home in Thessalonika to attend military high school and the staff college, from where he passed out in 1902 and joined the Young Turks. His familiarity with French political thought led Kemal to see France as the model for Turkey, and he dismissed the sultan's rule as passive and incompetent. Although brought up to be a good Muslim, like most military cadets he regarded religion as something for women. Certainly, the young Kemal's life showed little indication of Islamic influence; he learned to waltz, which he declared to be an essential accomplishment for a staff officer, drank beer and *raki* – 'what a lovely drink this is, it makes one want to be a poet' – and he cherished the human rights he associated with the French Revolution.

The new regime quickly demonstrated its liberal credentials by abolishing censorship of the press, disbanding Abdulhamit's internal intelligence service, offering an amnesty to political prisoners and dismissing the most corrupt government officials.[29] However, it had to weather two unsuccessful wars against the Italians in Tripoli in 1912 and against several Balkan states in 1912–13 that threatened the existence of the empire. Despite this, the CUP managed to win elections in 1912 and 1913. It succeeded in making sweeping improvements, especially in Istanbul, where the provision of trams, gas, electricity, water and telephones made it much more like a European capital. Further reorganisation of the armed forces created an effective body that proved itself during the First World War, when the Turks repelled British offensives at the Dardanelles and forced the surrender of an entire British army at Kut in Mesopotamia. Above all, the government subordinated religious interests to the state, by imposing secular family law, introducing state training for judges in religious courts, making Islamic judges paid state officials subject to the Ministry of Justice, and subjecting their decisions to appeals in the secular courts. This did not change the status of Islam

1. The Mezquita, Cordoba, Spain. Before 785, when this famous mosque was built, Muslims and Christians worshipped on the same site. In the sixteenth century a cathedral was planted in the middle of the mosque: 'You have destroyed something that was unique in the world,' complained King Carlos I.

2. The 'Rainbow Portrait' of Queen Elizabeth I, *c.*1600, incorporates Islamic fabrics and jewels that were fashionable at the Tudor court. The combination of trade and political collaboration with the Ottoman Empire made Islamic culture interesting and acceptable in this period.

3. General William Palmer, British Resident at Lucknow, with his
Muslim wife Fyze (seated), their children and several of Fyze's relations,
painted in 1785. It signifies the extent to which British men embraced
Muslim society in eighteenth-century India.

ONE BUBBLE MORE!!

4. This *Punch* cartoon of 1877
is an example of Victorian
stereotyping of Muslims and
represents the typical Victorian
disparagement of Turkey's
capacity for reform. In fact, the
Ottoman Empire was engaged in a
prolonged phase of modernisation
at this time.

5. The Shah Jahan Mosque, Britain's first purpose-built mosque erected at Woking, Surrey, in 1889 because land was cheaper there than in central London. It was intended as a study centre for Indian students in Britain.

6. This *Punch* cartoon of 1910 reflects British anger towards Turkey for growing closer to Germany in the run up to the First World War. Her decision to side with Germany in 1914 marked the end of the long tradition of Britain propping up the Ottoman Empire against Russian expansion and Balkan nationalism.

THE TEUTONISING OF TURKEY.

German Kaiser. "Good Bird!"

7. Norman Hassan, an Arab merchant seaman who lived at South Shields, with his English wife, pre-1914. In the long term such men won acceptance through their patriotic role as merchant seamen in two world wars.

8. Winston Churchill, as colonial secretary, Gertrude Bell and T.E. Lawrence at the Cairo Conference in 1921, where they drew up the boundaries of modern Iraq, considered how far they could retain British control over the new country, and enjoyed themselves on visits to the pyramids.

9. General Allenby, high commissioner in Egypt, with King Faisal, who was recommended by the archaeologist Gertrude Bell – the government's best-informed Middle Eastern expert – and newly chosen by Britain as King of Iraq, 1921.

10. Mustafa Kemal Ataturk, the Turkish president, meets King Edward VIII on his Mediterranean tour with Mrs Simpson, 1936. The encounter symbolised the improved relations between Britain and the new secular Turkish state.

11. Mohammed Mossaddeq, the democratically elected Iranian president, antagonised Britain by proposing to nationalise his country's oil revenues and was deposed by MI5 and the FBI in 1953, thereby putting Iran on the path of autocracy that eventually led to the Iranian Revolution in 1979.

12. Sir Anthony Eden with President Nasser and Sir Ralph Stevenson, Cairo, February 1955. Although Eden was well informed about Islamic society and comparatively sympathetic, he did not get on well with the Egyptian president; the encounter went badly and set the two on course for the Suez Crisis in 1956.

13. The Aziziye Mosque in Stoke Newington, London, a former cinema converted in the 1980s. It is a good example of the success of Islam in meeting the needs of the Muslim population while also fitting into changes in British society; its domes reflect 1930s cinema style yet seem appropriate for a modern mosque.

14. The Ramadan countdown calendar by Beacon Confectionery, Nuneaton, sold by Morrisons supermarkets in 2018. Very similar to a Christian Advent calendar, its thirty windows record Islamic values such as 'piety', 'good manners' and 'charity', as well as including small pieces of chocolate. It is a striking symptom of Christian–Muslim convergence in modern Britain.

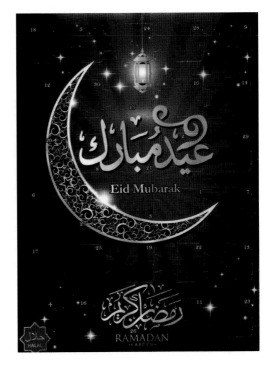

Halal Pies & Pastries

Traditional British pies and bakes, made Halal

Our aim is to provide products which meet the needs of the wider community so, for our Muslim customers, we produce two ranges of Halal pies & pastries, slices and other savoury bakes at our pork free production facility. The ranges sit under different Halal accreditation bodies.

15. The website of Lewis Pies of Swansea promoting its halal products. The eighty-year-old pie-and-pasty-maker turns its business entirely over to halal products two days of the week, and is approved by the Halal Authority Board and the Halal Monitoring Committee. Its halal pies and pasties are bought by several British football clubs.

16. Mo Farah, who arrived in Britain as an immigrant from Somalia, wins a gold medal for Britain at the 2012 Olympic Games en route to becoming one of the Muslim celebrities in British society.

as the religion of the Ottoman Empire, but it did place it under the control of the state.

◉ ❀ ◉

Among the major Muslim communities, Persia stands out for being relatively slow to adopt Westernising strategies. It experienced the same stimulus of external invasions – notably Nadir Shah's raid in 1722 – and repeated Russian incursions into Georgia, Armenia and Azerbaijan, but the impact proved to be modest. This was partly a consequence of Persia's geographical position, which left it relatively isolated from the ideas and technology of Europe. Although involved in Silk Road trade, Persia did not experience the extensive European contact that Indian Muslims had via the British Raj, or Indonesians via the Dutch; and unlike Egypt and Turkey, it largely escaped the impact of the French Revolution. Moreover, Persia already enjoyed a comparatively strong sense of national identity, based on the Persian language, a glorious history and pride in a distinctive culture. The effect was consolidated by the central role of Shiism, which commanded the loyalty of the population and remained independent of the temporal authority.[30] Distrustful of both the shah and the Europeans, Shias did not especially want to know about Western Europe, and they lacked the relaxed attitude towards Islam that characterised the Ottomans.

The other key factor in Persian modernisation was simply accidental. The country experienced a succession of rulers who were unwilling or unable to force change on the country. Fath-Ali, the shah from 1798, was famous for having fathered 260 children; but he left military and external policy to his son and heir, Abbas Mirza, who showed much more interest in the European states – perhaps partly because he was based in Tabriz, in the north-west, dangerously close to the Russian border. A good Muslim, Abbas Mirza was moderate and tolerant towards Jews and Armenians. He was quick to appreciate that Persia's army was medieval, a collection of tribal levies, with no real infantry, lacking discipline, and equipped with bows and arrows and archaic artillery that had a habit of exploding and killing the baggage animals. Abbas Mirza employed both French and British advisers, and Britain shrewdly paid him a subsidy to be spent on British weapons and uniforms. Like reformers in Egypt and Turkey, he delved into the Qur'an to find passages that appeared to endorse military innovations calculated to defend Islam.[31] As a result, by 1812 Persia was part way to building a modern army; but then the British withdrew their advisers and pressured Persia into making a settlement with Russia. The upshot was the Treaty of Golestan, which confirmed Russia's possession of the Iranian Caucasus and gave her a naval monopoly on the Caspian Sea. This humiliation for the Persians went a long way to discrediting Westernisation, as it appeared to mean allowing the Europeans to gang up on them.

From 1811 onwards, a handful of Persian students were dispatched to London to learn military tactics, medicine and languages, and some craftsmen studied British gun manufacturing and the printing press. However, this had a very marginal impact, by comparison with the extensive innovations and developments in Egypt in the same period. In Persia, religious zealots proved to be far more antagonistic towards imports from Europe. Attempting to restore prestige to his policy, Abbas Mirza launched a war of revenge on the Russians in 1826; but he was defeated and forced to concede even more territory in northern Persia, to grant the Russians exclusive trading rights in the Caspian Sea and to pay a large indemnity. He died in 1833, and under a new shah the modernisation came to a halt. His successor, Nasser al-Din, was a 17-year-old who ruled for the next 48 years. Initially he left control in the hands of an older and experienced man, Mirza Taki Khan Farahani, known as Amir Kabir. A ruthless reformer, Amir Kabir collected the taxes more effectively and instituted a postal service, hospitals, town planning, manufacturing and the cultivation of sugar cane and cotton. But by 1851, his conservative enemies had managed to undermine him with claims that he sought to depose the shah and was plotting with foreigners. As a result, Nasser al-Din dismissed him and had him murdered in his bathhouse in 1852; after just three and a half years of reforms, this effectively put an end to Persia's modernisation for the next 40 years.

Indeed, during the later nineteenth century the country went backwards, partly because the financial problems of the shah's government led him to make concessions to British and Russian pressure. Although Persia had comparatively little in the way of resources – oil had not yet begun to attract the Western powers – the development of cotton interested the British. When the shah gave a British bank the right to issue bank notes, the Russians demanded the same privilege. In 1872, the shah granted monopoly rights to build railways, roads, dams, mines and factories to Baron Reuter, a British entrepreneur, in a deal described by Lord Curzon as 'the most complete surrender of the entire resources of a kingdom into foreign hands that has ever been dreamed of'.[32] Although this was dropped when the Russians protested, other inducements were granted to the baron. In 1891, the shah allowed another British businessman, a Major G.F. Talbot, a 50-year monopoly concession over the sale and export of tobacco; in return for a mere £15,000, he could siphon off the tobacco profits to Britain. Thereupon the farmers hid their crops and angry demonstrations occurred in Persian cities. The clerics issued a *fatwa* banning smoking until the monopoly was cancelled, and it, too, was withdrawn (with compensation for Talbot). Russia was allowed to export goods duty free and to veto British loans. But in effect the shah had destroyed his own reputation by appearing to be a tool of the foreigners.

It was not until 1906 that Persia underwent a constitutional revolution designed to introduce representative institutions to the country. Modelled on the Belgian constitution of 1831, it inaugurated a system that lasted until 1925. The election of the Majlis, or assembly, had the effect of stimulating the formation of political parties and newspapers (up from six in 1906 to a hundred). Crucially for the supporters of democracy, the *ulema* backed constitutionalism, thereby creating a synthesis quite unlike that prevailing in Western countries, where reform had been attained by secular means. Constitutional reform in Persia involved an alliance of the religious and the secular that was designed to curtail the powers of the monarchy, which was seen as arbitrary and pro-Western.[33] However, the *ulema* did not want to undermine the primacy of Islam. They saw unqualified freedom of speech as a threat to religion, and so the constitution was amended to exempt anything offensive to religious sensitivities, to require permission to publish anything on Islam, and to punish the publication of anti-Islamic material. The *ulema* were less concerned about individual liberties than about protecting the believers. Yet despite these qualifications, pre-war changes in Persia were enough to demonstrate that Iranians were far from being unsuited to constitutional forms of government.

However, foreign economic penetration continued, culminating in the Anglo-Russian Entente of 1907, which effectively gave Russia the north of the country around Teheran as a zone in which to seek concessions, while Britain had the same privileges in the southern sphere around Bandar Abbas. For all practical purposes, Persia was now under foreign control. The effect was to undermine the credibility of modernisation and constitutionalism, by associating it closely with the interventionism of foreign powers. Britain's malign role in the pre-1914 era sowed the seeds for her unhappy relationship with Iran later in the century. The failure of the constitutional revolution to reverse the decline of Iran paved the way for a resumption of monarchical control under Reza Khan after 1921. He offered strong, centralised control, faster economic development and a nationalist rationale which was similar to that of Ataturk. However, he left no room for democratic institutions. At best, Reza's authoritarianism had the effect of keeping the democratic ideal alive among many Iranians.

The record of democratic innovation and the strategies for modernisation among the Muslims of Turkey, Egypt, Persia and India before 1914 were evidence of a significant desire to adapt to Western ideas during the nineteenth century. Significantly, Britain was not the major influence, except in India: the goal of a centralised, efficient state presiding over a body of citizens owed much more to French thinking. The limitations on change were partly financial, in that most Muslim countries became encumbered by huge debts in this period, and partly cultural, in that they lacked a ready-made set of administrators to implement the new ideas, until a younger generation had been educated. Although innovation provoked Islamic opposition when autocratic rulers imposed changes too quickly, religious or ideological opposition was not the major obstacle.

On the whole, the modernisers managed to sustain their claims that Westernisation could be consistent with Islamic traditions. Moreover, although change occurred in instalments over many years, especially under the Ottomans, it is questionable whether it was as slow as it appeared. By the second half of the century, the Ottomans had a system of cabinet and parliamentary government, albeit severely limited by the extensive powers retained by the monarch, which was not unlike the system that had prevailed in Britain during the seventeenth and eighteenth centuries. By 1914, Turkey was no longer the sick man of Europe, but a part-Westernised Asian empire.

CHAPTER EIGHT

THE GREAT WAR AND THE RE-DRAWING OF THE OTTOMAN EMPIRE

During the 14 years before the outbreak of the First World War, Britain comprehensively revised her diplomatic alignments, readjusted her military strategy and rearranged her armed forces to meet the threat posed by the European powers. In the process, she signed an alliance with Japan and ententes with France and Russia, she concentrated her fleet in the North Sea and the Channel, and developed a plan to prevent Germany from imposing a quick defeat on France by mobilising a new British Expeditionary Force. However, there remained one flaw in all this: she had not really considered the Ottoman Empire or, indeed, the wider question of her relations with the Muslim societies in Turkey, Persia, Egypt and especially India. This oversight was a by-product of her new strategy, which frankly made security in Europe the chief object and in effect downgraded the importance of the imperial world. As a result, Britain failed to take full account of changes in the Middle East, Asia and Africa engendered by the Great War.

Yet the Edwardian period was already having a stimulating effect on these regions, notably through the dramatic defeat of Russia by the Japanese in the war of 1905. This was the first time an Oriental power had beaten an advanced Western one. Moreover, Japan had not simply created a modern army and navy; she had also managed to adopt a system of constitutional, parliamentary government, which Russia had rejected, while still maintaining her traditions and values. Modernisation did not mean simply copying Europe.

Also, 1903 saw the foundation of the Pan-Islamic Society of London by Abdullah al-Mamoun Suhrawardy and Mushir Kidwai, a symptom of the shift in Muslim opinion against Britain in several countries and of the divided loyalties of those within the empire. Continuing economic exploitation and the pressure exerted by Christian missionaries had contributed to the growing perception of the West as the enemy. Pan-Islamism appealed because it suggested that, by uniting the huge Muslim populations, it might be possible to resist the power of Europe. To promote this goal, a new journal, *The Firmest Bond*, was published by Jamal al-Din and circulated in many Muslim countries. Admittedly, the drive for solidarity eventually came to little, because of the split between Turkey and the Arabs; after the war, the Turks adopted an independent course and eventually abandoned the Caliphate.

While Muslims were turning against the West, Britain effectively, if not explicitly, abandoned her traditional supportive stance towards the Ottomans. The change had been long developing, but the Edwardian Liberal governments accelerated the trend. It has been suggested that Winston Churchill, a rising force in those governments, wanted an alliance with the Ottomans.[1] But in truth, the impetuous and erratic Churchill had no consistent view, sometimes appearing pro-Turk and at other times anti-Turk. When the cabinet discussed the future of Turkey in 1915, it entertained a bizarre range of alternatives, which simply underlined the fact that by this stage Britain had no coherent view. Churchill was in any case rather late, for by 1900 the prime minister, Lord Salisbury, had concluded that the traditional policy of propping up the Ottomans was futile, and after 1900 Britain practically ceded her role as defender of Turkey to Germany.

By contrast, from the German point of view a connection with Turkey made complete sense: no territorial disputes complicated relations between them and they enjoyed a common enemy in Russia.

Moreover, as the prospect of an eventual conflict with Britain drew closer, the Germans appreciated that they could destabilise the British Empire by promoting pan-Islam. Visits by the German Kaiser Wilhelm II in 1889 and 1898 had initiated the process of conciliating the sultan and winning concessions and investment opportunities. Turkey offered the chance for Germany to extend her economic penetration of the Middle East and to increase the pressure on Britain in Asia. In 1903, Germany had won the right to build a railway from Istanbul to Basra: the 1,280-mile Hejaz railway through western Arabia was completed in 1908, with the option of exploring for oil 15 miles on either side of the line. German banks also financed electricity and telegraph services for Istanbul. By 1910, Germany supplied 21 per cent of Turkish imports, including steel and munitions.

From the Turkish perspective on the eve of the First World War, Germany was the only power willing to support her in the aftermath of the Balkan wars of 1912–13. They shared a common enemy in Russia, and this rationale had become especially compelling once Britain and France became Russia's allies. Already Russia sat threateningly across Turkey's Anatolian frontier and – were she to win the First World War – she would seize even more Turkish-populated territory. Such considerations made a Turkish alliance with the Allies in 1914 improbable, though not impossible. Following the domestic revolts of 1908 and 1913, the sultans had been displaced by the Young Turks, led by Enver Pasha, a rising army officer who had been so highly impressed by a visit to Germany that he concluded that Turkey would be capable of facing up to her enemies only if she emulated German military methods. As a result, General Liman von Sanders led a German delegation to Turkey in 1913.

The necessity for military reform was underlined by the aggression of the other powers in the pre-war years. The French used their entente with Britain to grab Morocco. In 1911, Italian forces occupied Cyrenaica (Libya) and Tripolitania and won recognition of their occupation of the islands of the Dodecanese. In the Balkan wars of 1912–13, the Greeks, Bulgarians, Romanians and Serbs were responsible for large-scale atrocities, massacring Muslim and Jewish peasants in their villages: altogether

27 per cent of Muslims in the Ottoman Balkans were killed and 35 per cent became refugees fleeing towards Istanbul.[2] The Turks were deprived of Albania, Western Thrace, Macedonia, Thessaly, Epirus and Kosovo, effectively ending their European empire and leaving a small rump in Eastern Thrace around Istanbul.

Meanwhile, the incompetence with which the British government handled Turkey was all of a piece with the general treatment of Muslims prior to and during the First World War. The decision of the Ottoman sultan, who was also the caliph, to declare a *jihad* against the British had dangerous implications for the huge Muslim population in India, which is why Curzon warned against it: in effect, Indian Muslims were being urged to rise up and drive the British out of their country. To the delight of the Germans, *agents provocateurs* had already entered India to encourage a rebellion. The hostile reaction to the anti-Turkish policy largely superseded recent British efforts to conciliate Muslim opinion through the creation of a new Muslim-majority province in East Bengal and the separate Muslim representation under the Morley–Minto reforms of 1909.

As for Iran, despite growing evidence of anti-Westernism, Britain persisted in treating it as a colonial territory. Following the constitutional revolution of 1905, the elected parliament vetoed foreign loans, including a £400,000 Anglo-Russian loan. But for Britain, the rise of a parliamentary state was irrelevant: the effective end of Iranian independence seemed a price worth paying for the 1907 entente with Russia. In the north, now declared a Russian sphere of influence, Cossack troops dispersed parliament, while the south around Basra was pronounced a British sphere, in effect a colony manned by Indian troops. The effect of this interventionism was to strengthen nationalist sentiment, which, with the backing of the clerical leaders, was Islamic in character.

British policy in Iran was driven largely by the need to safeguard trade in the Persian Gulf, and especially by the security of oil supplies and the pipeline to Abadan, which carried 275,000 tons of oil. To this end, an Indian expeditionary force arrived at Basra as early as November 1914. There was also an element of prestige. British control of Mesopotamia boosted her reputation in India; indeed, some officials wanted Mesopotamia to become an Indian colony, once the Turks had been ousted. Churchill, as first lord of the admiralty from 1911, was much taken with the idea of fuelling the new battleships with oil, which would allow them to stay at sea longer. But the drawbacks were formidable. Whereas Britain had plenty of coal, she had no oil, except what was available in remote, unstable parts of the world. Presently, the oil was obtained via two companies, Shell and the Anglo-Persian Oil Company. Although Shell was British controlled, the Anglo-Persian managed to convince the naïve Churchill that, as 60 per cent of Shell's shares were Dutch owned, it was a foreign company. The upshot was that Churchill nationalised Anglo-Persian, giving it a monopoly as state supplier.[3] Characteristically (if absurdly), Churchill cut the Persian government out by reaching deals with the local Bedouins to safeguard the oil supply. The scheme made a profit for British taxpayers for several generations, but it also accentuated the imperial exploitation of Iran and thus embroiled Britain in controversy for years to come. Although Iran remained neutral during the war, this was ignored by the Allies, who simply landed more troops at Basra in order to protect the oilfield at Ahwaz. The sad truth about Britain's treatment of Iran – which was exemplified by Churchill – is that she felt happier dealing with wild, romantic tribesmen than with the sophisticated, urban Muslims who were increasingly coming to the fore in the cause of secularism and modernisation.

Unfortunately, during this period of rising nationalism in Muslim societies, British policy in the Middle East largely lacked coherence, lurching unrealistically from pro-Turk to anti-Turk under the influence of the impulsive Churchill. He dispatched Rear Admiral Arthur Limpus to lead a naval mission in Istanbul, and he offered to build two warships at a reduced price for the Turks. However, when Churchill met Enver in 1909, he showed no interest in the Turks' idea of a new settlement. As a result, the Turks concluded a secret treaty with Germany in August 1914, by which the Germans undertook to support the Ottomans militarily if they found themselves at war with Russia. It was this that gave the Turkish government the confidence in the crisis following the assassination of the Austrian archduke to mobilise its armed forces and cancel interest payments on its foreign debt. Even so, Enver remained undecided about the war and kept the country neutral for a time. However, the British blundered in their dealings with the Turks. They were just completing the building of Churchill's warships, the *Sultan Osman* and the *Reshadieh*, already paid for by public subscription at £7 million. Handing over the ships would have been a good way of conciliating Turkey and keeping access to the Black Sea – and thus communications with Russia – open. Unfortunately, Churchill appropriated the ships for Britain's own needs, without compensation. This folly handed a propaganda coup to the Germans, who shrewdly offered the Turks two first-class vessels, the *Goeben* and the *Breslau*. In this way, Germany added virtual control of the Turkish navy to her existing control of the army. The German–Turkish ships sailed through the Mediterranean, evading the Royal Navy's pursuit, to appear at the Dardanelles, whereupon Enver allowed them through into the Black Sea. In this dire situation, the best that Churchill and Grey, the foreign secretary, managed to do was inform the Turks that 'if Turkey remains loyal to her neutrality' she would keep her empire – more of a threat than a reassurance. This was in any case disingenuous, as Britain had been cheerfully signing away Turkish territory in the recent Balkan wars. Not surprisingly, the Turks responded by expelling the British naval mission from Istanbul, and in September they closed the straits and mined them.[4] In October, the German commander of Turkey's fleet sailed around the Black Sea, sinking Russian ships and bombarding Russian ports. It only remained for Turkey to declare a *jihad* – and thus war – on Britain, France and Russia on 11 November.

There was nothing inevitable about this historic rupture between Britain and Turkey, for the Turks were genuinely undecided about which side to join. However, it proved to be a crucial decision. If the Germans won the war, as seemed likely in 1914–15, Turkey stood to gain territorially and economically. But by placing Turkey on the losing side, the decision led inexorably to the dissolution of the Ottoman Empire, to the emergence of a secular, national state in 1923 and to the end of the

Caliphate. For Britain, the rupture proved disastrous. In the short term it brought military humiliations. In the long term it hugely complicated her policy, for it entangled her more deeply than ever in an unending process of redrawing the boundaries of the Muslim world and trying to manipulate its rulers – a habit that would persist for the next century, resulting in a series of political and military disasters.

Once hostilities had been declared, the kaiser ordered German agents to be dispatched to India, Afghanistan, Persia, Libya and Morocco to stir up anti-British sentiment and, in the case of the amir of Afghanistan, to join Turkey by declaring war on Britain. The significance of these efforts was much exaggerated by British representatives, and until Gandhi took the lead in the Indian national movement, Muslims did little except volunteer to serve in the British army. Nonetheless, the mere thought of Muslim subversion reignited the fears of politicians at home, who realised they had bungled. As Asquith wrote: 'few things would give me greater pleasure than to see the Turkish Empire finally disappear from Europe'. Before long, British irritation with Turkey led to the resurrection of the excitable effusions of the late-Victorian era, notably on the part of Asquith's successor as prime minister, David Lloyd George. In speeches reminiscent of Gladstone, Lloyd George actually referred to 'the British crusade' against the Turks and claimed of the intervention in Palestine that 'we are undertaking a great civilising duty'. When British troops entered Jerusalem in December 1917, he hailed the victory for 'the embattled hosts of Christendom', while *Punch* depicted Richard the Lionheart, whose attempt to recover Jerusalem had failed, saying 'My dream comes true.' At the end of the war, Lloyd George's sentimentalism led him into a wholly unrealistic expectation that Britain could restore her position in the Eastern Mediterranean by using the Greeks as a substitute for the ally she had lost following the defeat of Turkey.

But what to do about the immediate Muslim threat? The obvious move was to overthrow the anti-British regime in Istanbul by launching an offensive at the Dardanelles. Britain felt vulnerable in the Eastern Mediterranean due to her reliance on the Suez Canal for communications with India and the East, and she could hardly tolerate a hostile power now posing a strategic threat. Moreover, once the main conflict became bogged down in trench warfare in France and Flanders, the more imaginative ministers, notably Lloyd George and Churchill, urged that Britain should use the flexibility the navy gave her to launch offensives on other fronts, with a view to knocking away the props that supposedly sustained Germany in central Europe. For the historically minded and boyishly enthusiastic Churchill, the Dardanelles was an especially appealing target. In January 1915, the Russians, under pressure on both their Turkish and Austrian fronts, appealed to Britain to do something to divert Turkish troops away from them. This seemed compelling, since, if Russia were defeated, the Turks would be able to transfer forces to Egypt; but if Britain gained control of the Black Sea, she would be able to supply munitions to the Russians, who had plenty of men but an inadequate industrial base.

The energetic Churchill persuaded the cabinet to adopt his idea of forcing the Dardanelles, although it was more of an aspiration than a real plan. The assumption was that battleships would silence the Turkish forts at the entrance to the Dardanelles, which would allow the passage of the fleet and thereby trigger chaos at Istanbul and the overthrow of the government. This was rather optimistic, especially as the politicians, including Churchill, greatly underestimated the military competence of their opponents. The Turks made resilient soldiers, whose effectiveness had lately been enhanced by German training, German officers and German repeating rifles, which put them on a level with the European forces. By contrast, neither the naval experts in the shape of Admiral Jackie Fisher nor the military ones in the person of Lord Kitchener thought the task would be easy. They were right. The obsolescent battleships sent to the Dardanelles carried big guns suitable for reducing the Turkish forts; but they were very vulnerable to mines and submarine attack, and the guns' limited trajectory meant that they were unable to focus on forts higher up, above the shore. By early 1915, it was clear that the naval effort was failing. Fisher and Kitchener had correctly warned that the campaign would require the landing of troops. In India, meanwhile, the prospect of failure threatened to humiliate Britain in the eyes of both Muslim and Hindu communities. Therefore, British troops landed on the Gallipoli Peninsula in April and August 1915, but they managed to establish only small beachheads against an effective Turkish opposition. By January 1916, after suffering 200,000 casualties, the British forces were evacuated, leaving the straits closed and the Turks triumphant.

Things went just as badly in Mesopotamia, where British reinforcements were supposed to protect shipping in the Persian Gulf and the oil refineries at Abadan. From their base at Basra, British forces under General Sir Charles Townshend advanced up the Tigris towards Baghdad; but their lines became stretched and subject to guerrilla attack. The retreating Ottomans fought near Baghdad and completely defeated Townshend, who could have retreated to Basra, but foolishly chose to make a stand at Kut al-Amara. Under siege at Kut, the British troops were soon in such a hopeless position that they were fed on opium, as the only way of staving off their hunger. Attempts were even made to bribe the Turkish general to let the British go. After a long siege, they surrendered in April 1916 – a further humiliation that underlined the competence of the Turkish infantry and their commanders. The Mesopotamian campaign had cost 38,000 casualties, and some 13,000 soldiers became prisoners of war.

In view of the fact that the Turks had begun the war facing invasion from four directions – by Russia in Anatolia and by the British at Gallipoli, Mesopotamia and Syria – they had done surprisingly well. However, the empire remained very vulnerable, and the British found an alternative strategy by engineering an Arab revolt against Turkish rule. Whether Arab discontent amounted to a real national movement at this time is a matter of some controversy. Well-informed contemporaries, like Gertrude Bell, argued that 'there is no nation of Arabs' and considered that most would have remained within the framework of the Ottoman Empire.[5] The chief impetus for self-determination came not from urban Arabs, but from the Hashemites, who were the leading force in the Hejaz, a remote rural region stretching from Akaba down the Red

Sea to the borders of Yemen. In the Hejaz, the inspiration for a rebellion against Turkey came from Sharif Hussein, the amir of Mecca, who was effectively a nominee of the sultan and now saw the British as a potential ally in his bid to break free of Ottoman control. In initiating the Arab revolt in June 1916, Hussein was motivated by personal ambition, rather than the nationalist cause.

The Turks felt confident of suppressing the revolt, because Hussein had only 6,000 troops – although during 1916 he received subsidies of £200,000 a month from Britain to keep the revolt going. However, Hussein's son, Abdullah, understood that the key to victory lay in control of the Hejaz railway, which enabled the Turks to transfer troops quickly to wherever they were needed. The guerrilla war to sabotage the railway was the work of the Arabs, in conjunction with T.E. Lawrence, whose expertise on Arab society had resulted in his appointment to British Intelligence in Cairo in 1914; in 1916, he was employed by the Arab Bureau to coordinate dealings with the Arabs. Lawrence became the Arabs' key military adviser, shrewdly focusing their strategy on soft targets, such as railway lines and supply convoys, rather than battles with the Turkish infantry. A typical British Orientalist, Lawrence disliked the intelligent, sophisticated Abdullah, preferring his Arabs to be innocent and cooperative, like his cook and servant, Salim Ahmad, with whom he was in love.[6] Although by nature homosexual, Lawrence remained passive in his relationships, being afraid of physical contact of any sort.[7] But as he liked men much more than women, Lawrence found Arab society comfortable, since it provided opportunities for the intense male friendships he had previously enjoyed in England.

Lawrence and the British officials in the Middle East and at home understood perfectly that Sharif Hussein was willing to collaborate with Britain as the best way of obtaining a substantial Arab state from the ruins of the Ottoman Empire. In negotiations with Sir Henry McMahon, the high commissioner in Egypt, Hussein made it clear that he aspired to be king of an Arab state including Syria, Palestine, Jordan, Iraq and the Arabian Peninsula. The British were so desperate for success against the Turks that they gave Hussein a military alliance and McMahon promised that 'Great Britain is prepared to recognise and uphold the independence of the Arabs in all the regions lying within the frontiers proposed by the Sharif of Mecca'. However, on the British side there was some vagueness about the territorial extent of a future Arab state, though the only exceptions they specified were the small Arab sheikhdoms on the Persian Gulf and the oilfields of Basra and Baghdad.

Although the British gave the impression that they supported Hussein's claims to an Arab kingdom, they were deceiving him. One complication was Hussein's rival, Ibn Saud, based in the Najid area, who also aspired to control the peninsula and won British backing and subsidies. Then there were Britain's commitments to the Jews, which were also inconsistent with her obligations to the Arabs. In addition, McMahon knew quite well that Britain had already agreed that France could annex Syria in 1915. Consequently, the foreign secretary, Sir Edward Grey, suggested that the French send a delegate able to settle French borders in Syria. The delegate was Charles Georges-Picot, who insisted that France must have all of Syria and that a large Arab state was unrealistic: 'Such a state will never materialize. You cannot transform a myriad of tribes into a viable whole.'[8] However, as the British government was keen to reach a deal with the French, they sent Sir Mark Sykes, an MP who posed as an expert on the Middle East, to take over the negotiations with Picot; the two proceeded to draw lines across the map defining the French and British spheres. Sykes compromised by excluding Lebanon and Mediterranean Syria from any Arab state. He agreed to extend the French zone from Syria eastwards to Mosul, thereby conveniently creating a buffer between British and Russian territory, while leaving Britain the Mesopotamian districts of Basra and Baghdad and parts of Palestine. This left the large inland desert areas including Aleppo, Damascus and northern Arabia, where Britain and France were 'prepared to recognize and uphold an independent Arab state or a Confederation of Arab states'.[9] The Sykes–Picot Agreement of January 1916 was kept secret from Hussein, who thought Britain had offered him much more – in particular that he was to inherit Palestine from the British. British duplicity towards the Arabs did not become widely known until November 1917, when the *Manchester Guardian* published, under the headline 'Russia and Secret Treaties', secret papers including the Sykes–Picot Agreement that the Bolsheviks had released on seizing power in Russia.

⬤ ✤ ⬤

The main qualification to be made about British strategy is that the Arab revolt proved to be of very minor significance in the defeat of Turkey. Despite British subsidies, neither Hussein nor Ibn Saud mobilised more than small numbers of unreliable troops and, but for the romantic myths spun by Lawrence in *The Seven Pillars of Wisdom*, the revolt would have been largely ignored. However, the Turks were eventually pushed back in 1917. From the south, British forces captured Baghdad in March 1917, and General Edmund Allenby, advancing from Hejaz to Damascus, rode up to Jerusalem's Jaffa Gate in December, where he dismounted and walked into the Holy City, hoping to emulate Christ and highlight the contrast with the kaiser, for whose entry in 1898 a lump of the city walls had been dismantled. The Turks finally surrendered in October 1918 and signed an armistice at Mudros. The terms included the demobilisation of their troops and the destruction of their fortifications and weapons. Although nominally committed to President Woodrow Wilson's Fourteen Points, which respected the idea of self-determination, the Allies promptly violated their agreement by occupying several parts of Turkey and by encouraging a Greek invasion of Smyrna (Izmir) in May 1919. Britain and France simply intended to divide up Anatolia to suit their own interests. At last the British appeared to have attained their long-standing aim of dismembering the Ottoman Empire without the risk that Russia would take advantage of it.

Decked out in Arab dress, T.E. Lawrence appeared at the Paris Peace Conference in January 1918 and posed as spokesman for the Hashemite Arabs who had fought in Hejaz. In fact, Lawrence despised Arab nationalism and was well aware of the Sykes–Picot Agreement; he knew that Britain's promises to Hussein were made to be broken.[10] At Paris, Lloyd George showed Faisal, another son of Sharif Hussein, the Sykes–Picot Agreement. As Faisal commented: 'in this way we had to face the bitter truth'. The conference divided Turkish territory into temporary mandates

177

over Mesopotamia and Palestine for Britain, and over Syria and Lebanon for France. What was actually to be done remained to be seen. In the event, President Woodrow Wilson fell ill, America withdrew and Britain and France proceeded to have their way with the territories. Eventually the Arabs realised that they had been cheated of a strong Arab state in favour of a series of small, weak ones. The French effectively occupied their mandates and suppressed Arab nationalism there; when Faisal was promoted as king of an independent Syria in 1920, the French simply drove him out.

Meanwhile the British combined three former provinces of the Ottoman Empire to form a new Iraqi state based on Baghdad. Iraq, however, proved to be an unstable mix of Sunni Muslims, Shia Muslims and Kurds, who, despite being the fourth largest ethnic group, saw their claims to self-determination ignored. At the Cairo Conference in 1921, Churchill accepted the Kurds' case for independence, but was persuaded that Kurdistan was somehow an integral part of Iraq and that if they left, the Shias would gain too great a preponderance. The British decided not to consult the local population, thereby provoking anti-British demonstrations which spread from Basra and Baghdad to Mosul and Kirkuk and forced the authorities to make up their minds how Iraq was to be run: was it to be independent, under British control, semi-independent with Britain attaching advisers to each ministry? Or should Britain simply evacuate the country? The autocratic high commissioner in Baghdad, Captain Arnold Wilson, simply wanted to rule Iraq as though it were India. However, by 1920 his views had come up against the domestic pressure to cut costs by getting out of Iraq without delay. Wilson was also undermined by another of the amateur eccentrics who were attracted to the Middle East: Gertrude Bell. An experienced traveller and archaeologist, Bell gained official roles in the face of the disapproval of misogynist officials simply because she was more knowledgeable about the region than anyone else. Though sympathetic towards the Arabs, she feared the consequences of a British withdrawal and tried to mediate between the nationalists and Wilson.[11]

In 1921, the pace was increased by the appointment of a new colonial secretary, Winston Churchill, who met up with Bell and Lawrence at the conference in Cairo, along with 40 British experts. As Churchill virtually hero-worshipped Lawrence, he was susceptible to the latter's influence. The starting point for Churchill, who had a history of seeking reductions in defence expenditure, was the £37 million that Britain currently spent on the Middle East; at a time when the Lloyd George coalition was drastically cutting military costs, he was keen to find a way out. 'I am going to save you millions,' he told the reporters. Thus, when the Kurds living in the north of the country refused to accept their place in Iraq, Churchill, an enthusiast of air power, sent aeroplanes in to bomb their villages; this was not very effective, but much cheaper than using troops. Always apt to jump at novel ideas, Churchill resorted to air power in several Muslim territories, including Somaliland, and in the Third Anglo-Afghan War he used it as an economical way of controlling a remote territory. But Churchill was terribly naïve. He failed to appreciate that when Afghan tribesmen faced aeroplanes, they flattened themselves against a rock-face, as it was too dangerous for the pilots to come in close for fear of hitting the mountainside. It was easier to bomb villages, but the idea that this enabled Britain to control the population was simply unrealistic. There was no substitute for troops on the ground.[12]

Meanwhile the eccentric trio of Lawrence, Bell and Churchill wanted Iraq to have an Arab government, so long as it remained largely under British control. This, they decided, meant finding a suitable person to be king. There were half a dozen possibilities, but Gertrude Bell rather liked Hussein and his family. She and Lawrence advised Churchill that Faisal, Hussein's younger son, would offer a cheap and quick solution. He was now available, as the French had banned him from Syria, where he had aspired to be king. Churchill, Bell and Lawrence put the case – admittedly a strong one – for Faisal: he was a war hero and pro-British; and his father was a thirty-seventh-generation descendant of the Prophet. Faisal duly came to Iraq, toured the country, received pledges of support and was crowned in August 1921. This appeared to be a good compromise, as it enabled elections to be held in 1922. Moreover, Bell believed that she would be able to guide him.

At the Cairo conference, Churchill also decided to settle the new Arab state of Transjordan under an elder son of Hussein, Abdullah. It was agreed that Jews would be able to settle west of the River Jordan, but Britain would remain in control by virtue of her mandate. This was condemned as a mistake by Bell, who described it as 'a stupendous barrier to honest dealing with the Arabs'.[13] She was correct, as it resulted in the Arabs rejecting the mandate and the Balfour Declaration, and massacring Jews in their settlements in 1922. However, Cairo did offer the Arabs a concession by defining the River Jordan as the boundary of Palestine, which meant that land east of it was in Transjordan, effectively halving the area that came under the remit of the Balfour Declaration.

As for the Turks, not only had they lost the former Ottoman territory in the Balkans, the Caucasus, the Crimea, Arabia and Egypt, they were even under threat in Anatolia itself. The French seized southern Anatolia, the Greeks much of the west, and the Armenians claimed most of the east; the Allies contemplated leaving the centre under an American League of Nations mandate, which, sensibly, the Americans refused to accept. Although 14.5 million of the population of 17.5 million were Turkish Muslims, the Allies, cynically disregarding the principle of self-determination, proposed to carve up the territory for Greeks, Italians, French and Armenians.[14] In 1920, the Turks accepted the Allies' wishes by signing the Treaty of Sèvres, a punitive measure that restricted Turkey's army to 50,000 men and her navy to a handful of ships; she was allowed no air force at all. Turkish finances were placed under an Allied commission and the Turks were left with Istanbul and a small slice of north-west Anatolia. This was far harsher than the treatment of the other defeated powers, and it created a long-term legacy of resentment towards Britain among many Turks. But at the time, the British were carried away by their success: 'Turkey is no more,' claimed an exultant Lloyd George. Unfortunately, Lloyd George and Churchill suffered from a complete misunderstanding of the Turkish nationalist movement, which they saw as pan-Islamic; they assumed that, as Muslims, the Turks were driven wholly by religious sentiment – a delusion that has persisted into the twenty-first century – and failed to recognise nationalism as a political force unrelated to pan-Islamism.

However, by imposing such a vindictive treaty, the Allies effectively ensured that Turks would rally around the nationalist movement. Even in the West, it was confidently predicted that Sèvres would not last three years; however, Lloyd George accepted Greek assurances that the army was capable of enforcing it. The Turkish resistance began initially with self-defence units in the villages and attacks launched from mountain retreats, using munitions smuggled into the country. The leadership of this movement fell to Mustafa Kemal, a revolutionary officer who had helped in the overthrow of the sultans and a military hero who had checked the British at Gallipoli. Withdrawing to the Black Sea coast in the centre of Anatolia, Kemal rejected the authority of the government in Istanbul as incapable of defending Turkish interests. He forged a new organisation called the Turkish Nationalists. Meanwhile, the British forcibly dissolved the parliament, imposed martial law and condemned Kemal to death; but this foolish action simply helped the nationalist cause, as it exposed the Istanbul government as a tool of the foreign powers and led Turks to unite behind the new movement. From 1920 onwards, the country looked to a Grand National Assembly under the presidency of Kemal, who drew the various Turkish forces together to resist the foreign occupation. He signed an agreement with the Russians, who supplied the Turks with much-needed armaments and allowed the transfer of troops from east to west. This reinforced the British conviction that he was engineering a pan-Islamic–Bolshevik alliance. First the Turkish forces defeated the Armenians in the east, and then the French, who decided to withdraw and repudiate the Treaty of Sèvres.

However, the main problem lay with the large Greek forces that had advanced from Izmir into the heart of Anatolia, massacring Turks and creating a million refugees. The Greek invasion was supported by the British navy and by Lloyd George, who believed that Greece would secure the straits and the Eastern Mediterranean for Britain. He was, in effect, reinventing traditional British strategy, by replacing Turks with Greeks. Yet this was delusional, for Greece enjoyed a population of only 4 million and had too few resources to be capable of dominating the straits, as the Ottomans had once done. By 1921, the Greeks had been checked and forced into a headlong retreat from Anatolia; in 1922, their troops were evacuated from Izmir.

Meanwhile British troops remained in the straits zone with a view to preventing the reoccupation of Istanbul. In September 1922, Turkish forces approached the nearby town of Chanak (Canakkale) defended by just 3,500 British troops. Determined to deny the Turks European territory, the cabinet proposed to send reinforcements and appealed for assistance from Britain's allies. They were surprised when the French, Canadians and Australians sensibly declined to help. Despite this, Lloyd George and Churchill, by now in a fairly irrational mood, believed they could bluff their way out. They issued an ultimatum to Kemal to withdraw and advised the general at Chanak, Sir Charles Harington, that though he could retreat to Istanbul, he must not allow the Turks to cross into Europe. By risking another war in this way, Lloyd George severely undermined his own credibility. A month later, at a meeting of Conservative MPs, their ex-leader, Andrew Bonar Law, argued that Britain could not 'act alone as the policeman of the world'; thereupon the MPs voted to split with the prime minister and Lloyd George's coalition collapsed.

Fortunately, Kemal, who could have overcome the small British force, did his best to be conciliatory: 'Our nation is not opposed to the English. On the contrary it acknowledges and respects them as the greatest, the most just, most civilised and humane nation in the world.'[15] He held his fire, correctly believing that it would not be necessary to fight the British, whose position was now very weak militarily, diplomatically and even politically, as domestic opinion rallied to oppose another war. Meanwhile Harington sensibly withheld the ultimatum, advising the cabinet 'I do not think Mustafa wants to attack us.' In this way, he saved the politicians from their own folly. Chanak thus proved to be one of the very few occasions in history when the British stopped short of what would have been another futile war in a Muslim country. A settlement (the Treaty of Lausanne) was reached, granting the Turkish state Anatolia, Istanbul and Eastern Thrace on more or less her pre-1914 European boundaries, along with an exchange of people between Greece and Turkey. The Ottoman Empire was now at an end. This concluded the War for Turkish Independence, although British troops did not finally leave Istanbul until October 1923 and the straits remained demilitarised for 13 years.

⟨⟩ ❖ ⟨⟩

At the end of October 1923, a new Turkish Republic was formally declared, with a capital at Ankara and a president, Kemal, whose prestige had been hugely enhanced by his decisive role in achieving independence, chosen by the assembly. Turkey was now a coherent state that had left behind many of the complications of the Ottoman Empire. It is easily forgotten that the foundations of the secularism imposed by Kemal Ataturk lay in the pre-war period. As the Ottomans steadily lost their non-Turkish provinces, their state had increasingly become ethnically unified. Moreover, the growth of anti-Westernism in the political sphere did little to inhibit social changes that reflected Western cultural influence. It is a measure of the gradual Westernisation that by 1907 only 2 per cent of married men had more than one wife and that in Istanbul the average Muslim household had fewer than four members.[16] Other symptoms of Westernisation included the writing of novels, which had not been a tradition, photography, the use of knives and forks and the wearing of wrist-watches to improve punctuality. Turkish women began to read women's magazines, to go shopping without men, to discard the veil in public and to walk in front of their menfolk, as in France.[17] At least in Istanbul, the ground had been prepared for Ataturk's revolution.

But Kemal intended to go further in transforming Turkey into a modern secular society informed by the example of France, by abandoning the Caliphate. He pointed out that there was a distinction between the functions of the caliph, as a successor of the Prophet, and of the sultan or temporal ruler; the Ottomans had seized these functions by force and had held onto them for six centuries, but as the Turkish people had now recovered their sovereignty, there were no religious grounds and no pragmatic justification for retaining the office. In 1924, the last caliph-sultan, Abdulmecid, left the country protesting that his deposition had no legal authority; but the lack of reaction in Turkey suggests that the institution was now regarded as an irrelevance.

More controversy attached to the position of the Islamic establishment. Although the constitution designated Islam as the official religion and Turks comprised the majority in the new state, Kemal insisted that non-Muslims were not required to conform. Nonetheless, 1,100,000 Greek Orthodox citizens left Turkey for Greece, while 380,000 Muslims migrated from Greece to Turkey. The traditional religious schools or madrasas which were now redundant would be replaced by secular Turkish-language schools, and as textbooks were to be written in Turkish, there would be no need to learn Arabic. There was to be a single unified system of education, and the state would no longer deal with Islamic law and religious foundations. In 1924, the religious courts which handled marriage, divorce and inheritance were abolished. The official prohibition on alcohol was also dropped, though it had clearly not been much enforced. In 1925, the assembly replaced the traditional Muslim solar calendar and the practice of numbering the hours from sunset with the 24-hour clock and the dates of the Christian era. A new penal code was introduced, based on Italian law, and a civil code based on Swiss practice, which improved women's rights by abolishing a husband's sole right to impose divorce. Women did not gain the parliamentary vote until 1934 – only 16 years after Britain and 14 years *before* France! In 1928, Turkey adopted the Latin alphabet and phonetic Turkish spelling, thereby eliminating the Arabic script and making it easier for Turks to learn European languages. Kemal also devoted much attention to the headgear used by Turks. In the nineteenth century, the traditional turban had given way to the fez, which allowed the forehead to touch the ground during prayers, but suffered from the disadvantage that it lacked a rim to shade the wearer from the sun. As a radical moderniser, Kemal argued that Turks should wear a hat that would be common to all classes of people. He disparaged the practice of women covering their faces, which was uncomfortable in hot weather. 'Let them show their faces to the world and see it with their eyes,' he argued. 'Don't be afraid.'[18] Although veils were not banned, they were discouraged, and the middle-class minority who had used them easily gave up the habit.

Over time, Kemal lost interest in his earlier aim of establishing the compatibility of Islam and modern society: his emphasis came to be more on a comprehensive policy of Westernisation, inspired by the example of revolutionary France. Kemal was prepared to offend strict Muslims, even to the extent of having statues of himself erected across the country. Nor was the political system a British one, based as it was on voting for local electoral colleges, which then chose the national deputies. Despite this, Kemal protested his sympathy for Britain, and the new country managed to put relations onto a friendly footing. The chief complication was the territorial dispute over Mosul, which Turkey claimed. Eventually, in 1926, a tripartite treaty involving Britain, Turkey and Iraq ceded Mosul to Iraq, which was easier for the Turks to accept than allowing British control. The threat posed by Italian fascism to both British and Turkish security in the Mediterranean between the wars reinforced their friendship. The culmination came in 1936, when Edward VIII, cruising the Mediterranean with Wallis Simpson, visited Istanbul to be greeted by Kemal. His action was taken as a symbolic way of burying the anti-Turkish tradition associated with Gladstone and Lloyd George.

On the other hand, while the Turks effectively resolved their national status, the winding up of the Ottoman Empire triggered an almost unending series of ramifications and complications in British relations with Muslims in Palestine, Transjordan, Egypt, Iraq and Iran – and not least in India. As Curzon, Kitchener and Edwin Montagu, the secretary of state for India, had warned, the Anglo-Turkish conflict shook the loyalties of the 60 million Indian Muslims who saw the sultan as the caliph and protector of their holiest places at Mecca and Medina. They thought it especially offensive to use Indian Muslim troops against their co-religionists in the Middle East. The viceroy, Lord Hardinge, found it politic to criticise Asquith for rashly proclaiming the end of the Ottoman Empire. Admittedly, the anticipated revolt was slow in coming, as 1,300,000 Indians, including many Muslims, volunteered to fight for the Allies in Mesopotamia, Palestine and Syria, without apparently taking much notice of the sultan's call to *jihad*. Yet in Egypt some Muslim troops deserted to the Turks and the Raj seemed precarious. As one Indian official warned: 'It is only necessary for a feeling to arise that it is impious to serve the British for the whole of our fabric to tumble like a house of cards without a shot being fired.'[19] In 1915, Pathan troops, who held strong religious objections, refused to embark at Rangoon when they realised they were going to fight in Mesopotamia; and in 1916, Muslims at Basra refused to march up the Tigris in view of their 'strong religious scruples against fighting in the vicinity of the holy places of Baghdad and Kerbela'. In 1919, when Britain fought a third war with Afghanistan, the amir declared *jihad* against the British, and in 1923 a *fatwa* pronounced it a sin against the Prophet to assist the government of India.[20]

That this was a turning point in British relations with Indian Muslims was underlined by domestic complications. Muslim sensitivity to the anti-Islamic drift of British policy was accentuated by wider wartime problems, notably increases in the land revenue and the inflation of food prices, which nearly doubled between 1914 and 1919. Even so, the Indian National Congress supported Britain in the war and left it to independent initiatives by B.G. Tilak and Annie Besant, who felt that Britain had taken Indians' loyalty for granted, to launch an agitation under the Home Rule Leagues. British assumptions that Hindus and Muslims would never cooperate against the Raj were alarmingly undermined by the rapprochement between Hindu and Muslims leaders at Lucknow in 1916, when Congress and the Muslim League jointly demanded self-rule and the former accepted separate electorates for Muslims. Meanwhile M.K. Gandhi had begun experimenting with a series of local agitations over material grievances at Champaran in Bihar, Khaira in Gujarat and in Ahmadabad. Emboldened by his success, Gandhi then launched nationwide campaigns during 1919 in protest against the Rowlatt legislation (which allowed trials in private without a jury) and the Amritsar Massacre. Although support was patchy, Gandhi extended his organisation from 1919 to 1920 by means of the *Khilafat* campaign, *Khilafat* being the Indian version of 'Caliphate'. Indian

Muslims demanded the preservation of the Ottoman Empire and the continued control of Mecca and Medina by the sultans. Urging Hindus to join the *Khilafat* agitation through fasting, strikes and boycotts of British imports, Gandhi largely merged his various campaigns into one during the summer of 1920.

For the British, this was a dangerous novelty, as it brought the two communities together and involved the Muslims of hitherto obscure rural districts. There were undoubtedly tensions in this relationship, not least because many rank-and-file Muslims felt no commitment to Gandhi's non-violent principles; but the campaign brought large numbers of people into politics for the first time.[21] The Muslim leaders now understood that they could bring real pressure to bear on the British if they could demonstrate Hindu backing. *Khilafat* also gave Gandhi a crucial strategic role as the leader capable of uniting Indian nationalists, and in the process he thoroughly undermined British tactics. Admittedly, the abandonment of the Caliphate by Turkey in 1924 went some way to discrediting Gandhi's strategy, but the habit of cooperation had now been established. Thereafter, the inter-war period saw a series of British instalments of reform designed to involve Indians in the system, as in 1919 and 1935, complemented by nationalist agitations, as in non-cooperation in 1920–22 and civil disobedience from 1932 onwards. But the events of 1919–20 had struck a huge psychological blow at British power, by showing that India was not as diverse as was thought, and that Congress now enjoyed the organisation and credibility to promote agitations when it wanted to, and also to fight elections success-fully when appropriate. Consequently, although Gandhi's desire for Hindu–Muslim brotherhood was over-optimistic, he retained signifi-cant Muslim support, even after the idea of a separate state for Muslims had been launched.

As the nationalist campaign gained mass support, British officialdom looked increasingly at the elements likely to counter it, notably the princes and Muslims. This led politicians such as Churchill, previously a fanatical anti-Muslim in the context of Turkey, to reinvent himself as pro-Muslim. The immediate explanation lay in his extreme hostility towards Gandhi and Congress, which he regarded as Hindu. His prejudice was underpinned by his Victorian classification system, according to which Islam enjoyed a relatively high place on account of its Judaeo-Christian origins, compared with less civilised people such as Hindus. He was much influenced by a contemporary work by Katherine Mayo, *Mother India* (1927), which attacked the social customs associated with Hinduism, as the British had in the years prior to the mutiny of 1857. In fact, Churchill knew little about the India of the 1930s, and his campaigns to prevent concessions to self-government during 1932–35 entirely failed for lack of domestic support.

Another major complication arising out of the Anglo-Turkish conflict lay in Palestine and involved a new British commitment to a long-term settlement for the Jewish people. Though ostensibly a dramatic wartime development, the origins lay in the growth of Zionism during the later nineteenth century. The idea of Zionism gained traction from the persecution suffered by Jews living in eastern Europe, especially after the assassination of Tsar Alexander II in 1881, in which some Jews were involved. The pogroms resulted in Jewish immigration into Britain and widespread sympathy for their plight. The idea of establishing a homeland for them entered British politics in 1903, as a result of a meeting between Leopold Greenberg, editor of the *Jewish Chronicle*, and Joseph Chamberlain, the colonial secretary. Accepting the principle, Chamberlain focused on where the homeland might be situated. Zionists spoke of the Sinai desert and Cyprus, but Chamberlain suggested East Africa, which was referred to as the 'Uganda Offer'. One of the leading Zionists, Dr Chaim Weizmann, moved to Manchester University in 1904, which brought him into contact with Arthur Balfour, who was then Tory prime minister and a Manchester MP, and Winston Churchill, also a Manchester Liberal MP, who was sympathetic towards the Jews. From the 1890s onwards, Balfour showed himself appreciative of the Jews, whom he described as 'the most gifted race that mankind has seen since the Greeks of the fifth century'.[22] Unfortunately, Balfour was an intellectual and a sentimentalist who never really grasped the practicalities of the idea of a homeland in

Palestine. By contrast, Gertrude Bell, who did know the country, argued 'to my mind it's a wholly artificial scheme divorced from all relation to facts'.[23] At the time, most leading British Jews believed that Jews represented a religion, not a nation, and were largely opposed to Zionism.

Despite the famous link between Balfour and the Zionist cause, much of the backing for a Jewish homeland came from Liberal sources. The Edwardian Liberal governments included three Jewish ministers, Rufus Isaacs, Herbert Samuel and Edwin Montagu. During the war, it was Samuel who put the idea before Grey, the foreign secretary, and C.P. Scott of the *Manchester Guardian*.[24] Weizmann and others advanced the argument that if Palestine became a British dependency following the disintegration of the Ottoman Empire, it would be possible to promote Jewish immigration with a view to safeguarding the Suez Canal. This was the line Samuel adopted in cabinet in 1915: Palestine could not be allowed to fall under the control of another power. In this way, Zionism was now presented as a British interest. During 1916, Weizmann became more appreciated by the government, partly because of his role in promoting the production of munitions. A high proportion of Jews volunteered to fight, and by 1917 five battalions of the Royal Fusiliers had been constituted as a distinct unit known as the 'Jewish Legion'. To the approval of the press, they marched off, keen to fight the Turks in Palestine.[25] In December 1916, when Lloyd George became prime minister and Balfour foreign secretary, Weizmann enjoyed access to the most influential men, strengthened by the new role of two Zionists, William Ormsby-Gore and Sir Mark Sykes, as political secretaries to Lloyd George.

By 1917, when British forces were close to an advance into Palestine, the future role of the Jews loomed larger. Essentially, the Zionists wanted a British protectorate over Palestine, with a view to allowing Jewish settlement there. But when the idea of a Jewish state was discussed in cabinet, it was strongly resisted by Edwin Montagu, who argued that it would undermine the position of Jews in Britain and disadvantage them in countries where they did not enjoy equal rights.[26] He pointed out that Zionism was not strongly rooted among Jews, but was essentially a product of their persecution in Russia. Curzon, conscious of the hostile reactions of Muslims in India, asked how Britain was to remove the Muslim population already living in Palestine:

> I do not myself recognise that the connection of the Jews with Palestine, which terminated 1,200 years ago, gives them any claims whatsoever. On this principle we have a stronger claim to France.

Eventually, at a meeting in October 1916, the cabinet modified the idea by committing itself to a homeland (rather than a state) for the Jews, and insisted 'nothing shall be done which may prejudice the civil and religious rights of existing non-Jewish communities in Palestine'. Even Balfour conceded that this did not imply the early creation of a Jewish state.[27]

Though less than he wanted, the Balfour Declaration was enough for Weizmann because of the prospect of a British protectorate. Now that the Russians (who had supported the French over Palestine) had dropped out of the war, it proved easier for Britain to get her way. Yet it was not quite certain what she would do. Extensive unrest among the Palestinian Arabs led many British officials in Palestine to conclude that the declaration had been a serious mistake. Their views were corroborated subsequently by recognition that it added to the injustice done to the Palestinian Arabs and initiated decades of conflict and misery in the Middle East. It ranks among the most ill-considered foreign policy statements ever made by a British government.

Despite the misgivings, however, Weizmann did his best to keep ministers up to the mark by warning them that the Germans were busily cultivating the Zionists. At the San Remo Conference in 1920, the British mandate was confirmed on the understanding that Britain would encourage large-scale Jewish immigration. The prejudice against the Palestinians among many politicians seems irrational, but it reflected the survival of Victorian notions about the hierarchy of races. And a superior group of 'real Arabs' was distinguished – the Bedouin of the desert areas, so beloved of such Englishmen as Wilfrid Blunt and T.E. Lawrence – from what were regarded as the degraded, inferior Palestinian Arabs, for whom the politicians showed little sympathy or consideration. They believed that the enterprise of the Jews would benefit Palestinians by extending greater prosperity to them.

Herbert Samuel was appointed British high commissioner in Palestine, but by 1921 he had begun to disappoint the Zionists by declaring that Britain would not allow a Jewish government to rule non-Jews. He also argued that immigration must be restricted to what was economically viable. It was a sign of Weizmann's influence that in this situation he went direct to the government and persuaded Lloyd George, Balfour and Churchill to reaffirm the Balfour Declaration. The British based their rule on an assumption that the Arabs would have to take second place to the minority community, and that the Jewish colonists 'for special reasons will be entitled to a position more than mathematically proportionate to their numbers'.[28] Somehow the British believed the two communities could live together amicably, as they had under the Ottoman Empire. All this appears hopelessly naïve, but at this stage no one foresaw either the extent to which Jews would migrate to what appeared an unattractive region or the extent of Arab desire for self-determination. By and large, the British representatives in Palestine sympathised with the Arab majority, but were usually over-ruled by pro-Zionists in London. Balfour foolishly dismissed Arab protests, saying they were 'nothing compared with what I went through in Ireland'.[29]

In 1922, Palestine had an estimated 600,000 Muslims, 83,000 Jews and 71,000 Christian Arabs. Although the number of Jews had risen to 108,000 by 1925, this represented a peak – and in 1927 twice as many left the country as arrived, largely as a consequence of the economic depression. Samuel tried to be fair in a situation in which the Jews were triumphalist and the Arabs had started organising demonstrations. However, by 1936 the Arabs numbered 983,000 and Jews 382,000 (an increase of 170,000 during 1933–36 as a result of persecution in Nazi Germany). They steadily bought up fertile farmland from the more affluent among the native Palestinians. The Arab community refused to participate in elections or to join an advisory council offered by Samuel. This may have been unwise, as it left the officials in charge and hindered any community development.

By 1936, the British were losing control of the situation in Palestine, despite the presence of 25,000 troops. They faced a general strike, attacks on the troops, the blocking of roads and the cutting of telephone wires. Britain responded by treating the Arab revolt as an internal insurrection by civilians. This meant that international law did not apply, and so the death penalty could be passed on anyone carrying ammunition. There followed a brutal suppression involving the destruction of property and livestock, the shooting and bayoneting of civilians even in villages that had not rebelled, the use of machine guns and incendiary bombs by the RAF against villages, and the torture of prisoners.[30] The London government responded by establishing a royal commission under Lord Peel, but the Arabs boycotted it. With little scope for manoeuvre between the British commitments and Arab protests, the commission opted for a partition of Palestine. When this was rejected by the Arabs, the resulting return to terrorism was brutally put down by British troops, so that by 1938 the country was effectively ungovernable. The authorities tried to suppress the rebellion by hanging leading Arabs, confining others to concentration camps and attacking them with four squadrons of Bomber Command. In desperation, the British appointed another commission, which modified Peel's report by reducing the Arab population of a Jewish territory to 38 per cent.

All this had damaging long-term results. By the late 1930s, the government was backing away from a partition altogether – so much so that a White Paper in 1939 considered establishing a Jewish homeland in a variety of places including Madagascar, Tanganyika and British Guiana. Jewish immigration and land purchase were to be severely restricted for five years. In effect, Britain had begun to distance herself from the Balfour Declaration and to alienate Zionists from British authority. Meanwhile, the Muslim Brotherhood began forming branches in Palestine during the 1940s. The effect of the mandate was that Britain was seen as the enemy of the Palestinians and of the Muslim cause more generally. After the war, the regimes in Egypt and Jordan, though Arab nationalist, helped to suppress opposition, leading to the emergence of a new Islamist movement in the form of the Palestine Liberation Organisation by the 1970s and Hamas in the 1980s.

In Iraq, Britain pursued the opposite course, as she was anxious to withdraw so as to cut defence costs. To this end, Churchill employed the RAF to bomb rebel Kurdish villages into submission, a tactic denounced by George Lansbury MP as 'this Hunnish and barbaric method of warfare against unarmed people'. As a result, agreements were reached in 1922 and 1924 to accelerate the devolution of power to King Faisal's government. Although elections were held in 1924, the system involved indirect election and the authorities ensured unopposed returns for approved candidates. The only real controversy was with Turkey over the Mosul area, but this was settled by a League of Nations commission in 1925, which left the territory with Iraq. Coincidentally, in 1925 concessions to exploit the oil around Mosul were granted to British, American, Dutch and French companies, with a share of the royalties, though not ownership, going to Iraq. However, Iraq was not yet an independent country. Not until 1932 did the British government agree to end the mandate and to promote Iraq's membership of the League of Nations – though even then it retained oil rights and military bases. From 1932, Iraq was independent, though with a pro-British government that contained British advisers. Faisal remained unhappy about the agreement with Britain, because it precluded the unification of the Arab states, to which he had always aspired. Iraq remained an unstable state split between Sunnis, Shias and Kurds, and consequently revolts among the Shias led the army into regular interventions and produced an authoritarian government. An army coup in 1936, the first of many, left the monarchy in place, but largely ended constitutional rule.

The revolts among Arabs in Palestine made Britain unpopular in both Iraq and Egypt, where an accelerated withdrawal also took place. When Turkey entered the war, Britain terminated the rule of the khedive. McMahon, the high commissioner, declared Egypt a protectorate, imposed martial law and censored the press. But it remained uncertain whether Egypt was now part of the British Empire. Egypt became a huge war camp, where 12 per cent of the troops stationed there were habitually disabled by venereal disease. Britain used Egypt as the base for launching the campaigns in the Dardanelles and Mesopotamia, which obviously enhanced the importance already attached to the country because of the Suez Canal; for the first two years of war, large British forces were tied down defending it.

Yet the military build-up did nothing to mitigate the problem posed by growing Egyptian nationalism, indeed Egyptians were naturally antagonised at being dragged into a conflict with the caliph without consultation. Farmers resented the compulsory wartime acquisition of their animals, the reintroduction of forced labour and government control of the price of cotton, which deprived them of the benefit of wartime inflation. As a result, by 1918 Egyptians had developed a new nationalist party, the Wafd, whose leader, Saad Zaghloul, demanded autonomy from the British, in line with the Anglo-French promises of Arab self-determination. When his request to be allowed to go to London to present Egyptian demands was refused, his Egyptian ministers felt obliged to resign. In 1919, Zaghloul and his colleagues were charged with sedition and exiled to Malta, an action which simply provoked extensive rioting and attacks on Europeans. The authorities stamped on any sign of revolt, including public meetings, deploying armoured cars and aeroplanes. Lloyd George sent General Allenby as the new high commissioner to maintain control, but was surprised when he sensibly released the nationalist leaders. However, this move encouraged the nationalists to demand immediate British withdrawal and did nothing to stem the revolt. The authorities were shocked when a commission of inquiry under Lord Milner recommended that Egypt should become an independent constitutional monarchy. Bit by bit, the British were being forced to recognise that they were losing the moral high ground and that the country could no longer be coerced; Allenby, Milner and Curzon had all reached the same conclusion. However, many officials still believed Britain had made too many concessions and ministers were inhibited by fears about losing control of the canal.

By 1920, the combination of Egyptian unrest and pressure from Allenby had forced Britain into negotiations over self-government conducted by Lord Milner. This was intended to be more apparent than real, in view of what Milner called 'native incompetence and corruption'. Subsequently, Britain terminated the protectorate and made a unilateral grant of independence in 1922 under the nominal control of King Faud whom the British had installed in 1917. This concession was, however, qualified by Britain's retention of control over foreign and military affairs, and by the presence of a British high commissioner until 1936. Again, Zaghloul was exiled – this time to the Seychelles. The 1923 constitution gave Egypt universal suffrage and an elected senate and chamber of deputies, although Faud, who bitterly resented being a constitutional monarch, enjoyed the right to dismiss his ministers, dissolve parliament and appoint some senators. In 1924, the Wafdists won a majority and Zaghloul became premier, though Faud and his son, Farouk, constantly tried to rule without them. Zaghloul continued to demand full independence, the withdrawal of British troops and the end of British control of the canal.

Egypt was suffering from a tripartite split between a constitutional system, an imperial presence and a king aspiring to rule autocratically. Although a new treaty was signed in 1936, Britain still maintained 10,000 soldiers in Egypt, but withdrew them to the Canal Zone and Sinai. She also retained the right to use any Egyptian ports, airports and roads in the event of war. This left Egypt in control of her own troops, intelligence and embassies for the first time; but it was a sign of the unchanging mentality that when the new king, Farouk, began talks with the Italians in 1936, his palace was promptly encircled by British tanks and he was forced to submit to cooperation with Britain or else abdicate. Not surprisingly, the Muslim Brotherhood, which was founded in 1928 by Hassan al-Banna, denounced the 1936 treaty for denying Egypt real independence.

Although Britain had no mandate in Persia, she had drawn the country into the imperial system through her entente with Russia and the Anglo-Persian Oil Company. The Russian Revolution made British control less complicated, but only temporarily. Although the region supplied only

22 per cent of British oil requirements in the late 1930s, this was expected to grow, and the government became concerned as American and French companies entered the field. As the Royal Navy was now more dependent on oil than any other navy (except for the American), the authorities intended to defend the new interest. In the absence of a mandate, Curzon argued that control must be retained by maintaining an army and influencing the Persian government. The British Resident in Persia, Sir Percy Cox, negotiated the Anglo-Persian treaty of 1919, which proclaimed the country independent – though in practice it remained subservient to Britain by virtue of loans, munitions, political advisers and army officers.

However, by this time the British were very unpopular, and the local commander, General Ironside, believed that withdrawal was the best policy. Accordingly, he gave Colonel Reza Khan to understand that he would not be resisted if he took over. Consequently, in February 1921, Reza Khan entered Teheran with his Cossack troops and was proclaimed army commander and then prime minister. In some ways, Reza's rule, which lasted until 1941, was similar to that of Ataturk, in that he promoted a modernising, secular policy. He reconvened the Majlis, which agreed to make him shah in 1926. He reduced the role of the *ulema* and the *Sharia* courts, outlawed the wearing of veils and required men to wear European clothes, including hats. In 1935, he resurrected the traditional name of the country as Iran. Yet all this did nothing to diminish the power of the Anglo-Iranian Oil Company. In 1933, Reza managed to negotiate an increase in the royalties paid to the government from 16 to 20 per cent, but was obliged to extend the concession from 1961 to 1993. He found the best way of countering British influence lay in cultivating ties with Germany, with the result that the Germans became Iran's largest trading partner, an ominous indication of her detachment from Britain during the Second World War and beyond.

In the inter-war period it became clear that Britain's relationship with Islam had reached new depths, as a result of her attempts to extract herself from the dilemma in which she had been placed by the First World War. Among the controversies, the only positive aspect was that her deteriorating relations with Turkey had been largely resolved by abandoning traditional attempts to prop that country up. Despite the revival of anti-Turk rhetoric by Lloyd George and (intermittently) Churchill, the Turks themselves had finally put things onto a stable foundation, not least by emerging as a useful buffer against Bolshevik Russia. However, beyond that Britain's meddling in the affairs of the Middle East following the dismemberment of the Ottoman Empire had introduced a raft of fresh complications, notably through her disappointment of Arab expectations. She had created a series of weak Arab states that often lacked stability and the necessary resources. Iraq was a shaky assortment of three communities. Kurdish aspirations had been frustrated. Arabia was scarcely under the control of Sharif Hussein. Egypt continued its struggle with British imperialism. Palestine had been destabilised by the Balfour Declaration. British policy towards Muslims entirely lacked consistency: it encouraged them towards nationalism in India, but tried to suppress it in Egypt, and largely failed to recognise it in Turkey. Yet the habit of interfering had become deeply ingrained because of the needs of imperial strategy and the Suez Canal, and this was accentuated by the importance of oil. The consequences were to resonate for decades to come.

CHAPTER NINE

ISLAM, DEMOCRACY AND NATIONALISM AFTER THE SECOND WORLD WAR

'There does seem to be something about Islam or at least the fundamentalist version of Islam ... that makes Muslim societies particularly resistant to modernity.'[1] Francis Fukuyama's comments in 2001 reflect the typical American prejudices of the time: but are they empirically or historically sound? Long before the outbreak of the Second World War, a number of Muslim societies had embarked on a transition towards modernised, secular, parliamentary states, and sometimes in the face of Western obstructionism. In Turkey, Egypt and Iran, for example, the process of reform had largely been blocked by Britain, rather than promoted, and any further advance was threatened by the role of Western imperialism in several countries. This makes any assessment of how far Islam was compatible with the evolution of democracy complicated, and any sweeping observations by Western commentators of dubious value. Although elective institutions have already emerged in several countries, there is a common assumption that in Muslim societies religion plays a negative part in the development of democracy; indeed, some observers uphold the idea of 'Islamic exceptionalism' – in effect the view that Muslims are uniquely resistant to liberal democracy and secularism.[2] Democratic institutions left by departing Western regimes, so the argument runs, have failed to survive everywhere except in Turkey; they have been superseded by autocracy and one-party states. Islamists in particular are thought to endorse democracy, before subsequently suppressing democratic opposition as subversive and irreligious.[3]

Another obvious limitation of the negative view is that it focuses on a few Muslim countries around the Mediterranean, and ignores those in the Far East, such as Indonesia, not to mention those that do not have a Muslim majority, such as India. Neither of those countries is consistent with the conventional assumptions. Moreover, the negative view tends to overlook the fact that Oriental societies have good grounds for regarding the Western model of parliamentary democracy as suspect – not least because the United States and Britain have a record of collaborating with Muslim autocracies and undermining and overthrowing democracies when they choose left-wing or anti-Western governments. This is notoriously the case in countries such as Iran after 1945.

Moreover, critics of Islam, seeing the question from a narrowly Anglo-American stance, fail to recognise that there is an *Asian* critique of the Western model. From the perspective of M.K. Gandhi, who was no Muslim, Western society was seen as suffering from major flaws: it was too influenced by militarism and excessively dominated by materialism. Although Gandhi appreciated many aspects of British life, he declined to participate in conventional British-style elections, which he regarded as calculated to lead to undue centralisation and to hierarchies of power. There is, of course, nothing eccentric about this critique, which has been strongly endorsed by Western feminists in recent years. Such perspectives serve as a reminder that conventional Western critiques of Islam, including academic ones, are quite narrow and often superficial.

In the short term, the Second World War made a dangerous reality of the nightmare that had long been anticipated by Britain's military forces. Her dilemma – too few resources for her extensive commitments – had been obvious since the 1890s, but prior to 1914 the Liberal governments had diagnosed the strategic problem, rearranged naval and military forces, and devised a viable plan to stop Germany seizing Paris in the early weeks of war. During the 1920s and 1930s, however, Britain relied more on bluff and on hopes that the Americans would step in eventually. She abandoned her alliance with Japan, leaving the Far East and India wide open to invasion. In the Mediterranean, the admirals were scared of the Italians, as their behaviour in the 1935 Abyssinian crisis showed. They failed to develop an expeditionary force for the Continent and faced the prospect of mass attack on their vulnerable cities and factories from bombing raids. Fortunately, Hitler never regarded an invasion of Britain as a priority, and once Britain began to out-build Germany in fighter aircraft the chances of an enemy landing became increasingly unlikely.

Yet while the Allies spent much time during the Second World War debating whether and when to open a western front (as opposed to invading Italy), and how long to leave the Russians to take the strain of the German offensives in the east, the non-European world was winning its freedom. Britain extended democratic elections in Jamaica and the Gold Coast, and made promises of independence to Malta and Ceylon. She placed troops in Egypt to retain control of the Suez Canal. In the Far East, the Japanese exploited anti-European nationalism when they swept through the Philippines, New Guinea, the Dutch East Indies (Borneo, Sarawak, the Celebes, Sumatra, Java), French Indo-China (Vietnam, Laos and Cambodia) and Burma (Myanmar) during 1942–45. For Muslims, the Japanese occupation had huge implications in 1949 when Java and Sumatra gained independence as Indonesia, the world's largest Muslim country. Although 2.5 million Indians, including Muslims, fought on Britain's side, the empire almost slipped from her grasp following the fall of Singapore, Hong Kong, Malaya and Burma in 1942. Having spent the entire nineteenth century worrying about an invasion of India across the north-west frontier, which never material-ised, Britain faced the prospect of an advance from Burma into the north-east of the country. Once a military asset, India had become a huge military liability. Moreover, British humiliations in Singapore and Europe seriously undermined the prestige on which her precarious control had rested in the eyes of Indians and many other colonial people.

The effects of these setbacks were exacerbated by official incompe-tence. A mediocre viceroy, Lord Linlithgow, declared India to be at war with Germany without any consultation. Since the Congress leaders fully endorsed the need to defeat fascism, and since Congress was now governing most of the provinces, this was an unforced error on the part of Linlithgow, who succeeded in offending those people who were cooperating with the system. He also presented the nationalists with a good excuse to return to confrontation. As some thousands of Indian troops, captured by the Japanese, were being trained to fight Britain and win freedom for their country, Britain had to make Congress a very attractive offer to retain its cooperation. However, in 1942 Churchill, reluctant to recognise the changed situation, sent Stafford Cripps with an offer of post-war independence, but on terms that allowed for the break-up of the country into several new states. Gandhi dismissed the offer as 'a post-dated cheque on a failing bank' and initiated the 'Quit India' campaign. As a result, Britain steadily lost control during the rest of the war. A major famine in Bengal undermined what little credibility she retained. Industrial strikes, mutinies in the armed forces, demoralisation among the police and rioting between Hindus and Muslims indicated that the endgame was now being played out, though without any precise plan for the terms on which independence would be granted.

In the post-1945 period, India has offered a corrective to assumptions about the supposed incompatibility of Islam with democracy. Notwithstanding its Hindu majority, India (with 150 million Muslims in 2000) is one of the largest Muslim countries in the world. How did Muslims respond to Westernisation and democracy in a society in which they constituted around 20–25 per cent of the population? Since the late-Victorian period, Indian Muslims had experienced freedom of the press, the formation of pressure groups and the organisation of non-violent campaigns designed to change government policy. They had generated three alternative strategies. One, associated with Sayyid Ahmad Khan, held that Muslims should organise to win concessions from the British; a second involved joining the national movement to oust the British; and the third involved violent opposition associated with the Wahabis, who carried out several assassinations of officials in the 1870s. Although Indian Muslims were part of an international community that looked to Mecca and the Ottoman Caliphate, they were, from 1885 onwards, also an integral part of the national movement. As early as 1888, the annual meeting of the Indian National Congress included 412 Hindus and 161 Muslims; in 1889 the meeting had 498 Hindus and 300 Muslims.

Wartime experience accelerated the evolution of Muslim politics in India in two main ways. First, Britain's conflict with Turkey enabled Gandhi to mobilise Muslims in his *Khilafat* campaign; and second, the Montagu–Chelmsford Reforms announced in 1918 expanded the provincial legislative councils, which were to be 70 per cent elected and included reserved representation for Muslims. Apart from their intrinsic importance, the reforms proved to be significant in two ways. They were not an event but a process, for they were to be reviewed and extended after ten years. Also, they failed to deflate the spirit of radical nationalism generated during the war, partly because expectations had been raised by Gandhi and partly because of several punitive actions by the British, notably the Amritsar Massacre and the Rowlatt legislation, and imprisonment without a trial for crimes of sedition.

Although the British had undoubtedly cultivated Muslim separatism as a foil to Hindu nationalism, this reflected their assumption that the Raj would last for many years to come. It did not imply a willingness to create a separate state for Muslims: on the contrary, the British felt very reluctant to split the country, the civil service, the armed forces and the finances that had been built up over decades after the confusion of the eighteenth century. In any case, the idea that the sub-continent held a Muslim nation was very slow to emerge both among the British and the Indians themselves. Muslims were divided by language and culture, by social status and by the Sunni–Shia split. Their main concentrations in Bengal and the North-Western Provinces were several thousand miles apart. And their one common rallying point, the Caliphate, had been removed by the Turks in 1924.

Although the Muslim League had existed since 1906, the demands it made were limited to increasing Muslim representation and creating new Muslim-majority provinces: there was nothing more radical. Nonetheless, successive British reforms inevitably promoted the idea of Muslims as a separate community, not least because some of their leaders argued that under a parliamentary democracy they would inevitably be disadvantaged as a permanent minority. Congress's leaders always rejected this view, on the basis that Muslims were well represented in its ranks. As late as 1929, the Muslim League leader, M.A. Jinnah, sought only a series of safeguards for Muslims under an independent India, including a federal system, residual powers for the provinces and separate electorates. The idea of a separate state for Muslims was not advanced until 1930 by Sir Mohammed Iqbal. It was to comprise the Punjab, Sind, Baluchistan and the North-West Frontier Province; to this list were added Kashmir in 1933 and Bengal in 1937. In itself, this bit-by-bit process indicates that a Muslim state was far from being an obvious goal.

A sophisticated urban lawyer, Jinnah was more attuned to Britain than to India. In 1931–33, while attending the Round Table Conference in London, he attempted to be adopted as a Labour Party candidate. When that failed, he tried as a Conservative, but was considered to be too much of a 'toff'. Jinnah was primarily a nationalist, and only nominally a Muslim. In the elections of 1937 (following the 1935 Government of India Act), the League won only 109 of the 482 seats reserved for Muslims. Subsequently, elected Muslims took part in coalitions with other parties in the new provincial governments. Thus, at this stage Muslims still appeared to be heading for a future as part of an independent, democratic India. Eventually, however, Jinnah averted this by arousing Muslim fears about their fate under a 'Hindu Raj'. The Congress leaders ignored this, naively believing that their electoral successes were an indication that Indian voters would increasingly divide on normal ideological lines, rather than on religious ones.

Not until 1940 did Jinnah and the League officially demand a separate state from the British, and even then this was widely regarded as a bargaining ploy to win further concessions. As authority collapsed in the later stages of the war, the British reluctantly conceded a modified version of Jinnah's demands; but there was nothing inevitable about it all: it simply reflected the lack of resources – and by 1946–47 of political will. However, the concession represented a blunder in the redrawing of the Islamic world, as the new Pakistan was never viable or coherent, combining as it did Bengal with the North-Western Provinces, several thousand miles apart. The Muslims of the two regions spoke different languages and enjoyed quite different cultures and traditions. Another major miscalculation by the British was to allow the existing princely states to join India or Pakistan at the whim of their rulers. As a result, the Hindu maharajah of Kashmir took his state into India, even though Muslims comprised 80 per cent of its population. This was a disastrous decision that led to Pathan troops immediately crossing the border from Pakistan, a ceasefire line in 1948 and years of instability and violence on the Indian side.

Nor did democracy in the new Pakistan prove to be a success. Elections and periods of civilian government alternated with control by the army, which was called in when the police failed to keep order and imposed martial law. Even the civilian politicians proved to be highly autocratic – starting with Jinnah, who set a precedent by grabbing all power for himself. The first civilian phase ran from 1947 to 1958, when General Ayub Khan launched a coup. Meanwhile the domination exerted by the Punjabi Muslims rapidly turned East Bengal, where the Muslim League was routed in the first elections, into a new colonial dependency. In the elections of 1970, the Awami League won 160 out of 162 seats in Bengal, while in western Pakistan the rival Pakistan People's Party won only 81 of 138. As a result, Mujab-ur-Rehman, the Awami League leader, claimed the right to form a national government. However, the west of the country had nothing but contempt for Bengalis, whom they refused to regard as true Muslims. This provoked a violent breakaway during 1971, leading to repression by the army, intervention by India and finally the creation of the state of Bangladesh.

This left Pakistan ostensibly a more coherent country, although still not entirely viable, as several provinces sought to break away. In the second civilian phase – from 1971 to 1977 – Zulfikar Ali Bhutto showed himself as dictatorial as the army had proved. His Pakistan People's Party was largely a vehicle for personal ambition, as was usual for the political parties.[4] Bhutto removed critics in favour of sycophants, intimidated opponents, used troops to suppress provincial opposition and rigged the 1977 elections.[5] When he called out the army to check the resulting protests, it sided with the generals, leading to a coup by General Zia ul Haq, who remained in power until 1988, when he died in an air crash. In a third democratic phase – from 1988 to 1999 – power was shared between Benazir Bhutto and Nawaz Sharif, she being a liberal and he pro-Islam and the army. Both faced corruption charges and used power for personal gain. In 1999, General Pervez Musharraf forced Nawaz Sharif out of power at gunpoint. Three times during this period, governments were dismissed by the head of state using Zia's Eighth Amendment to the constitution. By this time, the Pakistan army was of the view that it could allow the civilians to govern from time to time, and the standing of the parliamentary system was so low that the judiciary usually validated military intervention.

Indian experience tends to be overlooked in the dismal post-independence history of Pakistan. Despite the migration of some 5 million Muslims into the new Pakistan, independent India retained no fewer than 36 million Muslims, who became participants in the robust democracy of the new state. With an elected lower house, a nominated upper chamber and a cabinet and prime minister responsible to the legislature, Indian parliamentary democracy resembled that of Britain, qualified by the role of a president and powerful elected provincial governments that reflected regional languages and traditions. Congress remained faithful to its commitment to socialism, secularism and democracy, respecting all the religions of the sub-continent. While Lord Mountbatten briefly stayed on after independence as governor-general, Congress chose a Muslim, Dr Zakir Hussein, to be India's third president. In national elections, Muslims frequently stood as Congress candidates, but they also developed local parties in the provinces. In Kerala, for example, where a fifth of the population was Muslim, the Muslim League almost invariably participated in coalition governments. In short, any suggestion of incompatibility between Islam and parliamentary democracy is exploded by the Indian post-war experience.

Did the experience of Muslims in India hold any significance for Muslims elsewhere, or was India a special case? Indian independence involved a complete break with the past, whereas in the rest of the Muslim world Britain continued to cling to her traditional role and the complications that entailed. Although the government in the immediate post-war years was Labour, the foreign secretary – much admired even by his opponents – was Ernest Bevin, an old-fashioned imperialist, whose thinking (especially regarding Iran) was much influenced by his experience as a trade union leader trying to eliminate communist influence. Bevin's perception of Russian aggrandisement, combined with the withdrawal of American troops and his obsession with oil supplies from the Middle East, made his policy a conventional and conservative one. Unfortunately, the delusional post-victory mood carried over into the 1950s, enhanced by Churchill's return to office in 1951. Now over 80 and with attitudes derived from the 1890s, he was not well placed to promote the necessary policy adjustments. Consequently, Britain's dealings with Muslims after 1945 reflected continuity, rather than adaptation to changed circumstances. Although the loss of India actually removed one of the traditional reasons for her Middle Eastern strategy, she still regarded the Suez Canal as a uniquely British interest, despite the obvious fact that numerous other countries also relied on it for their trade. The countries of the Middle East were at most only informally part of the empire, but the British continued to assume that they should manage the region via a series of client relationships. It was as though Britain needed a substitute for India.

Continuity of outlook towards Muslim societies was obvious in the case of Iraq. Ostensibly, Iraq appeared to be a functioning democracy, with elections, parties and a free press; but the country had never had the opportunity to develop a culture of democracy. In 1921, when Britain offered a referendum on the form of government, people were puzzled. 'Why should I be involved?' one tribal sheikh was heard to enquire.[6] In the 1920s, Churchill had bequeathed a territorially incoherent country, handicapped by a defective political system presided over by King Faisal. The monarchy was autocratic, it harassed the political parties and rigged elections. Power was entrenched with the feudal

206

sheikhs, who, as late as 1950, held 35 per cent of the representation. A nominated senate was able to overthrow governments. Cabinets came and went, but each was staffed by the same collection of elderly, discredited men. The constitution could be suspended so easily that from 1931 until 1958 it became routine to rule through emergency legislation.[7] Britain could have acted to check this authoritarian system, but she conspicuously failed to do so. When elected assembly members refused to accept the 1924 Anglo-Iraq Treaty, the British intimidated them by dispersing the assembly and closing down the political parties. The British also collaborated with the government to determine the list of candidates to be returned.[8] During the Second World War, when some Iraqis collaborated with Germany and Italy with a view to winning independence, Britain suppressed them by force; nothing much mattered, other than maintaining her strategic and economic interests.

As a result, by the 1950s Iraq remained an unstable country under a political system that lacked legitimacy among its people. Eventually, in 1956 a National Union Front was formed to mobilise popular opposition and prepare for the overthrow of the monarchy. This was accomplished to popular acclaim by the military in July 1958. Iraq was declared a republic and Islam made the official religion. Yet the coup brought no stability. In 1963, the socialist-nationalist Ba'ath party seized power in cooperation with the army. Ahmad Hassan al-Bakr became president until 1979, when his deputy, Saddam Hussein, replaced him. Saddam proceeded to arrest, expel and execute his opponents, and in 1980 he plunged into a disastrous eight-year war with Iran, with the encouragement of Britain and the United States.

Britain also found it difficult to adjust to nationalism and democracy in Egypt, where the nationalists aspired to restore the Caliphate and to promote pan-Islamism through the creation of a major Arab state. However, although the Foreign Office was regarded as 'Arabist', it proved ineffective. British politicians never really understood Egyptian thinking and adopted an antagonistic approach to nationalism. After visiting the country, one American diplomat reported: 'The British are detested. The hatred against them is general and intense. It is shared by everyone in the country.'[9] This resentment had been accumulating ever since the

British occupation in 1882, surely one of the earliest – but most damaging – examples of British meddling in the Muslim world. In addition, the post-war era added three specific irritants to the relationship. First, Egyptians blamed Britain for the creation of Israel in 1948, which they saw as a betrayal of Arab aspirations. Second, they resented the incorporation of Turkey into NATO in 1952, as a ploy intended to keep the Muslim world divided. Third, they saw the Baghdad Pact of 1955 as designed to maintain Western control over the region, by ensuring that countries such as Iraq and Turkey joined it. Egypt, now the most influential Arab state, emerged as Britain's chief opponent and did its best to frustrate much of her strategy for managing the Middle East.

Yet for Anthony Eden, who was foreign secretary in 1951–55 and prime minister in 1955–57, the Baghdad Pact assumed supreme importance, because it ensured the security of the entire Middle East. In 1955, Britain persuaded Iraq and Turkey to initiate the process leading to the Baghdad Pact. But to the Egyptians, this smacked of British manipulation, a new means of extending her domination of the region. Although Pakistan and Iran subsequently joined the pact, Egypt declined to do so and used her influence to keep the other Arab states outside. When a British general visited Amman to discuss Jordan joining the Baghdad Pact, riots broke out fuelled by expressions of support for Egyptian President Nasser. Membership completely undermined Iraq's security arrangements and destabilised the monarchy, which was (as mentioned above) eventually overthrown in a coup in 1958. In effect, any association with British sponsorship proved to be a fatal flaw. By abstaining from joining, Jordan and Saudi Arabia avoided this outcome and kept on the right side of Egypt. The United States, making a similar judgement about the toxicity of the British connection, also refused to join.

Britain's dwindling influence among Middle Eastern Muslims was also reflected in Iran, where Reza Shah had openly flirted with the Nazis during the 1930s. The shah welcomed German engineers and technicians as an alternative to the much-disliked British. Consequently, the

British regarded Iran's relations with concern during the Second World War, leading to an Anglo-Soviet occupation of the country in 1941. This proved timely, for in 1942 the Germans moved south-east, hoping to take Baku and the Caucasian oilfields. The main reason for this initiative lay in the strategic importance of Iran as the best remaining link between Britain and the Soviet Union, allowing Western arms to be transported by road and rail to equip the Russian armies facing the Germans.[10]

Following the abdication of Reza Shah in favour of his son Mohammed, the monarchy protested its intention to rule constitutionally; and indeed, in 1944 Iran held elections for a genuinely representative Majlis for the first time since the 1920s. These years saw a resurgence of party-political activity, especially from the Tudeh, a communist party that campaigned against Western influence in the country. Britain antagonised communist-nationalist opinion, oblivious to the popular resentment over the high proportion of oil revenues she received. Her role was further complicated by intervention by the Americans, a rival to British influence, who were busy sending advisers and technicians and training the army.

Although all foreign troops had left the country by 1946, the government was undermined by popular demonstrations and fears that the shah intended to return to autocratic rule. In this situation, a new democratic leader, Mohammed Mossaddeq, emerged as the focus of opposition to the shah's policy. Educated in Paris and Switzerland, he was a genuine advocate of parliamentary government and freedom under the law, as opposed to the centralisation favoured by the shah. An eccentric figure, Mossaddeq smoked opium, made public appearances in his pyjamas, and delivered speeches from his bed. But he also enjoyed immense credibility as a champion of Iranian national integrity; he had left the country back in 1919 in protest against the Anglo-Persian Agreement and had been imprisoned as an opponent of Reza Shah.[11]

In 1949, Mossaddeq gathered a coalition of the Majlis deputies, known as the National Front, behind a demand for the nationalisation of Iran's oil. Since 1945, Iran had been receiving barely £6 million in oil royalties, while the British took £16 million. In 1951, the Majlis voted for nationalisation and Mossaddeq was named as prime minister. Although this was popular among Iranians, the British adopted a very intransigent attitude. The Anglo-Iranian Oil Company, supported by the Americans, imposed a blockade on the export of oil; however, as nationalisation enjoyed huge support in Iran, the Attlee government backed off. Then Churchill's return to the premiership brought Britain and America into a form of cooperation during 1952. Along with the monarchy and the army, they hatched a plot, backed by the CIA and MI6, to remove Mossaddeq from power. In 1953, he was arrested, convicted of treason and kept under house arrest until his death.[12] The Western-backed coup brought the democratic experiment to an end and led to the restoration of the shah's government.

It may be said that almost all British interventions in the Muslim world have proved counter-productive; but in the case of Iran, that would be a considerable understatement. In the immediate short term, the coup, carried out with oil in mind, actually led to a *reduction* in the British share of Iranian oil from 53 to 24 per cent. In the longer term, it identified Britain and America as the enemies of Iran. It also aroused strong anti-Western feeling throughout the Middle East, and in particular stimulated Egypt's Nasser to nationalise the Suez Canal in 1956. Few foreign interventions have proved so disastrous. The autocratic, secular and pro-American bias of the shah's rule eventually united all sections of Iranian society, culminating in widespread demonstrations and mutinies in 1978–79.[13] The shah had united Islam and nationalism in opposition to Western interference. In February 1979, he left the country, to be replaced by the Ayatollah Khomeini, who had been exiled back in 1964. The resulting Islamic Republic of Iran represented the culmination of the mistaken policy of imperialism followed by Britain and the United States since the mid-1950s. British interests would have been better served by coming to an agreement with Mossaddeq (who, after all, wanted to sell Iran's oil to the West), rather than propping up an autocratic, anti-Soviet, secularist regime. Even after 1979, however, Britain and the United States seemed unable to learn their lessons. They encouraged Iraq to attack Iran in a bloody war that lasted from 1980 until 1988.

⬤ ✿ ⬤

Britain's inability to adjust to the emergence of nationalism and modern-isation among Muslims involved her in similar disasters in Egypt. Although Egypt remained formally neutral during the Second World War, this was largely academic, as Britain quickly invoked Article VIII of the 1936 treaty, which placed all Egypt's facilities under her control; German nationals were interned and a virtual state of martial law prevailed. This would not have damaged Anglo-Egyptian relations too badly, had it not been for the Italian entry into the war in June 1940, as a result of which Egypt was bombed and General Wavell took command of the 55,000 British troops to counter the expected Italian invasion. In the crisis, the British treated King Farouk with contempt and compelled him to dismiss his pro-Italian ministers. As a result, by 1945 most Egyptians wanted Britain to evacuate her troops and to unite their country with the Sudan. They felt humiliated by the treatment of their fellow Arabs over the Palestine issue, and in consequence thousands joined the Muslim Brotherhood. The Brotherhood developed several methods for putting pressure on the British: by organising a guerrilla campaign against the troops, withdrawing the labour force from the Canal Base and denying them supplies of fresh food.

A debate then took place between modernisers and traditionalists, both stimulated by the example of Turkey. Egyptian reformers felt reluctant to follow Turkey all the way, especially in her abandonment of Islam and the Caliphate, which they believed should now fall to Egypt. In effect, the nationalists fell into two complementary camps: the 'Free Officers' in the army and the Muslim Brotherhood. Hassan al-Banna, the Brotherhood's leader since its foundation in 1928, was an orthodox Muslim not well disposed to Turkish secularism. He originally intended to revive and purify Islam. Determined to eliminate foreign oppression, he sent missions to many Muslim countries in North Africa and the Middle East. Although the Brotherhood found its early support among poor Egyptians, after 1934 it moved its headquarters to Cairo and recruited students, academics, civil servants and officers. The failure of the parliamentary system, dominated by the corrupt and pro-British

Wafd governments, promoted the growth of the Brotherhood, whose membership swelled to 2 million. In the 1930s, it had begun paramilitary training and gathering arms for a secret terrorist movement against the British.[14] In the army, the radical movement led by Colonel Gamal Abdel Nasser was less orthodox, seeking to unite pan-Islamism with secular nationalism. Though a good Muslim, Nasser was less concerned about the Caliphate and more interested in achieving Western prosperity for his country. He did, however, agree with the Brotherhood about the role of Egypt in restoring unity and power to the Muslim world after the demise of the Ottomans. From the late 1930s, the officers had been plotting to liberate Egypt from both the British and the monarchy, and by the end of the war Nasser's command of the cells in the army enabled him to achieve this.

In July 1952, a coup deposed King Farouk, and the new regime announced the end of the monarchy and the dawn of the Egyptian Republic. General Neguib became president and prime minister, with Nasser as his deputy. They initiated an agricultural revolution, by reducing rents and redistributing land from major landowners to peasant farmers. The British were irritated by the willingness of the Americans to deliver arms to the new regime in the belief that it was an effective means of checking communism in the Middle East. Reluctantly, Churchill made an agreement with Egypt in 1954 providing for the withdrawal of all remaining troops, and Anthony Eden, the foreign secretary, believed that the Egyptians would appreciate that their interests lay in cooperating with Britain. However, relations deteriorated – partly because the British bought less of Egypt's cotton, partly because of her refusal to cooperate with British plans for a Middle East Defence Organisation, and partly because of the Baghdad Pact, which Egypt saw as a way of dividing the other Arab states and of weakening her policy towards Israel. For their part, the British felt they had done their best to restore relations and were withdrawing troops, but were continually rebuffed; they failed to grasp that the rationale for the Egyptian regime lay in mobilising anti-British sentiment as a means of strengthening Arab nationalism.

Relations reached their nadir over Suez in 1956, a largely unnecessary crisis. By any realistic assessment, Britain's role at Suez was now superfluous: despite the presence of 20,000 troops, the base had become a white elephant. The Egyptians could sabotage the canal at any time by withdrawing local cooperation and sinking ships. Back in 1936, Eden had recognised that in 20 years' time Britain would have to compromise when the treaty expired. As foreign secretary, he had been the author of the 1954 agreement on withdrawal from the Suez Canal Base by 1956. A comparative liberal and a student of Oriental languages, Eden spoke Arabic and had read the Qur'an in the original; more than any other leading politician, he seemed ready to come to terms with Egyptian nationalism.[15] However, the press criticised his policy as one of scuttle; many Conservative colleagues derided it as a sell-out; and Churchill (who was heard to comment that he had not known that Munich was situated on the Nile) maliciously undermined him, both while he was prime minister and after his retirement in 1955.[16] The combination of political pressures and poor health may have led Eden to abandon his sensible, liberal instincts.

When Eden met Nasser in February 1955 things went badly, largely because the Egyptian leader felt he was being patronised. For his part, Eden remained vulnerable to criticism among Conservatives, who accused him of appeasement, a charge to which he was very sensitive; coming to office after Churchill, he felt the need to show that he, too, could see off a dictator. In March 1956, the British felt humiliated when King Hussein of Jordan dismissed General John Glubb as commander of the Arab Legion, a post he had occupied for 17 years. British reactions were over the top, for there was no reason why an independent country should employ a foreigner in such a role. But Eden saw it as symbolic of British influence and persuaded himself that Nasser had been responsible for the decision.[17] During 1956, the Egyptians continued to spread anti-British propaganda while British troops were preparing to leave, and Nasser broke his word on extending the company's concession within days of their departure.

However, Eden's reaction to these events was emotional and irrational. One official even claimed that at one point he declared he wanted Nasser murdered.[18] The Western powers then compounded the situation. Britain, the United States and the World Bank had agreed a $270 million loan to Egypt to build the Aswan High Dam, but the Americans reneged, apparently expecting to bring Nasser to heel. However, the Egyptian president responded by turning to the Soviet Union instead. He also delivered a famous speech at Alexandria in July – broadcast throughout the Arab world – in which he denounced the 74 years of colonial domination in Egypt. He entertained ambitions as an Arab leader to gain control of Sudan, Syria, Yemen and Jordan – that is, a large Arab state – and to achieve the destruction of Israel. Nasser then nationalised the canal, with compensation for the shareholders, and proposed to divert the dues raised from ships to the Aswan project. These actions symbolised Egyptian independence and Nasser's prestige; in Egyptian eyes, the Canal Company was a fraud, which exploited Egypt and left it with a mere 7 per cent of the profits.

In this situation, the British government saw the issue in terms of economics: two-thirds of West European oil passed through the canal; the Egyptians might block it by sinking ships; and in any case, they could not operate it efficiently themselves – an absurd proposition. However, British aims extended further, for the cabinet agreed that the immediate object of intervention was to destroy the Egyptian government. Although Eden bore the blame for the Suez fiasco, his leading colleagues, notably Harold Macmillan and Lord Home, both of whom subsequently became prime ministers, showed judgement just as poor when they claimed that Britain must 'not become another Netherlands' and would be 'finished' if she allowed Nasser to get away with nationalisation. The newspapers, with the honourable exception of the *Observer*, adopted a hysterical anti-Nasser line, replete with references to Mussolini and Hitler. In this mood, the cabinet threw judgement to the winds by deciding in favour of a clumsy and misguided plan for military intervention. The Israelis were to attack Egypt, allowing Britain and France to claim that the canal was in danger and thus have plausible grounds for intervention. There were sound alternatives to this madcap scheme: the issue could have been referred to the United Nations, or the Egyptians could simply have been left to run the canal (which, in the event, they did perfectly well).

However, the cabinet miscalculated by assuming American support, failing to appreciate that the interests of the United States were not directly involved. In fact, the military operation was a success, in that the Israelis captured Sinai, the Egyptian air force was destroyed and British and French troops advanced along a third of the canal. Yet despite this, the initiative rapidly turned into a fiasco. Nasser sank ships in the canal; a plan to assassinate him failed; and the United Nations censured the Anglo-French operation by a vote of 63–5. Above all, Eden's colleagues backed away – notably Macmillan, previously a hawk, who suddenly decided that oil sanctions were too great a risk. Crucially, the government was undermined by British economic weakness, in that the crisis provoked a run on sterling and the Americans declined to support the currency. In this situation, Eden lost his nerve and announced the withdrawal of the troops after only six weeks. His credibility was destroyed by the evidence that he had twice lied: first by denying any collusion to attack Egypt; and second by denying he had foreknowledge of the Israeli moves. He resigned in January 1957.

Was the Suez Crisis a major turning point? Seen in the narrow, domestic context it proved to be of comparatively minor significance for Britain. Only two junior figures, Anthony Nutting and Edward Boyle, resigned, and Eden's successor, Macmillan, proved to be adept at repairing relations with the United States when he met President Eisenhower in Bermuda in March 1957. Macmillan was largely responsible for re-creating the Special Relationship, effectively making Britain a client of the United States. But this had several damaging consequences: in particular, it resulted in Britain's exclusion from the European Economic Union by France in the 1960s. Although Britain conducted several interventions designed to slow the process of decolonisation, Suez was an exceptional case of over-reach. The disaster at Suez did not directly accelerate decolonisation, in that only three colonies gained independence in the later 1950s. However, by bringing Macmillan to power, it indirectly speeded up the granting of independence to no fewer than 26 territories in the 1960s. To some critics, this looked suspiciously like panic rather than a measured withdrawal from empire. Most of all, the crisis exposed the limitations of British power and aroused almost universal opposition; only Australia and New Zealand were willing to support the old country.

In the Middle East, the affair hugely undermined British influence, while strengthening Nasser's position in Egypt. By discrediting Britain, the crisis created a vacuum that was filled by the United States and the Soviet Union. In Iraq, Syria and Libya, pro-British regimes fell and the countries turned to the Soviet Union for aid and armaments – the very opposite of what the British had intended. Admittedly, both super-powers had already become involved, but after 1956 they enjoyed far greater opportunities. Nasser's successful defiance of imperialism made him a hero among Muslims and stimulated anti-imperialism generally in the Third World.

Conversely, it can be argued that Nasser's ambitions were checked by Suez, in that he would otherwise have gone on to take over Iraq, Jordan, Syria, Lebanon and even the Gulf States and Saudi Arabia. But such arguments seem preposterous, as they greatly exaggerate Egyptian power. More modestly, the Egyptians reopened the canal in April 1957 and Nasser granted Britain and France the right to use it on the same basis as he had offered before the crisis. Subsequently, British governments never so much as mentioned the impossible situation supposedly created by nationalisation. From this perspective, Suez offers a dramatic example of another counter-productive British intervention in Muslim affairs. Despite some concessions to Egyptian opinion, the British had persisted in seeing Egypt as a backward Muslim country and found it difficult to recognise the reality of nationalism in an Islamic state.

The fraught relations between Britain and the Middle Eastern Muslim countries in the 1950s throw some light on modern Western perspectives on Islam and its capacity to respond to Western ideas. It is tempting to start from the assumption that the development of liberal democracy is necessarily grounded in a secular society, without which it is not sustain-able. But although this idea grows out of European experience, it is hardly universal. The example of the United States – by progressive European standards still remarkably dominated by religion – immediately casts doubt on the notion. In fact, the historical evolution of liberal democracy has often been associated with religious politics, such as the Enlightenment and the European Reformation. In Britain, campaigns by radical Protestant groups, especially the nonconformist churches, from the seventeenth to the nineteenth century, promoted the idea of individual liberties, which is generally seen as integral to Western democracy. Islamic movements have sometimes fulfilled a similar role to Protestantism in promoting a transition to modernism and democracy.[19] In Islamic societies such as Turkey, Iran and Egypt, this transition occurred over a much shorter period than in Europe, and usually under the destabilising influence of external pressure.

For example, in Egypt the pressure for democracy came from the Muslim Brotherhood, which, despite its Islamic traditions, developed not as a conventional Western political party, but as a social-support, grass-roots organisation for poor people, and in the process became capable of winning popular support in elections. Starting from a base among uneducated people, the Brotherhood won backing from young, university-educated Egyptians who combined a belief in modernisation and meritocracy with Islam.[20] Islamists in countries like Egypt were alienated by the wealth and corruption enjoyed by the existing power-holders backed by the West; by contrast they adopted the moral high ground, embracing a humble lifestyle closer to the ordinary people. This was the mood that Khomeini and others capitalised upon in Iran. The experience of Egypt and Iran explains why Muslims have often felt sceptical about secularism and modernism: these policies failed, and moreover were associated with corruption, repression or imperialism. In Iraq, Britain's largely malign influence was used over many decades to suppress democracy and maintain autocracy. Muslim countries, including Turkey, Egypt and Iran, simply do not fit the Western model. In Turkey, Muslim intellectuals have been part of the movement for a liberal democratic system, and the Justice and Development Party (AKP) under Recep Tayyip Erdogan has managed to combine Islamism with a secular policy that includes joining the European Union.[21] In Egypt, observers do not recognise Islam as part of the engine leading to modernism, partly because the country appears to lack what are usually seen as the necessary preconditions for democracy: the growth of a large middle class, a market economy and rapid growth. In India, however, these changes tended to *follow* the attainment of liberal democracy rather than precede it.

Iran is commonly perceived as a classic example of an illiberal society influenced by religious doctrine, where Islam places a check on the trend towards democracy. Yet Iran enjoyed a period of democratisation that was abruptly terminated in 1953 by a Western-backed coup designed to restore the monarchy. The subsequent phase of repression and modernisation naturally stimulated the rise of political Islam, because it offered the obvious vehicle for resisting autocracy. Similar experience affected many Muslim countries – from Algeria to Tunisia, Iraq, Syria and Yemen. In Iran, the events of 1951–53 had the effect not only of alienating many young people from the shah, but also of disillusioning them with politics and reform generally. It was almost inevitable that they would to some extent return to religion as an alternative, more authentic, means of expression. As the shah rigged elections, disbanded the National Front and employed the CIA and the Israeli secret service, Mossad, against opponents, he only compounded the reaction against Western values. The Western powers have exacerbated things by routinely backing autocratic regimes against elected ones in Egypt, Iran and Palestine, where they supported the secular Mahmoud Abbas and his Fatah party against the elected Hamas government in 2007.

In some ways, Indonesia offers the most striking case of Islamic adaptation to liberal democracy in the post-1945 world. With 231 million people, of whom 90 per cent are Muslim, it is the largest Muslim country. By comparison with the countries of the Middle East, it has always practised a flexible version of Islam, as the people have always blended Hindu, Buddhist and local religious practices with those of the Muslims; Java in particular was regarded as only nominally Muslim. However, during the later nineteenth century, resentment towards the alien rule of the Dutch had the effect of strengthening the influence of Islam, which became the rallying-point for protest. Symptoms of this included the prominence of Arab traders and an increase in the numbers undertaking the pilgrimage to Mecca. The Dutch authorities, who were ignorant of Islam, imposed new regulations designed to obstruct the

Hajj.[22] The pilgrims were exposed to a much stricter Muslim environment than they were used to, and they were impressed both by the extent of Islam and by the oppressive attitude of European powers towards it. After 1918, the number of pilgrims to Mecca continued to increase, reaching 52,000 by 1926. Muslims also became increasingly critical of cultural penetration by Europeans, and especially by Christian missionaries. As a result, Islam played an increasing role in Indonesia's political evolution. By the 1930s, a number of Muslim organisations had emerged; but they were eclipsed by the communist party creating thereby a political base for Indonesian Islam. During the 1940s, Muslim support was mobilised by three organisations: the Nahdlatul Ulama, a traditional Islamic body; Masjumi, a modern Islamic socialist party; and Darul Islam, which opposed the government by violent means. The first two aimed at a government that would promote Muslim values and embody Islam in the national constitution.[23]

Its rich array of natural resources made Indonesia attractive to the Japanese during the Second World War, but the brutal requisitioning of labour and food supplies greatly accelerated demands for independence. As a result, within days of the Japanese surrender an Indonesian republic was proclaimed; and although the Dutch returned to their former colony, the country finally won its independence in 1949. Sukarno was elected president in 1945 and 1955, but he declared martial law and maintained a military dictatorship until 1965. His successor, President Suharto, continued his system until 1998. After independence, Sukarno promulgated a new religious ideology known as the Pancasila. Although his intention was to marginalise the communists, many Muslims reacted against the ideology, seeing in it a threat to the pre-eminence of Islam as the official religion of the country. However, an attempted communist coup in 1965 forced Muslims to cooperate with the government, and Muslim organisations subsequently worked with the army. President Suharto attempted to curtail Islamic influence by reducing Muslim control in education and marriage, backing the Pancasila and outlawing the Masjumi party. In consequence, from 1966 to 1998 Islam became a key force in resisting Suharto's repressive regime.[24] Radical Islamic groups came out in violent opposition. Eventually Suharto restored

Muslim influence and several Muslim parties agreed to accept the Pancasila. After Suharto's overthrow in 1998, Indonesia adopted a form of proportional representation. Every five years the assembly meets to select a new president and modify the constitution. In this way, Indonesia has emerged as a classic case of a tolerant, secular society with a liberal democratic system, but that is at the same time Islamic. That it attracts little attention in the West is symptomatic of the biased perspective on Islam.

CHAPTER TEN

MUSLIMS AND THE CRISIS OF BRITISH NATIONAL IDENTITY

In the Victorian period, Muslims commonly arrived in Britain as merchant seamen or as students from India; but of the 8,000–10,000 Muslims living in Britain by 1945, as many as 5,000 were thought to be converts rather than immigrants.[1] By 1914, the most significant concentrations of Muslim immigrants were Arab seamen from Yemen, the Aden Protectorate and Somaliland who had arrived at ports including Cardiff, South Shields, Liverpool and Hull. Like other seamen, they were badly exploited by the ship-owners who routinely overloaded unseaworthy vessels that frequently sank. They also faced demands from the National Union of Seamen for their deportation. Originally temporary workers, the Arabs were mostly young men, but by the inter-war period they had become residents. In South Shields, they associated with local women, who often found them attractive and married them, thereby generating moral panics, protests about 'half-caste' children and segregation via slum clearance and re-housing schemes.[2] However, the Arabs played a major part in the national effort as merchant seamen in both world wars, and during the post-1945 period prejudice against them dwindled through sheer familiarity. In the North-East they obtained employment in iron and steel and were re-housed all over South Shields, rather than being concentrated in limited districts. Young Arabs adopted local customs and values and frequently used the surnames of their English mothers.[3] In effect, they largely lost their Arab and Muslim identity and disappeared into the local community.

However, after the Second World War these long-standing Arab communities were overtaken by much more extensive Muslim immigration from the Punjab and Bangladesh, mostly comprising young single men attracted by economic opportunities in the textile industry and in catering. In addition, smaller numbers, driven by political instability, arrived from Turkish Cyprus, Yemen, Somalia, Eritrea, Egypt, Iraq and, in the 1970s, from East Africa, where successful Muslim businessmen faced discrimination from the Ugandan and Kenyan governments. Despite pressure from within the Conservative Party to restrict immigration, the governments of the 1950s felt reluctant to intervene – partly for fear of antagonising the Commonwealth and partly because they recognised the economic value of immigrant workers, who had proved vital in keeping public transport and the National Health Service going. Although many came from a background in agriculture, they showed the characteristic flexibility of immigrants, by filling gaps and by starting small businesses especially in shopkeeping, restaurants, the wholesale trade and taxi-driving. The competitive pressure on corner shops and the long hours of work created opportunities for immigrant families to fill. In Dewsbury, for example, 37 off-licences were run by a few Pakistani families, even though they were themselves mostly teetotal.[4]

However, the politicians succumbed to pressure for restrictions in 1962, by which time a more sluggish economy had reduced the need for labour. They enacted the Commonwealth Immigrants Act. Yet, as an attempt to limit immigration, it proved a complete failure. The Act provoked a rush of entries before it came into force, and it also provided for the admission of relatives of those already here. The result was an increase in Muslim immigration from the Indian sub-continent: between 1955 and 1960 there were only 17,000 immigrants from Pakistan, but during the 18 months prior to the 1962 Act some 50,000 arrived. The legislation also caused a major change in the character of the community: originally largely single men in temporary residence, it became dominated by permanent families. The change was accentuated by the fact that many immigrants came from quite small areas, such as Mirpur in Pakistan and Sylhet in Bangladesh, and also by the *Biradari* system, whereby new immigrants joined people from their local villages, clans or extended families. This had the advantage of creating a means of material support and reassurance in the face of discrimination, but also had the effect of isolating them from the host community.

Nor did the 1962 legislation do anything to reduce racial discrimination; on the contrary, it legitimised the exploitation of anti-immigrant sentiment by Conservatives, especially in the West Midlands prior to the general election of 1964. The Birmingham Conservative leaders deliberately made immigration a major issue in 1964, thereby gaining a 4.2 per cent swing in their favour at an election in which the national trend favoured Labour; in 1964, the Conservatives won three seats in this way – at Smethwick, Perry Barr and Slough. The most notorious of these was Smethwick, where virulent anti-immigrant propaganda over several years was backed by the local newspaper, and even the Labour Party operated a colour bar.[5]

On the other hand, at the national level the political parties engaged in a truce for several years, as they felt embarrassed about the 1962 Act and anti-immigrant propaganda. However, this was dramatically disrupted in 1968 by a notorious speech delivered by a senior Conservative, Enoch Powell, who claimed that attempts to restrict immigration had failed; he warned that 5 per cent of the population would be 'coloured' by 2000.[6] Powell used inflammatory language, repeated unsubstantiated anecdotes about immigrants, prophesied violence and advocated voluntary repatriation. But above all, he regarded immigration as a threat to British culture and tradition, frankly refusing to accept that anyone with a black face could be British – a claim that now seems almost bizarre, but at the time was widely accepted. Admittedly, the Tory leader, Edward Heath, sacked Powell; but his outburst gave further respectability to prejudice, and opinion polls suggested that anything between 67 and 82 per cent of voters endorsed his views.

Thereafter a succession of right-wing extremist parties emerged to mobilise this opinion, beginning with the National Front, which was formed in 1967 and openly voiced racist opinions. As a result, there was an increase in attacks on black and Asian people. By 1976, the National Front had initiated provocative marches through the Muslim districts of Bradford, and subsequently their tactics were copied by the British National Party and the English Defence League. Between 1978 and 1987, 49 Asians were the victims of racist killings, but the police usually ignored racist violence and were more inclined to arrest the victims than the perpetrators.[7] This led young Muslims to conclude that the older generation had passively accepted discrimination for too long. But as yet it was difficult for them to use the political system to defend themselves, not least because the Labour Party, in power from 1964 to 1970, was effectively two parties on the issue. In 1968, Labour's home secretary, James Callaghan, afraid of losing working-class votes, restricted the entry of Kenyan Asians unless they could prove a 'patrial' tie with a British resident. On the other hand, Harold Wilson's Labour government passed the Race Relations Act in 1965, which established the Race Relations Board with a view to giving legal redress against discrimination in housing and employment. As home secretary, Roy Jenkins strengthened the Act to cover indirect discrimination, and promoted equal opportunities, accepted cultural diversity and enjoined mutual tolerance. In effect, the politicians had recognised the need to take some deliberate steps to protect immigrant communities, to foster their own cultures and to check popular prejudice against them – even while pandering to it. In the long run, the legislation proved to be a success in discrediting racial discrimination in Britain.

The census published in 1982 estimated a Muslim population of 690,000, including 371,000 from Pakistan, 93,000 from Bangladesh and 63,000 from Arab countries. This rose to around a million by 1991, and 2 million by 2000. Muslims had largely settled in London's East End, Lancashire, Yorkshire, the West Midlands, Clydeside and South Wales. Ready to work for low wages, they supplied a labour force for declining textile towns such as Dewsbury, Huddersfield, Blackburn and Burnley. In order to find security, housing and employment, immigrants had followed their families and had thus become concentrated: by 2002, Muslims comprised 11 per cent of the population in Manchester, 15 per cent in Birmingham, 17 per cent in Bradford, 12 per cent in Leicester and 14 per cent in London.[8] The impact of this concentration was accentuated by the role of popular newspapers, including the *Sun*, *Daily Mail*, *Daily Express* and *Star*, which over several decades focused attention on the supposed threat posed by the ethnic communities. On successive days in December 2000, the *Mail* ran alarmist headlines: 'The British Cities Where Whites Will Be in the Minority' and 'Babyboom That Could Put Whites in the Minority'.[9] The effect of years of press propaganda was to instil an exaggerated idea of the extent of immigration in the minds of many people. As a result, by 2014 the public believed that Muslims alone comprised 21 per cent of the UK population, when the true figure was under 5 per cent.[10]

Alarmist reporting about the threat to British traditions was symptomatic of the politics of nostalgia, a tactic that helped proprietors to sell popular newspapers in a dwindling market. However, something more sinister was also at work. The populist press employed an age-old strategy designed to serve the political ends of its proprietors and editors. It had long been used to some effect in the United States, where the condition of the poor whites in the South had been exploited by blaming the equally poor blacks, when the true interests of both lay in combining against the reactionary forces that held them back. Similarly, in Britain most newspapers were owned by wealthy (and often foreign) entrepreneurs who were anxious to maintain right-wing governments and the tax advantages they brought. This required keeping disadvantaged people in all sections of society divided from one another. There were several ways of doing this: for example, by exploiting the fears of men about female employment; pitting employees who suffered from dwindling private pensions against those who retained state pensions; setting home owners against those who rented council houses; and playing those who refused to work in low-paid jobs off against those who did. The resentment thus aroused helped avert the danger that the disadvantaged would combine at the ballot box to vote for a more equal society. Muslims became natural victims of this strategy during the later decades of the twentieth century because of their relative poverty. The effect was exacerbated during the 1980s and 1990s, as Britain moved back into an era of mass unemployment and skilled manual jobs disappeared. As late as 2016, when overall unemployment stood at 5.4 per cent, it was 12 per cent among Muslims.

However, by the 1970s, many Muslims were no longer *immigrants*, as they had been born in Britain; and by 1994, 52 per cent of people of Pakistani descent and 44 per cent of Bangladeshi descent were British born and spoke with the accents of Yorkshire, Lancashire and the East End. They were also young: 47 per cent of people of Pakistani origin and 43 per cent of those of Bangladeshi origin were under 16. As a result, they were in many ways accommodated to British society; for example, 78 per cent of Pakistani men and 75 per cent of Bangladeshi men were rated competent in English.[11] Despite their experience of prejudice, they became involved in a gradual process of integration into mainstream society; in this period they largely thought of themselves as 'black' or as Asians, rather than as Muslims. While this seems to be at odds with received views about the Muslim community as different and separate, it overlooks the common ground and the interaction. Growing up in the Yorkshire textile town of Dewsbury during the later 1970s, Sayeeda Warsi became very familiar with the local culture through her school friends and her English neighbours. She was aware of the differences between the communities and her Pakistani heritage, but also developed aspirations to participate in mainstream British society. Her father had arrived in 1962, expecting to return 'home' eventually to a house in Islamabad. But that was 'an experiment which for almost everybody failed'; meanwhile he acquired a family, built up a business and became committed to life in Britain.[12] This was promoted by her mother, who took English classes, learned to drive and encouraged her daughters to go to university. 'My parents embraced and encouraged us to embrace what they saw as good within Britain, always keen for us to experience what they viewed as moments of great advancement. A family outing to the newly opened Humber Bridge was one such moment.'

In addition, first-generation British Muslims had been fairly relaxed about social behaviour and religious observation; most of the men wore European clothes, while some consumed alcohol and engaged in pre-marital sex. However, the growth of the female population after 1962 had the effect of reinforcing the most distinctive aspect of Muslim society as a community squarely based on a conventional family life. That meant avoidance of drugs, low alcohol consumption, female modesty and dislike of sexual excess. Yet none of this represented a problem or a challenge to convention. Muslim marriage was very stable, with divorce rates of around 3–4 per cent, and very few babies were born out of wedlock.[13] In short, their social habits placed Muslims comfortably within the conventional, even traditional, British value system.

Nor was Muslim experience particularly unusual, as Britain had an established record of accepting immigrant communities – notably the Irish during the Victorian era and the Jews from the 1890s onwards. The Jewish community, which numbered around 300,000 by 1914, was allowed to retain and cherish its own culture, establish its own organisations, and develop distinctive roles in business and employment, while also participating as British citizens through politics, trade unions, the media, sport and the armed forces. This was symptomatic of British *multiculturalism*: by 1900 it was a British tradition, though the term was not then used. Even earlier, a similar approach had been adopted towards the Welsh by Gladstone, who deliberately cultivated the distinctive language, education and culture of Wales, while involving the Welsh people in British national institutions. The success of multiculturalism became evident in the contribution that Jews made to the national effort in times of national crisis, including the Boer War and the First World War, in which 41,000 Jews volunteered to fight.[14] In 1951, the Mass Observation surveys reported that although anti-Semitism had not disappeared, most people accepted that Jews fitted comfortably into British society. The experience of Muslim immigrants since the 1950s has been similar to that of earlier Irish and Jewish arrivals, involving settlement focused on certain towns, the creation of community organisations, a gradual increase in employment and education, legal protection against discrimination, and participation in national politics. Nor is the British approach as eccentric as the controversy over multiculturalism suggests. Today Australia boasts that it is the world's most successful multicultural society, while in 1988 Canada actually passed a Multicultural Act as a way of promoting national identity. However, as contemporary critics of multiculturalism are not very familiar with British history, this pattern of accommodation has not been widely recognised.

The second generation of Muslims were not in Britain as temporary economic migrants, and consequently were less passive than their predecessors, more confident and aware of their opportunities and rights in Britain. For them, integration into mainstream society went hand in hand with an increasing assertiveness in the face of prejudice and an awareness of their identity as Anglo-Asians. By the 1980s and 1990s, the younger generation were becoming alienated from their parents due to familiarity with a secular society; many regarded the world of the mosque as boring. Sayeeda Warsi became aware of differences with her parents: 'The famous double life that many young Asians lived was tiresome . . . We were staying. Britain was home, it's where I belonged, it's where I wanted to matter.'[15] Inevitably, the behaviour of the communities began to converge. For example, by 1990, 54 per cent of Pakistanis and Bangladeshis were in non-compulsory education, compared with 56 per cent among the white population. There was a sharp fall in family size, another indication of a gradual adoption of local behaviour.[16] Muslims also began to reflect mainstream practice in other ways: more women in their twenties remained unmarried and, with their better language skills and qualifications, they were more likely to be in paid employment. One young woman with a job in the City explained: 'I may be Muslim and Pakistani by origin. But I am British. I want money, the good life, the works. I love the West, the freedoms and the lack of hypocrisy.'[17] Some Muslim women used the *hijab* as a way of symbolising their female identity, resisting the pressure to adopt wholly Western dress and indicating to Muslim men that they must be treated with respect.[18] This was an intelligent way of demonstrating their qualified acceptance of the culture of both societies, rather than a sign of their subordination.

Other Muslims developed different but viable compromises between the complete adoption of British customs, on the one hand, and the retention of their traditions on the other. The cricketer Mushtaq Ahmed, for example, worked in England from 1995 and initially adapted almost too well to his new life. However, he eventually decided that he was neglecting his family and was succumbing to the excessive materialism and extreme liberalism of British society.[19] In the event, he rediscovered his religion and settled down in the belief that it was possible to be a devout Muslim *and* to adapt to British life. Mushtaq Ahmed's experience was indicative of the fact that Muslims were primarily a family-oriented community and could be offended by the materialism, alcoholism, female immodesty and flagrant sexuality typical of modern Western society. But did this attitude represent a threat, or did it give Muslims the potential to reinforce traditional British values? The confusion was unintentionally reflected by the *Daily Mail*, which reported in 2000 on the case of an English girl who had left home voluntarily to live with an Asian family, subsequently became a Muslim and married a university-educated Muslim computer engineer. She explained that she was happy about dressing modestly, not having sex before marriage and 'knowing for certain that my husband would never look at another woman and not drink or gamble'.[20] She may have been reacting against the experience of her mother, who had had two broken marriages, and anticipated a more stable and domestic life in Muslim marriage. However, the *Mail* ran the story under a typically crass headline: 'My Daughter Was Seduced by Islam'. It reported that she wore 'long shapeless clothes' and was 'already tied down with a baby'. In effect, she had adopted the conventional values and the lifestyle commended to readers by the *Mail*! But the newspaper refused to recognise this, as it hardly fitted with its Islamophobic agenda, designating Muslims as a threat.

⬣ ❈ ⬣

In many ways, the early generations of Muslims managed to effect a limited accommodation with British life by filling gaps in the labour force, starting small businesses and adopting some of the social habits of the host community. They practised Islam, but were not ostentatiously Muslim. Unfortunately, during the 1980s this process of gradual assimilation began to become complicated, though not completely disrupted, by a combination of underlying political trends and dramatic short-term contingencies. The period saw a renewed attack on immigrants generally by the New Right. As premier between 1979 and 1990, Mrs Thatcher helped to legitimise fears about what she called 'swamping' by immigrants. Tirades about multiculturalism in reactionary journals like the *Salisbury Review* became a routine feature of the decade. This encouraged a succession of extreme Islamophobic organisations to move in from the margins to seek wider respectability and support. Back in the 1950s, the League of Empire Loyalists had recruited Sir Oswald Mosley's former supporters and a few Tory MPs, but it soon petered out. It was followed by Colin Jordan's White Defence League, which was overtaken by the National Front in 1967 and later by the British National Party, UKIP and the English Defence League. Provoked by economic decline, a feeling of betrayal by the Conservative leaders for taking Britain into the European Union, and an underlying sense that Britain was losing her national identity, their recruits began to gain a footing in the mainstream. They raised the question: can you be Muslim and British simultaneously? Eventually this pressure had the effect of forcing many Muslims to begin to identify themselves more as *Muslims*, which they had not generally done previously. This was not the result of multi-racial policies, whose impact was actually slight, but simply of the pressure of underlying trends and events.

Consequently, the explanation for the deterioration in relations between Muslims and British society during the later decades of the century cannot be found simply in terms of religion, as it was one symptom of a wider malaise in a society struggling to retain its national identity, handicapped at one level by underlying economic and political trends and at another by the impact of immediate contingencies. Among the former, it is significant that the effects of Mrs Thatcher's economic experiment during the 1980s and 1990s involved two major economic depressions and the eventual loss of around 2 million manufacturing jobs in steel, coal, engineering and shipbuilding. This had huge social and political consequences for a whole generation whose fathers had enjoyed well-paid, skilled, manual employment, but found themselves caught in a dilemma: they were under-qualified for work in the expanding service industries and unwilling to accept poorly paid work in the agricultural, retail and hospitality sectors. An almost inevitable result was a search for scapegoats, in the shape of immigrants, for depriving them of employment; though in reality, the work undertaken by immigrants was either in areas like engineering and construction (where Britain failed to produce enough qualified people) or in sectors where pay was so low and conditions so hard that British workers refused to accept them. The resulting sense of grievance was accentuated by another by-product of the Thatcher–Blair era involving a huge increase in the cost of housing, the sale of 1.5 million council houses (many of which passed into the hands of buy-to-let landlords who charged exorbitant rents) and restrictions on local authorities that prevented them from replacing the lost houses. This was another social disaster, creating a generation that found it difficult either to obtain social housing, to afford private sector rents, or to take out mortgages. A generation that had taken home ownership for granted saw it slipping away. Again, it proved all too easy to claim that immigrants were being favoured in housing, when in fact they shared a common interest in measures to check rent rises and policies to build social housing.

Among the immediate contingencies affecting the Muslim community was the publication in September 1988 of Salman Rushdie's book, *The Satanic Verses*. The author already enjoyed a reputation for provocation arising from *Midnight's Children*, which led Indira Gandhi to sue for libel on behalf of her father, Jawaharlal Nehru. In *The Satanic Verses* Rushdie went further, treating the Qur'an as the work of Mohammed masquerading as the Prophet of God. He gave a fictional account of the origins of Islam in which he resurrected a term used by medieval Christians – 'Mahound' – for the Prophet. Rushdie had not written a measured criticism of Islam, but a deliberately derogatory account, an unpleasant throwback to an earlier era. Muslims justifiably regarded it as insulting to the Prophet and to their religion.

Admittedly, *The Satanic Verses* became available in most Muslim countries, the chief opposition to it emerging from India and Saudi Arabia. The book assumed much greater significance in 1989, when the Ayatollah Khomeini issued a *fatwa* against it and a price was put on Rushdie's head. In this situation, the publishers, Penguin, rebuffed pressure to withdraw the book, while the British government managed to get the worst of both worlds by resisting pressure to ban the book, while also criticising Rushdie. They felt rather torn, in that they disliked Rushdie for his betrayal of his religion and his adopted home, but were also reluctant to respond to Muslim feelings because they saw Iran as the chief force behind the campaign. In effect, neither liberal opinion nor Muslim sentiment was placated.

The Rushdie affair proved to be a damaging episode, which has been regarded as a watershed for the British Muslim community. Muslims asked why the government failed to extend the laws on blasphemy to cover their religion, as well as Christianity. The problem lay in the fact that by this time, many people regarded the blasphemy laws as anachronistic and were thus slow to appreciate how strongly Muslims felt; they had been caught in the evolution of Britain into a largely secular society. But the resulting sense of grievance among Muslims remained strong. Sher Azam, chairman of the Bradford Council of Mosques, summed up its significance: 'We used to have questions about who we are and where we were going. Now we know. We've found ourselves as Muslims.'[21] In this way, the affair united several generations and led some young Muslims who had previously been non-religious and comfortable with British culture to reconsider their identity. Previously, they had regarded themselves as 'black', not even as Asian, let alone as Muslims; Rushdie forced them for the first time to respond to the pressure to choose between rival loyalties and make a commitment to Islam.[22]

Another by-product of the refusal of the government to ban *Satanic Verses* or to extend the laws on blasphemy to cover Islam was to stimulate attempts to promote an umbrella organisation for Muslims. In 1992, Kalim Siddiqui advocated the creation of a Muslim parliament, on the basis that Muslims' interests were being neglected, their values were under attack, and their self-confidence required restoration. However, the parliament was not elected and nor was it regarded by most Muslims as representative; indeed it looked like a way of discouraging Muslims from entering mainstream politics.[23] By the time of Siddiqui's death in 1996, the Muslim parliament had failed to mobilise enough support. However, after further rebuffs from the government a new Muslim Council of Britain (MCB) was formed that year to represent all Muslim opinion. This was comparable to earlier Jewish initiatives in founding the Board of Deputies of British Jews.

Between 1997 and 2005, the MCB enjoyed positive relations with the government and was consulted by officials. By 2016, it represented some 500 mosques, schools and charities, and its opinions were widely quoted in the press. However, the MCB fell out with the Labour government over its support for Hamas and Tony Blair's pro-Israeli sympathies. In 2016, David Cameron's government, reacting to the shock of the 7/7 attacks in 2005, decided that it was too 'Islamist' – meaning too critical of official policy – to be genuinely representative of Muslim opinion. It was inevitable that the MCB would create some distance between itself and the government, gaining more credibility among Muslims from official disapproval. Offended by the continuous stream of negative and inaccurate reports about Muslims, the council began to seek corrections from media organisations, though with only limited success: by the end of 2016, 20 retractions had been won and a further 20 were being considered by the press regulator. In 2016, the MCB decided to challenge the government's Prevent strategy, which was designed to check recruits to terrorism, by launching its own programme. It argued that Prevent imposed an ideological test that cast all critics of foreign policy as extremists or potential terrorists. In time, the scope of the MCB was extended. In 2018, it joined with the Board of Deputies of British Jews and 60 bishops of the Church of England to demand the scrapping of the government policy that allowed families to claim tax credits only for their first two children; all three religious leaders argued that this was responsible for increasing child poverty.[24] In effect, the emergence of such organisations signified that Muslims were moving into the political mainstream. While maintaining an independent organisation, they were also adopting an alternative or complementary strategy for raising their political profile, by working through the conventional political parties.

Yet although the experience of Muslims in British society in the late twentieth century resembled the earlier experience of the Jews and the Irish in some ways, there was one major historical difference. When immigrants arrived in Britain between the 1850s and the 1920s, they encountered a country still in its heyday as a great industrial, naval, imperial and monarchical power, enjoying a secure idea of its national identity, its political system and its purpose as a nation. However, during the 1970s, 1980s, 1990s and the early 2000s, this confidence largely unravelled as the institutions that had sustained national identity disappeared or became discredited, traditional values dwindled, loyalty to the Union broke down, and the external role of the United Kingdom became a matter for deep division. This had the effect of leaving British society much more vulnerable and uncertain about how to respond to new arrivals, changed conditions and Britain's reduced status in the world. These doubts were crystallised by the celebrations for the Millennium, which forced the British to look back into their past and forward to a future as a middle-ranking European power – a prospect that many older people simply refused to accept.

In this situation, Muslims found themselves caught in the crossfire. Religion certainly comprised one aspect of the dilemma over national identity – not because of any direct clash between Islam and Christianity, but because the arrival of Muslims in large numbers coincided with a period in which the churches were in headlong decline. In 2016–17, some 52–53 per cent of Britons told the British Social Attitudes survey that they had no religious affiliation. Only 1.1 million people, or 2.6 per cent of the population, regularly attended Church of England services, an embarrassing position for the Established Church. Just 14 per cent identified with Anglicanism, 8 per cent with Catholicism, 10 per cent with other Christian denominations and 8 per cent with non-Christian faiths.

This decline triggered a counter-attack against the threat of secularism and the demise of Christian marriage and conventional morality. Propagandists of the extreme right invariably claimed to be defending Britain as a Christian country against foreign influences, ignorant of the fact that the trend to a more secular society pre-dated the arrival of Muslims by many decades. As long ago as 1836, Britain introduced civil marriage and emancipated all religious groups from the Anglican monopoly; Jewish marriages could be registered by the Board of Deputies of British Jews – an early case of multiculturalism. In 1857, divorce was removed from the traditional control of the church courts and placed into the civil sphere. The role of the Church in education was gradually whittled away by the Education Act of 1870, the extension of secondary education and the opening of university education to non-Anglicans. The massive development of commercial leisure activities added to these symptoms of a long-term shift towards a secular society. As a result, by 2000 no one could plausibly claim that the Anglican Church any longer exercised a significant influence over morals and behaviour in Britain; at best it followed social trends by accepting female clergy, homosexual relationships and marriage for divorcees. Anglicanism's political role as the Established Church was also undermined, as it had lost its traditional authority on the right wing of politics, where it was regarded as too liberal. Its surviving political role in the shape of 26 bishops sitting in the House of Lords had become a complete anachronism, barely obscuring the fact that Anglicanism had practically ceased to be the national Church.

Consciousness of this weakness in conventional religion left many people very sensitive to what appeared to be a fast-growing religion, thereby corroborating claims about Islam subverting Western culture. Symptomatic of this reaction were the efforts to prevent the building or opening of new mosques. At Golders Green, proposals to convert the old Hippodrome into a community centre and mosque in 2017 were attacked by local Jews as dangerous and likely to 'result in violence and terrorism'. Yet it had been used by Christian Evangelicals for ten years before being bought for a Muslim centre.[25] In 2018, a Leeds businessman raised £60,000 to renovate a derelict building in Stornoway, on the Isle of Lewis, and use it as the first mosque on the Outer Hebrides to serve a handful of families, including some refugees from the war in Syria. This was opposed by the Free Church of Scotland (Continuing). According to the Rev. David Blunt:

> We object to the promotion of all false religion . . . If a mosque ever opens, Islam will be able to promote itself in our midst through public worship, despite its belief and practices being alien to the religious convictions of the vast majority of our community. Islam is also incompatible with, and indeed a threat to, our religious and civil liberties.[26]

These intolerant remarks, reminiscent of medievalism, underlined the isolation of the reverend and his ignorance about Islam. In fact, local opinion was generally supportive. James Maciver of the Free Church of Scotland, which has the largest congregation on Harris, welcomed local Muslims for integrating well: 'I come at this from the point of view of liberty of conscience . . . I have no right to come between someone's conscience and their god.' His remarks were a reminder that objections to building mosques were sporadic rather than systematic. However, the negative view was symptomatic of Christianity on the defensive. It helps to account for the anger and frustration expressed in the *Daily Mail* in 2000 because Britain failed to mark the Millennium by celebrating 2,000 years of Christianity.

Fears about the decline of Christianity also generated absurd scare stories, of which the most entertaining and long-running involved a supposed conspiracy to suppress the traditional Christmas with something called 'Winterval'. The notion arose in 2000 in the *Mail* which found it a useful weapon with which to attack Labour local authorities.[27] But when BBC Radio Four investigated no fewer than 17 reports of the introduction of Winterval, they were completely unable to find any factual basis for the claims! It was, in any case, an inherently absurd idea, as Jesus had always been honoured by Muslims as one of the great prophets, and although Muslims disagree over whether it is acceptable to celebrate the Prophet's birthday, some Sunnis do so. However, the

Winterval idea was like other pieces of popular fiction, such as the 'Angels of Mons' in the First World War; it endured because some people wanted to believe it.

Yet if the alarmists and Islamophobes had had a better knowledge of British history, they would have had no difficulty in seeing where Winterval stood in the evolution of the British Christmas. The authors of the secular British Christmas were really the Victorians, who pioneered the indulgent, modern penchant for Christmas cards, Christmas crackers, Christmas trees and Christmas shopping. By 1890, commercialism was so advanced that the *Jewish Chronicle*, a completely patriotic and pro-English publication, explained to its readers that the purely Christian meaning of Christmas was now somewhat in the background: 'The great winter festival . . . is in these days far less a religious than a national institution.'[28] The newspaper urged Jews simply to share Christmas with their Christian neighbours, especially as agnostics celebrated it as much as anyone else.

However, the *Mail*, never deterred by lack of evidence, was reluctant to lose a good story. It reported: 'Stores Attacked over Christmas Opening', blaming Sainsbury's, Woolworths, the Co-op and Budgens for proposing to open over Christmas in places such as Slough, Balham, Southall, Lewisham, Roehampton and Horley to appease the non-Christian communities and multicultural sentiment. On investigation, however, the shoppers in these places, who all boasted traditional English names, were enthusiastic about Christmas opening, a sign that the real reason was that Christmas had succumbed to English commercialisation and to the impatience of consumers unable to wait for the Boxing Day sales.[29]

Yet despite the lack of evidence, Winterval could not be allowed to die. 'We get this every year,' complained Luton's press officer in 2006. 'It just depends how many rogue journalists you get in any given year. We tell them it's bollocks.'[30] Undeterred, the eccentric writer A.N. Wilson alleged in 2006 that Christmas was being abolished by 'the crazy gang who constitute the local council at Luton'; the *Sun* complained about 'the dead hand of political correctness [which] is throttling the life out of the festive spirit'; and George Carey, former archbishop of Canterbury, and Mark Santer, bishop of Oxford, foolishly lent respectability to the claims.[31] These clerics were symptoms of the inability of a declining Christianity to react intelligently to other religions. 'The narrative at this time of year has been that Muslims don't like Christmas,' commented Lady Warsi, who admitted: 'my own party [Conservative] has done that in the past . . . we would try to find "Labour banning Christmas" stories and invariably it would have an ethnic link.'[32] She was correct. As late as 2010, the Tory MP Guy Opperman floated claims about the Labour Northumberland County Council attacking Christmas, for which he failed to produce any evidence.[33]

Yet rather than relying on baseless smears, journalists seeking evidence of the modern British Christmas might have visited the Christmas markets that were flourishing all over the country, a celebration of the British passion for food and drink. In Manchester's huge market they would have seen large numbers of Lancashire Muslims enjoying the event, along with everyone else. To see them was to realise that Muslims posed no threat to the British Christmas, which they celebrated as a secular festival, along with the rest of the population. At Christmas 2017, Tesco's Christmas television advertisements even featured a Muslim family celebrating, evidence, according to Tesco, of 'the many ways our customers come together over the festive season'. Some Muslims used the holiday to fit in a trip to Mecca, but many simply organised celebrations, including turkeys, trees and crackers. In effect, the influence of press and politicians had been largely outflanked by a combination of commercial pressures and social change.

Religious decline was, however, only one element – and not the most important – in Britain's loss of her sense of national identity. Following Indian independence in 1947, the process of decolonisation advanced slowly during the 1950s but accelerated in the 1960s. As little controversy was generated, it began to appear that imperial sentiment had never run very deep and the loss was therefore not traumatic. But despite this impression, the British had not really come to terms with loss of empire, and they cast around to fill the gap. In the 1950s, Empire Day became Commonwealth Day, but it made little impact, as the Commonwealth loomed large among the political elite rather than the population at large. Sections of the Establishment searched for a substitute for empire, which some thought they had found by joining the Common Market; but this option never attracted great popular enthusiasm. Alternatively, some politicians cultivated the Special Relationship with America as an expedient for retaining the status of a Great Power, though the complications the relationship caused for prime ministers including Attlee, Eden, Macmillan, Wilson, Thatcher and Blair made it a dubious expedient. In the economic sphere, there was some continuity, as traditional imperial markets were retained. But the empire had also functioned as a crucial safety valve by siphoning off men from the domestic economy and finding them prestigious and well-paid employment. However, by the 1960s that safety valve had disappeared. During the 1950s, so long as the consumer economy generated jobs and rapid economic growth, this was not a great problem; but by the 1970s, as unemployment increased and economic growth slowed, the loss of the opportunities empire had traditionally offered made a major impact. The British began to look for scapegoats.

For the immigrant communities themselves, the underlying dilemma posed by Britain's imperial withdrawal lay less in prejudice or poverty and more in psychology. By the 1970s, it was becoming clear that the British had largely written empire out of the national script, leaving many people in ignorance and uncertain whether the withdrawal from empire had been a success or a defeat. The confusion was nicely captured by the controversy aroused when the mayor of London, Ken Livingstone, questioned why one of the plinths in Trafalgar Square was permanently occupied by a Victorian general, Henry Havelock. To his critics, this represented an attempt to discredit the imperial past. Yet Livingstone had a point, for Havelock had been a military mediocrity who, during the Indian Mutiny in 1857, had tried to relieve the siege of Lucknow by marching his men up the road from Kanpur three times without success. He had no claim to fame in terms of achievements or talents, but sat on a plinth because of his association with a famous imperial setback. The episode underlined how sensitive a topic empire had become. Even historians complicated the issue by producing research suggesting that the economic value of empire had been greatly exaggerated. Empire also raised embarrassing moral questions about the wealth made from the slave trade, the methods used to suppress nationalist movements in places such as Kenya, and the cultivation of the idea of the British as a super-race. Yet the imperial record was far from being all negative, Britain's role of fostering the world's largest democracy in India being among the most notable achievements. However, the British were slow to build museums devoted to empire and to incorporate the subject in the school curriculum. The caution was symbolised by the failure of the Victoria and Albert Museum to realise a proposal for exploiting its vast but largely unseen Indian holdings, by establishing a new institution in Bradford at the centre of a large Hindu and Muslim population.

This inability to come to terms with the loss of empire left British Muslims in a particularly uncomfortable position. It came as a complete surprise to Ziauddin Sardar to discover that his grandfather and father had both served with distinction in the British army: his grandfather during the First World War, along with 800,000 other Indians, and his father in the Second World War, when he had joined 2.5 million of his compatriots. The Muslim Khudadad Khan (see above) was awarded the Victoria Cross in 1914, the first of 31 VCs won by Indian soldiers in the two world wars. Yet despite this record, Muslims appeared to enjoy no place in these chapters of British history. In Ziauddin Sardar's words: 'The Britain that greeted me was the eradication of memory, the obliteration of history.'[34] For many years there was no memorial either to those Indians who had fought in the armed forces or to those who had served and died in Britain's merchant navy. As Sardar commented, it was as though the British Asian immigrants had been reconstructed as a new people without a history, when they were in fact an integral part of British history. Eventually, in November 2002, the contribution of men from the former empire was recognised by the construction of memorial gates at the top of Constitution Hill in London. This was largely the achievement of Lady Flather, Britain's first female Asian peer, whose father had been a medical orderly in the Mesopotamia Campaign. 'We believe that the memorial should become a symbol for today's multi-racial Britain,' she declared. 'By remembering our shared sacrifice, we are certain that we can build together a truly cohesive society based on mutual respect and understanding.'[35] Here was some evidence that multi-racial Britain was belatedly coming to terms with its past.

The accumulating doubts about British national identity were crystallised by the unhappy attempts to celebrate the Millennium. In the past, Britain had managed such events without too much difficulty. She had successfully carried off the Great Exhibition of 1851, Queen Victoria's jubilees in 1887 and 1897, the British Empire Exhibition in 1924 and the Festival of Britain in 1951. They had been organised with some sense of pride in the past and some confidence about the future. But as 2000 approached, Britain floundered uncertainly. The government came up with the idea of a Millennium Dome to be built on a derelict site in East London, but investors showed reluctance to support the project, which was covered with derision. It became 'the embodiment of misconceived, shallow ideas about national identity,' as Yasmin Alibhai-Brown put it.[36] The hapless Dome simply symbolised British uncertainty about what was to be celebrated and where Britain was going in the future. The doubts culminated on the evening of 31 December 2000, when the prime minister, Tony Blair, and the queen engaged in an uncomfortable celebration on the north bank of the Thames. As midnight arrived, it became apparent that Her Majesty did not know the words of *Auld Lang Syne*, and nor did she realise that she was supposed to cross arms with her prime minister. Their awkwardness somehow symbolised the challenge that the occasion presented to the British.

There were alternative ways of marking the Millennium, including a complete anachronism championed by the *Daily Mail* and its journalists, who wanted the event to be celebrated as 2,000 years of Christian history, in order to 'rekindle our sense of the sacred'.[37] Vainly attempting to exploit the politics of nostalgia, promote Christianity, marriage and family, and attack female emancipation, gay sexuality, the multi-racial society and liberalism generally, the *Mail* saw the Blairite Millennium as anathema. It was infuriated by the whole celebration, as it highlighted the extent to which the newspaper had lost touch with the values and culture of modern society. Yet the right had already attempted to breathe life into this strategy and had failed. Earlier in the 1990s, Prime Minister John Major launched a 'Back to Basics' campaign, designed to rekindle faith in traditional values, family life and conventional morality. But it had blown up in his face, as revelations about the immorality of many of his own colleagues emerged, and it seemed to demonstrate that even in the Conservative Party the *Mail*'s morality no longer flourished. Major's failure, leading up to his massive electoral defeat in 1997, became part of a generalised right-wing thesis about the threats to British life posed by liberalism, Europe, immigration and multiculturalism.

The Millennium thus marked the culmination of a period of perceived national decline since the 1960s, which increasingly manifested itself in negative responses to external threats. One alternative strategy lay in withdrawal from the European Union and the recovery of national control that it was hoped this would bring. To that extent, the Millennium was a step towards the EU referendum of 2016. Another sign of the mood was a sharp rise in English nationalism in the face of the steady loss of confidence in the Union with Scotland and the growth of support for independence north of the border. Scottish separatism was complemented by the rise of nationalism in England, which in turn complicated efforts to respond positively to groups such as Muslims and other ethnic communities.

The significance of Britain's unravelling national identity was corroborated by the contrast with Scotland, where, despite a highly imperial history, society appeared more at ease. In Scotland, relations with the Muslim community were better, there was far less hostility to immigration and also a notable readiness to welcome Muslims into politics via both Labour and the Scottish National Party (SNP). In 2017, Labour in Scotland came close to electing a Muslim as its leader. Remarkably, 64 per cent of Asians voted for Scottish independence in the 2014 referendum. Their integration into SNP politics reflected a long-term strategy under Alex Salmond, who had consistently respected and cultivated the interests of Scots Muslims. In 2007, when Bashir Ahmad became the first non-white member of the Scottish parliament, he took his oath in English and Urdu, a small sign of multiculturalism that would have provoked irritation among English reactionaries. The SNP also gained credibility with Scots Muslims through its strong opposition to the Iraq War and sympathy for the Palestinian cause; Dundee was twinned with Nablus and Glasgow with Bethlehem. Bashir Ahmad founded 'Scots Asians for Independence': 'It doesn't matter where you come from. What matters is where we are going together as a nation.'[38] Tasmina Ahmed-Sheikh, who founded the Scottish Asian Women's Association, explained: 'I'm a Scot first. Then I'm a Scot-Asian Muslim.'[39]

Part of the explanation may lie in the more relaxed approach towards immigration, as so many Scots have been migrants themselves. This is reinforced by current concerns about the declining population and appreciation of newcomers for their contribution to economic growth. But the Scottish response is also more fundamental. Alex Salmond once explained that 'Scottishness is a very unthreatening identity, easy to adopt.' Scots can be more relaxed, because they have become more confident about their own identity, less subject than the English to hang-ups about empire and divisions over Europe. Following the election and the devolution referendum of 1997, they embraced a devolved parliament that won additional powers and sustained two viable governments, first a Labour–Liberal Democrat coalition, followed by an SNP administration. The experience with devolved government boosted Scottish confidence and sense of purpose at a time when the English were becoming more divided and uncertain about their political system and their role in the world. Consequently, Scots have managed to accommodate the Muslim community, rather than seeing it as a threat.

CHAPTER ELEVEN

ISLAMOPHOBIA

The origins of what is variously known as Islamism, Islamic fundamentalism and radical Islamism lie in the 1960s, in the ideas of a handful of Muslims in Pakistan, Egypt and Iran who believed that Muslims had been led astray from their religion by nationalist movements. Their critique emerged as a political movement in the early 1970s, culminating in the Iranian Revolution in 1979. Although some Muslims were critical of Western morality and politics, Islamism was not primarily anti-Western: it was essentially a reaction against what were widely seen as the corrupt, authoritarian and secular regimes that controlled much of the Muslim world. The aim was to evict them, return to a purer form of Islam and re-create an Islamic state. In view of the exaggerated reputation it enjoys in the West, it is worth remembering that this movement has largely been a failure.[1] Yet while fundamentalism appeals to only a small minority, it is also the case that large numbers of Muslims have become aggrieved by the policies of the Western powers. The explanation for this can be found in long-term frustration with the consistently pro-Israeli policy of Britain and the United States over Palestine, in addition to the proximate causes in the shape of two Afghan wars, the genocide in Bosnia, the Rushdie affair and the first Gulf War in 1990, which made many Muslims see themselves as the victims of Western aggression and interventionism.

By 2000, two generations of Palestinians had been displaced from their land in Palestine since 1948, confined to refugee camps and forced to endure the illegal confiscation of Arab land by the Israelis. This led to the emergence of the Palestine Liberation Organisation (PLO) and Hamas. Unfortunately, the British and Americans relied on cooperation with Jordan on the West Bank and with Egypt in Gaza to suppress Islamist movements, thereby placing themselves at odds with the Muslim population. They failed to promote a state for the Palestinians and allowed Israel to undertake military incursions into Palestinian territory, to build on Arab land and to surround the Palestinians with a massive blockade that crippled its economy. Britain continued to supply Israel with arms, and in 2014 she refused to condemn the aggressive Israeli response to rocket attacks by Hamas – a response that led to huge loss of life among Palestinians. This provoked the resignation of the Conservative government's one Muslim minister, Sayeeda Warsi, who accused the prime minister of losing all moral authority. She warned that David Cameron's acquiescence in the Israeli attacks would become 'a basis for radicalisation [which] could have consequences for us for years to come'.[2]

Another major element in the growing disillusionment among Muslims lay in the conflict that resulted from the break-up of the former Yugoslavia, which involved massacres of Muslims by Serbs in Bosnia. Britain and the United Nations were slow to intervene, claiming that to send arms to help them would only prolong the conflict. However, this enabled extreme Islamists in Britain to convince impressionable young Muslims that the only way of saving their co-religionists in Bosnia was to establish an Islamic state in the Balkans. They reportedly argued that 'if we had the Islamic state, the caliph would send the Islamic army to slaughter the Serbs'.[3] Certainly the Bosnian War acted as a catalyst for the radicalisation of British Muslims. The intelligence services were fully aware of British Muslim reactions, but turned a blind eye and even encouraged Afghan jihadis to travel to fight in the Balkans. This promoted the mobilisation of a generation of young Muslims, gave respectability to the idea of an Islamic state and allowed Islamists to put down roots in some communities. The followers of Hizb ut-Tahrir extended its campaign by, for example, visiting public libraries to check the electoral roll and identify Muslim voters: 'We were against democracy, and the first Islamist group to declare voting in general elections *haram*.'[4] However, Hizb ut-Tahrir represented only a very small extremist fringe, and when its volunteers visited the homes of ordinary Muslims they were usually met with hostility and abuse.

Antagonism over Anglo-American pro-Israeli policy was exacerbated by the Iranian Revolution of 1979, which cast the West as enemies of Muslims – a sad culmination to decades of inept intervention, notably in 1953, when Britain and America displaced the country's elected leader. Common sense dictated recognising Iran as a regional super-power, but instead the Western powers cast around for ways of containing the fundamentalist regime in Teheran. To this end, they built up Saddam Hussein of Iraq as a rival and encouraged him to wage war against Iran in 1980. Though Saddam's was a brutal and ruthless regime, Britain and America had no objections to it so long as he could be used as a tool for their aims. Another costly intervention, the war proved horribly counter-productive, as it not only failed to overthrow the fundamentalist regime, but also enhanced Saddam's ambitions to such an extent that he risked an invasion of Kuwait in the confidence that the West would allow him to get away with it. This triggered further Western military intervention to free Kuwait, which, as usual, was accomplished; but, as Saddam remained in power, victory left the United States all too well aware that it had not resolved matters. It was consequently looking for another excuse to intervene.

The result was two disastrously counter-productive Western interventions – in Iraq and Afghanistan. Britain's wars in Afghanistan in 1839, 1879 and 1919 had demonstrated that it was not too difficult to transport a Western army to Kabul, but it was subsequently almost impossible to control the country and difficult to extricate the troops. Afghanistan remained essentially a medieval state (or in Western thinking a failed state), in that it comprised regions under local warlords and tribal loyalties that were not easily controlled from Kabul. Yet in the twentieth century no one had learned the lessons of the past, and the Russian experience largely repeated that of earlier invaders. The Russians were concerned about external Islamic influence on their own Muslim population in Central Asia and about American meddling in Pakistan; they therefore aspired, like the West, to manipulate unstable Muslim regimes. In 1973, the Russians had armed the Afghan revolution that overthrew Zahir Shah, who had ruled for 40 years; but on finding that his successor, President Daud, maintained his links with the West, they had him killed and replaced with a pro-communist regime in 1978. However, the Afghan regime appealed for more Russian backing. The railway system enabled the Soviets to supply what eventually became an army of 140,000. The Russians apparently assumed that it would be sufficient to control the towns and the main roads connecting them, thus allowing them to withdraw in favour of a new regime. This has been described as an 'impractical aspiration' rather than a strategy, although it was largely repeated by the American invasion after 2000.[5] After 1979, they occupied every part of Afghanistan, but by 1989 admitted failure and withdrew, leaving 1.5 million dead.

Unfortunately, the Russian blunder had lured the American and British governments into a fresh miscalculation. Complacent about the local attacks on the Russian regime, they tried to exploit Russian discomfiture by recklessly arming the Taliban fighters. This effectively boosted the Islamic fundamentalists, so that when the Russians eventually quit in 1989, the Taliban were able to take over the country. But a Taliban Afghanistan was worse than a Russian one. Victory had the effect of enhancing Islamic fundamentalism not only in Afghanistan, but throughout the Muslim world. It gave inspiration to the PLO and Hamas to believe that if poor, unsophisticated Muslim forces could defeat a Western superpower, then God must be on their side. It gave some credence to delusions about the restoration of Islam to the dominance it had enjoyed in an earlier era. In this way, another Western intervention blew up in the faces of the politicians.

Western intervention in Afghanistan, combined with the role of American troops in Saudi Arabia, the state that controls Mecca, and anger over fresh Israeli retaliations in Gaza, led to a series of strikes by Islamists against the United States, culminating in the attack orchestrated by Osama Bin Laden on the Twin Towers in September 2001. In turn, this provoked two wholly disastrous responses by the American and British governments. Undeterred by the lessons of the Russian failure and the success of the Taliban, President Bush and Tony Blair embarked on fresh bombing campaigns and invasions of Afghanistan in 2001 and an invasion of Iraq in 2003, in the belief that they could eliminate terrorism by direct military means. In Britain, the new Afghan War aroused little controversy, as few realised how long it would last. It had the effect of compounding the impression that the West was engaged in a general crusade against Islam, a claim given credence by Bush's foolish rhetoric. Yet in reality, the Taliban had no ambitions outside Afghanistan and posed no threat to the West. It was Pakistan that invited Bin Laden into the country, whereas the Taliban told him to desist from attacks in Africa and elsewhere.

Over the next 17 years, the United States deployed 100,000 troops, spent £740 billion and lavished more money on 'nation building' in Afghanistan – all to no effect. The fighting largely went round in circles: official propaganda repeatedly claimed that an advance had been made, only to find that the Taliban forces recovered the lost villages later. Governments led by Tony Blair, Gordon Brown and David Cameron regularly redefined British objectives – establishing democracy, emancipating women, eradicating opium cultivation – in order to conceal from the public that nothing was really being achieved. They poured troops into Helmand province, but failed to gain lasting control. Yet Helmand was merely one of 34 Afghan provinces! One of the reasons for failure was that from 2004, the Taliban revived by encouraging the farmers to expand the cultivation of poppies for opium: production rose from 180 tonnes in 2001 to 8,000 tonnes by 2007. Afghanistan became the world's largest heroin producer, generating 80 per cent of Europe's supply. This proved profitable for the cultivators, required nine times as many workers as conventional crops and generated enough revenue to enable the jihadists to sustain a prolonged campaign; the Taliban could pay each new crop of fighters a decent wage. As a result, the NATO governments became anxious to find ways of extracting their troops without complete loss of face. By 2018, the Afghan War had resulted in a stunning 17-year defeat for the Western powers.

An easier objective, at first sight, was the invasion of Iraq in 2003, undertaken with a view to removing the regime of Saddam Hussein. The motive lay essentially in President Bush's regret that America had stopped short of this in the earlier Gulf War. The attack on the Twin Towers presented him with an opportunity. Yet this intervention was especially perverse since, although Saddam's regime was obnoxious and tyrannical, it was aggressively secular, not Islamic. There were no Islamic terrorists there – at least until attracted by Western interference. In fact, it was the Western allies, Saudi Arabia and Pakistan, that harboured and materially supported terrorism.

Supported by almost all the British political establishment at the time, this was arguably the worst foreign policy mistake in modern times, and it illustrates as nothing else the incompetence of Britain's dealings with the Muslim world. Much of the controversy was generated by the appreciation that the invasion was illegal, though this was a marginal consideration. The real flaw consisted in its *futility*: it served no national purpose and proved, as usual, to be counter-productive. Blair's government intimidated the public and parliament by claiming that Iraq had chemical weapons and the capacity to deliver 'weapons of mass destruction'. This was quite false, but distorted 'intelligence' was produced by way of corroboration, and this was swallowed uncritically by most newspapers: '45 Minutes from Attack' warned the *London Evening Standard*, and 'He's Got 'Em, Let's Get Him' advised the *Sun*. The propaganda destroyed Blair's credibility and severely undermined public faith in officials and experts for years to come.

The long-term consequence of this disastrous invasion was to transform what had been an unpleasant but strong regime into a highly unstable state racked by civil war; the upshot was mass migration across Iraq's borders. For the fundamentalists, their tactics seemed to succeed, by drawing Western governments further into military interventions and by reckless rhetoric about the threat posed by Islam. Despite their failures, Western politicians continued to back the wrong horses throughout the

Muslim world. Although they urged Muslims to adopt democracy, they continued to oppose secular, democratic radicalism wherever it appeared, preferring to think that they could use conservative, religious elements to their advantage. This problem was exacerbated by the obsession of the Western governments with terrorism, which only diminished their ability to accommodate their policies to the democratic movements that were arising in the Middle East. Blind to the danger of backing repressive regimes against grass-roots Muslim movements, the United States and Britain made themselves seen as enemies all over the region. Consequently, when Bush and Blair began to urge Muslims to adopt democracy, they commanded little credibility. Indeed, the United States had an impressive record of suppressing democracy whenever it resulted in the election of a left-wing or anti-American government, and its intervention proved to be a major cause of radicalisation in Muslim societies. Thus, Islamic militancy in Egypt, Saudi Arabia, Pakistan, Morocco, Jordan, Malaysia and Indonesia was to a large extent a reaction to American backing for repressive regimes. For years, the West supported repressive regimes – especially in Egypt, Iran, Iraq and Saudi Arabia – whose rulers did their best to strangle democratic movements. They failed to appreciate that Islamism was not primarily a movement directed against the West, but rather a movement designed to overthrow the autocratic and corrupt Muslim regimes that controlled much of the Middle East.

This view of Western ineptitude was corroborated by the emergence of the 'Arab Spring' in 2011. This movement for democracy came as a complete surprise to the battalions of Western experts and authorities on the Muslim world, not to mention the civil servants and politicians. During this phase, Muslims protested against autocratic regimes in Tunisia, Egypt, Libya, Yemen, Bahrain and Syria. The Arab Spring resulted in some hasty and ill-considered retreats, leaving Western policy in serious disarray. In Tunisia and Egypt, the West withdrew its backing from repressive regimes, but it continued to support those in Bahrain and Saudi Arabia; it refused to intervene in Syria, but conducted air strikes in Libya.

This inconsistency exposed graphically the ineptitude and confusion in the approach of Britain and America to the Muslim world. Western governments proved reluctant to emancipate themselves from the traditional mindset. For example, they accepted the rationale offered by Hosni Mubarak of Egypt that regimes like his were essential for suppressing the Muslim Brotherhood. The British government found it hard to recognise the Muslim Brotherhood as a genuine grass-roots social movement that enjoyed an impressive record of welfare work on behalf of ordinary Egyptians; the Brotherhood's members were content to operate within the political system once freed from imprisonment and torture. As a popular movement, it was one that the West had to deal with in the long term. Labelling it 'extremist' or 'Islamist' was simply irrelevant. This view was corroborated in Britain by the experience of Bob Lambert, a former Metropolitan Police officer, who reported that Muslim Brotherhood activists were quite compatible with a democratic culture and helped to counter the influence of al-Qaida in London. From practical experience, he concluded that attempts to demonise the Brotherhood as extremists were simply misguided.[6] Yet in 2014, Prime Minister Cameron threatened to ban the Brotherhood because of its supposed links with violent extremism. He instigated an inquiry under Britain's ambassador to Saudi Arabia, which, like the Egyptian regime, regarded the election-winning Brotherhood as a mortal threat. Thus, Britain maintained her misguided record in Egypt. In democratic elections, the Muslim Brotherhood won 40 per cent of the vote, and with its supporters installed a new government; but Britain then stood by as the elected head was deposed by force, and acquiesced in the restoration of authoritarian control by al-Sisi. The official mindset still found it difficult to recognise that in countries like Egypt, young, educated Muslims could be both modernisers and Islamists, hostile to the corrupt, opulent, secular regimes and keen to develop a stricter, more moral alternative form of politics. Misled by Islamophobic propaganda, Britain and America were unable to come to terms with what they called 'Islamism'.

What were the consequences of the Anglo-American invasions of Afghanistan and Iraq? They had appalling effects in the Middle East, where 500,000 died in Iraq alone. After 17 long years, the Afghan War had still not been won. Meanwhile, the Iraq War, though successful in changing the regime, had triggered a series of damaging results. It turned a secular state into a fundamentalist one and manufactured terrorist havens by attracting recruits in from the Middle East and Pakistan. Extremist organisations such as al-Qaida stepped aside from the barrage of Western military force, only to extend its organisation to fresh centres such as Yemen and Somalia. By 2010, when American forces were leaving Iraq, al-Qaida returned to rebuild its organisation in the form of the Sons of Iraq. Moreover, the invasion wholly frustrated American aims, in that it actually advanced the influence in the Middle East of Iran, which became a regional superpower equipped with nuclear weapons and a readiness to take on regimes such as that in Syria. When elections were held in Iraq, it proved impossible to form a government for seven months, until Iran intervened to bring the parties together.[7] For America, this was a humiliating outcome that underlined the futility of trying to deny Iran her role as a regional superpower.

Yet worst of all, the Western interventionism had the effect of destabilising Iraq, thereby generating a wave of immigration into Europe that greatly exacerbated domestic problems for Britain and other EU countries. Nor did Britain's politicians learn the mistakes of Iraq. In 2011, David Cameron, apparently striving to be the poor man's Blair, cheerfully embarked on another war against an unpalatable regime in Colonel Qaddafi's Libya. In conjunction with the French, Britain bombed Libya and destroyed the regime; but once again, intervention proved to be counter-productive, since the removal of the regime destabilised the country and led to years of civil war, bombings, assassinations, the kidnapping of the prime minister and the seizure of oil terminals by warlords. Worst was the blowback from the chaos that engulfed Libya via the expulsion of 40,000 Libyan troops, who took their weapons across the Sahel region of Africa, where they stimulated rebellions in countries such as Mali and Nigeria to the benefit of Boko Haram. As a result, thousands of people in African countries to the south began to travel to Libya in order to emigrate to Europe. They became Cameron's immigrants. Like Blair, Cameron had blundered into another counter-productive intervention in a region he did not understand.

For Britain, the second damaging effect of the Muslim wars was domestic. The failure of interventionism to make the public safe from terrorism was used to justify reactionary moves to undermine traditional British liberties, backed by a wave of irresponsible scaremongering and propaganda designed to suggest that Islam posed a threat to British values and politics. Well before the attacks on the World Trade Center, President George Bush had made fatuous announcements about a 'war on terror' and a new 'crusade' against the Middle Eastern Muslim powers. Successive prime ministers, including Blair, Cameron and Theresa May, routinely responded to every case of terrorism by claiming that it posed a threat to the British way of life and to liberal democracy itself. This was completely unfounded, but served to legitimise a whole series of extreme measures.

Unfortunately, a few academics lent authority to the politicians' claims. In a 1993 article, the late Bernard Lewis had launched the idea that Europe was in the throes of a conflict between civilisations, and in *The Crisis of Islam* (2003) he referred to 'the politics of rage', resurrecting Victorian Orientalist perceptions of Islam as a religion driven by hatred of Christendom and the West. The Islamophobic writing was extended by Samuel P. Huntington, a Harvard professor, in *The Clash of Civilizations* (1998). Huntington's rather unsophisticated thesis held that the world had always been dominated by a struggle between the forces of barbarism and the forces of progress, and this would continue in the future because of improved communications and globalisation. Yet Huntington's claims revealed more abut the mentality of Americans, always prone to paranoia, than about Islam. In particular, the fall of the Soviet Union had deprived right-wing extremists of the external threat on which they usually relied for propaganda, and left them seeking an alternative.

For anyone with a rudimentary knowledge of modern European history, the line of argument in the scaremongering literature was depressingly familiar. In the 1920s, fears about internal subversion and the spread of Bolshevism provoked the publication of *The Jewish Peril*, a work based on the notorious forgery, *The Protocols of the Elders of Zion*, which had appeared in Russia in 1905. It described a centuries-old conspiracy of Jews, animated by a hatred of Christianity, that aimed at subverting and destroying Western states by spreading corrosive ideas, including liberalism, socialism and communism. In the neurotic mood of the 1920s, it gained respectability, including endorsements by *The Times* and the *Morning Post* as 'a most masterly exposition'. Exposure as a forgery made little impact, as the ground had been so well prepared by Edwardian propaganda about Jewish influence, and society remained rife with anti-Semitism at all levels until the Second World War. It is extraordinary how the main elements in inter-war anti-Jewish propaganda reappeared in modern Islamophobic material, indicating a deep-seated need to identify external threats and subversion in Europe and the United States.

Once the theme of Islamic subversion in Europe had become fashionable, it was enthusiastically adopted in several scaremongering and opportunistic books, including Christopher Caldwell's *Reflections on the Revolution in Europe: Immigration, Islam and the West* (2009), Melanie Phillips' *Londonistan: How Britain is Creating a Terror State Within* (2006) and Michael Gove's *Celsius 7/7* (2006). Caldwell's was a scurrilous attempt to raise the spectre of a Europe overrun and subverted by Muslim immigrants. In contrast to such studies as James Fergusson's *Al-Britannia: A Journey Through Muslim Britain* (2017), Ziauddin Sardar's *Balti Britain* (2008) and Sayeeda Warsi's *The Enemy Within: A Tale of Muslim Britain* (2017), these authors were largely ignorant of the lived realities of Muslim communities. The reactionary novelist Martin Amis, not known as an authority on Islam, vented his spleen on Muslims by resurrecting Victorian propaganda about Islam as culturally backward, inward looking and in terminal decline. He insisted – in the face of all the evidence – that Muslim countries were unable to sustain democratic rule, and warned that 'the West confronts an irrationalist, agonistic, theocratic/ideocratic system which is essentially unappeasably opposed to its existence'.[8] Even in the respectable *Times Literary Supplement*, one reviewer claimed 'few would deny that after the collapse of Communism the rise of Islam poses a powerful challenge to the triumph of liberal democracy'.[9] Inevitably, some of the most unpleasant symptoms of Islamophobia appeared in the *Daily Mail*. In 2018, one of its notorious columnists, Katie Hopkins, astonished readers by claiming that a road accident outside London's Natural History Museum was a terrorist attack. Faced with evidence that this was wholly false, Hopkins showed her irrationalism: 'I stand by the idea that it's a terror attack. It's my personal opinion.' After the Manchester Arena attack in 2018, Hopkins called for a 'final solution' for British Muslims.[10] This crass association with the Holocaust provoked a huge backlash from the public. Hopkins was accused of hate speech and her contract with the *Mail* was terminated. Not surprisingly, Islamophobic literature rapidly lost credibility, though in 2018 Douglas Murray attempted a *réchauffé* of the old discredited material in *The Strange Death of Europe: Immigration, Identity, Islam*, claiming that Europe was godless, dying and 'exhausted by history', that London was no longer a white majority city and that migrants were raping and terrorising the population. It was indicative of the intellectual quality of this writing that Murray even blamed Muslims for the closure of British pubs. Explanations for pub closures actually lie in low supermarket prices, excessive rents charged by the brewers, and the fact that 30 per cent of those under 24 had become teetotal; but this was irrelevant for those who chose to use Muslims as all-purpose scapegoats.

In the process, Islamophobia moved into the mainstream via a series of extremist groups, including Britain First, The Infidels of Britain, the South East Alliance and Liberty GB, filling the gap left by the decline of the English Defence League. In 2018, the leader and deputy leader of Britain First, Paul Golding and Jayda Fransen, received prison sentences for a series of hate crimes against Muslims. But the biggest anti-Muslim organisation was UKIP. One of its MEPs, Gerard Batten, believed that Muslims should have to sign a special code of conduct and warned that Europe was mistaken in allowing 'an explosion of mosques across their land'.[11] However, by 2017–18, UKIP had declined dramatically, shrinking to become a small, fanatically Islamophobic party. Unfortunately, its rise had posed an attractive alternative for working-class voters, a trend that frightened some Labour candidates into pandering to right-wing extremism. At the election of 2010, the Labour candidate at Oldham East, Phil Woolas, was so desperate to save his seat that he allowed his agent to dispatch emails warning: 'If we don't get the white folk angry he's gone . . . Repeat the target, the mad Muslims . . . we can use the campaign to galvinise (*sic*) the white *Sun*-reading voters.'[12] Although Woolas was subsequently unseated by the courts for these tactics, some Labour MPs defended him, a symptom of how far the party had been demoralised since the 1960s, when Harold Wilson had condemned racist methods at general elections.

Meanwhile the extreme right had retained the footing it had enjoyed within the Conservative Party since the days of the Monday Club. When Sayeeda Warsi was appointed vice-chairman, she was shocked to discover how much prejudice existed towards Muslims. Muslim groups were turned away from party conferences and not allowed to hold fringe meetings. *Conservative Home*, a party website, published a ten-point list of conditions that Muslims should meet before being allowed to become Tory candidates.[13] However, in the early days of David Cameron's leadership he was keen to make the party more inclusive and to recruit Muslims, such as Sayeeda Warsi, who appreciated Conservatism for its association with entrepreneurialism.[14] Unfortunately, by 2012 Cameron had abandoned his strategy, under pressure from the far right, and the party had decided that, as Muslims were not very likely to vote Conservative, they didn't matter much.

Politicians like Warsi were also undermined by a network of anti-Muslim activists who used Facebook and Twitter to manipulate opinion by propagating fake news, designed to promote the idea of Islam as an imminent threat every time a terrorist attack occurred. Within 48 hours of the Manchester attack, for example, Tommy Robinson (Stephen Yaxley-Lennon), former leader of the English Defence League, added 40,000 followers to the 100,000 he already had. A contributor to the 'Gates of Vienna' blog, Paul Weston, wrote about an impending civil war with Muslims. In 2014, a scare was started to the effect that a member of the cabinet was an undercover fundamentalist, secretly co-opted to penetrate the heart of British government – a classic piece of fiction designed to attack Sayeeda Warsi, who had been appointed a minister by David Cameron. In March 2017, after the Westminster terrorist attack, a Twitter user displayed a photograph of a Muslim woman supposedly

ISLAMOPHOBIA ❖

ignoring people who were helping the victims, though it subsequently emerged that this was a fake account created in Russia.[15] The negligence of the social media platforms left society wide open to such propaganda.

⬣ ❄ ⬣

Yet Islamophobic propaganda on social media platforms could not entirely obscure the dearth of empirical support for its sweeping claims. What progress had the Islamic conspiracy to take over Europe actually made? How many Britons were being converted to Islam? In what ways had the political system been undermined by Muslims? In what sense was the economy controlled by Muslims? Which aspects of British foreign policy were determined by Muslim influence?

The most obvious flaw in the propaganda is that Islamism has been a failure across most of the world. Never very secure or coherent, it has regularly been suppressed, only to re-emerge in another part of the world; but it has never become representative of the great majority of Muslims. Even Iran, the foremost example of an Islamist state, is one that the Western powers have belatedly learned to deal with: President Obama reached an agreement over its nuclear policy that was widely welcomed in the West and is still backed by the EU, though abandoned by Donald Trump.

Islamophobia clearly involves sweeping exaggerations and generalisations, which gain credibility only through regular repetition by leading politicians. Contrary to popular impressions, the British population includes under 3 million Muslims (or 4.8 per cent), and there are only modest conversions to Islam of perhaps 5,000 a year. Although the birth rate is higher among Muslims, it is falling and effectively converging with that of the majority of the population, rendering absurd the claims that Muslims are set to become a majority. Nor is there much evidence that the vacuum caused by the decline in conventional religion is being filled by Islam; if anything, attendance at classes on mindfulness and meditation at Buddhist centres in the main cities indicates the most expansive religious movement in Britain today.

Another flaw in Islamophobia consists in the unwise stance taken by successive prime ministers, including Tony Blair, David Cameron and

Theresa May, who have routinely and unthinkingly repeated claims to the effect that the British way of life is threatened by Islamic terrorism. Yet the security of prosperous, well-defended Western states is really not in danger. To claim so is an over-reaction: it flatters the terrorists, gives them credibility and thus enables them to make young recruits. The former head of MI6 at the time of the Iraq invasion, Sir Richard Dearlove, condemned the government for exaggerating the threat of Islamist terrorism. It was a problem in the Middle East, he said, but Britain was only 'marginally affected' because it was not the main target. The scale and extent of the threat becomes obvious when seen in the perspective of Irish terrorism in the 1970s and 1980s. Between 1969 and 2015, 3,583 people were killed by Irish terrorists. The numbers killed or injured in Islamic terrorist attacks represent only a tiny fraction of those targeted by the IRA. Between 2007 and 2016, for example there were 26 deaths from terrorism: 23 by Irish terrorists, two by far-right terrorists and one by allegedly Muslim terrorists. Yet no one suggested that the IRA posed a serious threat to liberal democracy; indeed, the governments of the period treated them as criminal, rather than political.

Exaggeration also extends to the number of terrorists, which remains highly uncertain. Since the eighteenth century, when the French revolutionary period led the British state to pay people to report on spies and subversives, it has been evident that the more money that is spent on intelligence, the more subversives are discovered! The same applies today. After 2000, MI5 identified only a few dozen domestic terrorists, a figure promptly raised by Blair to a suspiciously round 250. The figure was subsequently lifted to 800 in 2005, 1,200 in 2006, and then to 1,600. Between 2001 and 2010, a total of 1,834 people were arrested in connection with terrorism; but of these, 1,000 were released without charge, 422 were charged with terrorism-related offences and only 237 were convicted. The figures suggest that we have little real idea about the extent of the problem. All we do know is that after the collapse of the Soviet Union, the security services lost their main purpose and struggled to find a new one in tackling drugs, money laundering, weapons of mass destruction and terrorism. The authorities have worked overtime to manipulate public opinion by regularly raising the 'threat' level, but this has largely had the effect of making the public cynical about official claims.

Islamophobic propaganda also relies on claims that Islam poses a threat to liberal democracy. This is not to deny that liberal democracy is under pressure. Several respected authors, including A.C. Grayling in *Democracy and Its Crisis* (2017) and David Runciman in *How Democracy Ends* (2018), have recently addressed the question. It is agreed that Britain's democracy suffers from long-term weaknesses, including the demise of local newspapers, the narrowing of ownership of the national press under a handful of right-wing proprietors, and the intimidation of the BBC by the agenda set by the red-tops. The democratic system is losing credibility as a result of the internet, the manipulation of social platforms by extremist organisations, the dissemination of false information, and the interference of Russia in the American presidential election and the British EU referendum. In 2018, the Electoral Commission, acknowledging that British democracy was under threat, called for reforms of the law following a series of online political campaign scandals, misinformation, misuse of personal data, illegal expenditure and foreign interference.[16]

However, amid all this evidence, no one has found any empirical basis for blaming Islamist influence for undermining democracy. Prime ministerial rhetoric on the subject is simply perverse, as it ignores Britain's role in propping up anti-democratic regimes in Muslim countries. Scaremongering about Islamist movements ignores their aims, which are not primarily concerned with the West at all, but with toppling the corrupt, authoritarian, secular regimes in the Middle East and eradicating American influence in the region – entirely legitimate and rational objectives that have often been thwarted by the Western powers. In any case, the claims simply ignore the evidence that Muslims have become fully involved in the British political system and have been participants in Western-style democracies in countries such as India for decades. Indeed, one by-product of the Iraq War was to provoke huge protests, such as the February 2003 demonstration in London, when some 2 million people joined with Muslims in common outrage at the government's action.

⬛ ✤ ⬛

In the case of British terrorism, it is now widely recognised that the country itself was not the target of terrorism by such regimes as that in Iraq; rather the interventionism of Blair and Bush made it a target. As the former head of MI5, Eliza Manningham-Buller, told the Chilcott Inquiry, Blair's policy 'radicalised, for the want of a better word, a whole generation of young people . . . who saw our involvement in Iraq and Afghanistan as being an attack upon Islam'.[17] She had already warned the government of the likely consequences and of 'the danger of over-reliance on fragmentary intelligence in deciding whether or not to go to war'. However, the governments of the 1990s and 2000s were unwilling to recognise that terrorism was largely a home-grown phenomenon or a by-product of avoidable errors by the politicians themselves. They preferred to see it simply as an intractable ideological problem – as a fundamental clash of cultures, reflecting the incompatibility of Muslim and Western society. Yet to target an ideology was really to stick a label on the problem without being able to explain it. It led to the proscription of individuals who criticised official foreign policy and of democratic organisations like the Muslim Brotherhood. Tony Blair and Gordon Brown, anxious to outflank the Conservatives on law and order (even if this meant pandering to the *Daily Mail* agenda), saw tough measures on terrorism as reinforcing their wider strategy. They unleashed a general attack on civil liberties in the name of protecting national security, and overlooked Britain's experience of dealing with terrorism in Northern Ireland. Although internment without trial there had proved counter-productive, the Blair governments reintroduced it for Muslim terrorists. Yet Britain's leading academic expert on terrorism, Paul Wilkinson, pointed out that it was not necessary to suspend the rule of law in order to maintain an effective counter-terrorism policy: the key to defeating domestic terrorism lay in acquiring good intelligence, which was frustrated once the community became alienated.[18]

Despite this advice, Blair and his home secretaries, David Blunkett and John Reid, enacted a mass of terrorist legislation between the late 1990s and early 2000s. Suspects were interned without trial in Belmarsh prison, until this was ruled illegal by the law lords; one victim, Babar Ahmad, was imprisoned from 2004 to 2012 without any charge being brought against him. Imprisonment without trial was an odd policy from those who claimed to want to uphold British values. Draconian terrorist legislation led to tourists being apprehended for taking photographs in central London, to train-spotters being interrogated for acting like the reconnaissance for terrorist cells, and to the arrest of an elderly Labour Party member for heckling Jack Straw at the party conference in 2005 – all effectively undermining public support for anti-terrorist policy. This oppressive legislation was backed with an array of initiatives designed to intimidate Muslims and critics of government foreign policy. Under the Prevention of Terrorism Act 2000, police were allowed to stop and search people without suspicion. In 2009, no fewer than 101,248 searches were made, yet only 594 people were even arrested – and none were prosecuted, let alone convicted! Muslims were 42 times more likely to be victims of stop-and-search than the rest of the population.[19] In 2010, West Midlands Police instituted a covert scheme to install 49 CCTV cameras and 169 number plate recognition cameras in two Muslim wards, Sparkbrook and Washbrook, in Birmingham; they deceived the local councillors by claiming the cameras were intended to detect drugs. Once exposed, these policies were hopelessly counterproductive because they alienated the Muslim community. These measures may not have turned Britain into a police state, but they led her half-way down the road to it.

Official policy on Islamic terrorism also suffered from great difficulty in identifying its targets, partly because the repeated extension of the surveillance of private emails effectively left the police swamped with far more information than they could manage. Yet independent reviewers concluded that the authorities could have prevented a number of attacks – not by more intelligence, but by making better use of what was already available. By 2017, the intelligence services had compiled a database of some 23,000 'persons of interest'. Of these, they prioritised 3,000 and gave the highest priority to 500. However, recruitment and radicalisation remained hard to detect – partly because it happened quite quickly, it was not usually linked to mosques and it relied on easily acquired weapons.

In turn, this raised questions about the circumstances that led some Muslims to become terrorists. The press and the politicians focused on radical imams and extremist mosques, but things turned out to be more complicated. Ed Husain gave an account in *The Islamist* (2007) of how, at the age of 16, he embarked on five years as an extremist in London colleges under the influence of Omar Bakri and Hizb ut-Tahrir. He eventually realised how little religion was really involved, became disillusioned and rejected fundamentalism.[20] Thereupon he switched to a career in banking which proved congenial, and before long 'Islamism was a distant memory'.[21] For the authorities, this was an appealing account, though one that did not quite add up. In particular, Husain's sudden embrace of high finance apparently raised in him none of the questions it would undoubtedly have forced upon a devout and well-informed Muslim. If his account tells us anything, it is that the seedbed for radical Islam exists among young, impressionable and poorly informed youths who are susceptible to rapid switches from one extreme to another.

As is often the case in political movements, the extremists were those who had converted to the cause – often young men with troubled lives who became involved in crime or who were looking for a cause and some excitement. The violence involved in Islamic extremism was a way of proving their loyalty and winning approval from the new community.[22] As a result, by 2016 some 12,500 young, disaffected Muslims were confined to prisons, where, rather perversely, they were exposed to a more austere version of Islam from the 200 Deobandi chaplains recruited by the authorities. Representing a highly conservative school in Islam, the Deobandis opposed female emancipation, believed that all science could be found in the Qur'an and insisted that Muslims must accept the opinion handed down to them without question. Their influence was almost calculated to deepen the inmates' alienation from mainstream society.

On the other hand, much of our information about the most notorious terrorists suggests that they were successful and fitted into society. The three leaders of the 2007 London bombings, Mohammed Sidique Khan, Shehzad Tanweer and Hasib Hussein, were born in Beeston, an unremarkable suburb of Leeds. Khan was a quiet youth, not obviously religious or political, who worked as a teaching assistant in a primary school, was married and had a business degree.[23] The authorities had little idea why such a person should become a suicide bomber. Many such men had rejected the culture of the older generation; they were Muslims, but had largely adopted Westernised habits. Some were detached from their society and became involved in criminal activity involving gangs and drugs, but many terrorists were educated, in employment, apparently well integrated, and not especially religious. The killers of the soldier Lee Rigby had actually been brought up as Christians. Official efforts to identify radical imams as the cause of terrorism also proved to be very wide of the mark. Khalid Masood, the Westminster attacker, had lived a quiet life and had not even converted to Islam until his early fifties. The common factor was a feeling that Muslims had been unfairly targeted by the Western powers: Sidique Khan explained that he had been alienated by the Muslim deaths entailed in British foreign policy: 'Our words have no impact upon you, therefore I'm going to talk to you in a language that you understand.'[24]

Not surprisingly, many such recruits failed to show up in intelligence reports or, at most, were seen as low risk. Khurram Butt, the London Bridge ringleader, was an extremist from East London who was so well known that he had even featured in a Channel Four documentary on extremism.[25] The attackers at Westminster, Finsbury Park, Manchester Arena and London Bridge were all under surveillance of some sort, and the attacks at Woolwich, Manchester and Westminster could all have been stopped with better intelligence. The perpetrators had not been recruited through mosques or radicalised by imams' hate-filled sermons. In fact, they did not even become religious until after joining jihadist groups. Imams frequently remind their followers that Islam condemns terrorism, suicide and the killing of innocent people; indeed it can be argued that those who make a serious study of the religion are better equipped to resist the appeal of extremism and violent radicalisation.[26] The young recruits to Hizb ul-Tahrir spoke fluently about the new Islamic state, but when it came to reciting the Koran or maintaining basic Muslim etiquette, they were clueless.[27] As they prepared to go to

Syria in 2014, the Birmingham terrorists, Yusuf Sarwar and Mohammed Ahmed, notoriously resorted to Amazon to buy copies of *Islam for Dummies*!

This picture recurred in 2015, when the collapse of the Iraqi state and its army led to the emergence of the so-called Islamic State and a civil war in Syria. An estimated 800 British jihadis had left to fight for the Islamic State of Iraq and Syria (Isis) by 2016.[28] Investigation of the British jihadis revealed their background and motivation. One Lancashire jihadi, known as Abu Jamal, had grown up in Britain as anything but a good Muslim. He smoked, drank, enjoyed clubbing and had girlfriends. If he had a religion, it was Manchester United. Slowly he learned more about Islam by attending classes, but becoming a good Muslim did not mean rejecting Western society. His motivation was external. He was shocked by the civil war in Syria and felt he had to do something. As it appeared that Britain was on the side of the Syrian opposition, by fighting to remove President Bashar Assad he was in effect following the advice given earlier by David Cameron, who had advocated military intervention.[29] Yet despite his experience, he was not going to pose a threat to British security on returning home; he accepted that he was still a British citizen born and bred. The case of Abu Jamal underlined the extent to which the authorities largely missed their target because they saw religious fanaticism everywhere.

Unfortunately, as the politicians remained unable to learn from their experience in the Middle East, the problem of domestic terrorism remained intractable. It became a habit to seek fresh military intervention for each new problem. Yet by 2013, the Taliban was resurgent in Afghanistan, and al-Qaida had spread through the Arab world into Iraq and Syria. British forces had been rescued from Helmand by the Americans and were obliged to leave Iraq via Basra under cover of darkness. As a result, the public lost confidence in interventionism. When David Cameron proposed intervention against Assad in 2013, he was defeated in the House of Commons. However, as the problems of the original invasion of Iraq persisted, he returned to the bankrupt policy by embarking on air strikes against Islamic State targets in Iraq in September 2014, this time with parliamentary approval. A year later, in

December 2015, nothing had been achieved, but Cameron decided to bomb Syria – this time backed in the Commons by 397 votes to 223. Critics enquired how the bombing would make Britain's streets safer from terrorism. As Cameron knew perfectly well that bombing without ground troops would be ineffective, he resorted to fictitious claims that some 70,000 anti-Isis troops were available 'based on detailed analysis updated daily'.[30] Like his predecessors, Cameron continued to walk into the traps set by Isis. Retaliation with bombs that killed civilians and extravagant rhetoric about Islamism helped ensure a constant supply of new recruits to the cause. A more intelligent strategy would have required preventing the Gulf States from supplying weapons to terrorists in Syria and Iraq, helping Turkey to seal its border against the flow of new Isis fighters and reintegrating the Sunnis of Iraq and Syria who were the mainstay of Isis.

These attempts to identify potential terrorists through intelligence were complemented by a campaign – the Prevent programme – designed to divert them by giving remedial treatment. This was doubly flawed, as it appeared to treat Muslims generally as the target and to define the problem as an *ideology* that could be combated and even eradicated. In a notorious speech at Munich in 2011, Cameron insisted: 'We have got to get to the root of the problem . . . that is the existence of an ideology, Islamist extremism.' Unfortunately, there was too much emphasis on symptoms, rather than causes. In 2005, a controversy surrounding the wearing of the *hijab*, the *niqab* and the *burqa* by Muslim women was provoked by the former foreign secretary, Jack Straw, who complained about women appearing at his constituency surgeries dressed this way. The issue was significant in two ways. First, it suggested something about the British approach that was reassuring. In France, legislation was enacted to ban the *hijab*, consistent with the French tradition where people enjoy a much clearer and stricter idea of national identity and require greater conformity than has ever been the case in Britain. By contrast, no attempt was made to limit the wearing of the *hijab* by legislation in Britain (where the French response seemed over the top). After Straw fluttered the dovecotes, the issue largely died down until 2018.

Second, inaction in Britain also reflected the fact that concern about Muslim dress was completely out of all proportion. There are some situations in which there is a legitimate objection to the *niqab* – in court, for example, where witnesses should show the jury their full face; but it is within the powers of the judge to have it removed. Beyond such cases, women of all sorts simply exercise their choice. The writer Gary Younge quoted the example of a family in which the mother and daughter chose not to wear the *hijab*, while two other daughters voluntarily adopted it.[31] Such cases offer a useful corrective to the propaganda surrounding the *hijab*. In fact, few British Muslims wear veils; and those that do, adopt them out of choice not through coercion. Like other young people, Muslims sometimes decide to indicate their stance or opinion by means of the clothes they wear; the hijab thus becomes a sign that a woman wishes to dress modestly and rejects the flaunting of the body characteristic of Western society. Some believe it confers respect and 'they don't want men looking at them'.[32] In Blackburn, Waqas Siddiqui explained: 'It is mostly the younger girls who are buying them . . . because when people criticise your religion, you hold on to it a bit more. You retreat back into what you're comfortable with.'[33] Consequently, whenever the issue is raised it has the effect of increasing sales! One can only conclude that the British avoidance of a ban is pragmatic and rational: it would be an unnecessary provocation. Even football, not the most progressive of sports, has adopted a relaxed attitude. In 2007, FIFA banned female footballers from wearing the *hijab*, claiming variously that it could strangle a player (for which there was no empirical evidence) and that it imported religious symbolism into the game (although such symbols were allowed for male players). But in 2014, the ban was dropped, along with prohibitions on Sikh and Jewish headwear. Tacitly the British seem to have recognised that a ban on female dress is a solution in search of a problem. This was corroborated in 2018, when Boris Johnson foolishly described women wearing *burqas* as 'letter boxes' and as 'looking like bank robbers'.[34] Significantly, however, he denied wanting to introduce a ban. Johnson's motive was widely recognised as part of his strategy for keeping himself in the news and in the running for the Tory leadership, and consequently the issue rapidly faded from public attention.

In contrast to their relaxed attitude towards *burqas*, the government decided to focus on the process it believed to be responsible for placing Muslims under the influence of Islamism – education. In 2015, David Cameron announced a crackdown on the madrasas, where about 200,000 Muslim children spent two hours each evening studying the Qur'an. He called on Muslims to integrate and adopt British values. Nothing could have illustrated better the confusion of government policy, for the Conservatives were actually encouraging the establishment of religious schools of all sorts – Catholic, Jewish and Muslim. In this they ignored the long-term experience of Northern Ireland, where segregation in schools had kept the communities divided.

Moreover, it proved difficult to apply Cameron's policy. At Waltham Forest, the council trained teachers to spot Islamist attitudes among pupils as young as ten.[35] In addition NHS trusts, local authorities and prisons were placed under a statutory duty to prevent people being drawn into terrorism (practically impossible to fulfil), and the government tried to persuade universities to inform on students' opinions. Schools were sold software designed to monitor pupils' internet activity for language associated with extremism. The results were both sinister and bizarre. One man who visited an accident and emergency department with burns on his hands was referred to the police on suspicion of experimenting with bomb-making. Many teachers were out of their depth in trying to identify signs of incipient Islamism. One four-year-old said 'cooker bomb' when trying to pronounce 'cucumber'. A ten-year-old suspect wrote 'terrorist house' when he meant 'terraced house'. Four-year-olds were being monitored for radicalisation. As one academic commented: 'They're pre-lingual, let alone pre-political. It's bonkers.'[36]

After its launch in 2005, the Prevent programme was revamped in 2011, 2013 and 2015 – an indication that even the authorities recognised it was not working. During 2015–16, some 7,631 people were referred to the official counter-extremism programme, but as the MCB

noted, the great majority were simply misidentified. On further examination, the referrals were rejected: threats were seen where none existed.
Less than one referral in ten came from the general public, and the
police accepted that many of those actually at risk of radicalisation were
not being referred at all. In 2016, the police chief leading the campaign
against terrorism, Simon Cole, complained that official policy on
extremism was so flawed that it risked creating a 'thought police', and
was unenforceable because it made the police the judges of 'what people
can say and cannot say'.[37] He felt the government was extending the
definition of 'extremists' so as to include people who did not in fact
advocate terrorism as it really had no useful working definition of
extremism. In this way, Prevent risked alienating people who could have
provided valuable information. In Dewsbury, for example, the five anti-
terrorism officers sent in by the council were seen as spies who 'never
seem to engage with the community'.[38] In November 2016, no fewer
than 26 mosques in Luton (i.e. almost all of them) told the council's
chief executive that as the Prevent strategy was unfair and counter-
productive, they were withdrawing their cooperation with it.[39] Prevent
was widely discounted for defining Muslims as the problem, for being a
cover for spying on the innocent, and for treating all critics of government foreign policy as potential extremists.[40] Its ineffectiveness was
borne out by the fact that only 5 per cent of all those referred to Prevent
actually received specialist support to turn them away from extremism.

In 2016, a report by the House of Commons Women and Equalities
Committee complained about the government's failure to provide
adequate financial and ministerial support for its counter-terrorism
strategy. David Cameron criticised Muslim women because 22 per cent
had limited or no English – the correct figure was only 6 per cent – and
initiated a £20 million scheme to help them learn, though his government had already cut £205 million from schemes to teach English to
immigrants![41] Lady Warsi reminded him that failure to learn English
was not a cause of Islamism, arguing that 'responses to foreign policy are
a greater driver of radicalisation'. Meanwhile, mosques began to take
counter-action by organising open days, so that non-Muslims could
visit. On a trip to An-Noor Community Centre in Acton in 2015,

where the mosque enjoyed a reputation for extremism, James Fergusson found it had been under surveillance since 2007. He heard a sermon on the dangers of materialism, which he thought could have been given in the Church of England. A camera recorded everything, so that the mosque could refute any accusations of extremism.[42]

As 33 per cent of Prevent referrals came from schools and colleges, including no fewer than 2,127 children under the age of 15, the controversy increasingly focused on the younger generation. But experts complained that there were no clear guidelines to help teachers identify radicalisation. Many of the suggested indicators – like changes in dress and reluctance to talk to teachers and parents – were simply routine teenage behaviour.[43] Nonetheless, the extent to which Islamophobic propaganda spoke to public fears was underlined by the Trojan Horse affair in 2014, when an anonymous letter sent to Birmingham city council alleged that 25 state schools in Birmingham had been infiltrated by Islamic extremists, who were trying to take them over. The education minister, Michael Gove, something of a witchfinder-general for Islamism, promptly sent in the inspectors and appointed the former head of anti-terrorism at Scotland Yard to find 'evidence of extremist infiltration in schools'. Yet the West Midlands Police said there was nothing to investigate, and the report found no evidence! Subsequently it emerged that the original letter was a fake and the claims baseless.[44] The whole thing had been 'a witch hunt triggered by a hoax', in the *Guardian*'s words.

Yet Michael Gove was not deterred. The government tried to ban 15 teachers for applying undue religious influence, though after legal action the ban was overruled by the courts. Following the Trojan Horse affair, Ofsted, the supposedly neutral schools inspectorate, was turned into a major arm of official policy on Islamism. It threatened six London schools with closure for failing to promote British values (even though its inspectors were not empowered to do that).[45] In Bradford, Ofsted, under direction from Gove, placed five schools in special measures for not teaching enough about the threat of extremism. One Birmingham school, Park View (which had recently been rated as 'outstanding'), was suddenly rated 'inadequate or failing'. In other Birmingham schools, the inspectors identified a series of failings: gender segregation, placing girls at the back of the class, curtailing the teaching of biology, banning music, putting an emphasis on Arabic, and banning Christmas trees. Every point was found to be false![46] In 2016, when Ofsted criticised a Birmingham school for segregating boys and girls at age nine and put it in special measures, the decision was overturned when the school challenged the inspectors' finding at a judicial review.[47] As gender separation was a traditional practice in many British secondary schools and private schools, Ofsted's action appeared almost comically discriminatory. In 2018, Ofsted recommended that inspectors should question Muslim primary-school girls if they were wearing the *hijab*. Over a thousand teachers and faith leaders immediately demanded a retraction and condemned Ofsted as 'kneejerk, discriminatory and institutionally racist'. In effect, Ofsted shifted its judgements so abruptly that it appeared to educational critics to be following a political rather than an educational agenda. Moreover, its interference had damaging effects. At Park View, the government renamed the school, removed the Muslim governors and placed it under academy control. As a result, there was an exodus of teachers, a reliance on supply teaching and a sharp deterioration in examination results.

However, the government felt that it could disregard Muslim reactions to its oppressive policies because it enjoyed the backing of the major newspapers. One of the most shocking scandals erupted in 2017, when *The Times* produced a lurid front-page headline based on a case in Tower Hamlets: 'Christian Child Forced into Muslim Foster Care'. This rapidly created hysteria in the press. 'Which individual at Tower Hamlets was responsible for the abuse of this little girl?' demanded the *Mail*'s Katie Hopkins. It was indicative of the mood that the claims were immediately believed. In the *Sun*, Trevor Phillips, the former equalities chief, excitedly described Tower Hamlets' actions as 'akin to child abuse'. Yet on investigation, the catalogue of alarmist claims circulated by the press turned out to be wholly false.[48] The episode was an indication of how polarised discussion of Muslims had become in some quarters, and showed that it had become routine for media bigotry to pander to popular fears.

The Islamophobic policies of this period reflected the politicians' inability to recognise that their habit of perpetual intervention in

Muslim countries had become counter-productive and that their own illiberalism left them poorly placed to insist that Muslims must embrace British values and liberal democracy. Their professed belief in British values sat uneasily with the detention of suspects without charge, trials without jury, the cultivation of dictators like Qaddafi and Mubarak, and the suspension of human rights in favour of rendition. Neither Tony Blair for Labour nor David Cameron for the Conservatives had much grasp of traditional British values and political history, and consequently they struggled to offer Muslims a plausible guide to national identity. Fortunately, while the political leaders floundered, social and commercial forces were making them less relevant in wider British society.

CHAPTER TWELVE

MUSLIMS IN THE BRITISH MAINSTREAM

Amidst the din generated by Islamophobia, it is not easy to recognise that there is an alternative narrative about the evolution of the three-million-strong British Muslim community and its role in society today. The alternative account does not make many headlines for two main reasons. First, it does not fit the agenda of most of the newspapers and other media outlets, which flourish on the dramatic story of violence and subversion. And secondly, it comprises a rather disparate concatenation of underlying social, political and commercial changes that are not easily represented as a neat, single process. But it involves one significant trend, namely a gradual *convergence* between the Muslim and the non-Muslim communities in Britain. For the historian, there is no great surprise here, for history is punctuated by quiet social revolutions that have often occurred in spite of politicians, the press and the opinion leaders who command massive attention, especially in a world driven by instant, 24-hour news. Yet the influence of politicians is far more limited than one might suppose from the relentless prominence they enjoy day by day.

Elderly critics of British society are often heard to complain that the country is not what it used to be in the 1950s. And they are correct, for society has changed in all kinds of ways. In particular, there has been a steady evolution of a more liberal society encompassing, among other

272

things, the spread of feminist attitudes among both men and women, a growing tolerance of differences in sexuality (including same-sex sex and gay marriage), less racial prejudice (as manifested, for example, in a high rate of inter-racial marriage in Britain and a million mixed-race children) and a pronounced extension of liberalism among the younger generations, accelerated by the huge spread of university education, which has been a major and apparently inexorable engine of social change. All of which causes immense frustration in the pages and columns of the *Daily Mail*, the *Sun*, the *Daily Express* and the *Daily Telegraph*. Yet although such titles constitute the bulk of newspaper sales, they have had remarkably little influence on the underlying pattern of social change, partly because their loyal readers die in great numbers each year. In 2016, the referendum vote to leave the EU represented a rare triumph for reaction, but it was a blip on the graph, not a sign of long-term change. This enables one to put into perspective the stream of misrepresentation and scaremongering about Islam and Muslims, the spread of poisonous material via social media platforms, and the toxic compound of heavy-handedness towards Muslims at home and incompetent meddling in Muslim states abroad. The market for alarmist books about the takeover of Europe by Islam has begun to collapse for lack of empirical support, leaving plentiful scope to consider how Muslims have been finding their way into the mainstream of British society.

The view promoted back in 1968 by Enoch Powell that it was impossible to be black and British has by no means disappeared, but today it does seem increasingly anachronistic. It has been superseded by alternative questions, such as how far is there a British Muslim identity today? In 2016, a report by Policy Exchange found that 'British Muslims as a whole continue to live somewhat more separately than other large ethno-cultural minorities'.[1] However, the report contradicted itself by recognising that in their everyday lives, Muslims are increasingly part of the mainstream, acknowledging that no fewer than 93 per cent of Muslims had a strong attachment to Britain, and explaining that their

attitudes on major issues were largely in line with the rest of the population. Indeed, opinion polls suggest that British identity is stronger
among ethnic communities generally than among indigenous English
people, who have retreated somewhat from the idea of Britishness in
recent decades. This makes sense, because 'English' is a racial-cultural
identity, whereas 'British' is a political one that encompasses the four
countries that comprise the British Isles. Moreover, around 70 per cent
of Muslims are under 25 and are British born, and so they enjoy fewer
links with their families' countries of origin and are better adapted to the
Western lifestyle. As a result, they increasingly describe themselves as
'British Asian', though this identity is less likely to be used by those of
Somali, Iraqi, Iranian or Syrian origin. Assertions about Muslims as a
separate community have been regularly contradicted by polls for
Populus and NOP, which record that half of British Muslims do not
attend mosques; that few fast for Ramadan; and that many visit pubs,
though they do not drink at home. The idea that they are radicalised by
fanatical imams in mosques has largely been exposed as a myth. In effect,
opinion poll findings suggest that Muslims have been steadily absorbed
into mainstream society. This, of course, helps to explain why the intelligence services have found it difficult to identify young Muslims who
engage with terrorist organisations: their radicalisation is not primarily
religious in nature, although it can adopt the language of religion, as
protest movements have often done.

As a result, Britain is now experiencing a remarkable two-way interaction between the communities: on the one hand more deliberate
efforts by Muslims to participate in the mainstream, and on the other,
fresh initiatives, often commercial in character, by society to recognise
and respond to the Islamic presence. Since 2005, observers have coined
the phrase 'Muslim Cool', referring to Muslim participation in music
(Islamic rap and hip-hop), the arts, the media and fashion. This involves
a synthesis of Western youth culture and the Islamic faith. Many
mosques have been thrown open to non-Muslim visitors. The Liverpool
Abdullah Quilliam Mosque, founded in 1893, opened its doors to offer
a barbecue and soft drinks to people of all denominations. 'This is the
first time any mosque has screened the World Cup,' commented its

chief executive. 'The mosque welcomes people of all walks of life and football brings people together and this encourages community cohesion.' Among the 2,000 mosques in Britain, several now enjoy listed-building status, including the London Central Mosque in Regent's Park, the Shah Jahan in Woking, Surrey, the Fazl Mosque in south London, and a mosque in one of Liverpool's Georgian terraces which is

> an example of Liverpool's capacity to embrace different cultural and faith communities as well as evidence of the social and cultural diversity that developed as a consequence of the city's role as an internationally significant port and trading centre.[2]

In Birmingham, where Muslims comprise a quarter of the population, 100,000 people gathered on Small Heath in June 2017 for the start of Eid, marking the end of the holy month of Ramadan. Once the mass prayer was over, they turned to fairground rides, miniature golf, clay-pigeon shooting and rodeo bull-riding. In effect, a Muslim festival was becoming a conventional carnival.

This process has been underpinned by the steady social convergence of the two communities. The poverty that afflicted 54 per cent of first-generation Muslims remains a serious problem, but now affects only 25 per cent of the third generation. The Muslim birth rate is falling towards the British average, and there are 77,000 one-parent Muslim families, alongside 260,000 married families with dependent children. Convergence is also obvious in the educational experience of young Muslims. By 1990, 54 per cent of those of Pakistani and Bangladeshi family origin were in post-compulsory education, compared with 56 per cent of the white population; and the rapid spread of universities in London, the North and the Midlands has accelerated the trend, by making university education available locally for many Muslims. Women now comprise up to 43 per cent of Muslim students.

There has also been an organisational-political convergence, especially among young progressive Muslims. In 2017, Qari Asim, a leading Leeds imam, proposed creating a national council to issue progressive religious rulings for young people that 'embed Islam in a twenty-first century British context' and promote an interpretation of Islam that is in line with British values. He said it would offer guidance on controversial issues, such as 'forced marriages, [female genital mutilation] and honour killing', since 'these practices are not sanctioned by the faith of Islam but they are cultural practices that have penetrated the Muslim community of particular backgrounds'.[3] This trend is being accelerated by the emergence of female pressure groups, including the Bradford-based Muslim Women's Council, which aims to establish the first mosque managed by women, and the Birmingham-based Muslim Women's Network, which campaigns against women's exclusion from among the trustees who manage mosques. For many years, women were barred from leadership roles in the Labour Party – largely by male Muslims, who persuaded the local parties to deny them nominations. In 2005, running as a Conservative, Sayeeda Warsi was defeated at Dewsbury in the face of opposition from Muslim men. Eventually, however, the Labour Party felt obliged to respond, because of the extensive role enjoyed by Muslim women in the Respect Party, under the leadership of Salma Yaqoob from 2003 to 2012. She highlighted complaints that women were being disenfranchised by men's control of postal votes, and she helped Respect gain Bradford West from Labour in 2012. At the general election of 2017, eight of the 15 successful Muslim candidates were female.

Nor is convergence a one-way process. The rather futile debate about multiculturalism tends to obscure the extent to which British society is recognising and adapting to the presence of a non-English community, sometimes almost unconsciously and sometimes deliberately. As the British have largely ceased to be a religious people, the symptoms of this process must be found elsewhere – for example, in the susceptibility of modern British consumers to the appeal of leisure, entertainment, food and drink. The evidence is all around us. Barbecues and Christmas markets are not British traditions, and yet they are being enthusiastically adopted by Muslims and non-Muslims alike. Every year thousands of British people enjoy holidays in Turkey, where they encounter a friendly and charming people who are also well adapted to Western entrepreneurialism and practise democracy, despite the autocratic character of their current regime. It is easy to overlook the fact that nearly all Turks are Muslims. The British fondness for holidays in the sun also entails contact with Muslims in India, Egypt, Tunisia, Morocco and Indonesia.

More significantly, the rise of a Muslim middle class and the expenditure of £31 billion annually by British Muslims has alerted business to an untapped market. As a result, commercial considerations are promoting some interesting cultural interactions. British farmers, for example, have become attuned to the fact that the best time to sell lamb coincides with Muslim festivals such as Eid, when prices rise by five to ten pence a kilo. 'The Muslim community seems to eat a fair bit of lamb and farmers are more mindful of them, when once upon a time they weren't,' observed one cattle-market director.[4] Not all commercial responses have been welcomed: the sale of a Muslim Barbie doll, dressed in a *hijab*, is not accepted as genuinely halal. A more impressive and successful example is Lewis Pies, an 80-year-old family firm from Swansea that has concluded that 'halal products, if well designed and marketed, can appeal to the general population where it is moving from niche to mainstream'. To this end, the firm has turned over a third of its business to halal products.[5] Two football clubs have even approached the firm to supply halal pies for consumption on the terraces. Lewis Pies has gone to some trouble to reassure the Muslim community: they market a whole range of items under the 'Trusty' label, indicating the approval of the Halal Monitoring Committee, and the 'Crescent' label, signifying the recognition of the Halal Authority Board. Specific days are wholly given over to making halal products, when halal representatives inspect the entire process.[6] The company responded to the spending power of Muslim millennials moved by a combination of Islamic faith and British consumerism, recognising that many Muslims wanted traditional British staple foods – such as shepherd's pie, but in a halal version.

Popular susceptibility to leisure, entertainment and food helps to explain how British society has become influenced by the celebrity culture during the last thirty years. Celebrity has been heavily promoted by newspapers, and especially by the BBC and other television companies, as a way of boosting audiences. The strategy involves programmes based frankly around prominent celebrities and using celebrities to front programmes on subjects about which they are ignorant; or alternatively it manufactures new celebrities from people who enjoy little or no claim on the title. Their success has been compounded by the mass use of social platforms that promote a sense of engagement between the public and famous people.

One of the indirect effects of the celebrity culture has been to make it increasingly easy for Muslims and others to enter the British mainstream without actually intending to do so, and without the process being widely recognised. For example, Mishal Husain, familiar and admired as a BBC radio and television broadcaster, has attained popular recognition without generally being identified as a Muslim. The same is true of the BBC economics editor, Kamal Ahmed – 'a very British man in Britain', in his own words.

By contrast, some Muslims – such as Gulam Khan and Shazia Mirza – have used comedy as a more direct means of confronting issues of race and religion faced by Muslims in the West, an expedient earlier followed by comedians with an Indian-Hindu background. Reportedly Britain's first female, Muslim, stand-up comedian, Shazia Mirza won a reputation by tackling controversial topics head-on. She tells her audiences: 'I'm Shazia Mirza. At least that's what it says on my pilot's licence.' Aware that sex is amusing for Muslims and non-Muslims alike, she ridicules the women who visit the Middle East to join Isis: 'They're not religious, they're horny. They're looking for a halal version of Brad Pitt.'[7]

Other Muslims have emerged via the British obsession with food. Millions of viewers avidly watch programmes featuring celebrity chefs and buy the spin-off cookery books. The winning formula has produced competitive programmes such as 'The Great British Bake Off', which successfully manufactures new celebrities from hitherto obscure people. One outstanding personality to emerge in this way is Nadiya Hussain, a widely admired 'British Bake Off' winner, whose easy charm and modesty made her an instant celebrity – and also a model Muslim operating successfully in the mainstream. The significance of Nadiya Hussain may be estimated by the hostile reaction her success provoked among reactionary journalists. In the *Daily Mail*, Amanda Platell nastily commented that rivals should have baked a chocolate mosque, while the *Sun*'s Ally Ross absurdly accused the BBC of waging ideological warfare on behalf of political correctness. But these rather pathetic jibes only underlined how far the reactionary press was losing touch with social change.

As a married woman and mother of three, Hussain is too reassuring a figure to be easily discredited. The critics were outmanoeuvred by Hussain herself, who appeared on *Desert Island Discs* and chose Marmite as her luxury item! As she says herself, she is 'as British as anyone else'. She also published a book, significantly entitled *Nadiya's British Food Adventure* (2017), that offered a shrewdly judged example of how to be both distinctive and familiar at the same time: 'the food of my childhood was a collision of two worlds'. Recognising Britain as a country of regions, Hussain's recipes visit Yorkshire, Lancashire and Scotland, giving traditional dishes like steak-and-kidney pie, Yorkshire pudding and baked beans the extra pizazz of Oriental ingredients and methods. They are calculated to satisfy the British taste for food that is both novel and reassuring. Her recipes include parathas stuffed with mashed potato and a sausage stew with garlic and spices: 'Sausages didn't used to be something that was widely available to people following a halal diet,' she writes. '[But] what an introduction it was! . . . I'd have a full English breakfast, a sausage and egg sandwich for lunch, toad-in-the-hole for dinner.'[8] In 2018, she began a new television series that tackled Cornish pasties and translated samosas into the traditional British fondness for a large pie. It is, of course, easy to disparage the significance of food, but that is to ignore its effect on popular culture. Nadiya Hussain's recipes rely on an intelligent strategy that reveals her as a recognisably successful British Muslim, but also makes it impossible, outside the enclaves of reaction, to typecast her as a Muslim. As the journalist Gaby Hinsliff commented: 'A cookery show can only take us so far towards a Britain at ease with itself, but every step counts.'[9] No fewer than

13.4 million people watched the 'Bake Off' final, a reminder that such popular expressions of Britishness reach more widely into society than the politicians.

The celebrity culture is also strongly reflected in sport, which has long constituted a central element in this country's national identity, not least because the British have traditionally taken pride in their role in creating – through the rules – modern sports including football, rugby, boxing, tennis, cricket, horse-racing, golf and even skiing. Sport has been widely considered to embody the key British qualities: respect for rules, discipline, team spirit, fair play and endurance. So much so that in the Victorian era some British people declined to engage in sports (such as rowing and football) with foreigners, preferring to keep things English![10] When the 'International Board' for football was constituted in 1886, it comprised England, Scotland, Wales and Ireland! Cricket, polo and pig-sticking became part of the imperial strategy designed to bind India to Britain – at least to the extent of teaching the princes English values and customs.

At a time when most of the traditional props to national identity have become irrelevant or have lost their force, sport has recently emerged as the most positive single element in Britishness. The decline of the traditional private gentlemen's clubs that controlled and restricted entry to many sports, combined with the huge increase in state funding since 1990, has accelerated this trend, by broadening the basis and boosting the success of British sport. Recent years have seen a renaissance in British sporting success – notably at the Olympic Games and in particular sectors, such as cycling, gymnastics and rowing. Although not initially recognised by the pundits, this has been a major achievement of Britain's multi-racial society. In 2018, 11 of the 23 members of England's surprisingly successful team for the football World Cup were black or of mixed race. Yet it has proved all too easy to overlook the extent to which Muslims have participated in this revival. At the London Olympics in 2012, Mo Farah leapt to fame and celebrity by winning a gold medal in the 10,000 metres – the first Briton to do so in the hundred years the event has been included in the Olympics – and draping himself in the Union flag. Farah had arrived in Britain aged nine as a Muslim refugee from Somalia.

Since the nineteenth century, boxing has been closely associated with Britishness, and enjoyed great popularity even when it was illegal; along with horse racing, it forged a link between aristocrats and the poor. In recent years, boxing has continued to produce characters, including Muslim stars such as Naseem Hamed, a flamboyant middle-weight fighter. The most potent figure is Amir Khan, who, aged 18, famously returned from the 2004 Athens Olympics with a silver medal to receive a civic reception from his home town, Bolton, where he subsequently trained with Bolton Wanderers. Decent and articulate, Khan was consistently unequivocal about his loyalties: 'I'm British. I went to the Olympic Games for Britain. I could have chosen to go for Pakistan if I was like that.'[11] Yet his experience in America forced him to recognise how race and religion had complicated his career: 'I know for a fact that if I were a white fighter maybe I would have been a superstar in Britain.' Despite his success, Khan was sometimes booed in the ring, and he became the target of crude prejudice vented in chatroom exchanges. But this did not prevent him recognising his responsibility as a role model for young Asians and as a bridge between the communities. 'I have to try to fix things between the Asian community and the British community . . . I have tried to break that barrier.'[12] He demonstrated his maturity prior to a 2009 fight with an American Jew, in which both boxers resisted the media-inspired temptation to play up race and religion by emphasising their respect for one another.[13] Khan's combination of success and patriotism has enabled him to occupy the mainstream and to counter the alienation of young Muslim men.

Cricket, with its imperial tradition of Indian and Caribbean players, has also proved to be a significant sport for Muslims. Early participants included Aftab Habib and Usman Afzaal. The experience of the renowned leg-spinner Mushtaq Ahmed was especially striking. Of Punjabi origin, Ahmed played for Sussex, Surrey and Somerset and took 185 wickets in 52 tests. He recalled how his team mates used to stop their tour bus to allow him to say his prayers: 'English people are very open-hearted, you know, they can accept your thing.'[14] In the run-up to the 2012 London Olympics, a Foreign Office video used Mushtaq Ahmed to highlight Britain's tolerant multi-faith society. Addressing young Muslim men, he argued: 'we're living in a country, England, we're praying five times, there's mosques. The freedom is there.' Ahmed became another ideal role model for young Muslims otherwise vulnerable to alienation and radicalisation.

Among the most interesting cricketers is Nasser Hussain, who arrived in England, aged seven, the son of a Muslim from Chennai and an Englishwoman from Cornwall. A sign that British Asians were developing middle-class lifestyles, Hussain received his education at a private school and married an English girl he met at university. His father insisted: 'I want them brought up in England. I want them to respect English ways.'[15] In 2000, Hussain was hailed even by the *Daily Mail*, which clearly appreciated his family's middle-class lifestyle and aspirations, as 'the most successful cricket captain in years'.[16] Hussain realised that as a result of his success at cricket, the England and Wales Cricket Board saw him as a means of boosting attendances. Evidently comfortable with both communities, he chided 'second and third generation Asians . . . [for] clinging to their sub-continental roots whereas I felt that there's a huge amount to gain by the Asian community nailing their colours to England's mast'. His identity was not in doubt: 'Having always considered myself to be totally English . . . I have never thought of myself as a role model for British Asians.'[17] Yet despite this evidence, the *Mail* could not quite bring itself to recognise his career as an endorsement of the multicultural society.

British Asian participation appears to have been closely associated with England's growing success at cricket, including the recapture of the Ashes from Australia in 2011; as England had previously won just three test matches in 25, this was seen as a national turning point. Her victory over Pakistan in 2000 was partly attributable to the performance of two bowlers who were the sons of Asian parents, Sajid Mahmood and Monty Panesar, a Sikh, who became a cult figure, leading fans to adopt fake beards and turbans in tribute to him. For earlier generations, cricket had offered a means of expressing their cultural heritage through support for Pakistan, but this changed. When Mahmood appeared, he was booed not by English fans but by visiting Pakistanis, who thought he should have been playing for their team. By the 2000s, British Asians were increasingly coming to appreciate that their sons would want to play for England. As one concluded: 'the future was British Pakistanis supporting England . . . It is possible to be both British and Muslim.'[18]

Gradually the success of cricketers such as Mushtaq Ahmed and Nasser Hussain has fed through into the younger generation, as is dramatically illustrated by the career of Haseeb Hameed. His parents left a village in Gujarat in 1969 to emigrate to Bolton, where they worked in the local cotton factories and lived in a two-up two-down house in a deprived part of the town. At an early age Haseeb would go from his mosque classes to play cricket, winter and summer. No fewer than three Hameed sons became able cricketers, but Haseeb was quickly recognised by the local coach as an outstanding talent.[19] Taken on by Lancashire, who gave him a cricket scholarship and a public-school education, he scored a century aged ten. In 2016, at the age of 19, Haseeb played for England against India, only the second teenager to do so since 1949. His story, rather than the media obsession with terrorism and multiculturalism, offers a striking parable for the British Asian community in the twenty-first century.

Although participation in mainstream sport has not been uniform, and indeed it is widely assumed that Muslims tend to be excluded from team sports, there is some surprising unacknowledged evidence of participation. In rugby league – a conservative sport played mainly by white men – Ikram Butt became the first Asian to play in the England team in 1995. Born to Pakistani parents, Butt grew up as a true Yorkshireman, playing rugby for Leeds, Featherstone, Huddersfield and Hunslet. A devout Muslim, he could not fail to realise that the English rugby shirt was emblazoned with the Cross of St George, a symbol of Christianity. Yet he founded the British Asian Rugby Association to encourage the participation of young Asians. 'No one was more proud to play for England than I was. England is my country and I would do anything for my country,' he wrote.[20]

Even less promising, on the face of it, is football, a sport long notorious for insularity and racism among both supporters and management. Football has been regularly discredited by fresh revelations about the prejudice harboured by the professional game, despite prolonged efforts to eradicate it. However, the racists have shifted their targets from the black Caribbean players who acted as the pioneers, encouraged by the Football Lads Alliance, a Muslim-hate organisation that joins forces with the English Defence League. Yet such initiatives indicate the waning of racism, for even in this most backward of sports, liberal attitudes are advancing. It comes as a surprise to know that 60 per cent of Bengali boys play football – a higher proportion than among native English – and that some have worked their way up into the professional game.[21] Mohamed ('Mo') Salah, an Egyptian national who plays for Liverpool and is known as the 'Egyptian King', is arguably the best player in the Premier League, and is certainly too successful for the fanatics and xenophobes to dismiss. In 2018 he was the Premier League's top goalscorer and his boots were presented to the British Museum, where they were displayed in the modern Egyptian section. Salah is well on the way to becoming a national celebrity. A good Muslim, he briefly prostrates himself on the ground after scoring a goal, while the Liverpool fans chant:

If he's good enough for you
He's good enough for me
If he scores another few
Then I'll be Muslim too.

Nor is Salah an isolated example. The top teams have recruited many Muslims, including Paul Pogba (Manchester United), whose 2016 transfer fee was £90 million and who donates much of his salary to charity; Riyad Mahrez (Manchester City); N'Golo Kante (Chelsea); Mesut Ozil (Arsenal); Yaya Toure (ex-Manchester City); Mamadou Sakho (Crystal Palace); Islam Slimani (Newcastle United); Mohamed Elyounoussi (Southampton); and Cenk Tosun (Everton).[22] In Britain's celebrity society, they help to undermine crude racial stereotyping among white football fans, and as they are pictured reading the Qur'an on football coaches, or even visiting Mecca, they also provide role models of success for younger British Muslims.

Politics offers a more precarious ladder into the mainstream. Some Muslims have questioned whether it is really possible for devout Muslims to participate in the political life of Europe as a minority community. This is a surprisingly unhistorical view, as in India they have done exactly that for many years. Yet some go further, arguing that elections are unknown to Islam, that democratic systems do not respect Islamic values or criteria, and that a Muslim can give allegiance only to another Muslim. Tariq Ramadan has claimed that 'Western Muslims vote rarely, if at all', though he produces no evidence.[23] This scepticism reflects the feeling that although Muslims have been granted full citizenship in European countries, in practice they must participate through political parties, which can be seen as undermining their loyalty to Islam. Traditionally, this perspective has divided Muslims from Christians, who have always had a clearer idea of the separation of the religious and the political authority.

Yet despite these reservations, there is no shortage of evidence that the negative view about Muslim political participation is quite erroneous. In the face of claims that the system was not Islamic, Iqbal Sacranie, former secretary of the Muslim Council of Britain, argued that Muslims had a duty to vote: 'We believe it is a necessity for us to relate to the wider society, to understand our neighbours, and to let them understand us.'[24] The registration of Muslims as voters rose to 75 per cent during the 1970s and had reached 85 per cent by 1991. It is estimated that around three-quarters voted in the 1997 general election, only slightly less than among the rest of the population.[25]

In local government it is comparatively easy for Muslims to win elections, partly because of the first-past-the-post system and the concentration of Muslim-majority wards in such places as Bradford, Leicester, Birmingham and Tower Hamlets (as was the case for Jews in an earlier generation). In Birmingham, 90 per cent of Muslims live in just five inner-city wards, for example.[26] As a result, Muslims have been increasingly represented in local government since the 1980s: by 2001 there were 217 councillors; and by 2018 there were over 300, concentrated in East London (Newham, Tower Hamlets, Waltham Forest), Bradford and Birmingham. The first Muslim mayors took office in Brent (1981) and Bradford (1985). An iconic figure in this development is the lord mayor of Sheffield, Magid Magid, who fled Somalia, aged five, with his mother and sister. His mother worked as a cleaner in Sheffield, while Magid took his degree at Hull, where he was elected president of the students' union. A digital marketing consultant, he was elected as a Green member of the city council in 2016.[27] His disregard for convention turned Magid into an instant celebrity. He wears his gold mayoral livery collar along with his black Doc Martens boots and yellow baseball cap. Although he became the target of hostility, his policy is to 'kill it with kindness and bury it with a smile. You could be the most racist person . . . [but] I will still be kind to you . . . I believe people can come around just by meeting people.'[28]

Meanwhile, at the national level Muslims have been elected on a largely secular basis, as representatives of their party (usually Labour), rather than their religious community: Mohammad Sarwar was elected an MP (Glasgow Govan, then Central) in 1997; Khalid Mahmood (Birmingham Perry Barr) in 2001; Shahid Malik (Dewsbury) in 2005, becoming the first Muslim minister in 2007; and Naz Shah, who defeated George Galloway in Bradford West in 2015. By 2017, there were 14 Muslim MPs – all Labour, apart from two Conservatives. This compares with the record of Jews, who returned 17 MPs in 1929 and 28 in 1945. Several Muslims have also been made peers, including Lord Nazir Ahmed, Lady Pola Uddin, Lord Waheed Alli and Lady Sayeeda Warsi.

Unfortunately, many politically ambitious Muslims have suffered from smears and innuendo, designed to deter them from standing or to secure their defeat. Yet the political parties recognise that they cannot entirely do without them, as is strikingly illustrated by the career of Sayeeda Warsi. A Muslim woman from a northern working-class background, articulate and personable, Warsi represented everything the Conservatives needed in their efforts to become a more inclusive, national party at a time when most Muslims voted Labour. Although the handful of Muslim candidates were unsuccessful in 2005, including Warsi at Dewsbury, David Cameron shrewdly saw her as an asset and appointed her a peer, Conservative vice-chairman and a junior Foreign Office minister. Nonetheless Warsi found it difficult to pursue her career in Conservative politics. Instead of welcoming her role as a Conservative Muslim, the reactionary press set about undermining her. The *Daily Telegraph's* Andrew Gilligan, employing the nudge-nudge style of journalism, claimed – 'Colossal Conspiracy in Whitehall' – that she was promoting the entry of Islamic radicals into the government.[29] Caught between routine prejudice among colleagues and the anti-Muslim bias of government policy, she found life increasingly uncomfortable. In 2011, she famously attacked newspaper critics for stereotyping Muslims as moderates and extremists, saying that 'Islamophobia has now passed the dinner-table test' – by which she meant that it had become respectable among the chattering classes. 'It is OK for non-Muslims . . . to make jokes about people with long beards or wearing burqas. If you were to replace the word Muslim with black or Jew, you would be jumped on straight away as racist or anti-Semitic.'[30] Her comments irritated some Conservatives and she lost her place in the government, but she won praise from the Muslim Council of Britain and the Muslim Youth helpline.

However, the party showed itself hesitant about tackling the problem. Admittedly, Conservatism suffered several problems in dealing with Muslims. For one thing, the socialist leanings in Islam were difficult to reconcile with market economics. Unlike Labour the Conservatives were reluctant to admit that the wars in Afghanistan and Iraq had been a mistake. In 2018, Miqdaad Versi of the Muslim Council of Britain compiled a dossier on Conservative Islamophobia, which included comments by candidates and MPs, and demanded an inquiry into the problem by the party chairman. 'I've been warning my party of its Muslim problem for far too long,' complained Lady Warsi, who claimed that nothing had been done after three years.[31] No action was taken against one MP, Bob Blackman, who was accused of using material drawn from Muslim-hate websites, although at the local government level a number of Tory candidates and councillors have been suspended from the party or have left. One Muslim who stood as a local candidate explained that 'a lot of Muslims share Conservative values', but he felt alienated by the prejudice and patronising attitudes he encountered towards Muslims.[32] However, beyond issuing general condemnations of Islamophobia, the Conservative chairman and party leader saw no need for further action. As only 11 per cent of Muslims had voted Conservative in 2017, this looked risky – as Theresa May appeared to recognise in 2018, when she demanded an apology from Boris Johnson for his clumsy jokes about Muslim women.

By far the most significant Muslim political career so far has been that of Sadiq Khan, a former human-rights lawyer who was elected Labour MP for Tooting, acted as campaign manager for Ed Miliband, and became the first Muslim to sit in a cabinet. Hard-working and moderate, Khan was difficult to attack. He readily criticised government policy towards Muslims (even to the extent of having a row with Tony Blair in 2006) without it apparently damaging his career; he showed that it was feasible to speak up on behalf of Muslims, while also entering Labour's mainstream. The culmination was Khan's selection as candidate for London mayor in 2016. He faced a racist smear campaign by the Conservative candidate, Zac Goldsmith, who deliberately sought to arouse anti-Muslim feeling. In this he was backed by David Cameron, Theresa May (home secretary) and Michael Fallon (defence secretary), who attempted to associate Khan with Islamic extremism.[33] The right-wing press systematically tried to discredit him. The *Sun* reported that Khan 'Gave Speech with "Black Flag of Jihad" Flying'; the *Daily Telegraph* claimed 'Khan Linked to Online Bin Laden'; *The Sunday Times* declared 'Labour's Khan Joined Radical Imam at Rallies'; and the *Evening Standard* suggested 'Sadiq Khan's Family Links to Extremist Organisations'. According to Sadiq Khan, Cameron 'set out to divide London's communities . . . [he] used fear and innuendo to try to turn different ethnic and religious groups against each other'.[34] Significantly, Cameron's disreputable smears of a critic of terrorism and extremism fell fairly flat, and Goldsmith's defeat went some way to discrediting this element in right-wing politics. Indeed, Sadiq Khan's comfortable victory was the best possible rebuttal to Islamist claims that democracy and Islam are irreconcilable or that the West is at war with Islam. His popular mandate represented a major setback for Islamophobic propagandists in Britain and a vindication of his own efforts to persuade Muslims to become involved in mainstream politics.

In 2018, a succession of resignations from Theresa May's cabinet brought Sajid Javid to prominence as the first Muslim to occupy one of the major offices of state, the Home Office. The significance of Javid's rise is not easy to assess. Born in Rochdale, he emerged from modest origins as the son of a bus driver who had arrived in Britain in the 1960s with, reportedly, one pound in his pocket. In some sense, his rise was even more significant than Khan's. Elected MP for Bromsgrove in 2010, Javid was no progressive, but rather a Thatcherite and former investment banker who was instinctively on the right of politics. As business secretary after 2015, he engineered a crackdown on trade union rights and sided with the Brexit cause. This suggests that he was shrewdly aligning himself with Conservative orthodoxy, rather than attempting to become a spokesman for Muslims. However, Javid also showed himself ready to challenge the prejudice within the Conservative Party. On the fiftieth anniversary of Enoch Powell's anti-immigrant speech, he frankly disparaged the ideas of a man widely admired on the right. As new home secretary, he promptly disowned the 'hostile environment' that Theresa May had tried to inflict on Commonwealth immigrants, which he stated was 'unhelpful', continuing 'it doesn't represent our values as a country'.[35] Referring to the treatment of long-standing immigrants, he said: 'I thought that could be my mum . . . my dad . . . my uncle . . . it could be me.' By setting a more liberal standard for Tory attitudes on race in this way, Javid may well have created a turning point in politics, although his determination to pander to media hysteria over small numbers of refugees crossing the Channel throws this into doubt.

❀ ❀ ❀

While Muslim participation in politics is unmistakable, the community's role in the economy is less obvious, though even more revealing as a
symptom of the interaction with mainstream society. But like politics,
economics raises questions for devout Muslims. From the 1880s
onwards, Islam became influenced by socialism, especially as more
Muslim students travelled to Europe. Already critical of Western capi-
talist exploitation in their own countries, they believed that equality was
central to Islam. Jamal al-Din al-Afghani regarded socialist self-suffi-
ciency as the model for Muslim communities, and he saw the Bedouin
Arabs as a prototype for this community. In Egypt, the modernisers
(including the Muslim Brotherhood) promoted socialist ideas, such as
community welfare; some frankly claimed that Islam endorsed socialism,
in that all goods ultimately belong to God and must be shared fairly.[36]
Egypt under Nasser, Syria under the Ba'ath party and Libya under
Qaddafi all had socialist regimes, and those in Algeria and Somalia
adopted a policy of 'Islamic socialism'. In Libya, socialism involved the
redistribution of wealth, the nationalisation of industry and improvements in public morality through restrictions on gambling and alcohol.
In effect, then, Islamic socialism reflects orthodox ideas taken from the
Qur'an but accentuated by the reaction against Western indulgence and
exploitation. In recent times, some Muslims have regarded the excessive
materialism of the West as indicative of a regression from the Christian
ideal towards paganism.

In this context, some have argued that for Muslims living in the
West, most financial transactions and investments are inconsistent with
being true to their religious principles. It has even been claimed that this
view has led some Muslims to abstain from economic activity.[37] There is
no agreement on whether it is legitimate to buy a house by borrowing
from a bank, and strict Muslims believe that banks receive an 'unearned
gain' by charging interest. The Qur'an places what appears to be a clear
ban on usury: 'Those who take usury will not rise up [on the Day of
Resurrection] except like those maddened by Satan's touch. For they
claim that trading is like usury, whereas Allah has made trading lawful
and prohibited usury.'[38] But does interest charged by a bank constitute
usury? As long ago as the 1920s, Muslims began establishing banks in

Egypt, Palestine and India; and today banks in Turkey and Egypt do charge interest.

Yet despite the notional limitations on economic activity, there has been a major growth in Islamic banking, partly as a result of the oil industry. In 2013, at the first meeting of the World Islamic Economic Forum to be held outside a Muslim country, David Cameron declared 'I want London to stand alongside Dubai as one of the great capitals of Islamic finance anywhere in the world.'[39] He unveiled Treasury plans to launch a £200 million Islamic bond, or *sukuk*, which was to be compliant with Islamic law and investment principles, and to inaugurate the first Islamic Market Index. This would enable London to secure a slice of global Islamic investments and become one of the capitals of Islamic finance.

The direction of change is indicated by the success of the Islamic Bank of Britain, founded in 2004 and based in Birmingham, which has been known as the Al Rayan Bank since 2014, when it was acquired by Masraf Al Rayan. The bank, which has branches in London, Birmingham, Manchester, Leicester, Bradford, Blackburn, Tooting, Luton, Wembley and Ilford, closes briefly on Friday afternoon to enable staff to attend *Jummah*, or prayers, and it is the leading provider of *Sharia*-compliant banking services. One survey revealed that only 36 per cent of Muslims currently use *Sharia*-compliant banking. Al Rayan's operations are based on Islamic law, which is taken from the Qur'an and from the example of the Prophet. This starts from the idea that money has no intrinsic value. As a matter of faith, a Muslim cannot lend money and expect to profit from the interest. In Islamic finance, wealth can be generated only through legitimate trade in tangible goods; the money must be used in a productive, not a speculative way. Thus, any gains from trade are shared between those who provide the capital and those who supply the expertise.[40]

It is worth noting that Islamic banking, as practised by Al Rayan, is far less marginal than one might suppose. It is a normal bank, providing the usual services to 80,000 personal, business and retail customers. It is open to people of all faiths and was the third fastest growing bank out of 155 in the UK in 2017. It also appeals to non-Muslims as an ethical bank. It is, for example, a living-wage employer. It does not use financial instruments that are based on speculation or that involve a high element of risk. Its investments are backed by tangible assets and it never invests in gambling, alcohol, tobacco, armaments or pornography.[41] These policies underline the extent to which the bank is well adapted to contemporary British thinking, representing a bridge between Muslim and non-Muslim communities.

As Al Rayan's example illustrates, in Britain traditional Muslim inhibitions about borrowing and investment can be respected within Islamic thinking. As it is acceptable to earn a share of a bank's profits by sharing in its risk, savings, investments and current accounts are all available, as are mortgages.[42] From the early days in Britain, many Muslims settled in the cheap Victorian terraces of Lancashire and Yorkshire, where, by the early 1990s, 64 per cent of them had become owner-occupiers.[43] Today the Al Rayan Bank offers savers of all faiths 4 per cent – the 'expected profit rate' – on its two-year savings accounts, and requires deposits of 5–10 per cent on house purchases. This enables Muslims to take out mortgages and become home owners – a habit that could hardly be more symptomatic of their assimilation into the value system of mainstream British society, with its obsession with property ownership. Yet even this evidence of convergence has been condemned by one of the *Daily Mail*'s most reactionary journalists, Melanie Phillips, who denounced it as 'a beachhead in the attempt to colonise British society for Islam'.[44] Perverse and mischievous in the extreme, Phillips illustrates how Muslims are damned if they do and damned if they don't by the Islamophobes.

Among the best-established British Muslim entrepreneurs have been Sir Anwar Pervez, chairman of the Bestway Group, and Lord Gulam Noon, who served as president of the London Chamber of Commerce. But recently they have been overtaken by large numbers of young Muslims keen to deploy their entrepreneurial talents and evidently not inhibited by ideological reservations. Islamic fashion has been popularised by Dina Torkia, who enjoys 700,000 YouTube subscribers, and Amena Khan, who has 400,000 subscribers. In 2007, from his flat in Notting Hill, Imran Amed founded a media and technology company whose website, 'The Business of Fashion', is eagerly received by half a million people in 190 countries, including the world's most influential designers; every September it publishes the BoF500, a power list for the fashion industry.[45] In 2017, Amed was awarded an MBE for services to fashion. Admittedly, Islamic fashion attracts criticism from those who feel it is diluting Muslim values, but its advocates see no incompatibility between styling tips and traditional female modesty.

'When a young Muslim consumer doesn't find a product they are looking for on the high street,' explained a representative from Ogilvy Noor, 'their instinct is to go and create it themselves.' Ogilvy Noor is an Islamic branding agency, founded in 2010 and pitched originally at the 7 million American Muslims, but now at the global market. It helps companies to understand Muslim values and thus to tackle the market, as otherwise consumers, 80 per cent of whom would prefer to buy brands that support Muslim identity, feel neglected.[46] In Britain, this philosophy has begun to generate a wave of businesses among young Muslim entrepreneurs. In 2000, Adeem Younis, a design student at Wakefield College in Yorkshire, wanted to become his own boss, and so he founded SingleMuslim.com, a Muslim marriage website, after coming under pressure from his family to marry. For Muslims, the site fills the space usually occupied by dating in pubs and clubs. With a staff of 30, SingleMuslim.com enjoys nearly a million users in the United Kingdom and has fostered 50,000 weddings.[47] His success has enabled Younis to initiate other ventures, including the charity Penny Appeal, which raised £14 million in 2017, and a new fund to provide seed capital for tech ventures. He was named Yorkshire and North East 'Young Director of the Year' in 2017 by the Institute of Directors.

At a more modest level, many young Muslims are creating business start-ups, especially in fashion, cosmetics, personal products and food.[48] For example, Aab is a fashion brand founded in 2008 with a view to offering women a range of clothing that is modest, but more fashionable and attractive than the traditional hijabs sold at market stalls: 'Our clothes have an unmistakable DNA. Carrying a modest silhouette, most garments flow below knee length, have longer sleeves and higher neck-lines.'[49] Using its own models to market its clothes, Aab is adapting to

Western practice while still retaining Muslim principles. Serendipity Tailormade markets halal-friendly holidays, hotels, tours and weddings, typically to 24–32-year-old professionals, thereby filling a gap left by the conventional companies. The company defines its aim as enabling Muslims to travel, but 'keep our faith while doing so'; it includes a travel prayer mat in its services.[50] Serendipity Tailormade also devotes some of its profits to charitable work, including schools, orphanages and schemes to provide access to Islam for the deaf. A particularly interesting business is the London Beard Company, whose products include halal beard oils and skin products, combs, scissors and pomade: 'We're here to cater for all types of beard growers, from the stubby geeks to the full flowing beardsmen.'[51] The company's website gives examples of its customers, who on one day in 2018 included not only Iram and Mohammed, but also Gavin, Duncan, Raj and Anjum – a striking illustration of its success in crossing the boundaries between Britain's different communities through the medium of consumerism.

Contrary to conventional assumptions, Muslim women also play a significant role in the new businesses. This may reflect a major cultural change in the Pakistani and Bangladeshi community: back in 1990, men outnumbered women in higher education by two or three to one; but by 2016, 25 per cent of women aged 21–34 had degrees, compared to 22 per cent of men.[52] Female Muslims receive explicit encouragement in the area of relationships and sex from a book, *The Muslimah Sex Manual: A Halal Guide to Mind Blowing Sex*, published in 2017 by an anonymous author. It offers advice to women on the basis that they should enjoy a varied sex life and be prepared to take the lead. The author argues that this is entirely consistent with the Islamic tradition in which 'there's an emphasis on enjoying physical relationships within the context of marriage, not just for procreation. It is the wife's right that her husband satisfy her sexually.'[53] Groups such as the Muslim Women's Network UK praised the book on the grounds that 'Islam places a responsibility on men to ensure women's pleasure; without advice, however, women are often left uncertain as to which sexual acts are permissible.'

The seedbed for Muslim entrepreneurialism since the 1990s consists in the 24 per cent of Pakistanis and 19 per cent of Bangladeshis who are self-employed.[54] The explanation for the high rate of self-employment is not hard to find. It reflects pressure to escape from discrimination in the more usual forms of employment, as well as a decline in the jobs available in traditional sectors, like textiles. Most immigrants began as manual labourers, with few qualifications, but they can now attain a higher status through participation in higher education. In addition, many of those whose families originally came from the Punjab, northern India and Bangladesh already enjoyed a culture of entrepreneurialism, which in Britain manifested itself originally in family-run small shops and restaurants in which wives assisted their husbands. A middle class of Asian businessmen emerged initially based on shop-keeping, but increasingly extending into fashion, computers, electronics and food manufacture. This Muslim entrepreneurialism has been partly responsible for economic revival in Leicester, where Muslims comprise 70,000 people, or a fifth of the city's population. Many came as immigrants from Gujarat with an established reputation for shrewdness in business, and helped to fill the gap left by the collapse of the local textile industry in the 1970s.[55] Encouraged by the city council, Leicester tends to celebrate the diversity of the ethnic communities, which now make up the majority of the population. The city boasts 40 mosques, for example. Leicester also reflects the extent to which Britain's communities have joined in a common celebration of food. All supermarkets stock Indian chutneys and meals, while the British Asians of Birmingham famously repackaged their traditions to suit English tastes by inventing the Balti curry. Food effectively helps to maintain a distinct culture, while also adapting to mainstream society. For example, Ali Imdad, a 'Great British Bake Off' contestant in 2013, followed up by starting Artisan, a dessert restaurant in Birmingham, recognising that Muslims may not visit bars and clubs, but may go out for 'mocktails' and desserts instead.

The success of new Muslim entrepreneurs has been complemented by growing evidence that global brands have recognised the potential of younger Muslims who enjoy an increasing disposable income and represent an untapped market. As Muslims have the youngest median age of any religious group (23 years), they have become major consumers. At the 2016 Muslim Lifestyle Expo event, it was reported that Muslims were influenced by their religion when making purchases, and that business had been slow to reach out to them.[56] One of the exhibitors was Asda, which – like other supermarkets – now sells halal meat. Indeed, Asda's website lists no fewer than 60 halal items, including chicken sausages, chicken noodles, lamb patties, meat samosas, turkey rashers, 'chorizo', shepherd's pie and other products aimed at Muslims, marketed under the 'Humza', 'Aisha', 'Tahira' and 'Ahmed' labels. Dolce and Gabbana market clothes designed to appeal to Muslims. In 2016, Marks & Spencer decided to sell 'burkinis' – that is, full-cover swimsuits. The H&M fashion chain even used a model wearing a hijab. The advertisers had identified global urban Muslims – or 'Gummies' – who were young, educated, engaged in the social media, tech savvy, and spiritual rather than religious.

More conventionally, the Ramadan economy in Britain is now estimated to be worth £200 million and, as many Muslims spend more than usual at this time, they are increasingly targeted by supermarkets and brands. In areas with substantial Muslim populations, Tesco, Sainsbury's, Asda and Morrisons run special offers and displays for the month of Ramadan, including food, chocolates and cosmetics. Morrisons have sold a Ramadan countdown calendar which, with numbered windows concealing sweets, is very like the Advent calendars sold in the month before Christmas, a neat example of how one culture impinges on another. In 2018, Westfield (London), Europe's largest shopping centre, hosted an Eid festival, with special offers, performances, pop-up food stalls and live catwalk shows.[57] Ramadan is, however, modified to suit British conditions. Gyms adjust their opening times to allow attendance between sunset and dawn. There is no shutdown, as in the Middle East, and only about half of Muslims reportedly take time off work. The celebrations and family visits for Eid at the end of Ramadan are spread out over several weekends. In effect, traditional Islamic practice is being adapted for life in Western society.

What conclusions are to be drawn from this survey of Anglo-Muslim relations?

At the official-political level, the conclusions are obviously negative. Governments continue to show little sign of recognising that the British habit of meddling in the affairs of Muslim societies around the world is almost invariably counter-productive. Policy-makers persist in seeing Muslims as a community driven primarily by religion and influenced by an ideology of Islamism, which must somehow be eradicated rather than engaged with.

On the other hand, when seen in a historical perspective, the experience of Britain's Muslim community is almost reassuringly familiar. Most of the features associated with earlier Jewish immigration have been repeated. The result today is that the Jewish community retains and celebrates its own culture and values, but is largely accommodated within British society through the economy, politics, sport, academia and entertainment. Yet that leaves plentiful scope for difference, as Jews range across a wide spectrum – from orthodox communities that live fairly self-contained lives to those who are largely indistinguishable from the mainstream of society. In the absence of a clear sense of British national identity, Muslims have inevitably suffered from a need to define themselves; but they are gradually doing so, as British Asians playing their part in sport, entertainment, politics and the economy. Like Britain's other ethnic communities, their experience reflects a long-term decline in prejudice in the face of the expansion of a multi-racial society. The old Powellite notion that only a person with white skin could be British has been steadily eroded by the prominence of Muslims in various aspects of national life. It is symbolic that Powell's old seat in Wolverhampton is today held by Eleanor Smith, an MP of Caribbean origin. A Muslim mayor of London and a Muslim home secretary were inconceivable back in 1968.

In particular, the propaganda about a 'clash of civilisations' has steadily lost whatever credibility it once had in the context of British society. This is partly because the proximate sources of danger to liberal democracy have been increasingly identified in such places as Russia, Hungary and President Trump's America. But by far the most potent trend is revealed in the evidence that Muslims and non-Muslims are steadily converging in their social behaviour, as was the case with earlier ethnic communities in British history. Through participation in the economy and the pervading consumerism that dominates British society today, a gradual process of assimilation appears to be inexorable. Over time, these influences have much more effect than the political personalities and political events that intrude so noisily upon the daily agenda.

NOTES

1 ISLAM: 'A KIND OF CHRISTIANITY'?

1. The phrase was first used by Thomas Carlyle (1795–1881) in 'The Hero as Prophet' (1841), p. 76.
2. Karen Armstrong, *Muhammad: Prophet for our time* (London: Harper Press, 2006), pp. 37–8.
3. Armstrong, *Muhammad*, pp. 41–3.
4. Qur'an 5:4; Andrew Rippin (ed.), *The Blackwell Companion to the* Qur'an (Oxford: Wiley-Blackwell, 2009), pp. 7–8.
5. Keith Kahn-Harris, *Judaism* (London: Hodder Education, 2012), pp. 11–15, 34–5; A.C. Bouquet, *Everyday Life in New Testament Times* (London: Batsford, 1953), pp. 16–17, 11–19.
6. Qur'an 16:57; 2:216; 5:92; P.J. Stewart, *Unfolding Islam* (Stroud: Sutton, 2008), p. 75; D.S. Roberts, *Islam: A Westerner's guide* (London: Kogan Page, 1981), pp. 134–5.
7. Qur'an 2:184.
8. John L. Esposito (ed.), *The Islamic World: Past and present* (Oxford: Oxford University Press, 2004), Vol. 3, p. 15.
9. Qur'an 4:40; Esposito, *The Islamic World*, Vol. 1, p. 128; Stewart, *Unfolding Islam*, p. 98.
10. Esposito, *The Islamic World*, Vol. 3, p. 29.
11. Qur'an 3:42.
12. Qur'an 7:15–19.
13. Chris Horrie and Peter Chippindale, *What Is Islam?* (London: Virgin Books, 2003), pp. 129–33, 136–8.
14. Roberts, *Islam: A Westerner's guide*, pp. 51–2; Horrie and Chippindale, *What Is Islam?*, pp. 148–51.
15. Christopher de Bellaigue, *The Islamic Enlightenment* (London: The Bodley Head, 2017), pp. 188–9.
16. Qur'an 4:10.
17. Rippin, *Blackwell Companion to the* Qur'an, pp. 8–11; Qur'an: 4:25.
18. Personal observation by the author, 1969–71.
19. Qur'an 4:34.
20. Rippin, *Blackwell Companion to the* Qur'an, pp. 300–2; Qur'an 36:21; 2:36.

21. Qur'an 2:240.
22. de Bellaigue, *The Islamic Enlightenment*, p. 195.
23. Qur'an 26:165.
24. Qur'an 7:80; Scott Siraj al-Haqq Kugle, *Homosexuality in Islam* (Oxford: Oneworld Publications, 2010), pp. 23–4, 66–7.
25. Kugle, *Homosexuality in Islam*, pp. 39–40, 50, 53, 56.
26. de Bellaigue, *The Islamic Enlightenment*, p. 196.
27. Kugle, *Homosexuality in Islam*, p. 200.
28. Christopher Lloyd, *English Corsairs on the Barbary Coast* (London: Collins, 1981), p. 124.
29. Linda Colley, *Captives: Britain, empire and the world 1600–1850* (London: Cape, 2002), pp. 128–9.
30. Christopher Tyerman, *The Crusades: A very short introduction* (Oxford: Oxford University Press, 2004), p. 79.
31. Rippin, *Blackwell Companion to the* Qur'an, pp. 311–15.
32. Bernard Lewis, *The Crisis of Islam* (London: Phoenix, 2003), pp. 11–17.
33. Roberts, *Islam: A Westerner's guide*, pp. 73–6.
34. Bernard Lewis, *The Arabs in History* (Oxford: Oxford University Press, 1993), p. 46.
35. Lewis, *The Arabs in History*, pp. 87–8.
36. Ehsan Masood, *Science and Islam: A history* (London: Icon Books, 2009), pp. 66–8.
37. Masood, *Science and Islam*, pp. 61–2.

2 THE MYTHS OF THE CRUSADES

1. Stephen Greenblatt, *The Rise and Fall of Adam and Eve* (London: The Bodley Head, 2017), pp. 7,121.
2. R.W. Southern, *Western Views of Islam in the Middle Ages* (Cambridge, MA: Harvard University Press, 1962), pp. 16–17; N. Matar, *Islam in Britain 1558–1685* (Cambridge: Cambridge University Press, 1998), pp. 121, 157.
3. Christopher J. Walker, *Islam and the West* (Stroud: Sutton, 2005), p. 62; Lewis, *The Arabs in History*, pp. 139–40; Southern, *Western Views of Islam*, pp. 19–22.
4. Quoted in Southern, *Western Views of Islam*, p. 36.
5. Quoted in Southern, *Western Views of Islam*, p. 101.
6. Jerry Brotton, *This Orient Isle: Elizabethan England and the Islamic world* (London: Allen Lane, 2016), p. 114.
7. Samuel C. Chew, *The Crescent and the Rose: Islam and England during the Renaissance* (New York: Octagon Books, 1965), pp. 224–6.
8. Marc Morris, *King John: Treachery, tyranny and the road to Magna Carta* (London: Hutchinson, 2015), pp. 178–9.
9. Tyerman, *The Crusades*, pp. 2–3.
10. Simon Lloyd, *English Society and the Crusade 1210–1301* (Oxford: Clarendon Press, 1988), pp. 74–7.
11. Lloyd, *English Society and the Crusade*, pp. 93–5.
12. Brotton, *This Orient Isle*, p. 67.
13. C. Hillenbrand, *The Crusades: Islamic perspectives* (Edinburgh: Edinburgh University Press, 1999), pp. 50–2; Niall Christie, *Muslims and Crusaders* (London: Routledge, 2014), pp. 21–3.
14. Hillenbrand, *The Crusades*, pp. 33–6.
15. Christie, *Muslims and Crusaders*, pp. 77–9; Hillenbrand, *The Crusades*, pp. 293–4.
16. Hillenbrand, *The Crusades*, pp. 274–80.
17. Christie, *Muslims and Crusaders*, pp. 73–6.
18. Brotton, *This Orient Isle*, p. 27.
19. Quoted in Tyerman, *The Crusades*, p. 52.
20. Roy Porter, *Edward Gibbon: Making history* (London: Weidenfeld and Nicolson, 1988), p. 114.
21. Quoted in Tyerman, *The Crusades*, p. 10.

3 THE IMPACT OF THE REFORMATION

1. Brotton, *This Orient Isle*, p. 9.
2. Colley, *Captives*, p. 115.
3. Andre Clot, *Suleiman the Magnificent* (London: Saqi, 2005), pp. 129–37.
4. Brotton, *This Orient Isle*, pp. 56–7.
5. Quoted in Brotton, *This Orient Isle*, p. 75.
6. Quoted in Brotton, *This Orient Isle*, p. 78.
7. Walker, *Islam and the West*, p. 113.
8. Peter Frankopan, *The Silk Roads: A new history of the world* (London: Bloomsbury, 2015), pp. 234–5.
9. Brotton, *This Orient Isle*, pp. 11–12.
10. Chew, *The Crescent and the Rose*, pp. 144–5.
11. Quoted in Chew, *The Crescent and the Rose*, pp. 395–6.
12. Chew, *The Crescent and the Rose*, pp. 443–4.
13. Chew, *The Crescent and the Rose*, pp. 36–7.
14. Chew, *The Crescent and the Rose*, p. 119.
15. Anna Pavord, *The Tulip* (London: Bloomsbury, 1999), pp. 13–14.
16. Frankopan, *The Silk Roads*, p. 245.
17. Quoted in Walker, *Islam and the West*, p. 110.
18. Chew, *The Crescent and the Rose*, pp. 164–9.
19. Qur'an 2:257; Matar, *Islam in Britain*, p. 106.
20. Walker, *Islam and the West*, pp. 145–8.
21. Colley, *Captives*, p. 44.
22. Colley, *Captives*, pp. 117–18.
23. Chew, *The Crescent and the Rose*, pp. 373–8.
24. Adrian Tinniswood, *The Pirates of Barbary* (London: Cape, 2010), p. 149.
25. Matar, *Islam in Britain*, pp. 16–17, 22.
26. Tinniswood, *Pirates of Barbary*, p. 42.
27. Colley, *Captives*, pp. 122–3.
28. Matar, *Islam in Britain*, pp. 15–16.
29. Brotton, *This Orient Isle*, p. 141.
30. Tinniswood, *Pirates of Barbary*, pp. 42–3.
31. Tinniswood, *Pirates of Barbary*, pp. 47–8.

4 INDIA AND THE ANGLO-MUSLIM LOVE AFFAIR

1. Richard Burton, *The Arabian Nights* (London, Macmillan, 1886), p. xix.
2. See a corrective in Philip Lawson, *The East India Company: A history* (Harlow: Longman, 1993), pp. 5–7.
3. P. Hardy, *The Muslims of British India* (Cambridge: Cambridge University Press, 1972), pp. 2–9.
4. Quoted in S.N. Mukherjee, *Sir William Jones: A study in eighteenth-century British attitudes to India* (Cambridge: Cambridge University Press, 1968), p. 119.
5. William Forbes (ed.), *The English Factories of India 1618–1669* (1906–27), Vol. I, pp. 39–40, in William Dalrymple, *White Mughals: Love and betrayal in eighteenth-century India* (London: Penguin, 2002), p. 17.
6. William Dalrymple, *The Last Mughal: The fall of a dynasty, Delhi, 1857* (London: Bloomsbury, 2006), pp. 64–66.
7. Ronald Hyam, *Empire and Sexuality: The British experience* (Manchester: Manchester University Press, 1990), p. 25.
8. Dalrymple, *White Mughals*, p. 6.
9. Dalrymple, *White Mughals*, p. 19.
10. Dennis Kincaid, *British Social Life in India, 1608–1937* (London: Routledge, 1973), pp. 43–4.

11. John Masters, *Bugles and a Tiger* (London: Michael Joseph, 1956), p. 174.
12. Masters, *Bugles and a Tiger*, pp. 153–4.
13. Quoted in Kenneth Ballhatchet, *Race, Sex and Class under the Raj* (London: Weidenfeld and Nicolson, 1980), p. 120; Hyam, *Empire and Sexuality*, p. 60.
14. Hyam, *Empire and Sexuality*, pp. 29–30.
15. David Omissi, *The Sepoy and the Raj: The Indian Army 1860–1940* (Basingstoke: Macmillan, 1994), pp. 49–50, 98, 101–2.
16. Omissi, *Sepoy and the Raj*, p. 129.
17. Masters, *Bugles and a Tiger*, p. 95.
18. Quoted in Omissi, *Sepoy and the Raj*, p. 66.
19. Hyam, *Empire and Sexuality*, pp. 128–9.
20. Hardy, *Muslims of British India*, p. 24.
21. Rippin, *Blackwell Companion to the* Qur'an, pp. 311–15.
22. Reginald Heber, *Narrative of a Journey through the Upper Provinces of India* (1828), pp. 393–4, quoted in Hardy, *Muslims of British India*, p. 33.
23. Hardy, *Muslims of British India*, pp. 37–46.
24. Hardy, *Muslims of British India*, p. 38.
25. Quoted in Hardy, *Muslims of British India*, p. 72.

5 BRITAIN AND THE MANAGEMENT OF ISLAMIC DECLINE

1. Quoted in Walker, *Islam and the West*, p. 174.
2. Edward Gibbon, *The Decline and Fall of the Roman Empire* (1776), Vol. III, p. 336.
3. Porter, *Gibbon*, p. 114.
4. Porter, *Gibbon*, pp. 130–1.
5. Thomas Carlyle, 'The Hero as Prophet: Mahomet and Islam', in *On Heroes, Hero-Worship and the Heroic in History* (1841), p. 43.
6. Carlyle, 'The Hero as Prophet', p. 64.
7. Carlyle, 'The Hero as Prophet', p. 54.
8. Carlyle, 'The Hero as Prophet', p. 76.
9. Fiona MacCarthy, *Byron: Life and Legend* (London: John Murray, 2002), pp. 544–5.
10. Quoted in Orlando Figes, *Crimea: The last crusade* (London: Allen Lane, 2010), p. 45.
11. Figes, *Crimea*, pp. 4–5, 17–21.
12. David Brown, *Palmerston: A biography* (London: Yale University Press, 2010), pp. 363–5.
13. Peter Mansfield, *The British in Egypt* (London: Weidenfeld and Nicolson, 1971), pp. 5–6.
14. Mansfield, *British in Egypt*, p. 19.
15. Mansfield, *British in Egypt*, p. 19.
16. Lord Cromer, *Modern Egypt* (London: Macmillan, 1908), pp. 4–7, 17, 538.
17. Cromer, *Modern Egypt*, p. 394.
18. Robin Neillands, *The Dervish Wars: Gordon and Kitchener in the Sudan 1880–1898* (London: John Murray, 1996), p. 75.
19. Quoted in John Marlowe, *Cromer in Egypt* (London: Elek Books, 1970), p. 251.

6 THE VICTORIANS, ISLAM AND THE IDEA OF PROGRESS

1. Nigel Yates, 'Pugin and the Medieval Dream', in Gordon Marsden, ed., *Victorian Values* (Harlow: Longman, 1990), pp. 80–2.
2. Edgar Johnson, *Walter Scott: The great unknown* (London: Hamish Hamilton, 1970), pp. 686–7, 738, 933–7.
3. Thomas Metcalf, *Ideologies of the Raj* (Cambridge: Cambridge University Press, 1994), pp. 75–7.
4. Metcalf, *Ideologies of the Raj*, pp. 75–7.
5. David Gillard, *The Struggle for Asia 1828–1914* (London: Methuen, 1977), p. 49.
6. Gillard, *Struggle for Asia*, p. 47.

7. Gillard, *Struggle for Asia*, p. 54.
8. Eugenio Biagini, *Gladstone* (Basingstoke: Macmillan, 2000), pp. 61–4.
9. Eugenio Biagini, 'The European mind of late-Victorian liberalism: W.E. Gladstone and Joseph Chamberlain', *Journal of Liberal History*, 98, Spring (2018), p. 15.
10. Burton, *Arabian Nights*, xix.
11. Burton, *Arabian Nights*, xix.
12. Burton, *Arabian Nights*, vi.
13. Wilfred S. Blunt, *The Future of Islam* (Dublin: Nonsuch Publishing, 1882, 2007 edn), p. 158.
14. Blunt, *The Future of Islam*, p. 12.
15. Blunt, *The Future of Islam*, pp. 172–3.
16. Blunt, *The Future of Islam*, pp. 175,191.
17. R.H. Davidson, 'Turkish attitudes concerning Christian-Muslim equality in the nineteenth century', *American Historical Review*, 4 (1954), p. 845.
18. Davidson, 'Christian-Muslim equality', pp. 850–1.
19. Davidson, 'Christian-Muslim equality', pp. 856, 863.
20. Karl Meyer and Shareen Blair Brysac, *Tournament of Shadows: The Great Game and the race for empire in Asia* (London: Little Brown, 1999), pp. 175–6.
21. Quoted in Meyer and Brysac, *Tournament of Shadows*, p. 177.
22. Gillard, *Struggle for Asia*, pp. 153–4.
23. W.S. Churchill, *The River War*, Vol. II (London: Macmillan, 1899), pp. 248–50.
24. Quoted in Warren Dockter, *Churchill and the Islamic World* (London: I.B. Tauris, 2015), p. 23.
25. Dockter, *Churchill and the Islamic World*, p. 17.
26. Churchill to Lady Randolph Churchill, 6 April 1897, in Randolph Churchill, *Churchill*, Vol. I (London: Heinemann, 1966), p. 332.

7 Islam – Westernising or Orientalist?

1. Pankaj Mishra, *From the Ruins of Empire: The revolt against the west and the remaking of Asia* (London: Allen Lane, 2012), pp. 100–1.
2. Kenneth Rose, *Superior Person* (London: Macmillan, 1969), p. 88.
3. Quoted in John Marlowe, *Cromer in Egypt*, p. 280.
4. Hardy, *Muslims of British India*, pp. 38–9, 80–8.
5. Ibid.
6. Quoted in Anil Seal, *The Emergence of Indian Nationalism* (Cambridge: Cambridge University Press, 1971), p. 318.
7. Quoted in ibid., p. 317.
8. Aijaz Ahmad, *Aligarh Muslim University: An educational and political history 1920–47* (Ghaziabad: Lata Sahitya Sadan, 2005), pp. 18–19.
9. Qur'an 22:63, 70; 67:1, 5; 71:15.
10. Mishra, *From the Ruins of Empire*, pp. 54–9, 92.
11. Shompa Lahiri, *Indians in Britain* (London: Frank Cass, 2000), pp. 161–2.
12. Lahiri, *Indians in Britain*, pp. 125–6, 177, 222.
13. Ahmad, *Aligarh Muslim University*, p. 19.
14. Ahmad, *Aligarh Muslim University*, pp. 62–3.
15. Ahmad, *Aligarh Muslim University*, pp. 28–9.
16. de Bellaigue, *The Islamic Enlightenment*, pp. 5–7.
17. de Bellaigue, *The Islamic Enlightenment*, p. 23.
18. de Bellaigue, *The Islamic Enlightenment*, p. 45.
19. de Bellaigue, *The Islamic Enlightenment*, pp. 37–8.
20. de Bellaigue, *The Islamic Enlightenment*, p. 31.
21. Lord Cromer, *Modern Egypt*, p. 540.
22. Mansfield, *British in Egypt*, p. 7.

23. Marlowe, *Cromer in Egypt*, pp. 258–9.
24. Justin McCarthy, *The Ottoman Turks* (Harlow: Longman, 1997), p. 202.
25. de Bellaigue, *The Islamic Enlightenment*, pp. 62–4.
26. de Bellaigue, *The Islamic Enlightenment*, p. 74.
27. McCarthy, *The Ottoman Turks*, pp. 295–6.
28. M. Nain Turfan, *Rise of the Young Turks: Politics, the military and Ottoman collapse* (London: I.B. Tauris, 2000), pp. 133–45.
29. Turfan, *Rise of the Young Turks*, p. 145.
30. de Bellaigue, *The Islamic Enlightenment*, pp. 77–9.
31. de Bellaigue, *The Islamic Enlightenment*, p. 115.
32. Quoted in Mishra, *From the Ruins of Empire*, p. 107.
33. Ali Gheissari and Vali Nasr, *Democracy in Iran* (Oxford: Oxford University Press, 2006), p. 118.

8 THE GREAT WAR AND THE RE-DRAWING OF THE OTTOMAN EMPIRE

1. Dockter, *Churchill and the Islamic World*, p. 53.
2. Paul Addison, *Churchill on the Home Front 1900–55* (London: Jonathan Cape, 1992), pp. 156–7.
3. Andrew Hyde, *Jihad: The Ottomans and the Allies 1914–1922* (Stroud: Amberley Publishing, 2017), pp. 21–3.
4. T.G. Fraser, *The Makers of the Modern Middle East* (London: Ginkgo Publishing, 2015), pp. 11–15.
5. Michael Asher, *Lawrence: The uncrowned king of Arabia* (London: Viking, 1998), pp. 102–3.
6. Asher, *Lawrence*, pp. 42–3.
7. McCarthy, *The Ottoman Turks*, p. 354.
8. Christopher Sykes, *The Man Who Created the Middle East* (London: William Collins, 2016), p. 255.
9. Sykes, *The Man Who Created the Middle East*, pp. 256–9.
10. Asher, *Lawrence*, pp. 240–1.
11. Liora Lukitz, *A Quest in the Middle East: Octavia Bell and the making of modern Iraq* (London: I.B. Tauris, 2006), p. 130.
12. For a lengthy, if implausible, defence of Churchill's bombing policy, see Dockter, *Churchill and the Islamic World*, pp. 115–20.
13. Georgina Howell, *Daughter of the Desert* (London: Macmillan, 2006), p. 399.
14. McCarthy, *The Ottoman Turks*, p. 373.
15. Quoted in Fraser, *The Makers of the Modern Middle East*, p. 265.
16. de Bellaigue, *The Islamic Enlightenment*, p. 159.
17. de Bellaigue, *The Islamic Enlightenment*, pp. 162–3.
18. Quoted in Andrew Mango, *Ataturk: The biography of the founder of modern Turkey* (London: John Murray, 1999), p. 434.
19. Omissi, *Sepoy and the Raj*, p. 130.
20. Omissi, *Sepoy and the Raj*, pp. 129, 140.
21. Judith Brown, *Gandhi's Rise to Power: Indian politics 1915–1922* (Cambridge: Cambridge University Press, 1972), pp. 210–16.
22. S.H. Zebel, *Balfour* (Cambridge: Cambridge University Press, 1973), pp. 39–41.
23. Quoted in Walter Reid, *Empire of Sand: How Britain made the Middle East* (Edinburgh: Birlinn, 2013), p. 142.
24. Fraser, *The Makers of the Modern Middle East*, pp. 50–4.
25. Reid, *Empire of Sand*, pp. 43–5.
26. Fraser, *The Makers of the Modern Middle East*, p. 92.
27. Zebel, *Balfour*, p. 247.
28. Zebel, *Balfour*, p. 239.
29. Zebel, *Balfour*, p. 241.

30. Matthew Hughes, 'The banality of brutality: British armed forces and the repression of the Arab revolt in Palestine 1936–39', *English Historical Review*, CXXIV (2009), pp. 313–54.

9 ISLAM, DEMOCRACY AND NATIONALISM AFTER THE SECOND WORLD WAR

1. Francis Fukuyama, *Wall Street Journal*, 5 October 2001.
2. Discussed in Nader Hashemi, *Islam, Secularism and Liberal Democracy* (Oxford: Oxford University Press, 2009).
3. See Lewis, *The Crisis of Islam*, pp. 96, 101, 112, 139–40.
4. Dominic Lieven, *Pakistan: A hard country* (London: Allen Lane, 2011), pp. 206–7.
5. Owen Bennett Jones, *Pakistan: Eye of the storm* (New Haven: Yale University Press, 2002), pp. 227–30.
6. Adeed Dawisha, *Iraq: A political history from independence to occupation* (Princeton: Princeton University Press, 2009), p. 45.
7. Dawisha, *Iraq*, pp. 151–4.
8. Dawisha, *Iraq*, pp. 161–2.
9. Quoted in David Carlton, *Britain and the Suez Crisis* (Oxford: Blackwell, 1988), p. 11.
10. Michael Axworthy, *Empire of the Mind: A history of Iran* (London: Hurst and Company, 2007), pp. 232–3.
11. Gheissari and Nasr, *Democracy in Iran*, p. 48.
12. Axworthy, *Empire of the Mind*, pp. 241–2.
13. Gheissari and Nasr, *Democracy in Iran*, pp. 55–8.
14. Tom Little, *Modern Egypt* (London: Ernest Benn, 1967), pp. 131–3.
15. D.R. Thorpe, *Eden* (London: Chatto and Windus, 2003), p. 382.
16. Thorpe, *Eden*, pp. 420–1.
17. Carlton, *Britain and the Suez Crisis*, p. 28.
18. Carlton, *Britain and the Suez Crisis*, p. 29.
19. Hashemi, *Islam, Secularism and Liberal Democracy*, p. 48.
20. Hashemi, *Islam, Secularism and Liberal Democracy*, p. 54.
21. Hashemi, *Islam, Secularism and Liberal Democracy*, pp. 155–7.
22. P.M. Holt, Ann Lambton and Bernard Lewis (eds), *The Cambridge History of Islam* (Cambridge: Cambridge University Press, 1970), Vol. 2, pp. 69–71.
23. Esposito, *The Islamic World*, Vol. 3, pp. 24–5.
24. Hashemi, *Islam, Secularism and Liberal Democracy*, pp. 158–65.

10 MUSLIMS AND THE CRISIS OF BRITISH NATIONAL IDENTITY

1. Humayun Ansari, *The Infidel Within: Muslims in Britain since 1800* (London: C. Hurst and Co., 2004), p. 138.
2. Richard I. Lawless, *From Ta'izz to Tyneside: An Arab community in the north-east of England during the early twentieth century* (Exeter: Exeter University Press, 1995), pp. 175–81.
3. Lawless, *From Ta'izz to Tyneside*, pp. 245–8.
4. Robert Winder, *Bloody Foreigners: The story of immigration to Britain* (London: Little, Brown, 2004), p. 298.
5. Birmingham Borough Labour Party minutes, 13 June 1962; Patrick Gordon Walker diary, 11 September 1962, Gordon Walker Papers 1/4; Martin Pugh, *Speak for Britain: A new history of the Labour Party* (London: The Bodley Head, 2010), pp. 331–2.
6. See Robert Shepherd, *Enoch Powell* (London: Hutchinson, 1996), pp. 325–69.
7. Kenan Malik, *From Fatwa to Jihad: The Rushdie affair and its legacy* (London: Atlantic Books, 2009), p. 40.
8. Ansari, *The Infidel Within*, pp. 176–7.
9. *Daily Mail*, 7 and 8 December 2000.
10. *Guardian*, 29 October 2014.
11. Ansari, *The Infidel Within*, p. 182.

12. Sayeeda Warsi, *The Enemy Within: A tale of Muslim Britain* (London: Allen Lane, 2017), x–xxiii.
13. Ansari, *The Infidel Within*, pp. 262–5.
14. See *Jewish Chronicle*, 2 January 1885, 5 and 12 January 1900, 7 August and 4 September 1914.
15. Warsi, *The Enemy Within*, xxii.
16. Ansari, *The Infidel Within*, p. 212.
17. From Alibhai Brown quoted in Ansari, *The Infidel Within*, p. 295.
18. Ansari, *The Infidel Within*, p. 289.
19. Mushtaq Ahmed, *Twenty20 Vision* (London: Granta, 2006), pp. 151–5.
20. *Daily Mail*, 1 December 1999.
21. Malik, *From Fatwa to Jihad*, p. 29.
22. Malik, *From Fatwa to Jihad*, viii–xxi; Gary Younge, *Who Are We?* (London: Penguin Books, 2010), pp. 173–4.
23. *Guardian*, 7 April 2018.
24. *Observer*, 15 October 2017.
25. *Guardian*, 10 April 2017.
26. *Guardian*, 17 April 2017.
27. *Daily Mail*, 22 December 2000.
28. *Jewish Chronicle*, 26 December 1890.
29. *Daily Mail*, 22 and 26 December 2000.
30. *Guardian*, 8 December 2006.
31. *Guardian*, 8 December 2006.
32. Warsi, *The Enemy Within*, p. 4.
33. Martin Pugh to Guy Opperman (copy), 12 October 2010.
34. Ziauddin Sardar, *Balti Britain* (London: Granta, 2008), p. 209.
35. Sardar, *Balti Britain*, p. 236.
36. *Independent*, 21 September 2000.
37. *Daily Mail*, 1 and 3 January 2000.
38. James Fergusson, *Al-Britannia, My Country: A journey through Muslim Britain* (London: Bantam, 2017), p. 253.
39. Fergusson, *Al-Britannia*, p. 255.

11 ISLAMOPHOBIA

1. Gilles Kepel, *Jihad: The trail of political Islam* (London: I.B. Tauris, 2002), pp. 13–14.
2. *Guardian*, 6 August 2014.
3. Ed Husain, *The Islamist* (London: Penguin Books, 2007), pp. 75, 82, 91.
4. Husain, *The Islamist*, p. 136.
5. Rodric Braithwaite, *Afgansty: The Russians in Afghanistan 1979–89* (London: Atlantic, 2011), p. 123.
6. *New Statesman*, 20 November 2011.
7. *Guardian*, 18 October 2010.
8. Martin Amis, *The Second Plane* (London: Little Brown, 2008), pp. 21, 78, 84.
9. Malise Ruthven, *Times Literary Supplement*, 20 October 2010.
10. *Guardian*, 28 November 2018.
11. *Guardian*, 5 February 2014.
12. *Guardian*, 8 November 2010.
13. Warsi, *The Enemy Within*, pp. 124, 212, 213.
14. Fergusson, *Al-Britannia*, p. 86.
15. *Observer*, 26 November 2017.
16. *Guardian*, 26 June 2018.
17. *Guardian*, 21 July 2010.

18. Paul Wilkinson, *Terrorism Versus Democracy: The liberal state response* (Cambridge: Cambridge University Press, 2001), pp. 82–3, 95.
19. *Guardian*, 20 October 2010.
20. Husain, *The Islamist*, pp. 146–9.
21. Husain, *The Islamist*, pp. 179–82.
22. Fergusson, *Al-Britannia*, pp. 51–2.
23. Malik, *From Fatwa to Jihad*, pp. 81–2.
24. Quoted in Warsi, *The Enemy Within*, p. 56.
25. *Guardian*, 9 June 2010.
26. Qur'an 5:28; Sardar, *Balti Britain*, pp. 304, 322; Fergusson, *Al-Britannia*, pp. 12, 84.
27. Husain, *The Islamist*, p. 146.
28. *Guardian*, 16 January 2016.
29. *Guardian*, 26 July 2014.
30. *Guardian*, 3 December 2015.
31. Younge, *Who Are We?*, p. 147.
32. Fergusson, *Al-Britannia*, pp. 186–8.
33. *Guardian*, 9 August 2018.
34. *Guardian*, 7 August 2018.
35. *London Evening News*, 3 February 2010.
36. *Guardian*, 11 June 2015.
37. *Guardian*, 25 May 2016.
38. Fergusson, *Al-Britannia*, p. 38.
39. Fergusson, *Al-Britannia*, pp. 247–8.
40. Warsi, *The Enemy Within*, pp. 87–8; *Guardian*, 10 August and 10 November 2017.
41. *Guardian*, 19 January 2016.
42. Fergusson, *Al-Britannia*, pp. 62–6.
43. *Guardian*, 21 March 2016.
44. *Guardian*, 4 June 2014; *Observer*, 8 June 2014.
45. *Guardian*, 22 November 2014.
46. Fergusson, *Al-Britannia*, p. 106.
47. *Guardian*, 12 July 2017.
48. *Guardian*, 2 September and 3 October 2017; *Observer*, 3 September 2017.

12 MUSLIMS IN THE BRITISH MAINSTREAM

1. *Guardian*, 2 December 2016.
2. *Guardian*, 13 March 2018.
3. *Guardian*, 19 August 2017.
4. *Hexham Courant*, 6 September 2018.
5. *Observer*, 25 June 2017.
6. See Lewis Pies website.
7. Fergusson, *Al-Britannia*, pp. 198–200; *Guardian*, 9 October 2015.
8. Nadiya Hussain, *Nadiya's British Food Adventure* (London: Michael Joseph, 2017), p. 83.
9. *Guardian*, 9 October 2015.
10. Martin Pugh, *Britain: Unification and disintegration* (Sandy: Authors Online/Bright Pen Books, 2012), p. 209.
11. *Guardian*, 5 December 2009.
12. *Guardian*, 5 December 2009.
13. *Guardian*, 23 October 2009.
14. *Evening Standard*, 22 March 2011.
15. Nasser Hussain, *Playing with Fire* (London: Granta, 2004), p. 29.
16. *Daily Mail*, 13 December 2000.
17. Hussain, *Playing with Fire*, p. 242.

18. *Observer*, 13 August 2006.
19. *Observer*, 20 November 2016.
20. *Guardian*, 28 October 2009.
21. Ansari, *The Infidel Within*, p. 225.
22. *Observer*, 25 February 2018.
23. Tariq Ramadan, *Western Muslims and the Future of Islam* (Oxford: Oxford University Press, 2004), pp. 158–9, 165.
24. Quoted in Ansari, *The Infidel Within*, p. 247.
25. Ansari, *The Infidel Within*, pp. 237–8.
26. Ansari, *The Infidel Within*, p. 213.
27. *Guardian*, 23 June 2018.
28. *Guardian*, 23 June 2018.
29. Warsi, *The Enemy Within*, p. 151.
30. *Guardian*, 21 January 2011.
31. *Guardian*, 4 July 2018.
32. *Guardian*, 1 June 2018.
33. *Guardian*, 1 March 2016.
34. *Observer*, 7 May 2016; *Guardian*, 6 May 2016.
35. *Guardian*, 1 May 2018.
36. Esposito, *The Islamic World*, Vol. 3, pp. 93–4.
37. Ramadan, *Western Muslims*, p. 188.
38. Qur'an 2:280.
39. *Guardian*, 29 October 2013.
40. Al Rayan Bank website.
41. Al Rayan Bank website.
42. Esposito, *The Islamic World*, Vol. 3, pp. 64–5.
43. Ansari, *The Infidel Within*, pp. 179–80.
44. Melanie Phillips, *Londonistan: How Britain is creating a terror state within* (London: Gibson Square, 2006), xiii.
45. *Observer Magazine*, 9 September 2018.
46. Ogilvy Noor website.
47. *Guardian*, 11 November 2017.
48. *Observer*, 16 October 2016.
49. Aab website.
50. Serendipity Tailormade website.
51. London Beard Company website.
52. *Observer*, 3 April 2016.
53. *Observer*, 16 July 2017.
54. Ansari, *The Infidel Within*, p. 194.
55. Fergusson, *Al-Britannia*, pp. 152–4.
56. *Observer*, 3 April and 16 October 2016.
57. *Observer*, 29 April 2018.

BIBLIOGRAPHY

Addison, Paul, *Churchill on the Home Front 1900–55* (London: Jonathan Cape, 1992).

Ahmad, Aijaz, *Aligarh Muslim University: An educational and political history 1920–47* (Ghaziabad: Lata Sahitya Sadan, 2005).

Ahmed, Mushtaq, *Twenty20 Vision* (London: Granta, 2006).

Amis, Martin, *The Second Plane* (London: Little Brown, 2008).

Anderson, Olive, *A Liberal State at War: English politics and economics during the Crimean War* (London: Macmillan, 1967).

Ansari, Humayun, *The Infidel Within: Muslims in Britain since 1800* (London: C. Hurst and Co., 2004).

Armstrong, Karen, *Muhammad: Prophet for our time* (London: Harper Press, 2006).

Asbridge, Thomas, *The First Crusade* (London: The Free Press, 2004).

Asher, Michael, *Lawrence: The uncrowned king of Arabia* (London: Viking, 1998).

Axworthy, Michael, *Empire of the Mind: A history of Iran* (London: Hurst and Company, 2007).

Baldock, John, *The Essence of Sufism* (London: Arcturus Publishing, 2016).

Ballhatchet, Kenneth, *Race, Sex and Class under the Raj* (London: Weidenfeld and Nicolson, 1980).

Bayly, C.A., *Indian Society and the Making of the British Empire* (Cambridge: Cambridge University Press, 1988).

Bennett Jones, Owen, *Pakistan: Eye of the storm* (New Haven: Yale University Press, 2002).

Biagini, Eugenio, *Gladstone* (Basingstoke: Macmillan, 2000).

Biagini, Eugenio, 'The European mind of late-Victorian liberalism: W.E. Gladstone and Joseph Chamberlain', *Journal of Liberal History*, 98, Spring (2018).

Blunt, Wilfred S., *The Future of Islam* (Dublin: Nonsuch Publishing, 1882, 2007 edn).

Bolt, Christine, *Victorian Attitudes to Race* (London: Routledge, 1971).

Bose, Mihir, *The Spirit of the Game: How sport made the modern world* (London: Constable, 2011).

Bouquet, A.C., *Everyday Life in New Testament Times* (London: Batsford, 1953).

Bourne, Kenneth, *The Foreign Policy of Victorian England 1830–1902* (Oxford: Clarendon Press, 1970).

Bradley, Ian, *The Call to Seriousness: The evangelical impact on the Victorians* (London: Allen and Unwin, 1976).

Braithwaite, Rodric, *Afgansty: The Russians in Afghanistan 1979–89* (London: Atlantic, 2011).

Brotton, Jerry, *This Orient Isle: Elizabethan England and the Islamic world* (London: Allen Lane, 2016).

Brown, Callum G., *Religion and Society in Twentieth-Century Britain* (Harlow: Longman, 2006).

Brown, David, *Palmerston: A biography* (London: Yale University Press, 2010).

Brown, Judith, *Gandhi's Rise to Power: Indian politics 1915–1922* (Cambridge: Cambridge University Press, 1972).

Brown, Judith, *Modern India: The making of an Asian democracy* (Oxford: Oxford University Press, 1985).

Brown, Judith M., *Gandhi: Prisoner of hope* (New Haven and London: Yale University Press, 1989).

Burke, Jason, *The New Threat from Islamic Militancy* (London: The Bodley Head, 2015).

Burton, Richard, *The Arabian Nights* (London: Macmillan,1886).

Caldwell, Christopher, *Reflections on the Revolution in Europe: Immigration, Islam and the West* (London: Allen Lane, 2009).

Carlton, David, *Anthony Eden* (London: Allen Lane, 1981).

Carlton, David, *Britain and the Suez Crisis* (Oxford: Blackwell, 1988).

Carlyle, Thomas, 'The Hero as Prophet: Mahomet and Islam', in *On Heroes, Hero-Worship and the Heroic in History* (1841).

Chandra, Bipan, *India's Struggle for Independence* (London: Penguin, 1988).

Chew, Samuel C., *The Crescent and the Rose: Islam and England during the Renaissance* (New York: Octagon Books, 1965).

Christie, Niall, *Muslims and Crusaders* (London: Routledge, 2014).

Churchill, Randolph, *Churchill* (London: Heinemann, 1966).

Churchill, W.S., *The River War* (London: Macmillan, 1899).

Clot, Andre, *Suleiman the Magnificent* (London: Saqi, 2005).

Colley, Linda, *Captives: Britain, empire and the world 1600–1850* (London: Cape, 2002).

Cromer, Lord, *Modern Egypt* (London: Macmillan, 1908).

Dalrymple, William, *White Mughals: Love and betrayal in eighteenth-century India* (London: Penguin, 2002).

Dalrymple, William, *The Last Mughal: The fall of a dynasty, Delhi, 1857* (London: Bloomsbury, 2006).

Davidson, R.H., 'Turkish attitudes concerning Christian-Muslim equality in the nineteenth century', *American Historical Review*, 4 (1954).

Dawisha, Adeed, *Iraq: A political history from independence to occupation* (Princeton: Princeton University Press, 2009).

de Bellaigue, Christopher, *The Islamic Enlightenment* (London: The Bodley Head, 2017).

Dockter, Warren, *Churchill and the Islamic World* (London: I.B. Tauris, 2015).

Esposito, John L., *The Islamic Threat: Myth or reality?* (Oxford: Oxford University Press, 1999).

Esposito, John L. (ed.), *The Islamic World: Past and present* (Oxford: Oxford University Press, 2004).

Fakhry, Majid, *The Qur'an: A modern English version* (Reading: Garnet Publishing, 1997).

Fergusson, James, *Al-Britannia, My Country: A journey through Muslim Britain* (London: Bantam, 2017).

Fieldhouse, D.K., *Economics and Empire 1830–1914* (London: Weidenfeld and Nicolson, 1973).

Figes, Orlando, *Crimea: The last crusade* (London: Allen Lane, 2010).

Flinders Petrie, W.M., *Egypt and Israel* (Basingstoke: Macmillan, 1910).

Foot, Paul, *Immigration and Race in British Politics* (London: Penguin, 1965).

Frankopan, Peter, *The Silk Roads: A new history of the world* (London: Bloomsbury, 2015).

Fraser, T.G., *The Makers of the Modern Middle East* (London: Ginkgo Publishing, 2015).

Gheissari, Nader Ali, *Democracy in Iran* (Oxford: Oxford University Press, 2006).

Gibbon, Edward, *The Decline and Fall of the Roman Empire* (1776).

Gilbert, Martin, 'A path to peace inspired by the past', *History Today*, 60, August (2016).

Gillard, David, *The Struggle for Asia 1828–1914* (London: Methuen, 1977).

Glubb, John Bagot, *The Great Arab Conquests* (London: Hodder and Stoughton, 1963).

Gove, Michael, *Celsius 7/7* (London: Weidenfeld and Nicolson, 2006).

Grayling, A.C., *Democracy and Its Crisis* (London: Oneworld Books, 2017).

Greenblatt, Stephen, *The Rise and Fall of Adam and Eve* (London: The Bodley Head, 2017).

Guillaume, Alfred, *Islam* (Harmondsworth: Penguin, 1968).

Haig, Christopher, *Elizabeth I* (London: Longman, 1988).

Hamid, Mohsin, *The Reluctant Fundamentalist* (London: Penguin, 2007).

Hardy, P., *The Muslims of British India* (Cambridge: Cambridge University Press, 1972).

Hasan, Mushirul, *Moderate or Militant: Images of Indian Muslims* (Oxford: Oxford University Press, 2008).

Hasan, Rumy, *Multiculturalism: Some inconvenient truths* (London: Routledge, 2010).

Hashemi, Nader, *Islam, Secularism and Liberal Democracy* (Oxford: Oxford University Press, 2009).

Haugaard, W.P., *Elizabeth and the English Reformation* (Cambridge: Cambridge University Press, 1968).

Hillenbrand, C., *The Crusades: Islamic perspectives* (Edinburgh: Edinburgh University Press, 1999).

Holmes, Colin, *John Bull's Island: Immigration and British society 1871–1971* (Basingstoke: Macmillan, 1988).

Holt, P.M., Ann Lambton and Bernard Lewis (eds), *The Cambridge History of Islam* (Cambridge: Cambridge University Press, 1970).

Holt, Richard, *Sport and the British* (Oxford: Oxford University Press, 1989).

Horrie, Chris and Peter Chippindale, *What is Islam?* (London: Virgin Books, 2003).

Howell, Georgina, *Daughter of the Desert* (London: Macmillan, 2006).

Hughes, Matthew, 'The banality of brutality: British armed forces and the repression of the Arab revolt in Palestine 1936–39', *English Historical Review*, CXXIV (2009).

Husain, Ed, *The Islamist* (London: Penguin Books, 2007).

Hussain, Nadiya, *Nadiya's British Food Adventure* (London: Michael Joseph, 2017).

Hussain, Nasser, *Playing with Fire* (London: Granta, 2004).

Hyam, Ronald, *Empire and Sexuality: The British experience* (Manchester: Manchester University Press, 1990).

Hyde, Andrew, *Jihad: The Ottomans and the Allies 1914–1922* (Stroud: Amberley Publishing, 2017).

Johnson, Edgar, *Walter Scott: The great unknown* (London: Hamish Hamilton, 1970).

Kahn-Harris, Keith, *Judaism* (London: Hodder Education, 2012).

Keay, John, *Sowing the Wind: The seeds of conflict in the Middle East* (London: John Murray, 2003).

Kedourie, Elie, *Politics in the Middle East* (Oxford: Oxford University Press, 1992).

Keegan, John, *The Iraq War* (London: Hutchinson, 2004).

Kepel, Gilles, *Jihad: The trail of political Islam* (London: I.B. Tauris, 2002).

Kincaid, Dennis, *British Social Life in India, 1608–1937* (London: Routledge, 1973).

Kinross, Lord, *Ataturk: The rebirth of a nation* (London: Weidenfeld and Nicolson, 1964).

Kostick, Conor (ed.), *The Crusades and the Near East: Cultural histories* (London: Routledge, 2011).

Kugle, Scott Siraj al-Haqq, *Homosexuality in Islam* (Oxford: Oneworld Publications, 2010).

Kyle, Keith, *Suez* (London: Weidenfeld and Nicolson, 1991).

Lahiri, Shompa, *Indians in Britain* (London: Frank Cass, 2000).

Lawless, Richard I., *From Ta'izz to Tyneside: An Arab community in the north-east of England during the early twentieth century* (Exeter: Exeter University Press, 1995).

Lawson, Philip, *The East India Company: A history* (Harlow: Longman, 1993).

Lewis, Bernard, *The Jews of Islam* (Princeton: Princeton University Press, 1987).

Lewis, Bernard, *The Arabs in History* (Oxford: Oxford University Press, 1993).

Lewis, Bernard, *What Went Wrong? Western impact and Middle Eastern response* (London: Weidenfeld and Nicolson, 2002).

Lewis, Bernard, *The Crisis of Islam* (London: Phoenix, 2003).

Lewis, Philip and Sadek Hamid, *British Muslims: New directions in Islamic thought, creativity and activism* (Edinburgh: Edinburgh University Press, 2018).

Lieven, Dominic, *Pakistan: A hard country* (London: Allen Lane, 2011).

Lings, Martin, *Muhammad* (London: Allen and Unwin, 1983).

Little, Tom, *Modern Egypt* (London: Ernest Benn, 1967).

Lloyd, Christopher, *English Corsairs on the Barbary Coast* (London: Collins, 1981).

Lloyd, Simon, *English Society and the Crusade 1210–1301* (Oxford: Clarendon Press, 1988).

Loyn, David, *Butcher and Bolt: Two hundred years of foreign engagement in Afghanistan* (London: Hutchinson, 2008).

Lukitz, Liora, *A Quest in the Middle East: Octavia Bell and the making of modern Iraq* (London: I.B. Tauris, 2006).

Lyons, Malcolm and D.E.P. Jackson, *Saladin* (Cambridge: Cambridge University Press, 1982).

MacCarthy, Fiona, *Byron: Life and legend* (London: John Murray, 2002).

MacMillan, Margaret, *Peacemakers: Six months that changed the world* (London: John Murray, 2001).

Malik, Kenan, *From Fatwa to Jihad: The Rushdie affair and its legacy* (London: Atlantic Books, 2009).

Mango, Andrew, *Ataturk: The biography of the founder of modern Turkey* (London: John Murray, 1999).

Mansfield, Peter, *The British in Egypt* (London: Weidenfeld and Nicolson, 1971).

Marlowe, John, *Mission to Khartoum: The apotheosis of General Gordon* (London: Gollancz, 1969).

Marlowe, John, *Cromer in Egypt* (London: Elek Books, 1970).

Mason, Philip, *A Matter of Honour: An account of the Indian Army, its officers and men* (London: Cape, 1974).

Masood, Ehsan, *Science and Islam: A history* (London: Icon Books, 2009).

Masters, John, *Bugles and a Tiger* (London: Michael Joseph, 1956).

Matar, Nabil, *Islam in Britain 1558–1685* (Cambridge: Cambridge University Press, 1998).

Matthew, H.C.G., *Gladstone*, Vol. 2 (Oxford: Clarendon Press, 1996).

McCarthy, Justin, *The Ottoman Turks* (Harlow: Longman, 1997).

McLeod, Hugh, *Religion and Society in England 1850–1914* (Basingstoke: Macmillan, 1996).

Metcalf, Thomas, *Ideologies of the Raj* (Cambridge: Cambridge University Press, 1994).

Meyer, Karl and Shareen Blair Brysac, *Tournament of Shadows: The Great Game and the race for empire in Asia* (London: Little Brown, 1999).

Milton-Edwards, Beverley, *Islamic Fundamentalism since 1945* (London: Routledge, 2005).

Mishra, Pankaj, *From the Ruins of Empire: The revolt against the west and the remaking of Asia* (London: Allen Lane, 2012).

Morris, Marc, *King John: Treachery, tyranny and the road to Magna Carta* (London: Hutchinson, 2015).

Mukherjee, Ramkrishna, *The Rise and Fall of the East India Company* (New York: Monthly Review Press, 1974).

Mukherjee, S.N., *Sir William Jones: A study in eighteenth-century British attitudes to India* (Cambridge: Cambridge University Press, 1968).

Nagus, Ralph and Eden Naby, *Afghanistan: Mullah, Marx and mujahid* (Oxford: Westview Press, 2002).

Neillands, Robin, *The Dervish Wars: Gordon and Kitchener in the Sudan 1880–1898* (London: John Murray, 1996).

Nicoll, Fergus, *Gladstone, Gordon and the Sudan Wars* (Barnsley: Pen and Sword Books, 2013).

Omissi, David, *The Sepoy and the Raj: The Indian Army 1860–1940* (Basingstoke: Macmillan, 1994).

Orga, Irfan and Margarete Orga, *Ataturk* (London: Michael Joseph, 1962).

Palmer, Alan, *The Banner of Battle: The story of the Crimean War* (London: Weidenfeld and Nicolson, 1987).

Pavord, Anna, *The Tulip* (London: Bloomsbury, 1999).

Pemble, John, *The Raj, the Indian Mutiny and the Kingdom of Oudh, 1801–1859* (Hassocks: Harvester Press, 1997).

Phillips, Jonathan, *The Second Crusade* (London: Yale University Press, 2007).

Phillips, Melanie, *Londonistan: How Britain is creating a terror state within* (London: Gibson Square, 2006).

Polk, William R., *Understanding Iraq* (London: I.B. Tauris, 2006).

Ponting, Clive, *The Crimean War: The truth behind the myth* (London: Chatto and Windus, 2004).

Porter, Roy, *Edward Gibbon: Making history* (London: Weidenfeld and Nicolson, 1988).

Pugh, Martin, *Speak for Britain: A new history of the Labour Party* (London: The Bodley Head, 2010).

Pugh, Martin, *Britain: Unification and disintegration* (Sandy: Authors Online/Bright Pen Books, 2012).

Ramadan, Tariq, *Western Muslims and the Future of Islam* (Oxford: Oxford University Press, 2004).

Rauf, Imam Feisal Abdul, *What's Right with Islam* (San Francisco: Harper Collins, 2004).

Reid, Walter, *Empire of Sand: How Britain made the Middle East* (Edinburgh: Birlinn, 2013).

Riley-Smith, J., *The Crusades: A short history* (London: Macmillan, 1987).

Rippin, Andrew (ed.), *The Blackwell Companion to the Qur'an* (Oxford: Wiley-Blackwell, 2009).

Roberts, D.S., *Islam: A Westerner's guide* (London: Kogan Page, 1981).

Roberts, J.M., *The Triumph of the West* (London: Guild of Publishing, 1985).

Rogerson, Barnaby, *North Africa: A history from the Mediterranean shore to the Sahara* (London: Duckworth Overlook, 2012).

Rose, Kenneth, *Superior Person* (London: Macmillan, 1969).

Said, Edward, *Covering Islam* (Cambridge: Cambridge University Press, 1981).

Sardar, Ziauddin, *Balti Britain* (London: Granta, 2008).

Sardar, Ziauddin, *The Islamic World* (London: Robinson, 2009).

Sardar, Ziauddin (ed.), *The Britannica Guide to the Islamic World* (Philadelphia: Running Press Book Publishers, 2009).

Sen, K.M., *Hinduism* (Harmondsworth: Penguin, 1981).

Shepherd, Robert, *Enoch Powell* (London: Hutchinson, 1996).

Southern, R.W., *Western Views of Islam in the Middle Ages* (Cambridge, MA: Harvard University Press, 1962).

Stewart, P.J., *Unfolding Islam* (Stroud: Sutton, 2008).

Stokes, Eric, *The Peasant and the Raj* (Cambridge: Cambridge University Press, 1978).

Sykes, Christopher, *The Man Who Created the Middle East* (London: William Collins, 2016).

Thomson, Andrew, *The Empire Strikes Back? The impact of imperialism on Britain from the mid-nineteenth century* (Harlow: Longman, 2005).

Thorpe, D.R., *Eden* (London: Chatto and Windus, 2003).

Tinniswood, Adrian, *The Pirates of Barbary* (London: Cape, 2010).

Turfan, M. Naim, *Rise of the Young Turks: Politics, the military and Ottoman collapse* (London: I.B. Tauris, 2000).

Tyerman, Christopher, *The Invention of the Crusades* (London: Cape, 1998).

Tyerman, Christopher, *The Crusades: A very short introduction* (Oxford: Oxford University Press, 2004).

Walker, Christopher J., *Islam and the West* (Stroud: Sutton, 2005).

Ward, Paul, *Britishness since 1870* (London: Routledge, 2004).

Warsi, Sayeeda, *The Enemy Within: A tale of Muslim Britain* (London: Allen Lane, 2017).

Wilkinson, Paul, *Terrorism Versus Democracy: The liberal state response* (Cambridge: Cambridge University Press, 2001).

❖ BIBLIOGRAPHY

Winder, Robert, *Bloody Foreigners: The story of immigration to Britain* (London: Little, Brown, 2004).

Yates, Nigel, 'Pugin and the medieval dream', in Gordon Marsden (ed.), *Victorian Values* (Harlow: Longman, 1990).

Younge, Gary, *Who Are We?* (London: Penguin Books, 2010).

Zebel, Sidney, *Balfour* (Cambridge: Cambridge University Press, 1973).

INDEX